The Political Forms of Modern Society

*M. + J. Walzer*

*October, 1987*

*Princeton*

# Social and Political Theory from Polity Press

## Published

David Beetham, *Max Weber and the Theory of Modern Politics*
Richard Bernstein, ed., *Habermas and Modernity*
Richard Bernstein, *Philosophical Profiles*
John Burnheim, *Is Democracy Possible?*
Stanley Cohen, *Visions of Social Control*
Robert A. Dahl, *A Preface to Economic Democracy*
David Frisby, *Fragments of Modernity*
Harold Garfinkel, *Studies in Ethnomethodology*
Anthony Giddens, *The Constitution of Society*
Anthony Giddens, *The Nation-State and Violence*
W. F. Haug, *Critique of Commodity Aesthetics*
John Heritage, *Garfinkel and Ethnomethodology*
J. N. Isbister, *Freud: An Introduction to his Life and Work*
Martin Jay, *Marxism and Totality*
Hans Joas, *G. H. Mead: A Contemporary Re-examination of his Thought*
Harvey J. Kaye, *The British Marxist Historians*
Claude Lefort, *The Political Forms of Modern Society*
Thomas McCarthy, *The Critical Theory of Jürgen Habermas*
Claus Offe, *Disorganized Capitalism*
Carole Pateman, *The Problem of Political Obligation*
Mark Poster, *Foucault, Marxism and History*
Barbara Sichtermann, *Femininity: The Politics of the Personal*
Julia Swindells, *Victorian Writing and Working Women*
John B. Thompson, *Studies in the Theory of Ideology*

## A Selection of Forthcoming Titles

Barry Barnes, *The Basis of Power*
Zygmunt Bauman, *Legislators and Interpreters*
Norberto Bobbio, *What is Socialism?*
Raymond Boudon, *Theories of Social Change*
Pierre Bourdieu, *Language and Symbolic Power*
Cornelius Castoriadis, *The Imaginary Institution of Society*
Anthony Giddens and Jonathan Turner, eds, *Social Theory Today*
David Held, *Models of Democracy*
Scott Lash and John Urry, *The End of Organized Capitalism*
Niklas Luhmann, *Love as Passion*
William Outhwaite, *Habermas*
Alan Ryan, *Political Philosophy: An Introduction*
Michelle Stanworth, *Feminism and Sociology*
John B. Thompson, *The Interpretation of Ideology*
Nigel Thrift, *Social Theory and Human Geography*
James Tully, ed., *Meaning and Context*
Sylvia Walby, *Patriarchy at Work*
Paul Willis, *To Labour: The Subjective Side of Capital*

Claude Lefort

# The Political Forms
# of Modern Society

Bureaucracy, Democracy, Totalitarianism

Edited and Introduced by
John B. Thompson

Polity Press

© Chapters 1–4, Droz 1971; chapters 5 and 6, Gallimard 1978;
chapters 7–10, Fayard 1981.
This English translation (except Chapter 5) © Polity Press, 1986;
Introduction © John B. Thompson, 1986;
Chapter 5 © *Social Research*, 1978.

First published in the United Kingdom, 1986 by
Polity Press, Cambridge,
in association with Basil Blackwell, Oxford.

Editorial Office:
Polity Press, Dales Brewery, Gwydir Street, Cambridge
CB1 2LJ, UK.

Basil Blackwell Ltd
108 Cowley Road, Oxford
OX4 1JF, UK.

*British Library Cataloguing in Publication Data*
Lefort, Claude
The political forms of modern society:
bureaucracy, democracy, totalitarianism.
1. State, The
I. Title   II. Thompson, John B.
320.1   JC11
ISBN 0-7456-0109-X
ISBN 0-7456-0110-3

Typeset by DMB (Typesetting), Oxford
Printed in Great Britain by TJ Press, Padstow

# Contents

# Preface and Acknowledgements

The essays in this volume were originally published between 1948 and 1981. They represent a selection of some of Lefort's most important work on the political, symbolic and historical characteristics of modern societies.

I am particularly grateful to Claude Lefort for his constant and generous assistance throughout the period of preparing this volume for publication. His openness to my suggestions, his responsiveness to my questions and his warm hospitality have made my task much easier and much more enjoyable than it might otherwise have been. Anthony Giddens and David Held provided me with many helpful comments and a great deal of editorial support.

I am also grateful to Librairie Droz, Éditions Gallimard and Librairie Arthème Fayard for their willingness to allow us to translate and reproduce the essays. Most of the essays originally appeared in various journals before being gathered together in the volumes published by Droz, Gallimard and Fayard. Details of previous publication are given below.

1 'The Contradiction of Trotsky', originally published as 'La contradiction de Trotsky et le problème révolutionnaire', *Les Temps Modernes*, 39 (1948–49); reprinted in Claude Lefort, *Éléments d'une critique de la bureaucratie* (Geneva: Droz, 1971), pp. 11–29.
2 'Totalitarianism Without Stalin', originally published as 'Le totalitarisme sans Staline: L'U.R.S.S. dans une nouvelle phase', *Socialisme ou Barbarie*, 14 (1956); reprinted in *Éléments d'une critique de la bureaucratie*, pp. 130–90.

3 'What is Bureaucracy?', originally published as 'Qu'est-ce que la bureaucratie?', *Arguments*, 17 (1960); reprinted in *Éléments d'une critique de la bureaucratie*, pp. 288–314.

4 'Novelty and the Appeal of Repetition', originally published as the postscript to *Éléments d'une critique de la bureaucratie*, pp. 351–62, under the title 'Le nouveau et l'attrait de la répétition'.

5 'Marx: From One Vision of History to Another', originally published as 'Marx: d'une vision de l'histoire à l'autre', in Claude Lefort, *Les Formes de l'histoire: essais d'anthropologie politique* (Paris: Gallimard, 1978), pp. 195–233.

6 'Outline of the Genesis of Ideology in Modern Societies', originally published as 'Esquisse d'une genèse de l'idéologie dans les sociétés modernes', *Textures*, 8–9 (1974); reprinted in *Les Formes de l'histoire*, pp. 278–329.

7 'Politics and Human Rights', originally published as 'Droits de l'homme et politique', *Libre*, 7 (1980); reprinted in Claude Lefort, *L'Invention démocratique: les limites de la domination totalitaire* (Paris: Fayard, 1981), pp. 45–83.

8 'The Logic of Totalitarianism', originally published as 'La logique totalitaire', *Kontinent Skandinavia*, 3–4 (1980); reprinted in *L'Invention démocratique*, pp. 85–106.

9 'The Image of the Body and Totalitarianism', originally published as 'L'image du corps et le totalitarisme', *Confrontation*, 2 (1979); reprinted in *L'Invention démocratique*, pp. 159–76.

10 'Pushing Back the Limits of the Possible', originally published as 'Reculer les frontières du possible', *Esprit* (1981); reprinted in *L'Invention démocratique*, pp. 317–31.

Most of the essays are published in this volume without alteration. However, I have edited some of the essays in Part I, in so far as they contained material which was repetitive or which was too closely tied to the original circumstances of their publication. All deletions are indicated by ellipses in square brackets.

The material has been translated by several individuals. Alan Sheridan translated essays 1, 2, 7, 8 and 9. Essay 5 was originally translated by Terry Karten and published in *Social Research*, 56 (1978), pp. 615–66; I am grateful to the editor of *Social Research* for permission to reprint this translation. I translated most of the remaining material and I revised the entire manuscript in order to render style and terminology consistent throughout the volume.

I accept responsibility for any errors or infelicities that may remain.

When Lefort quotes from texts which have been translated into English, the standard English translations are used wherever possible. Occasionally it was necessary, however, to alter the existing translation in order to stay close to the French text quoted by Lefort. All such alterations are clearly indicated in the notes.

J.B.T., Cambridge, August 1985

The editor and publisher are grateful to Penguin Books Ltd and Random House Inc. for permission to reprint extracts from *Capital* by Karl Marx, introduced by Ernest Mandel and translated by Ben Fowkes. Translation © Ben Fowkes, 1976.

# Editor's Introduction

Many people today would agree that the traditional resources of theoretical reflection are inadequate in face of the political realities of our time. The size and complexity of modern societies, the development of new forms of social stratification, political organization and military strength in different parts of the world, the emergence of new social movements and new forms of social conflict in the East as well as the West: these and other features of the contemporary world seem to call for new ways of thinking, fresh attempts to come to terms with current problems and to search for ways out of the apparent impasses in which we find ourselves today. While insights and inspiration may still be drawn from the traditional perspectives of Marxism and socialism, of liberalism and democratic theory, it seems clear that the value of these perspectives is limited in certain respects. For they bear the imprint of their formation in the eighteenth and nineteenth centuries; they are marked by the priorities and the prejudices, the aspirations and the fears, of those who were reflecting on the beginnings of modern industrial and political societies. The changes ushered in by the twentieth century have been enormous and no attempt to understand contemporary societies can be spared the effort of rethinking the nature of politics in the modern world.

This is an effort which, for more than thirty years, has animated the work of Claude Lefort. Lefort is one of the most original political theorists, and one of the most perceptive political analysts, in France today. Outside of France he is perhaps best known as an interpreter of the philosophy of Merleau-Ponty, who was his teacher in the early 1940s. He may also be known as one of the founding members, together with Cornelius Castoriadis, of the small left-wing group,

Socialisme ou Barbarie, which published a journal bearing that name throughout the 1950s. But Lefort's work represents much more than an interpretation of the philosophy of Merleau-Ponty, much more than an historical contribution to the dilemmas of radical politics. For Lefort has developed, in the course of an extended reflection on events in Eastern and Western Europe, a highly original account of the political forms of modern society. It is an account which stems from an awareness that the twentieth century has given birth to new forms of power and oppression, an awareness that, beneath the banner of eliminating all exploitation, new systems of exploitation have been installed. It is an account which is based on a critical interpretation of the work of Marx, an interpretation which acknowledges Marx's insight as well as his blindness, the strengths of his analysis of modern society as well as the inadequacies, the inconsistencies, the simplifications of his thought. It is an account which is rooted, finally, in a sensitivity to the history of political theory, a sensitivity to the ways in which this history is interwoven with the development of modern forms of politics while at the same time falling short of them, leaving a gap that can only be filled by the continuously renewed effort to rethink the political nature of modern societies.

The essays which comprise this volume span the entire career of Lefort. They attest to the development of his thought, while at the same time displaying a consistent and penetrating political vision. My aim in this introduction will be to sketch this development and to convey something of this vision. I shall not attempt to provide a comprehensive survey of Lefort's work; and some of his writings, such as those dealing with Merleau-Ponty and Machiavelli, will largely be left aside.[1] I shall also refrain from critical commentary; although I believe that there are many respects in which Lefort's views could be questioned, this is not the place to present my reservations.[2] Here I shall be concerned primarily to describe the context and the central themes of the essays which are included in this volume, in the hope that such a description will facilitate both the reception of his work in the English-speaking world and the recognition of his contribution to contemporary social and political thought.

## Problems of Politics and Bureaucracy

From his earliest to his most recent writings, Lefort has regarded the developments in post-revolutionary Russia and Eastern Europe as a privileged reference point for political reflection. Recently there has been a growing interest among social and political analysts in the shortcomings of what has been called 'actually existing socialism'.[3] For many years, however, Lefort's critical appraisals of the Soviet Union and Eastern Europe were out of tune with the views which prevailed in left-wing circles, especially in France. When those on the Left in France turned their attention to the East, they tended either to adopt a Trotskyist conception of the 'degeneration' of the Russian Revolution or to offer an apologetic, if somewhat ambivalent, defence of the Soviet path. But, for the most part, thinkers on the Left preferred not to look; they preferred to focus their critical attention on Western capitalist societies, where they could restrict themselves to refining or elaborating Marx's analysis, without calling into question the basic assumptions of Marx's approach or his conception of an alternative society. It is less easy to maintain this confident conviction when one's eyes are firmly fixed on the events which have shaken the Soviet Union and Eastern Europe in recent decades. The revelations of the purges and the forced labour camps in the Soviet Union, the about-turn signalled by Khrushchev's denunciation of Stalin, the uprisings of East Berlin, Hungary, Poland, Czechoslovakia: such events are the episodes of a dark history which has constantly preoccupied Lefort. It is a history which obliges one to abandon some of the basic assumptions of traditional approaches, including that of Marx, and which forces one to face some of the most lugubrious political realities of the twentieth century.

Lefort's first analyses of the Soviet Union and Eastern Europe were developed in the late 1940s and 1950s, when he was actively involved in the group Socialisme ou Barbarie. This group emerged out of a disagreement within the French Trotskyist Party, the PCI, which Lefort had joined while still a student in 1943. The disagreement was concerned primarily with the Trotskyists' analysis of the Soviet Union. Lefort and others had serious reservations about this analysis. The Trotskyists tended to regard the Russian bureaucracy as a parasitic and transitory caste which had been grafted on to a basis that was fundamentally socialist; they thus failed to grasp, in the view of Lefort and others, the nature of the new exploitative system which was emerging in the Soviet Union. This critique of Trotskyism was developed most forcefully by Cornelius Castoriadis, who arrived in Paris in 1945 as a refugee from the civil war in Greece. Castoriadis and Lefort met in 1946 and formed a small dissident group within the PCI. However, their differences with the official party line became increasingly pronounced and eventually, in 1948, they decided to leave the party. They formed an independent group and the first issue of their journal, *Socialisme ou Barbarie*, appeared in March 1949.[4] The group continued to publish the journal until June 1965, although some members (including Lefort) left the group before then. As an independent forum for political and theoretical debate, *Socialisme ou Barbarie* made an important contribution to the development, in the early post-war period, of a critical analysis of the industrial societies in Eastern and Western Europe.

Lefort's essay 'The Contradiction of Trotsky' was first published at the end of 1948 and highlights his differences with the Trotskyist approach. Lefort shows that Trotsky did not have the clear and consistent view of Stalinism, and of the Stalinist 'degeneration' of the Russian Revolution, which is often attributed to him by his followers. Trotsky compromised with Stalin for as long as possible, thus disarming and confusing the forces that were resisting Stalin's rise to power. Moreover, Trotsky's conception of the bureaucracy as a parasitical caste, a small troupe of traitors who would soon be ousted either by a revolutionary insurrection or by the restoration of capitalism, was altogether inadequate. For the Russian bureaucracy was part of a new social system which was based on determinate relations of exploitation. This argument, sketched in Lefort's essay, had been developed by Castoriadis in a lengthy analysis published in *Socialisme ou Barbarie* at roughly the same time.[5] Lefort argues that the emergence of this new bureaucratic system of exploitation can only be understood against the backcloth of the prior development of the Bolshevik Party in the specific circumstances of pre-revolutionary Russia. These circumstances necessitated and facilitated the concentration of power in the hands of party functionaries who were increasingly cut off from the masses. This tendency was accentuated in the post-revolutionary period, resulting in the crushing of the workers' revolt at Kronstadt in 1921, a repressive action that Trotsky himself supported. Trotsky's struggle against the bureaucracy was ineffective because he failed to see that this bureaucracy was an integral part of the new system of exploitation which was emerging in the Soviet Union.

Lefort develops and deepens his analysis of the Soviet Union in a long essay entitled 'Totalitarianism without Stalin'. This essay, originally published in 1956, was occasioned by the denunciation of

Stalin by the new Soviet leaders of the Twentieth Congress of the Communist Party. Today it may be difficult for us to appreciate the significance of this event. For many people at the time it came as a severe shock, a public acknowledgement that something had gone wrong – albeit temporarily, accidentally – in the great programme of building socialism; and the shock was particularly disturbing in France, since the French Communist Party, the PCF, had maintained (and continues to maintain) close ties with the Soviet Union. Lefort never harboured any illusions about the repressive character of Stalin's regime. He had consistently criticized the so-called 'progressive intellectuals', including Sartre, who had deemed it appropriate, for one reason or another, to lend their support to the PCF and the Soviet Union.[6] In 'Totalitarianism without Stalin' he takes the opportunity afforded by the new Soviet leaders' denunciation of their predecessor to develop a critique of Stalinism and of the system of which it is part. Lefort listens to the Soviet leaders' criticisms and promises, their diagnoses and declarations, and uses this material to provide a new and original analysis of Soviet society.[7] As Lefort recently remarked, in the 1950s it was scandalous for someone on the Left to suggest that the USSR was a totalitarian society. Today this suggestion would no doubt give rise to discussion and disagreement, but there is no hint of scandal; and Lefort's analysis remains a valuable contribution to contemporary debates about the nature of the Soviet system.[8]

According to Lefort, Stalinism must be seen as a phase in the rise of the totalitarian party, the origins of which stem from the pre-revolutionary period. Stalinism appeared when the party succeeded in concentrating all power in its hands, identified itself with the state and, as the state, subordinated all other institutions in society to itself and freed itself of all social control, while at the same time seeking to eliminate all opposition from within its ranks. This process occurred in the context of a tremendous social upheaval in which the old classes and strata of pre-revolutionary Russia were swept into a new hierarchy. This hierarchy was bureaucratically structured and dominated by a bureaucratic elite, which Lefort sometimes refers to as the 'new bureaucratic class'. The characterization of the Soviet bureaucratic elite as a 'new class' has, of course, been developed by other thinkers; one of the most well-known accounts is that of Milovan Djilas, whose book *The New Class* was originally published at about the same time as Lefort's essay.[9] But the interest of Lefort's analysis lies in the way that he describes this 'new class' and the new social system which was emerging in the Soviet Union. Lefort is well aware that the new class is very different from the bourgeoisie and that the new system differs in fundamental respects from the old liberal capitalist societies. In liberal capitalism the bourgeoisie maintained its dominance by virtue of its position in the economy, as the class of private owners of the means of production; there was a separation or division between the state and 'civil society',[10] and between different spheres of activity within civil society, even though the actions of the state were not altogether independent of the interests of the dominant class. In the case of the Soviet Union, by contrast, the unity of the bureaucratic class is not guaranteed by the economic activities of its members, but is established only by virtue of the integration of bureaucrats around the state and their subordination to the administrative apparatus. Hence the exercise of terror was not merely the accidental excess of a disturbed personality: it was an integral part, in Lefort's view, of the development of a new class whose unity and dominance could no longer be guaranteed by the mechanism of private appropriation. Moreover, by contrast with liberal capitalism, the separation between state and civil society is abolished in the Soviet system. The state has become, or seeks to become, consubstantial with society and to diffuse its presence throughout the social sphere.

Totalitarianism should not be seen, therefore, as a specific political regime or as an assortment of political institutions; it is not the same thing, in Lefort's view, as a political dictatorship, such as the one-time dictatorship of Franco. Rather, totalitarianism is a *form of society* in which all activities are interrelated and in which the separation beween different domains of social life is claimed to be negated. It is not so much 'a monstrous outgrowth of political power in society as a metamorphosis of society itself in which the political ceases to exist as a separate sphere'.[11] This 'homogenization' or 'unification' of society is supposed to be carried out by the party. Ideally the party has the task of diffusing politics throughout society and thereby effecting the fusion of society and the state. In reality it operates like a particular group whose function is to present an imaginary unity, to project the image of a society at one with itself. The activity of the party thus produces, in practice, a new separation between the political function and social life. The presence of the political is now felt in every sphere of social life; everywhere people run up against the norms of the party and confront it as an alien body whose power is imposed on society. The party thus creates new divisions, new lines of conflict, new forms of vulnerability, whereas it claims to abolish all division and to govern in the interests of society as a whole.

On the basis of this analysis Lefort assesses the significance of the declarations made, and the reforms introduced, by the Twentieth Congress. The denunciation of Stalin exposed the fallibility of the regime, but it would be imprudent to interpret this act as the sign of a fundamental change in the totalitarian system. The reforms announced by the new leaders – the reductions in prices, the improvement in working conditions, etc. – are important steps in themselves and will benefit many people; it is unlikely, however, that these steps will amount to anything more than an attempt to *ameliorate* totalitarianism, to make it more acceptable to those who live within it. The speeches of the leaders indicate that they are aware of a split which has grown up between the state and society, between the party and social life; with each new measure they seek to re-create a unity which would bind the members of society together in the pursuit of a common task. But this aim is ultimately incompatible with a system which is based, in the first place, on a deep division between a bureaucratic class and those exploited groups and classes which carry out the orders of the bureaucrats and, in the second place, on the strict subordination of all members of society to the state–party apparatus. Lefort does not rule out the possibility that this system may be shaken at some future date by internal or external activities or events, but he does doubt whether it would be fundamentally altered through the actions of the individuals who derive most benefit from it.

Lefort's critique of Trotsky and his early analyses of the Soviet Union make extensive use of the concept of bureaucracy and it is therefore appropriate that he should undertake a systematic analysis of this concept. 'What is Bureaucracy?' was first published in 1960 in the left-wing journal *Arguments*. It offers a rigorous analysis of the conceptions of bureaucracy which may be derived from Marx and Weber, points to certain difficulties in these conceptions and outlines an alternative approach which might enable one to come to terms with the *social* nature and *dynamic* character of bureaucracy in the modern world. According to the Marxist conception of bureaucracy, as developed by Marx in the *Critique of Hegel's Philosophy of Right* and

*The Eighteenth Brumaire* and by Lenin in *The State and Revolution*, the bureaucracy is a special body within society. It is 'special' because it plays a crucial role in maintaining existing social relations; and it is 'within society' because it derives its existence from the division of society into classes and it acts, on the whole, in the interests of the dominant class. While Lefort acknowledges that this account is illuminating in some respects, he criticizes the tendency to regard bureaucracy as subordinate to class. For this tendency makes it difficult to study bureaucracy for its own sake, to examine its intrinsic dynamics and development. It also makes it difficult to understand how the state bureaucracy could assume an active interventionist role in capitalist societies and how it could continue to exist – indeed, to expand considerably – in those societies which claim to have eliminated class relations.

Weber's analysis of bureaucracy has the merit, in Lefort's view, of treating this phenomenon as a distinctive form of social organization which involves relations of power, status and authority. It is a form of organization which may be found not only in the state but also in civil society, in industrial firms, schools, political parties and so on. Weber enumerates a series of criteria which define, in his view, an 'ideal type' of bureaucratic organization. But Lefort is critical of this formalistic approach; he argues that, if one tries to use this approach to analyse actual instances of bureaucracy in the state and civil society, many of Weber's criteria do not apply. Moreover, this formalistic approach obscures the ways in which the development of bureaucracies is always rooted in specific social conditions and always nourished by an internal dynamic of power. This dynamic involves a double movement: on the one hand, the bureaucracy proliferates distinctions and divisions, fragments and compartmentalizes activities, thus creating a complex and self-sustaining hierarchy of interdependent elements; on the other hand, the bureaucracy thus constituted tends to form a closed world that sets itself off from dominated groups and seeks to preserve its own material privileges. In terms of this dynamic one can begin to make sense of the development of the bureaucracy as the dominant group or class in the Soviet Union. Weber was certainly right to suggest that the Russian Revolution would not lead to the abolition of the state but would, on the contrary, facilitate the growth and bureaucratization of the state administration. Lefort argues, however, that Weber's formalistic conception of bureaucracy does not bring out with sufficient clarity the internal connections between the process of bureaucratization in the Soviet Union and the struggle for, and maintenance of, political power. The development of the state bureaucracy was foreshadowed by the bureaucratization of the Bolshevik Party in the pre-revolutionary period; and all post-revolutionary political leaders were necessarily supported by the state and party bureaucracies. In the wake of the revolution these bureaucracies fused political and economic power in a complex network of hierarchical organizations, a network which effectively excluded the majority of the population from decision-making processes. Yet these bureaucracies, by virtue of their own internal differentiations, are torn apart by conflicts and rivalries and require, in order to maintain their cohesion, a constant activity of political unification, an activity whose success is by no means guaranteed.

While Lefort's early analyses of totalitarianism and bureaucracy retain much of their theoretical value today, nevertheless in certain respects Lefort has moved beyond the framework within which these analyses were conducted. In 'Novelty and the Appeal of Repetition', which was written in 1970 and published as the postscript to *Éléments d'une critique de la bureaucratie*, Lefort discusses the considerations which led him to develop his views. One of these considerations derived from his experience as a political activist in the small left-wing group which was responsible for the publication of *Socialisme ou Barbarie*. From the outset Lefort's relationship to this group had been somewhat ambivalent. While he shared the general concern to develop a critique of bureaucracy in all its forms, not only in the Soviet Union but also in the industrial firms and working-class organizations in the West, he felt that some members of the group were inclined to view their activities in terms of the Leninist model of a revolutionary party. In Lefort's view, this contradicted their anti-Leninist commitment to proletarian autonomy, their conviction that the fate of the working class was the responsibility of that class, and it ran the risk of introducing bureaucratic structures into the group itself. For these and other reasons Lefort decided to leave Socialisme ou Barbarie in 1958.[12] In later reflecting on this experience he was struck by the fact that the micro-bureaucracy which began to emerge in their group was not based on any material considerations but rather on the possession of a certain knowledge and a certain capacity to inscribe every event in a 'mytho-history'. The Left is no stranger to the comforts of tradition. And this is a fact which merits reflection.

For it attests to the imaginary relation that we maintain with the past, 'the mythical function that we make it play in order to assure ourselves of a truth which is already given and which will not betray us, in order to conjure away, in sum, the indeterminacy which constantly re-emerges in the history that we live'.[13]

The second consideration which led Lefort to develop his views was his critical interrogation of the work of Marx. His earlier writings, while sharply critical of the more orthodox forms of Marxism, were nevertheless premised on the basic assumptions of Marx's approach. When Lefort argued that the state and party bureaucracies had assumed a position of dominance in the USSR, he took it for granted that this dominance was rooted in social relations of exploitation and that the exploited groups constituted a class which had the potential, indeed was destined, to lead a revolutionary struggle; the bureaucracy had replaced the bourgeoisie and developed according to different principles, but the position of the proletariat remained unchanged. Similarly, the processes of bureaucratization in the industrial firms and workers' organizations of the West did not call into question, but merely redirected and accentuated the proletariat's task of creating a society freed from all domination. However, as Lefort remarks in 'Novelty and the Appeal of Repetition', this emphasis on the proletariat is difficult to reconcile with the diversity of divisions and forms of conflict which characterize modern societies. The revolt which erupted in May 1968, for example, could hardly be forced into the framework of a single united movement struggling for the overthrow of the dominant class.[14] The demand for collective self-management continues to animate struggles in a wide – and increasing – range of spheres of life, but this demand is now severed from the privileged link that it once seemed to maintain with the proletariat.

However, it is not merely a matter of displacing the privileged role of the proletariat: the critique must be pressed to the heart of Marxist theory, to the system of concepts and relations which define what is fundamental in society and what is crucial to social change. Marx's emphasis on the concept of the mode of production, and on the social relations established in the processes of production and exchange, tends to underplay the significance of the *political* and *symbolic* dimensions of social life. These dimensions cannot be reduced to or derived from economic processes; political and symbolic forms are of a different order than economic activities, even if, in actual circumstances, they are interwoven with the latter. Of course, Marx did not ignore questions of politics and symbolism. His whole work was oriented, in a sense, towards political activity and his discussions of ideology and fetishism were among his most outstanding contributions. But Marx's approach to politics and symbolism was overdetermined by other aspects of his work; or more precisely, a careful reading of Marx's work would show that it does not offer a single, consistent approach to social life but rather several approaches which stand in a relation of tension with one another, sometimes contradicting one another and sometimes converging into an apparently unified vision. Lefort seeks to sustain this claim, and to develop his own approach to the analysis of political and symbolic forms, in the material assembled in Part II of this volume.

### History, Ideology and the Social Imaginary

The essay entitled 'Marx: From One Vision of History to Another' was based on a course of lectures given at the Sorbonne in 1965. It is a brilliant study of Marx's theory of history and of the tensions and inconsistencies inherent in his account. 'What attracted me in Marx', writes Lefort, 'was the ambiguity of his thinking and, more than that, his opposition to himself'.[15] Thus Lefort discerns an opposition in Marx's work between the notions of continuity and discontinuity in history. On the one hand, Marx presents a vision of history as a continuous, progressive process, through the various stages of 'pre-history' to the revolution which would usher in the classless society and mark the beginning of a truly human history. On the other hand, Marx also emphasizes a radical discontinuity in the historical process, a mutation which sets capitalism off from all precapitalist forms of society. Whereas all precapitalist modes of production were, as Marx puts it in *Capital*, 'essentially conservative', the capitalist mode of production is essentially revolutionary and carries out a rapid, almost feverish, transformation of social relations. Thus the capitalist mode of production is viewed by Marx as fundamentally different from all previous modes of production and the latter, taken as a whole, are regarded as capitalism's *other*.

The opposition between continuity and discontinuity in history is closely linked to another tension in Marx's work, that between the idea of a dissolution of all 'restricted social relations', on the one hand, and the idea of a force of conservation, a mechanism of repetition, which would ensure the permanence of a structure, on the other. Thus the emergence and development of capitalism rapidly destroys the localized, community-based social relations of precapitalist modes of production, sweeping individuals into great cities and factories, socializing production and creating the conditions for a genuine 'socialization' of society as a whole. Yet alongside this image of a progressive torrent of change, Marx sketches the image of a mechanism of repetition, a principle of petrification, which turns a society back towards the past. Just as the development of capitalism seems to demystify the relation to the past, sweeping away 'all fixed, fast-frozen relations, with their train of ancient and venerable prejudices and opinions',[16] just at that moment capitalism gives birth to the most extraordinary phantasies and illusions, concealing its own history by taking refuge in models of the past and spirits of the dead. Thus Marx offers an interpretation which is, as Lefort says, 'sometimes Darwinian, sometimes Shakespearean in inspiration'.[17]

Lefort explores these oppositions and tensions in Marx's work through a careful analysis of three texts. The first text is Marx's discussion of precapitalist modes of production in the *Grundrisse* of 1857–8. This discussion is of particular interest to Lefort because it seems clearly to project a discontinuous vision of history: Marx does not present a steady evolutionary progression but, on the contrary, seeks to bring out a kinship among precapitalist modes of production and to juxtapose them as a whole to the capitalist mode of production. In precapitalist societies, according to Marx, individuals were tied to the land and immersed in the community. They may have been owners or co-owners of property but they were not yet 'labourers', for the emergence of 'labour' required certain transformations which were only instituted by capitalism. Hence labour was not at the origin of property but, on the contrary, property was a precondition of labour. The ownership of property in precapitalist societies involved participation in the community, which was the basis of all appropriation. Thus the 'communal form' was preserved in the passage from one precapitalist mode of production to another. The development of productive forces does not alter the fundamental role of the communal form, but merely modifies the particular arrangements and relationships within which it is expressed. The stability of this form is accentuated by Marx's discussion of the Asiatic mode of production, in which individuals seem to be 'welded' to their communities and insulated from any risk of change. The preservation of the communal form in precapitalist modes of production thus attests to a kinship among these modes which sets them off from capitalism, as well as a stability which resists the apparently progressive advance of the forces of production.

The emergence of capitalism seems clearly to inaugurate an era of rapid and progressive social change; and yet Lefort shows, through an analysis of various passages in *Capital*, that the capitalist mode of production also appeared, in Marx's eyes, to be governed by mechanisms of preservation and repetition. According to Marx, the emergence of capitalism presupposed the formation of a free labour force separated from the means and materials of production, on the one hand, and the exchange of free labour for money, on the other. Only under these conditions does the 'labourer' exist as such, that is, as an individual severed from the environment which once served as a dwelling place as well as a place of work. The individual is now incorporated into a productive mechanism which develops according to its own laws. But while the 'natural' determinations of the communal form are thereby overcome, the development of the capitalist mode of production gives rise to its own kind of 'naturalization'. The roots of this process are to be found in the very movement of capital formation, whereby capital, land and labour seem to become separated from one another and detached from human beings, who no longer appear as the source of value but as the product of a mechanism which dominates them. Capital, land and labour – the three terms of the 'trinity formula' – now appear as abstractions, as 'pure phantoms', constituting an imaginary realm within society which conceals the social relations between labour and capital. Thus bourgeois society, which supposedly swept away the myths and prejudices of the past, turns out to be, in Marx's words, 'an enchanted, perverted, topsy-turvy world in which *Monsieur le Capital* and *Madame la Terre*, who are social actors as well as mere things, do their *danse macabre*'.[18] At the very heart of capitalism, Marx uncovers a movement which, far from expressing the progressive dissolution of all past relations and ideas, seems to reinstitute a demonic force governed by the mechanism of repetition.

The political significance of this mechanism is vividly displayed in *The Eighteenth Brumaire*, which is the third text analysed by Lefort. *The Eighteenth Brumaire* is a study of the events which led to the *coup d'état* of Louis Napoleon Bonaparte in 1851. There are moments in this study when Marx presents us with the image of a progressive history, animated by the logic of class struggle and by a revolutionary process 'which does its work methodically';[19] but above all what he presents us with is a history caught up in phantasy, governed by repetition and turned back towards the past. Thus, at one point, Marx seems to be explaining the action of the two main factions of the dominant class in terms of their respective interests, one faction being rooted in large-scale industry and the other in landed property. Yet Marx immediately adds that what prevented them from jointly exercising political domination was not so much this divergence of interest but rather the fear of appearing on the social stage with their true faces exposed, undisguised by the jewels of the crown. Moreover, Marx goes on to argue that the support given to Louis Bonaparte by the peasantry can be understood only in terms of the peasants' longing for the past. As a scattered, fragmented group of small land holders, a 'class which is not a class', the peasants cannot represent themselves but must be represented. They dream of a power which would bring them unity from outside; failing to recognize the real conditions of their misery, they are moved by the 'phantoms of the empire' and lend their support to the second Bonaparte instead of aligning themselves with the proletariat, even though the latter is, on Marx's account, their true ally.

These analyses highlight the extent to which Marx acknowledged – implicitly or explicitly – the importance of the symbolic, 'imaginary' aspects of social life in modern societies. He suggests that, in these societies, individuals are constantly confronted with what is new, but they are unable to face it with open eyes and instead take refuge in the images of the past. Thus *The Eighteenth Brumaire* opens with this celebrated passage:

> The tradition of all the dead generations weighs like a nightmare on the brain of the living. And just when they seem engaged in revolutionising themselves and things, in creating something that has never yet existed, precisely in such periods of revolutionary crisis they anxiously conjure up the spirits of the past to their service and borrow from them names, battle-cries and costumes in order to present the new scene of world history in this time-honoured disguise and this borrowed language.[20]

At the very moment when human beings are involved in the process of creating their own history, of undertaking unprecedented tasks, they draw back before the risks and uncertainties of such an enterprise and invoke representations which assure them of their continuity with the past. At the very moment when continuity is threatened, they *invent* a past which restores the calm. Thus the diffusion of representations in modern societies serves to conceal the fact that these societies are *historical*, that is, susceptible to continuous transformation and always open to the emergence of what is new. It also serves to conceal the fact that these societies are *divided*, that is, split apart along various lines which separate those who are dominant from those who are dominated. It is in terms of this double function of representation that Lefort develops his own account of the principal forms and transformations of ideology in modern societies.

'Outline of the Genesis of Ideology in Modern Societies' was originally published in 1974 in the journal *Textures*. It is an original attempt to rethink the concept of ideology and to demonstrate its relevance to the analysis of contemporary societies. The concept of ideology has been used in many disparate ways in recent years, so much so that it is now in danger of meaning little more than 'ideas' or 'system of beliefs'. Lefort is justly critical of this dilution; he is concerned to recover that sense in which 'ideology' once referred to the logic of dominant discourses, a logic which had to be disclosed through a process of interpretation and critique. This is a sense of 'ideology' which may be found in Marx's work, even if Marx did not develop a clear and systematic theory of ideology. Marx linked the notion of ideology, Lefort argues, to a 'triple denial': the denial of social division (in particular class division), the denial of temporal division (the difference between present and past), and the denial of the division between knowledge and practice. Thus Marx did not regard ideology as simply the product of a particular class, such as the bourgeoisie. Rather, he linked ideology to the fundamental *divisions* characteristic of modern societies, divisions which, for various reasons, cannot be expressed openly and without the aid of dissimulating devices. But if Marx was right to approach ideology in this way, there are other aspects of his work which tend to limit the fruitfulness of his approach. For, in the last analysis, he tends to understand social division in naturalistic terms, relating it back to a division of labour which arises 'naturally' between the sexes and which develops in accordance with a quasi-naturalistic evolutionary schema. He tends, in the last analysis, to treat the spheres of politics and symbolism as derivative from, or dependent upon, a 'real' process which unfolds at the level of production and class struggle, even though his historical studies, such as *The Eighteenth Brumaire*, attest to the fact that matters are much more complicated. Hence Lefort, while wishing to elaborate on certain themes in Marx's writings, is fully aware that in many respects Marx's work must be left behind.

In developing his account of ideology, Lefort proposes to restrict the application of the term 'ideology' to a certain kind of discourse which prevails in particular types of society. The types of society concerned are those which belong to the 'modern era', that is, those which emerged from the ruins of feudalism and which currently comprise the developed industrial societies of the East and the West. At the origin of the modern era lies a development whose significance Lefort regards as paramount. Gradually there emerged, during the late fourteenth and early fifteenth centuries, a discourse on politics and society which was no longer couched in theological or 'transcendental' terms, which was no longer subordinated, in other words, to the representation of 'another world'.[21] This 'discourse on the social', as Lefort calls it, is located *within the social*; it no longer claims to draw its legitimacy from a world or a being which lies beyond the social sphere. The emergence of a discourse on the social coincided with the development of a mode of production which radically transformed social relations and created a society which is constantly subjected to rapid change, a society which is 'open', 'indeterminate', 'historical'. Ideology, in Lefort's view, is that kind of discourse on the social which seeks to conceal the social divisions inherent in modern societies and their historical, indeterminate character; or as Lefort says, 'ideology is the sequence of representations which have the function of re-establishing the dimension of society "without history" at the very heart of historical society'.[22] Ideology may thus be conceived of as a specific regime of the 'social imaginary', if by the latter term we understand that creative, symbolic dimension of social life through which human beings represent themselves and their collective modes of co-existence.[23] But unlike other forms of the social imaginary, ideology cannot make reference to 'another world'. As a discourse on the social, ideology must remain within the social sphere, must avail itself of the resources of the social in order to carry out its task of sealing every crack. This is, however, a risky, conflict-laden undertaking. For ideology always runs the risk of appearing *as* a discourse, a particular discourse in the

service of a particular group or class; and hence its capacity to dissimulate social and temporal divisions is constantly threatened by
the possibility that the very attempt to dissimulate will become
apparent to all.

The general properties of ideological discourse are manifested in
the different forms of ideology which may be discerned in modern
societies. Lefort distinguishes three principal forms; these forms are
internally related in the sense that, by examining the reasons for the
failure of one form we may gain some insight into the mechanisms
which govern another. The first form of ideological discourse analysed by Lefort is the so-called 'bourgeois' ideology which reached
its peak in the nineteenth century. While it continued to be interlaced
with the remnants of religion, bourgeois ideology gradually broke its
links with religious discourse and discarded the reference to a
spiritual or mythical 'elsewhere'. In place of this 'elsewhere' it sub-,
stituted general, abstract ideas; the text of bourgeois ideology,
remarks Lefort, is written in capital letters: Humanity, Progress,
Science, Property, Family, Nation. These ideas are both representations and 'rules', in the sense that they imply a certain way of
acting which is consistent with the idea. The ideas thus give rise to
an opposition between the subject who speaks and acts in accordance
with the rule, and the 'other' who has no access to the rule and is
therefore deprived of the status of the subject. The opposition is
expressed in a series of dichotomies: worker/bourgeois, savage/civi-
lized, mad/normal, child/adult. Across these dichotomies there
emerges a 'natural being', a sub-social, sub-human sphere, the
image of which underpins the affirmation of a society above nature.
By drawing a distinction between society and that which lies below
it, in an underworld of seedy chaos which allegedly threatens the
social order, bourgeois ideology seeks to conceal any divisions which
exist within society. The strength of this ideology stems from the fact
that its discourses are multiple and disjoint. It does not 'speak' from
a single place, but multiplies and divides itself in accordance with
the differentiation of social institutions in bourgeois society (the
state, the legal system, the business firm, the educational system,
etc.). But the dispersion of the discourses of bourgeois ideology also
gives rise to the possibility of its failure. The ideology harbours
incompatible representations, internal discordances, and hence runs
the risk of revealing itself as a discourse of dissimulation. Moreover,
it is caught in the inescapable contradiction of a discourse which

strives to secure a point of certainty from which it can speak about the social world, producing abstract ideas which claim to transcend reality, and yet the *loss* of such a point of certainty lies at the very origin of ideology. Hence bourgeois ideology is destined to undergo a constant and ultimately futile process of displacement, a process which has, as Lefort puts it, no 'safety catch'.

The failures and contradictions of bourgeois ideology shed light on the nature of totalitarian ideology, which is the second form analysed by Lefort. Totalitarian ideology may be understood as an attempt to produce a unified discourse which explicitly asserts the homogeneity of the social domain, in lieu of relying on a multiplicity of disjointed discourses. An explicit quest for totalization replaces the implicit and interminable labour of occultation. In developing an account of totalitarian ideology, Lefort takes up and elaborates his earlier analyses of totalitarianism. Thus totalitarian ideology seeks to efface the boundaries between different sectors of society, and between civil society and the state; it seeks to diffuse power throughout society, without allowing power to appear divided. The idea of the 'organization' is therefore essential to this ideology, for it provides a way of assigning everyone a function within a smoothly operating machine. This ideology also implies the vision of a 'centre' from which social life is organized, a centre which is located within the state apparatus and which ultimately unifies knowledge and power. However, the ideal of a well-ordered and fully mastered social organization is constantly threatened by the occurrence of all sorts of events – economic, political and cultural – which escape the prediction of the leaders and are capable of displaying an organizational failure. Various means of defence are set in motion in an attempt to defuse these potentially disruptive events; the critique of bureaucratism and inefficiency are evident examples. A more fundamental mechanism of defence is to *exclude* the disruptive events, to treat them as representatives of the 'outside' of a society claimed to be homogeneous. The disruptive event or troublesome agent is cast out as an alien element, a representative of the anti-social. But, in the long run, this exclusion is unlikely to succeed. Disruptive events and troublesome agents constantly reappear; they haunt the organization, calling forth a discourse which seeks to explain away or suppress the unwanted element, a discourse which 'runs the risk of appearing as a generalized lie, as discourse in the service of power, the mere mask of oppression'.[24]

The third form of ideology considered by Lefort is what he describes as the 'invisible ideology'. This is the form of ideology, in his view, which currently prevails in Western industrial societies. It retains some of the principles of previous forms of ideology, while fusing them together in a new, more resilient system of dissimulation. As in totalitarianism, the new ideology seeks to secure the homogenization and unification of the social domain; but this project is severed from the affirmation of totality, rendered latent, implicit, 'invisible'. The project of homogenization is thus reconnected to the key principle of bourgeois ideology, which required the constant displacement of discourses, which tolerated their conflict and worked out compromises. However, whereas bourgeois ideology presented itself as a discourse on the social, distinct from the social discourse which is constitutive of everyday life, the new ideology seeks to merge with social discourse. It finds an excellent means of diffusion in the mass media, which reach a vast audience and draw everyone in to a conversation apparently open to all. The most banal programmes on radio and television, the chat shows and question times, become inner sanctums in a mass society, intimate worlds where the sense of distance and adversity has been abolished. Therein lies the imaginary, ideological dimension of mass communication: it provides the constant assurance of the social bond, attests to the permanent presence of the 'between-us', the *entre-nous*, and thereby effaces the forms of temporal and social division. Lefort extends this analysis to the language and imagery of advertising, which are pervasive features of a society oriented towards consumption. The consumer product is always located in a 'system of objects',[25] where what is new is merely different from other things; and the consumer is presented with a world in which everything can, in principle, be grasped. As a version of the new ideology, the discourse of consumption thus establishes a closed universe, repetitive and pre-arranged, but renders this discourse invisible by the very absence of a totalizing discourse. This does not mean, however, that the contradictions which disrupt the bourgeois and totalitarian ideologies are comfortably resolved in the new ideology. On the contrary, insists Lefort, the more this ideology seeks to coincide with social discourse – the more 'invisible' it seeks to become – the more it runs the risk of losing the function of legitimating the established order. The absorption of the discourse on the social into the social discourse is a way of preventing the former from appearing as a contingent discourse in the service of power; but it raises the possibility that power may now appear as groundless, as deprived of the legitimating support that ideological discourse previously sought to provide.

## Democracy and Totalitarianism

Lefort's analysis of the principal forms and transformations of ideo-logy helps to illuminate some of the connections which exist between the symbolic systems of modern societies. Each of these systems is governed by a 'logic', that is by specific aims and inherent contra-dictions, which can be discerned and related to the logic of other systems. This systematic, comparative approach also animates Lefort's most recent investigations. Once again the reference point of reflection is that form of society which has emerged in the Soviet Union and Eastern Europe. However, Lefort now examines this form of society from a somewhat different angle; rather than analys-ing it primarily in terms of bureaucratic organization or by com-parison with bourgeois ideology, he now approaches it by means of a contrast between democracy and totalitarianism. The notion of democracy is, of course, a complex and contested notion, a notion which today means different things to different people and yet which is, in one form or another, seemingly championed by all. Lefort's view of this notion is determined by several considerations. In the first place, he believes that the liberal democratic thinkers of the eighteenth and nineteenth centuries gave voice to experiences and articulated values which are worth re-examining and defending today. Hence Lefort rejects those arguments which seek to equate democracy with bourgeois democracy and to reject the whole out of hand. He proposes, instead, to return to the texts of the liberal democratic thinkers, to the texts of de Tocqueville, Guizot, Michelet, and to reappraise some of their ideas.[26] A second consideration which governs Lefort's approach is that democracy should be seen, not so much as a specific institution or cluster of institutions, but rather as a 'form' of modern society, that is, as a particular way in which society is articulated or 'instituted'. This mode of articulation or institution involves a certain configuration of power and a certain conception of its symbolic character. These and other characteristics of democracy can be highlighted – and this is a third consideration which governs Lefort's approach – by reflecting on a form of society which was not available to nineteenth-century thinkers, but which represents, as it were, an 'eclipse' of the democratic form. Thus the experience of totalitarianism is not tangential, in Lefort's view, to our understanding of democracy; on the contrary, it is the struggle of people in Hungary, Poland and Czechoslovakia, it is the battle of words and rights which is currently being fought by groups and individuals in the USSR and Eastern Europe, which teaches us what 'democracy' means today.

The emergence of the democratic form of society was the result of a series of transformations which began to take place in medieval and early modern Europe. Among these transformations was the gradual development of a system of states based on a notion of sovereignty and differentiated from the societies within which they exercised power. The sphere of political power was thus separated from society as a whole and from the spheres of economic activity, law, knowledge and so on. Political power was not only separated but also circumscribed. Its legitimacy was no longer based on ideas such as divine right but rather on 'the people'; and 'the image of popular sovereignty', observes Lefort, 'is linked to the image of an empty place (*lieu vide*), impossible to occupy, such that those who exercise public authority can never claim to appropriate it'.[27] This notion of power as an 'empty place' provides the key, on Lefort's account, to the nature of modern democracy. Democracy is sustained by the tension between two principles: on the one hand, power stems from the people; on the other hand, it is the power of nobody. The principle that power belongs to nobody is reflected in the contemporary institutionalized forms of competition between political parties, but the general significance of this principle goes beyond any particular institutional arrangement. The tension between these two principles is essential to democracy and it cannot be resolved without threatening or destroying democracy as such. This perspective sheds light, in Lefort's view, on the formation of totalitarianism. For totalitarianism *actualizes* the image of popular sovereignty by means of a party which claims to identify with the people and which, beneath the cover of this identification, seeks to *occupy* the place of power. Hence power ceases to be an 'empty place'; it is given a substantial reality and it seeks to subordinate the spheres of economic activity, law, knowledge and so on to itself, to absorb civil society into the state and to efface every form of social division. The indeterminacy characteristic of the democratic form of society, the uncertainty

associated with a place of power which remains 'empty', 'unoc-
cupied', 'open', is eclipsed by a political form which seeks to fuse
power and knowledge in a determinate social whole with clearly
defined goals.

The democratic form of society is linked with a particular notion
of 'right' which, once again, has emerged historically. The differentiation of the political sphere from society as a whole and the
development of a state of limited right implied the separation of
power and right: thus it is declared, for instance, that there are
rights inherent to 'man' which must be respected by the state. Doctrines of human rights have a long history and no doubt there are
many aspects of these doctrines which can be criticized. But Lefort
believes that, just as it would be unwise to conflate democracy with
bourgeois democracy and to reject the whole out of hand, so too it
would be shortsighted to dismiss the idea of human rights. That
some people influenced by Marx have been inclined to do so is not
surprising, for Marx himself was scathing in his critique of the
'rights of man' in *On the Jewish Question*. It is to this critique that
Lefort returns in the essay entitled 'Politics and Human Rights',
first published in 1980. For Marx, the doctrine of the 'rights of
man', such as it was espoused in the late eighteenth century, was
merely a cover for the dissociation of individuals in society and their
separation from a genuine political community. 'The so-called *rights
of man*', wrote Marx, 'are nothing but the rights of a *member of civil
society*, i.e., the rights of egoistic man, of man separated from other
men and from the community'.[28] Marx's conception of these rights,
his dismissive remarks on liberty, equality, security, the freedom of
opinion and so on, are the outcome of his conviction that these rights
are merely so many expressions of abstract bourgeois individualism.
Marx fails to go behind the rhetoric of individualism; had he done
so, he would have seen that these rights could not, in any case, be
regarded as merely individual, since their actualization always presupposes a social context. Had he done so, he might have been less
inclined to adopt a wholly negative attitude towards these rights and
he might have seen that, far from expressing merely the egoism of
isolated individuals in civil society, they express the refusal to allow
civil society to be absorbed by the state and they provide a basis of
opposition to the established order.

Lefort sees the struggle for human rights as a 'generative principle' of democratic society. By this he means that these rights do not

'exist' in democratic societies in the form of specific laws and institutions; rather, they animate institutions and engendre laws in so far as these institutions and laws are the outcome of struggles rooted in an *awareness of rights*. It is this general awareness of rights, over and beyond the specific content of any particular right, which is characteristic of modern democratic societies. This awareness is 'indeterminate' in the sense that the rights themselves are not fixed, like so many possessions which have been acquired once and for all. Their content changes with time, new rights emerge and give rise to new forms of struggle, always expressed in terms of right: the right to work, the right to equal pay, the right to live free from the threat of industrial pollution or nuclear destruction. These various forms of struggle, which are evident features of Western democratic societies today, are fragmented and disparate by nature. They emerge from different places within society, from different groups or different locales, and they do not tend to fuse together in a single, unified, overall project. They do not ignore the state, they often attack it or call upon it to respond in some way, but they do not seek a collective solution to their concerns through the conquest or destruction of state power. The new forms of struggle do not aim to take hold of the state and thereby to coincide with it; rather, they are more commonly concerned to maintain and nourish their own autonomy, or to acquire the mutual recognition of their rights and liberties, within a social space which is separated from state power. The Left has often found itself disarmed (or at least somewhat disturbed) in face of these new forms of struggle, captivated as it is by the image of a unified struggle for an alternative society, a society which would, as it were, 'accord spontaneously with itself'.[29] Lefort firmly defends the value of the initiatives taken by groups seeking greater participation in those aspects of social life which concern them and he regards such initiatives as an essential aspect of democracy. But he is also aware of the difficulties and dangers involved in any attempt to generalize these initatives to the level of society as a whole; and he is not taken in by the myths that the Left is inclined to spin in order to convince itself that these difficulties and dangers do not exist.

If the struggle for human rights is an inherent feature of democratic society, it also attests to a democratic impulse within totalitarianism. When Soviet dissidents or Polish workers voice their criticisms or issue their demands, they are not merely calling for specific policy changes on the part of the state: they are also implicitly demanding the *right* to criticize and to make demands. However much these dissidents or workers may insist that they have no wish to engage in politics, their actions are pre-eminently political. For their criticisms and demands call into question the very 'logic' of totalitarian power, which is to encircle the 'public sphere', to absorb civil society into the state and to identify itself with the 'body' of the people while at the same time constituting its 'head'. In 'The Logic of Totalitarianism' (1980), Lefort explores this 'logic' in more detail and examines why the Left has failed to understand the nature of totalitarianism. Faced with the realities of the USSR and Eastern Europe, the Left has always hesitated, divided itself, adopted inconsistent or hypocritical attitudes; it has allowed conservatives or liberals to take the lead in developing a critical approach. The ultimate reason for this failure, Lefort argues, is that the Left has always lacked a conception of political society. The Left has always tended to treat political power as secondary to the economy and has given insufficient attention to the transformations of the relations between state and society and to the symbolic dimensions of power. It is by analysing these transformations and dimensions that Lefort seeks (and for thirty years has sought) to formulate a critical conception of totalitarianism.

'The Image of the Body and Totalitarianism' is a remarkable account of one aspect of the system of representations characteristic of totalitarianism. The essay was first presented as a lecture to a group of psychoanalysts, and subsequently published in the journal *Confrontation* in 1979. The starting point of Lefort's account is the representation, basic to totalitarianism, of the 'People-as-One': internal division is denied, and yet at the same time an opposition is affirmed between the People-as-One and an 'Other' which is regarded as the Enemy of the People. This representation gives rise to a new image of the social body, the 'body politic'. The People-as-One forms a social body which is held together and sustained by a Power-as-One, a power which simultaneously embraces and stands for the whole. This Power-as-One is what Solzhenitsyn describes as the 'Egocrat';[30] it too is an 'other', but an omniscient, omnipotent, benevolent other who sacrifices himself for the sake of the social body. The Enemies of the People are altogether different. They are attacked with a fervour which amounts to a kind of 'social prophylaxis', 'as if the body had to assure itself of its own identity by expelling its waste matter'.[31] This image of the social body contrasts in an

interesting way with the image characteristic of the *ancien régime*.
Ernst Kantorowicz has analysed the way in which the image of the
king's body as a double body, incarnating the community and
underpinned by the body of Christ, developed through the Middle
Ages.[32] Lefort takes up this analysis and argues that the 'democratic
revolution', of which de Tocqueville spoke, involved not only a
'decapitation' of the body politic but also a 'disincorporation' of the
individual. The democratic revolution gave rise to a society which is
radically indeterminate and uncontrollable, a society whose identity
can no longer be defined in terms of the identity of a social body.
Totalitarianism, by contrast, seeks to banish the indeterminacy
which haunts democratic society by revitalizing the social body. But
the image of this revitalized body is quite different from that which
permeated the society of the *ancien régime*, for the Egocrat has lost the
religious dimension which characterized the double body of the king:
the Egocrat is located within society, while at the same time claiming
to lead it as if it were the omniscient head of the People-as-One.

It would be misleading to give the impression that Lefort is concerned only to analyse the logic and ideology of totalitarianism,
without regard to actual social, political and economic developments.
He has always insisted that one must study 'two sides' of totalitarianism: on the one hand, its ideal aim or project, together with its
characteristic system of representations; on the other, the actual
events and developments which take place in Eastern Europe and
the Soviet Union, and which indicate that all is not unfolding in
accordance with the ideal. Lefort devoted long essays to the uprisings in Hungary, Poland and Czechoslovakia in the 1950s and
1960s.[33] In 'Pushing Back the Limits of the Possible', with which
this volume concludes, he discusses the significance of the events
which have shaken Poland in recent years. The essay was written in
November 1980, at a time when the atmosphere in Poland was tense
and the future uncertain. Solidarity had conducted a series of
strikes; the government had made a string of concessions; an historic
agreement had apparently been reached between the two protagonists. But Lefort, writing in the midst of these developments, is not
optimistic: the government cannot, and will not, tolerate a situation
of double power. 'One would fail to recognize the profound
character of the conflict if one thought that the claims put forward
could be satisfied without striking at the supremacy of the party.'[34]
Lefort suspects that the government, in coming to an agreement

with the leaders of Solidarity, is merely playing for time, adopting a strategy which will temporarily defuse the situation while it decides how best to eliminate the threat. And now we know, sadly, that Lefort was right.

Even if the future of the independent trade-union movement in Poland is doubtful, the struggle which it has conducted is, in Lefort's view, of great significance. In certain respects the Polish movement, while perhaps less dramatic than the Hungarian and Czech uprisings, goes further than the latter. For it moves beyond the dilemma of reform or destruction of communist power and aims instead to assert the autonomy of civil society at a distance from that power. The Polish movement contradicts the logic of the totalitarian system from within, as it were, by reaffirming that distinction between state and civil society which the totalitarian system seeks to efface. The threat which this movement poses is thus considerable. With each demand issued by the workers, the right to make demands is brought to the consciousness of the Polish people, making them aware of their collective strength and their unlimited capacity to take initiatives. With each concession granted by the government, the gap deepens between the state apparatus and the workers, in such a way that the former can no longer appear as the representative of the latter. The Polish movement has disrupted the logic of totalitarianism, at least for a while. And Lefort had no doubt that, in the future, in one place or another and in some form that we cannot foresee, this logic will be disrupted again.

Lefort's writings over the last thirty years span a wide range of subject matter and address issues of great theoretical and political importance. While there are many respects in which his views could be contested, there can be no doubt about the pressing nature of his concerns. His attempt to develop a systematic perspective on the political and symbolic forms which have come to prevail in the twentieth century will become a reference point for anyone interested in the nature of modern societies. His critical analyses of the work of Marx and others will nourish the continuing debate about the strengths and weaknesses, the insights and illusions, of the great texts which have become part of the societies in which we live. While Lefort has been deeply influenced by these texts and shares some of the values commonly associated with the socialist and liberal traditions, he is well aware that these texts are flawed and that the resources of these traditions fall short of the political realities of our time. He asks uncomfortable questions, dismantles reassuring myths, forces us to face issues which many people would prefer to ignore. No one can read his work and fail to be impressed by the richness and originality of his reflection on the political forms of modern society.

# Part I

# Problems of Politics
# and Bureaucracy

# 1

# The Contradiction of Trotsky

Let us hold out our hands to each other and rally around our Party's committees. We must not forget even for a minute that only the Party committees can worthily lead us, only they will light our way to the Promised Land.

It was in these words, with the turn of phrase now familiar to us all, that as early as 1905 Stalin addressed the Russian workers on the occasion of their first revolution. It may well have been on that very same day, Trotsky notes, that Lenin despatched from Geneva the following appeal to the masses: 'Make way for the anger and hatred that have accumulated in your hearts throughout the centuries of exploitation, suffering and grief!'[1]

Nothing could be more typical of the two men, or better bring out the contrast between them, than these two statements, one made by a revolutionary for whom the oppressed masses are the essential force of history, the other made by a party militant, already a 'bureaucrat', for whom the party apparatus alone knows what the future is to be and is capable of bringing it about. For us who are familiar with the course that events have taken since then, this psychological opposition assumes a more general significance, for it forms part of a broader opposition that is essentially historical in character.

In his long book on Stalin, Trotsky tried to expose the character of his protagonist and the nature of his behaviour before his accession to power and to show how both were in a sense legitimated by history during the decline of the revolution, with the formation of a new social stratum, the bureaucracy. In substantiating his thesis. Trotsky used the traditional methods of the historian: he examined the documents, explored the annals of Bolshevism, cited eye-witnesses, interpreted

dates, placed side by side documents written prior to 1923 and the
commissioned panegyrics composed after the advent of the bureaucracy.[2] In the first phase of his political activity, Stalin is shown to
have been a 'provincial' militant, intellectually mediocre and politically inept. In Georgia, he never managed to bring together a Bolshevik
fraction to confront the Mensheviks within the social-democratic
fold; he attended the first Bolshevik Party congresses only in the
capacity of an observer, since he never managed to win a sufficient
number of votes to get elected as a delegate. At the London Congress,
the mandate that he claimed was shown to be fraudulent and he was
deprived of voting rights. He was able to join the Bolshevik Central
Committee only by co-option, that is, without ever having been
elected by the party militants. The uprising of February 1917 suddenly gave him, in Lenin's absence, an exceptional degree of power
which he used as badly as possible: he was in favour of supporting
the provisional government, the revolutionary war and, in the final
analysis, the revolution in two stages. He was one of those opportunistic conciliators whom the workers in the party wanted to expel,[3]
and whom Lenin was later to return to their places, when he put forward his famous April theses and rearmed the party with a view to
the seizure of power. These fragments of information enable Trotsky
to sketch a portrait of a rather uninteresting character, a 'functionary' as Trotsky says, by which he wished to stress Stalin's narrow
preoccupation with his work, his limitations as a theoretician and his
propensity for routine. Trotsky's intention is obvious: he wanted to
show that the 'qualities' which enabled Stalin to become the man of
the bureaucracy are precisely those which prevented him from being
a revolutionary figure.

The argument is clear enough and sufficiently supported with evidence. But, in that case, one cannot but be surprised that a political
writer of Trotsky's abilities should have believed it his duty to devote
such a large book to him, to undertake a task that consists very largely
of anecdotal history, almost of detective work, to prove that, throughout the pre-revolutionary and revolutionary period, Stalin was an
obscure figure, and that it was precisely this fact which enabled him
to emerge, in 1924, as a 'ready-made dictator'. Stalin's life was not
unknown to the public. In 1935 Boris Souvarine had published a
substantial work on Stalin,[4] to which Trotsky added little that was
new and of which, curiously enough, he pretended to be unaware.
If we assume that Trotsky felt that he had a duty to inform the

revolutionary vanguard about the background and development of the current dictator of Russia, then this duty had already been carried out. But Souvarine was not content, as Trotsky had been in his three hundred pages, to describe Stalin's behaviour. He had skilfully integrated this study into a much broader and more interesting analysis of the Bolshevik Party. The single-minded determination with which Trotsky stresses the mediocrity of his 'hero', and the subordinate nature of the posts that he occupied in the revolutionary apparatus has, of course, been taken as an indication of Trotsky's personal resentment and desire for self-justification. Trotsky, it is said, set out to compare his own situation and destiny with those of Stalin before the revolution; he wanted to bring out the enormous distance that separated himself from that obscure functionary of Bolshevism. However, if one knows anything about Trotsky's temperament one soon realizes that such concerns were quite alien to him and that such an interpretation is artificial. If one must speak of self-justification, it would be more appropriate to do so by giving this term a political sense. One might say, for instance, that Trotsky wished to show that he had been deprived of power not because of any lack of political intelligence, but by the overwhelming power of objective factors. And this power of objective factors could be proved by the very mediocrity of the new leader. The end of Trotsky's Introduction makes this interpretation a very tempting one. 'He [Stalin] took possession of power', writes Trotsky,

> not with the aid of personal qualities, but with the aid of an impersonal machine. And it was not he who created the machine, but the machine that created him. That machine, with its force and its authority, was the product of the prolonged and heroic struggle of the Bolshevik Party, which itself grew out of ideas. The machine was the bearer of the idea before it became an end in itself . . . Lenin created the machine through constant association with the masses, if not by oral word, then by printed word, if not directly, then through the medium of his disciples. Stalin did not create the machine but took possession of it.[5]

Trotsky was already expressing, in a different form, the same sentiments when, in *My Life*, he wrote:

> And the fact that today he is playing first is not so much a summing-up of the man as it is of this transitional period of political backsliding

in the country. Helvetius said it long ago: 'Every period has its great men, and if these are lacking, it invents them.' Stalinism is above all else the automatic work of the impersonal apparatus of the decline of the revolution.[6]

However I do not believe that this interpretation is entirely satisfactory either. Trotsky's study of Stalin does not strike me so much as a conscious attempt at self-justification; it seems to me, above all, to play the role of a substitute. When we open his *Stalin*, we are in no doubt that Trotsky has written under this title a new study of the USSR, that he has taken up again the whole problem of Stalinism and tried to give it an economic and social characterization: this was certainly his concern, as we know from his last published articles. It is what we expected of him. But this *Stalin*, this imposingly long work which laboriously follows the steps of the then anonymous master of the Kremlin, showing us that he was unable to direct a particular strike, or that while in deportation he went around with common-law criminals and was despised by the political prisoners: this work that one would have liked to regard as important is restricted to demolishing a legend in which serious people do not believe. I regard this work, therefore, as a kind of *aborted attempt*. Trotsky gossips quite unnecessarily about Stalin, because he would like to, but cannot, define Stalinism. Nothing could better confirm us in this belief than the second part of the book, which is intentionally more limited and insubstantial and which deals by allusion with events of the first importance:[7] this is because it concerns specifically the period of the crystallization and triumph of the bureaucracy, that is, not so much Stalin himself as Stalinism. But Trotsky could not claim that he had exhausted the subject in the two or three chapters that he devoted to it in *The Revolution Betrayed* and in *My Life*.

It is to this formative period of Stalinism that I should like to return, beginning with the scattered statements on the subject that are to be found in Trotsky's last work. By its inadequacies, its contradictions, by its silences as well, it calls for a critique that would put Trotsky back in his place as an actor in a situation which, when writing his book, he tries all too easily to master.

### Trotsky's Struggle against Stalin

A reading of *Stalin*, or of the earlier *The Revolution Betrayed* or *My Life*, would lead one to believe that the attitude of Trotsky and of the Left

Opposition, in the great period of 1923–7, was a perfectly rigorous one. It is as if Trotsky, 'bearer' of revolutionary consciousness, had been swept aside by the inexorable course of things that were then developing in a reactionary direction. There were a great many who, taking sides against Trotsky and in a way for Stalin, reproach-ed Trotsky only for not having been realistic enough, not having been able to 'adapt' the politics of revolutionary Russia to the dif-ficult circumstances of a capitalist world undergoing reconsolid-ation. They did not dispute that Trotsky had then adopted a clearly revolutionary attitude, but it was precisely this attitude that they denounced as abstract. In any case, it is not usually denied that the Left Opposition had a coherent strategy, whether it was justified at the level of revolutionary morality or whether it was regarded as in-opportune. Trotsky himself largely lent support to this view. In his works, he speaks of this period with perfect serenity, repeating that he acted as he had to act in the given objective situation. History, he says in essence, was taking a new course. No one could block the ebbing tide of the revolution. Thus, recalling the events of the decisive year 1927, he writes in *My Life*:

> We went to meet the inevitable debacle, confident, however, that we were paving the way for the triumph of our ideas in a more distant future . . . It is possible by force of arms to check the development of progressive historical tendencies; it is not possible to block the road of the advance of progressive ideas for ever. That is why, when the struggle is one for great principles, the revolutionary can only follow one rule: *Fais ce que tu dois, advienne que pourra.*[8]

It would be quite admirable, when one is in the midst of historical action, to retain such lucidity and to be able to stand above day-to-day events, perceiving what is permanent in the heart of what is immediately present. But one must ask whether Trotsky was as lucid when he was acting as he was when he was writing. For it is one thing to judge one's own past actions, to look back on a relatively closed period in which the most diverse actions seem to take on a single, absolute meaning; it is a quite different thing to act in an equivocal situation with an indeterminate future.

In his *Stalin* Trotsky defines once again the principles of the Left Opposition in its anti-Stalinist struggle:

> Numerous critics, publicists, correspondents, historians, biographers, and sundry amateur sociologists, have lectured the Left Opposition

from time to time on the error of its ways, saying that the strategy of the Left Opposition was not feasible from the point of view of the struggle for power. However, the very approach to the question was incorrect. The Left Opposition could not achieve power, and did not hope even to do so—certainly not its most thoughtful leaders. A struggle for power by the Left Opposition, by a revolutionary Marxist organization, was conceivable only under the conditions of a revolutionary upsurge. Under such conditions the strategy is based on aggression, on direct appeal to the masses, on frontal attack against the government. Quite a few members of the Left Opposition had played no minor part in such a struggle and had first-hand knowledge of how to wage it. But during the early twenties and later, there was no revolutionary upsurge in Russia, quite the contrary. Under such circumstances it was out of the question to launch a struggle for power.

Bear in mind that in the years of reaction, in 1908–1911 and later, the Bolshevik Party refused to launch a direct attack upon the monarchy and limited itself to the task of preparing for the eventual offensive by fighting for the survival of the revolutionary traditions and for the preservation of certain cadres, subjecting the developing events to untiring analysis, and utilizing all legal and semi-legal possibilities for training the advance stratum of workers. *The Left Opposition could not proceeed otherwise under similar conditions.* Indeed the conditions of Soviet reaction were immeasurably more difficult for the Opposition than the conditions of the Tsarist reaction had been for the Bolsheviks.[9]

The first observation to be made is that this interpretation of the years following 1927 is in contradiction with Trotsky's general theses on the nature of Stalinism. In all his works he has said that Stalinism is based on a proletarian infrastructure: it is reactionary, but it is a moment of the dictatorship of the proletariat. For example, in 'The Workers' State, Thermidor and Bonapartism' Trotsky writes:

This usurpation [of power by the bureaucracy] was made possible and can maintain itself only because the *social content of the dictatorship of the bureaucracy is determined by those productive relations that were created by the proletarian revolution.* In this sense we may say with complete justification that the dictatorship of the proletariat found its distorted but indubitable expression in the dictatorship of the bureaucracy.[10]

How, then, if one maintains Trotsky's general theses on the nature of Stalinism, could the struggle against Stalin, still regarded by him as a political struggle, require, as he says in his last work, a revolutionary upheaval? When Trotsky compares the situation of the Left

Opposition with that in which the Bolshevik Party found itself in its struggle against Tsarism, he implies—quite rightly, in my opinion, but in contradiction with all his theses—that the struggle against the bureaucracy could only be a class struggle. I can only agree with the conclusions that he draws from this: the maintenance of revolutionary traditions, the preservation of the cadres, the tireless analysis of events in order to instruct the most conscious workers. But it is no accident if these conclusions, whose true import he fails to grasp, correspond in no way to the real tactics which were his and those of the Left Opposition in practice.

Indeed it is striking to see, when one examines the events of this period closely, that the struggle of the Left Opposition against Stalin almost never assumed a revolutionary form and always developed around compromise. The problem is not the one that Trotsky poses, namely, whether it was possible or desirable to undertake a struggle for power. The question was to lead the struggle—or to lay the ground for the future—in a revolutionary spirit. The Bolsheviks were in retreat between 1908 and 1911 and postponed until later the struggle for the seizure of power; but, on the theoretical plane, they did not make the slightest concession to their adversaries. At no time did the Bolsheviks ever indulge in a policy of compromise or conciliation with Tsarism. By contrast, it is Trotsky himself who declared in November 1934, referring to his attitude to Eastman when the latter revealed on his own initiative the existence of Lenin's Testament: 'My statement at that time on Eastman cannot be understood except as an integral part of our line, which, at that time, was orientated towards conciliation and appeasement.'[11] In 1929 he was writing from the same point of view and in a much more brutal manner:

> Right up to the last minute, I avoided the struggle, for, in the first stage, it had the character of an unprincipled conspiracy directed towards me, personally. It was clear to me that a struggle of this nature, once begun, would inevitably assume an exceptional vigour and, in the conditions of the revolutionary dictatorship, might lead to dangerous consequences. This is not the place to try to find out whether it was correct *at the cost of the greatest personal concessions* to tend to preserve the foundations of a common work, or whether it was necessary for me to throw myself into an offensive all along the line, despite the absence, for such an offensive, of adequate political bases. The fact is that I chose the first solution and that in spite of everything I do not regret it.[12]

Trotsky speaks here in an intentionally vague way of 'personal concessions'. But it is clear that, given his situation, those conditions could only have a political character.

Without going into detail as to what those concessions were, in other words, what the Left Opposition's policy of 'conciliation and appeasement' actually was, something should be said about a period that Trotsky usually passes over fairly rapidly: the year 1923, when Lenin was still alive and preparing a 'bomb against Stalin' for the Twelfth Congress, when Trotsky was still regarded as the second most important Bolshevik leader by the majority of the party, and when, above all, Stalin had not yet succeeded in achieving complete control of the party apparatus and the newfound power of the bureacracy was still vulnerable. It is usually thought that the antagonism between Trotsky and Stalin was much more severe than that between Stalin and Lenin. Yet it appears, quite indisputably, according to Trotsky's own memoirs, that it was not he, at this time, who wanted to take up the struggle against Stalin, but Lenin. While fatally ill, Lenin had perceived, quite lucidly, the extreme danger that Stalin and his bureaucratic methods represented for the future of the party. The documents that he left and which are known as the *Testament* leave no doubt on this question. They show in the most striking way that Lenin had decided to launch a decisive struggle against the heads of the bureaucracy: Stalin, Ordzhonikidze and Dzerzhinsky. Trotsky's memoirs show just as clearly that, although he basically shared Lenin's point of view, he did not wish to trigger off decisive hostilities against the Stalinists. Relating a conversation that he had had at this time with Kamenev, who had already gone over to Stalin's side and was acting as his emissary, Trotsky writes:

'Sometimes,' I said, '*out of fear of an imaginary danger*, people are capable of bringing real danger down upon themselves. Remember, and tell others, that the last thing I want is to start a fight at the congress for any changes in organization. I am for preserving the status quo. If Lenin gets on his feet before the congress, of which there is unfortunately little chance, he and I will discuss the matter together anew. I am against removing Stalin, and expelling Ordzhonikidze, and displacing Dzerzhinsky from the commissariat of transport. But I do agree with Lenin in substance.'[13]

Apart from Trotsky's memoirs, the documents are there to show that, against Lenin's will, Trotsky turned the Twelfth Congress of the Bolshevik Party into a congress of unanimity; the 'bomb' concerning the national question that Lenin had advised Trotsky to explode at this congress was set aside. Again it is Trotsky who prides himself on having avoided any struggle with Stalin by contenting himself with amending his resolution instead of fighting it. Significant too was his refusal to present the political report to the congress in Lenin's absence. And the justifications that he gave are no less significant. His whole conduct seems to have been dictated by a concern not to present himself as a pretender to Lenin's succession. It is difficult to understand these preoccupations, these sentimental scruples on the part of a Bolshevik, when a vital political question was at stake.

In fact, Trotsky had refused from the beginning, even when in a superior position, to initiate a struggle to regenerate the party by attacking the bureaucracy. When he maintains that a struggle for power was impossible, it is difficult to believe him – at least in the case of the year 1923, when nothing had yet been decided. Indeed he himself was to write later:

> Would Lenin have been able to carry out the regrouping in the party direction that he planned? At that moment, he undoubtedly would . . . Our joint action against the Central Committee at the beginning of 1923 would without a shadow of a doubt have brought us victory. And what is more, I have no doubt that if I had come forward on the eve of the twelfth congress in the spirit of a '*bloc* of Lenin and Trotsky' against the Stalin bureaucracy, I should have been victorious *even if Lenin had taken no direct part in the struggle*.[14]

It is true that Trotsky adds: 'How solid the victory would have been is, of course, another question.' But even if one answers this question negatively, as he does by showing that the flow of history was then turning into the ebb of the revolution, the task of the politician could never be to compromise with the ebb.

Now, from that point on and 'to the very last minute', the Left Opposition practised a policy of 'conciliation' and 'appeasement'. Even this policy could not remain coherent, for even if the Left Opposition did not want a fight, the bureacracy did. Its triumph involved the annihilation of the former revolutionary leader, at the very time that this leader was seeking an understanding. So Trotsky was led to attack on several occasions; but his attacks bore the sign of his weakness. As Souvarine rightly remarks, Trotsky wore himself out in a vain polemic within the politbureau. In his articles (those that he published on the *New Course* in 1923, and the *Lessons of October* in 1924) he piled allusion on allusion and wrote in such a way that he could be understood only by the leadership of the party. None of his writing was intended to instruct the ordinary militants. Far more seriously, while the bureaucratic repression pitilessly tracked down the members or sympathizers of the Left Opposition, Trotsky did nothing to defend them; by his constantly shifting line he disarmed them politically; he gave them no platform for struggle, no theoretical element that might enable them to recognize themselves and to regroup.

This is not the place to follow in detail Trotsky's political development throughout this period, but we should highlight a few particularly important episodes. At the time of the Thirteenth Congress, the first to be completely 'fabricated' by the bureaucrats, Trotsky, after having defended his views of the State Plan, felt obliged to stress the unity of the party in terms that could not fail to throw all his supporters into confusion.

> None of us desires or is able to dispute the will of the Party. Clearly, the Party is always right . . . We can only be right with and by the Party, for history has provided no other way of being in the right. The English have a saying 'My country, right or wrong,' whether it is in the right or in the wrong, it is my country. We have much better historical justification in saying whether it is right or wrong in certain individual concrete cases, it is my party . . . And if the Party adopts a decision which one or other of us thinks unjust, he will say, just or unjust, it is my Party, and I shall support the consequences of the decision to the end.[15]

It was Trotsky who, in his *Stalin* of 1940, imposes upon himself the most categorical refutation of this view when he declares that a political party is neither 'a homogeneous entity', nor 'an omnipotent historical factor', but 'only a temporary historical instrument, one of very many instruments and schools of history'.[16] The true meaning of Trotsky's statement at the Thirteenth Congress emerges when one realizes that at that time he was aware of the complete bureaucratization of the organization and the mystification which prevailed at the congress. Indeed, shortly before, there had taken place a massive intake of new members to the party which came to be known as 'Lenin's levy' and which, Trotsky was to write later, was a 'manoeuvre . . . to dissolve the revolutionary vanguard in raw human material, without experience, without independence, and yet with the old habit of submitting to the authorities'.[17] This levy had been made in order to turn the party into a docile instrument in the hands of its general secretary. However 'Lenin's promotion', which, Trotsky was to say on another occasion, 'delivered a mortal blow to Lenin's party', was also approved by him during the Thirteenth Congress. Trotsky even pushed concession to the point of declaring that it 'brought the party nearer to being an elected party'.[18]

It is true that the struggle against Trotskyism had not yet come out into the open and, more importantly, that Stalinism was only just emerging as a *political* entity. Trotsky's concessions seemed all the more tragic when battle commenced. After the first phase of this battle, after Trotsky had triggered off a struggle in favour of the New Course, after he had been the object of a campaign of systematic attacks from the politbureau, after Stalin had put forward his view of socialism in one country,[19] Trotsky published an article in *Pravda* (January 1925) in which he denies ever having thought of opposing a platform to the Stalinist majority.[20] This was to state clearly that there was no fundamental divergence between him and this majority. Capitulation appears again in that year 1925, on the occasion of the Eastman affair. In a work entitled *Since Lenin Died*, the American journalist, a Bolshevik sympathizer, had taken it upon himself, as I have already indicated, to reveal the existence and the content of Lenin's Testament, which Trotsky, in agreement with the Central Committee, had thought good to conceal not only from the Russian masses, but also from the party militants and from communists throughout the world. Trotsky's declaration, at this time, would deserve to be quoted in full, so striking is the degree to which it reveals Trotsky's bad faith and the practice of the 'supreme sacrifice'. Trotsky accuses Eastman of 'despicable lying' and implies that he is an agent of international reaction. 'Comrade Lenin', he writes, 'did not leave a testament: the nature of his relations with the Party and the nature of the Party itself excludes the possibility of such a testament.' Referring to Lenin's letter on the reorganization of the Workers' and Peasants' Inspection (in which Stalin had the upper hand), Trotsky does not hesitate to declare: 'Eastman's affirmation according to which the C.C. was anxious to conceal, that is to say, not publish, Comrade Lenin's article on the Workers' and Peasants'

Inspection is equally erroneous. The different points of view expressed in the C.C., *if it is actually possible to speak of a difference of points of view* in this case, was of absolutely secondary importance.'[21] How could Trotsky speak in this way, when Lenin, on this very point, was making a fundamental attack, and when Trotsky was fully in agreement with him, as he has repeated a hundred times?

We cannot complete the balance sheet of this politics of conciliation without showing that, even on the theoretical level, Trotsky was confused. I have already shown that he did not regard the struggle against the theory of socialism in one country, when it was 'discovered' by Stalin, as a matter of fundamental principle. One must also recognize that Trotsky did not oppose the entry of the Chinese communists into the Kuomintang nor the tactics used by the British communists within the trade-union Anglo–Russian Committee. In each case, he took up the struggle against the Stalinist policy only when it was obviously turning into a disaster.[22] I said above that the tactics of the Left Opposition had helped to disarm the revolutionary vanguard in Russia; I should add, in the light of these examples, that it also had a negative effect on the revolutionary vanguard throughout the world. Trotsky said that Stalin appeared to the world one day as a 'ready-made dictator' — he forgot to mention his own responsibility in this regard.

Finally, it was in the last stage of the struggle between the Opposition and the Stalinist leadership, as this struggle became more violent, that the capitulations became more radical and more tragic. On two occasions, in October 1926 and in November 1927, the Left Opposition, which then had the support not only of Trotsky but also of Kamenev and Zinoviev, solemnly condemned itself, repudiated its supporters abroad and undertook its own dissolution. Finally, when there was no hope left for it, when Stalin had at his disposal a Congress (the Fifteenth) that obeyed him blindly, the Opposition made a final attempt to return to favour, and drew up a new condemnation of its own activity, namely, the Declaration of the 121. This is a document of the greatest historical importance, because it represents the last public action of the Left Opposition in Russia. The declaration begins by proclaiming that the unity of the Communist Party is the highest principle during the period of the dictatorship of the proletariat. We find the same terms that Trotsky had used in his speech to the Thirteenth Congress quoted above. The party is regarded as a divine factor in historical development, independently of its content and its line. The declaration thus under-lines the danger of a war against the USSR and declares that there is nothing more urgent than to re-establish 'the combatant unity of the Party'. One may find it extraordinary that the Opposition was seek-ing *above all* to preserve the facade of party unity, whereas the gravest dissensions were setting it against the leadership of this party. But the 121 had decided to regard their dissensions with the party as in-significant. Of course, on several occasions, they repeated that they were convinced of the correctness of their views and that they would continue to defend them, as the organizational statutes allowed them to do, after they had dissolved their fraction; but at the same time they proclaimed: '*There is no programmatic difference between us and the Party*'.[23] And they bitterly denied that they had ever believed that the party or its Central Committee had followed a Thermidorian course. Now, not only had the party completely lost its revolutionary and democratic character in 1927, but it had adopted the perspective of socialism in one country, that is, it had in fact renounced the perspective of world revolution.

### Bolshevism and the Rise of Bureaucracy

So that royal road, along which Trotsky, if his *Stalin* is to be believed, would have led the Left Opposition, never in fact existed. For five years Trotsky improvised a policy from day to day, a policy of harsh concessions, of revolt – when the domination of the bureaucracy became too unbearable – then of capitulations which led to new explo-sions. It is not possible here to follow the behaviour of the various representatives of the Opposition. But there were many defectors among them, not to mention Zinoviev and Kamenev, who had become professionals of capitulation. Of course, the face of Trotsky stands out from the group, for he was not a man to give in completely. But his responsibility can only be more striking. How could he blame the defectors when his entire policy tended to deny any 'programmatic difference' with the Stalinists? This policy can be summed up in the formula that he used in 1927: 'What separates us [from the bureauc-racy] is incomparably less than what unites us.'[24] It was a policy of *suicide*, since, despite all his practical declarations, Trotsky was not taken in by the bureaucratic degeneration, as a thousand details prove. His interventions in the higher bodies of the party and the notes that he himself mentions in his memoirs leave no doubt on the matter. He deliberately misled public opinion in the name of higher ends, that is, in order to defend the Soviet state in the world.

How can we understand that Trotsky, while perceiving the complete bureaucratization of the party and the reactionary character of the policies of its leaders, continued to feel at one with this party and its leaders? One can only answer this question by standing back and placing Trotsky and Trotskyism in their objective development. What is interesting, for me, is not to see whether Trotsky acted well or badly in a given situation, but to explain his attitude. In this sense, much of Souvarine's critique seems to me to be artificial. In many passages, he criticizes Trotsky for leading the struggle badly, for provoking the hatred of the leaders by inopportune polemics, for pushing Zinoviev and Kamenev in Stalin's direction instead of driving them apart, in general for being unable to wait for the bloc of his enemies to crumble, for being unable to play for time and manoeuvre as his adversaries were doing. I do not share Souvarine's point of view. Even if Trotsky had often been intransigent and clumsy, despite his general line of conciliation, this is merely a minor aspect of the question; and, in any case, he should not be criticized for being incapable of manoeuvring within the circles of leadership, but, on the contrary, for having all too often confined his actions to these circles. Indeed, Souvarine seems to appreciate this all too well when he levels his criticism, not at Trotsky's personality, but at the development of his positions.

If we are to offer an objective critique of Trotsky and of the Left Opposition, we must put aside evaluative criteria in favour of a concrete, historical point of view. Trotsky seems to adopt this point of view when he tries to reduce everything to some such explanation as 'the revolution was at an ebb'. In fact this explanation, though not incorrect, is unsatisfactory, for it is much too broad. The conception of the revolutionary ebb may enable us to understand the failure of the Opposition, but not its ideological disarray. It is because the explanation is too broad that Trotsky often invokes another one, this time too narrow: the machinations of Stalin and his supporters. In fact we can understand the policies of Trotsky and of the revolutionary leaders who surrounded him, after 1923, only by integrating them into the previous development of the Bolshevik Party.

For it is certainly Bolshevism that continued to be expressed in the Left Opposition, and what we have to try to explain is its inability to survive as a revolutionary ideology and strategy. In a passage in his *Stalin*, Trotsky attempts to elude the problem:

> Sterile and absurd are the Sisyphean labours of those who try to reduce all subsequent developments to a few allegedly basic original attributes of the Bolshevik Party . . . The Bolshevik Party set for itself the goal of the conquest of power by the working class. In so far as that party accomplished this task for the first time in history and enriched human experience with this conquest, it fulfilled a tremendous historical role. Only the bewildered with a liking for abstruse discussion can demand of a political party that it should subjugate and eliminate far weightier factors of mass and class hostile to it.[25]

One cannot but agree as to the prodigious historical role of the Bolsheviks. But the question is badly put. It is obviously not a matter of requiring the party to win some sort of triumph over the course of history, but to understand how the course of history is expressed through the structure and life of the party itself. The fact that the Bolshevik Party carried out the October Revolution must not lead one to deify it and to see its subsequent failure as a mere accident. The failure of the Bolshevik Party in 1923 must be understood in terms of the internal dynamics of that party. In no sense am I trying to minimize the role of objective factors, but rather to discern, on the basis of the Bolshevik experience, the enduring power which they may have.

I have no wish to go over again – enough books and studies of every kind have brought this out – the very particular character of Russia within the capitalist world prior to 1917, the backward nature of its economy and the lack of education among the masses. If this very situation, as has also been stressed, was favourable to the formation of a vigorous revolutionary party, the social contradictions having been carried to their breaking point, then it is no less true – and commentators have usually had little to say about this aspect of things – that it had fundamental consequences as regards the structure and functioning of the party. The development of the professional revolutionary in Russia was probably unique and unparalleled in other countries: the necessities of illegality in the face of the Tsarist autocracy, the habit of living under oppression and in great poverty, helped to create the type of revolutionary practitioner represented *par excellence* by the Bolshevik. But one must also see that, by the very logic of his situation, the professional revolutionary

was led to detach himself from the masses, to maintain only superficial relations with the real vanguard in the factories. Secrecy obliged
the revolutionary to live in small, relatively closed circles. This
climate was favourable to centralization, not to democracy. In his
*Stalin*, Trotsky supports this view:

> The negative aspect of Bolshevism's centripetal tendencies first
> became apparent at the Third Congress of the Russian Social-
> Democracy. The habits peculiar to a political machine were already
> forming in the underground. The young revolutionary bureaucrat
> was already emerging as a type. The conditions of conspiracy, true
> enough, offered rather meagre scope for such of the formalities of
> democracy as electiveness, accountability and control. Yet, un-
> doubtedly the committeemen narrowed these limitations considerably
> more than necessity demanded and were far more intransigent and
> severe with the revolutionary workingmen than with themselves,
> preferring to domineer even on occasions that called imperatively for
> lending an attentive ear to the voices of the masses. Krupskaya notes
> that, just as in the Bolshevik committees, so at the Congress itself,
> there were almost no workingmen. The intellectuals predominated.
> 'The "committeeman",' writes Krupskaya, 'was usually quite a self-
> confident person; he was fully aware of the tremendous influence
> wielded by the Committee's activities on the masses; the "committee-
> man", as a rule, did not recognize any internal party democracy.'[26]

Of course, this divorce between certain professional revolutionaries
and the masses was less marked in the great revolutionary moments,
but the effects were nonetheless very serious. They could be observed
on the occasion of the 1905 revolution, when the Bolsheviks refused
to recognize the Soviets that had been spontaneously created by the
workers. 'The Petersburg Committee of the Bolsheviks', notes
Trotsky, 'was frightened at first by such an innovation as a non-
partisan representation of the embattled masses, and could find
nothing better to do than to present the Soviet with an ultimatum:
immediately adopt a Social-Democratic programme or disband.'[27]
It may be said that, if the Bolsheviks did not bring about a series of
catastrophes, it was thanks to Lenin and to his exceptional ability to
discern the revolutionary significance of every situation. But even
Lenin's pre-eminence deserves reflection; one is struck by how insubstantial the best Bolshevik leaders appeared to be without him.
There is a veritable gulf between Lenin and the other Bolshevik

leaders, as well as a gulf between those leaders and the average militants of the party organization. Innumerable cases might be cited as evidence, but no doubt the best known is provided by the events of February 1917 when, with Lenin in exile, Kamenev and Stalin took over the leadership of the party in his absence. When Lenin returned and presented his April theses, he was almost alone against the entire party, finding support only among the Bolshevik workers of Viborg. It would not be an exaggeration to say that the strength of the party was hanging on a thread. Of course, the Bolshevik workers were the best guarantee of its power, but they could not by themselves run the party organization and, among the cadres, no one other than Lenin could.

This very special physiognomy of the Bolshevik Party became all the more apparent in the aftermath of the revolution and throughout the period of the civil war. Indeed the civil war, combined with economic chaos and the low level of education of the Russian masses, necessitated an increased concentration of power and an increasingly voluntarist political strategy in the face of an increasingly difficult situation. Souvarine describes perfectly the evolution, in these conditions, of the Council of People's Commissars, which soon became the blue-print of the Bolshevik Central Committee and did nothing more than give a constitutional form to its decisions. He also shows that the Central Committee in turn existed less and less as a 'college' and that real power was concentrated in the hands of an oligarchy within the politbureau. In all institutions, in the trade unions and in the Soviets, there was only one power and one policy, that of the Bolsheviks, who more and more became mere functionaries, alienated from the masses and from the workers in particular. The same logic led the Bolsheviks to eliminate all opposition. We know only too well the exceptional violence with which Lenin set about exterminating his adversaries, whether they were left-wing socialist revolutionaries or anarchists. Volin provides some striking information on this point. One sees the Bolsheviks fabricating compromising documents against the anarchists in order to inculpate them for criminal activities of which they were absolutely innocent. The terror that began by exterminating all the opposition parties and competing groups, and which culminated, within the Bolshevik Party itself, by forbidding the existence of factions, reached its paroxysm with the repression of the workers of Kronstadt who, once regarded as the revolutionary elite and fighting for demands some of which were confused but most of which were democratic, were treated as agents of counter-revolution and ruthlessly crushed.[28]

All the facts concur: the party which, from its origin and by reason of the objective situation, tended to develop towards a military structure and functioned as a body loosely linked to the masses began to accentuate these traits considerably during the post-revolutionary period. One cannot but follow Souvarine when he takes up Bukharin's definition of the party as 'entirely apart from and above everything'.[29] On the other hand, it seems to me that Souvarine oscillates between a (subjective) criticism of the leaders' attitude and an objective interpretation that links this development of Bolshevism to the given economic, social, national and world situation. I repeat, the first criticism has no significance for me; let us put aside that kind of value judgement. The political strategy of the Bolshevik Party between 1917 and 1923 was that of a revolutionary organization struggling desperately to preserve, until the outbreak of world revolution, a proletarian victory unprecedented in history. This strategy was essentially contradictory, since it led to the adoption of an anti-proletarian content in the name of the higher interests of the proletariat. But its contradictions were themselves objective, for they expressed the contradictions of the victorious Russian proletariat, stifled in its victory by negative factors on a national and international scale. The post-revolutionary period in Russia is the *tragic* moment of Bolshevism, torn apart between its ends and the nature of the forces that it tried to animate. This tragedy culminated in the repression of the workers of Kronstadt by Trotsky, who was led to crush them and to forge false evidence in order to persuade the whole world of their guilt. But this *moment of contradiction* was essentially transitory. Bolshevism could not remain split between its real behaviour and its principles; whatever the supreme ends at which it aimed, it could not survive if it were cut off from its real content –the proletarian masses that it represented. It could not remain without a social basis, as a pure will determined to force the course of history. At the very heart of the party, the contradiction was expressed as the difference between the strategy of Lenin and Trotsky, who side by side were 'steering towards world revolution', and the very body of the party, which was beginning to crystallize socially and was already taking on the form of a privileged caste.

It is only from this point of view that one can understand the defeat of Trotsky, his liquidation in 1927 and, above all, his ideological collapse from 1923 on. Trotsky's struggle against the bureaucracy lacked any basis because Trotsky himself was objectively an artisan of that bureaucracy. Trotsky could not reproach Stalin for carrying out an anti-proletarian and anti-democratic policy when he had himself inaugurated that policy. He could not criticize the repression practised on the Opposition when he himself had taken part in the repression of the 'Workers' Group' and 'Workers' Truth'. He was no longer free to find support among the vanguard of the factories because he had cut himself off from it. He had no overall platform against Stalin because he had allowed himself to be caught up in the contradiction that consists in directing the proletariat according to its higher interests and against its immediate interests. The turning-point of 1923 often seems difficult to understand. In fact, at this period the revolutionary character of Bolshevism was already hanging by a thread, in so far as the policies of Lenin and Trotsky were orientated towards world revolution. In the absence of this revolution, the thread could only snap. The contradiction was too intense and could not persist. Thus the rise of Stalin represents the eclipse of the contradiction and the emergence of a new term. In order to strengthen its hold, the new regime did not need to wage war against all the preceding values. They had destroyed themselves and, losing their true content, had already become, in a sense, the means of mystification. Thus Stalin could emerge without his policy seeming at first to be in opposition to Bolshevik policy. Thus the struggle he conducted against Trotsky could appear as a struggle between individuals. And Trotsky himself could declare that it was an 'unprincipled conspiracy, directed against him personally'. In fact it was an absolute break with the past, as the future was to show, but it appeared to be no more than an imperceptible transition, a question of individuals. Trotsky wanted to see the very existence of the party and the formal survival of the dictatorship of the proletariat as an historical guarantee of world revolution; he *wanted to believe* that this bureaucratized party, which was pursuing a counter-revolutionary strategy, was an essential element for the international proletariat. This is the significance of the strange declarations referred to above on the unity of the party and the significance, in general, of his conciliatory line. Such, too, was the significance of his intermittent shifts and changes. At one and the same time, he concealed the *Testament* and accused Stalin of abandoning Leninist policy; at one and the same time, he called for a 'new course', a true democratization of the party, and declared, despite its bureaucratization, that 'the Party is always right'. He was no longer free to act as a revolutionary because he participated in a process which led him to turn his back on the masses. He was no longer free to act as a bureaucrat because he always sought to act, whatever his tactics might have been, in accordance with the revolutionary ideal.

Perhaps these contradictions are most strikingly expressed in his hesitation over the dating of 'Thermidor'. In 1923, he rejected any analogy with the Thermidorian reaction. In 1926, he was predicting the possibility of a Thermidorian course; at the same time he violently attacked the Leftists of *Democratic Centralism*, who were declaring that Thermidor was already a fact. In November 1927, following a demonstration in the streets in which supporters of the Opposition were molested by Stalinist gangs, he declared that they had just witnessed a general repetition of Thermidor. In 1927, with the 121, he declared that he had never thought that the party or its Central Committee were Thermidorian. In 1928–9, he announced yet again that there was a Thermidorian threat; then, in 1930, he brusquely declared: 'With us, Thermidor has dragged on.' Finally, in 1935, in his pamphlet, 'The Workers' State, Thermidor and Bonapartism', he writes: 'The Thermidor of the Great Russian Revolution is not before us but already far behind. The Thermidoreans can celebrate, approximately, the tenth anniversary of their victory.'[30]

It was worth examining carefully Trotsky's attitude at the dawn of Stalinism, for it enables us to elucidate the (theoretical) policy to which he adhered until his death. I have said that Trotsky represented, between 1923 and 1927, the contradictions of Bolshevism. I should now add that he never emerged from this divided situation. Subsequently he transported into the domain of revolutionary theory the contradiction in which he had become objectively enclosed. Of course, he was forced by events to perceive the counter-revolutionary character of Stalinism, but he was not capable of taking an overall view of the new Stalinist society and of defining it. He transferred on to economic categories (collectivization, state planning) the fetishism that he had first professed with regard to political forms (party, Soviets). He declared both that 'in contradistinction to capitalism, socialism is built not automatically but consciously. Progress towards socialism is inseparable from state power',[31] and that 'the dictatorship of the proletariat found its distorted, but unquestionable expression in the dictatorship of the bureaucracy'.[32] He shows how bureaucracy found an autonomous economic and social base,[33] but he continues in all his works to maintain that bureaucracy is not a system of exploitation, that it is simply a parasitical caste. He writes, quite brilliantly, that 'the Russian Thermidor would have undoubtedly opened a new era of bourgeois rule, *if that rule had not proved obsolete throughout the world*',[34] thus indicating that the mode of exploitation based on private property had been superseded in the course of history without, for all that, resulting in the realization of socialism; and yet elsewhere he reiterates his view that the reign of bureaucracy was purely transitory and would inevitably collapse before the only two historical possibilities: capitalism or socialism. [. . .]

# 2

# Totalitarianism without Stalin

The new course of Russian politics ushered in since the death of Stalin and vividly illustrated by the Twentieth Congress has an extraordinary import that we cannot begin to understand unless we appreciate the social upheaval from which it stems. By revealing and recording this upheaval, it marks a decisive moment in world history. It has a properly revolutionary significance, for it pre-supposes – over and above the individual personalities performing on the Congress platform, inventing new devices of domination, speaking pompously of the construction of communism, cursing an ancestor who only yesterday was a sacred, civilizing hero, deciding one by one the tasks to be carried out by tens of millions of others – it presupposes the people themselves who cannot speak, but those whose new needs, new activities in production and new outlook have brought about a break with the past and the liquidation of the indi-vidual who was its unchallenged embodiment. The event is revolu-tionary because it indicates, not a change in political orientation of a conjunctural character, but a total transformation that affects the functioning of the bureaucracy as a class, the working of essential in-stitutions, the efficiency of planning, the role of the totalitarian par-ty, the relations between the state and society, because it expresses, at the deepest level, a conflict inherent in the system of exploitation based upon state capitalism. [. . .]

The Twentieth Congress, whatever significance may be attributed to it, suggests an unavoidable conclusion. The USSR can no longer appear as a world 'apart', an enclave in the capitalist world, a system impermeable to the criteria forged with the advent of capitalism. The trust or blind hatred that it has inspired in people, the ideological paralysis that it has imposed on the revolutionary vanguard for the past thirty years, cannot resist indefinitely the worthy speeches of the new leaders, who, driven by necessity, have brought out the profound kinship between all modern systems of exploitation. An iron curtain as important as that which impeded the movement of human beings and commodities has been lifted: this is the curtain woven by the imagination, the curtain through which a metamorphosed USSR seemed to elude every social law. A society without a body, always confused with the pure Will of Stalin (infinitely good or evil), it has aroused the strangest collective delusions of our time: a bourgeois delusion that turned the USSR into an infernal machine with perfectly oiled joints, crushing every social and individual difference and producing, under the orders of a reincarnated Ghengis Khan, a human robot entrusted with the annihilation of humanity; and a 'communist' delusion, fashioning the ideal image of the socialist paradise, in which the harshest contrasts in reality are transformed into harmonious and complementary parts. It has not been sufficiently recognized that these opposing delusions curiously intersect in the myth of a perfectly coherent system, designated as absolute totalitarianism or as socialism, but always presented as radically different from the capitalist system known to us. Trotskyism, it is true, presented a contrasting picture; but, content to graft the image of totalitarianism on to that of socialism, it added to its own myth the fictions of its predecessors. The USSR had built socialist foundations, which meant that it could not be seen as a system of exploitation; at the same time, it brought with it a dictatorship and gross social inequalities which deformed it; the proletariat was the master of a power of which it happened to be completely dispossessed. As in dreams where every metamorphosis seems natural, in the Trotskyist utopia socialism turned into its opposite without losing its identity. The product of this imbroglio was the short-term prediction of a collapse of the bureaucracy, a small caste of traitors, powerless to prevent a capitalist restoration or a proletarian resurrection.

No doubt events are powerless in themselves to destroy myths, but at least the myths will have to be transformed in order to be adapted to the upheavals which have occurred since the death of Stalin. The caste of which Trotsky spoke is still in power and consolidating its position, despite war and now despite a transformation of the government. If the leadership is revising its methods, it is neither as a result of pressure from invisible capitalist elements, nor as a result of the threat of foreign imperialism, nor in response to an uprising of the proletariat. So we must understand these developments in the context of a particular social structure. However, with the passing of its Ghengis Khan, the bourgeoisie has lost a marvellous explanatory key. Terror has been outlawed, the dictatorship has become more flexible and it is said that the individual rights of citizens will be guaranteed; the standard of living of the masses has improved appreciably and it seems likely that in a few years time it will catch up with those of the advanced capitalist countries; Stalin is denounced at last as a brutal tyrant who polluted the development of the regime. Better still, a whole series of measures have been adopted that clearly prove the Russians' desire to avoid war. The bourgeoisie is taken with vertigo: its image of the infernal machine seems ridiculous. How can it go on dreaming of an essential difference between the Western capitalisms and the USSR? Similarly, the 'communist' imagination has gone to pieces. It was said of Stalin that he was the lighthouse showing the route to socialism; it now seems that this proud light, of blinding strength, has drowned the oarsmen. He was the magnificent pilot steering among the reefs swarming with imperialist agents; it now seems that he invented those agents, transforming at will any opponent into a bandit, that he himself planted the reefs and that progress would have been more flexible and more rapid without him. He was the strategic genius who succeeded in breaking the most powerful army in the world; he is now shown to have been a blundering dictator whose incompetence very nearly led the USSR to disastrous defeat. The regime may claim that it is intact, now that it has rid itself of his burdensome *personality*.

But how can one preserve the image of socialist harmony? According to the myth there was a perfect correspondence between the socio-economic system and the political leadership: the system was socialist and Stalin was a genius, each reflected the other. There could therefore be no criticism without attacking the whole: each of Stalin's political acts was perceived as correct for the excellent reason that it could not be wrong, since in every case it expressed objective necessities. This myth has now been exploded. The fact that Stalin's policy for the last twenty years or more includes a series of 'errors' – some of them enormous – implies that objective and subjective no longer reflect one another, that historical necessity is broken, that criticism is now possible. Who will decide how far such criticism can go? Only Stalin is in question, Khrushchev implies. But Stalin embodied the politics of the USSR. Who, then, will say where error begins and where it ends? And who will say where politics begins and where it ends? Who will determine the supposed frontier between the objective and the subjective? Can the political and social system be dissociated from the economic system? When the state concentrates all power into its own hands, when it defines the direction and volume of production, when it lays down the regulations for work, when it determines the hierarchy of social status by the incomes and benefits that it grants to each individual, it is strictly absurd to separate political activity from social life as a whole. Khrushchev tries in vain to circumscribe the area opened to criticism: if Stalin's personality is no longer sacred, then the entire leadership past and future, the regime as a whole, lose their divine right to historical truth. The system becomes, like any other social system, an object of analysis and critique.

The collapse of the Stalinist mythology — even before one tries to offer an interpretation based on an analysis of the USSR — indicates the extraordinary import of the latest twist in Russian affairs. This twist cannot be compared to any of those that occurred during the Stalinist era, however fertile in zigzags that era may have been, nor can it be reduced to the triumph of one faction over another. For in the past, the brutal interventions of Stalin always had the same function. Within the USSR itself, they served to reassert the primacy of the state leadership at the expense of any social group or any faction of the bureaucracy that threatened the cohesion of the regime. On the international scale, they served to reassert the interests of the USSR at the expense of those of the local bureaucracies, in such a way that the power relationships between the national communist parties and the respective bourgeoisies that they confronted were necessarily subordinated to the particular strategy of the USSR in the world. There is little to add to Trotsky's analysis of the Stalinist zigzags; the brutal purges carried out among managers of the collective farms, among technicians, military personnel and trade unionists, the sudden switches in policy on China, Germany or Spain, illustrate the tortuous course of the Stalinist dictatorship, imposed on each occasion without prior warning on all 'communists' everywhere. The French reader may remember in particular the abrupt changes of direction that marked the history of the French Communist Party and which hurled it successively from the war against the socialists before 1934 to the Popular Front, from the all-out war against the bourgeoisie and the imperialist war to participation in that war on the basis of a fervent nationalism, from collaboration with the bourgeoisie inside a government that emerged from the Liberation to violent opposition to former allies. But what Trotsky could not explain was that at each turning-point, and in spite of the local losses suffered by the communist parties, the unity of the bureaucratic leadership was categorically reaffirmed, all the troops came together on the new terrain with the same cohesion as on the old. For the cohesion of the Stalinist camp was the expression of an essential feature of the national bureaucracies that Trotsky misunderstood: the strict subordination of their policy to that of the USSR could not be explained by the treason of the leaders, by the personal links that bound them to the ruling caste in the USSR or by some other accidental factor; it stemmed from the very nature of the communist parties which were essentially similar to the Russian bureaucracy, and which were trying to open up the way for a new dominant stratum, to wrest power from the bourgeoisie at the same time as it imposed a new mode of exploitation on the proletariat. Subjected to the pressures, different in each situation, exerted by both the bourgeoisie and the proletariat, the communist parties were able to crystallize their own elements and become aware of the historical opportunities offered by the growing concentration of capital only by keeping their eyes constantly fixed on the USSR, whose regime provided them with an image of their own future. If Stalin's twists and turns were necessarily ratified by the national communist parties (whatever temporary effects they may have had on them), it was because the interest of those parties was actually subordinated to that of the mother body, the only one capable of imposing on them the ideological unity of which their own social situation could provide no more than a sketch. And, similarly, as I shall have occasion to repeat, totalitarianism in the USSR was justified in principle, even in the eyes of the factions that it decimated, by the function that it played in ruthlessly sacrificing their interests to the cohesion of the bureaucracy as a whole.

The change of direction carried out by the new leadership is radically different, since it calls into question the very principles on which all previous policy changes were based. Totalitarianism is challenged; collective leadership is praised. It is implicitly admitted that the policy of the USSR can be contested, since it is explicitly recognized that Stalin's policy was wrong. The methods by which the former dictatorship annihilated its opponents and subordinated the interests of satellite countries to its own are rejected. The past, which was once presented as an ineluctable sequence of historical truths and had been lived as such, is now turned into an object of examination. [. . .]

In this sense, the policy changes of the Twentieth Congress have inaugurated a new, irreversible course; the *monopoly of truth* built up by Stalinism has been broken, whatever the new leaders do to restore it. For decades, the rules of organization and the rules of thought for all communist militants have been golden rules. Disquiet, disarray, individual criticisms were always absorbed in the ultimate vision of the Stalinist universe, a universe governed by a necessity in which every action was mechanically linked to every other. Did the Stalinist policy of participation in government seem contrary to the interests of the French workers in the wake of the Liberation? It *could not* be so; the conquest of the state by the communist parties in Eastern Europe proved that it was revolutionary. Did not this conquest of the state, the nationalizations and collectivization, seem to be carried out without any transformation of the situation of the proletariat in production? The socialist import of those measures was guaranteed by the support that the USSR gave them and the example that it provided of a regime towards which the people's democracies could gradually progress. In the USSR itself, were not social inequalities, working conditions and police suppression a cause for concern? These features resulted, it was said, from the isolation of the USSR, which was constantly threatened by imperialism and its agents. In such a system of thought there was no possible hold on events, since the cause could be traced back closer and closer to Stalin's policy and this policy was in turn justified by the objective conditions that it had to confront and that it alone was capable of appreciating in all their complexity. There was, therefore, no other possibility (except challenging everything) than to regulate one's activity in accordance with that of the leadership: as a militant, one was a Stalinist from head to toe, with no other possible reference than that provided by the party. One was equipped once and for all with a system of reflexes that enabled one to act in any situation, whatever it may be, whether it concerned the Atlantic Treaty, trade-union tactics, biology, literature or psychoanalysis.

It is precisely because Stalinism constituted such a mechanically regulated universe that the criticism being made today cannot allow itself to be confined to an isolated sector. Just as at the end of the Middle Ages criticism directed merely at the methods of the Church began to lift the weight of the sacred and led to the collapse of religious totalitarianism, so too the mere questioning of Stalinist policy brings one ever closer to a re-examination of each problem and shakes the foundations of modern totalitarianism. But it is not only the 'communist' militants, and particularly the intellectuals, who have been aroused from their torpor; the new course of the Russian bureaucracy cannot fail to exert a very strong influence on the behaviour of the proletariat as a whole. For although it is true that the action of the proletariat is profoundly determined by the conditions of exploitation, by its struggle to wrest control of its own labour from capitalism, this action also depends on its assessment of the social forces against which it has to fight, its assessment of the historical opportunities that are offered to it. In this sense, the cohesion of Stalinism has long been perceived as an insurmountable barrier. Consciously or not, workers felt paralysed by their bureaucracy. The difficulty of destroying a powerful apparatus which had been constructed in order to struggle against capital, but which had become increasingly rigid and distant from the masses, was exacerbated by the fact that this apparatus had become a world force whose historical cohesion was apparent to all. With the decline of this cohesion, the bureaucracy begins to lose the fantastic dimensions that it has acquired. It is no longer inevitable. It is exposed as conflict-ridden, prone to error, vulnerable. The authority accorded to the leaders maintained a sense of powerlessness in the proletariat; it now becomes aware of its weakness and is led to examine its own sources of strength. One cannot conclude that the crisis of the communist parties could *in itself* set off a proletarian offensive, but it seems clear that, when placed in conditions of struggle, the proletariat would situate itself in a new relation of force with the bureaucracy.

I have quite deliberately tried to stress the immense possible repercussions of the liquidation of Stalinism and the new Khrushchev direction before examining the factors that have determined them. This is because, in my view, the event in itself opens up a new field of possibilities. Though ideological, it is more than ideological, in so far as Stalinism is in itself both an ideological phenomenon and a social phenomenon, a system of thought and a system of action. I am nonetheless aware – need I repeat it? – that future changes depend, in the final analysis, not on a transformation of attitude, but on new struggles and new forms of working-class struggle. We are already witnessing all the ruses by which the militant tries to hide from himself the starkness of the event, to overcome his vertigo, his eyes obstinately turned away from the Stalinist ditch. Attempts are being made to minimize the change; it is repeated that self-criticism is a sign of vitality, as if the liquidation of Stalin were not the liquidation of the past; one clings to Lenin as if one could quietly transfer one's faith from one god to another; and above all one loudly sings the praises of the new-found flexibility of the dictatorship, the liberalization of the regime and the improvement in living conditions, as if the unchanged Truth had only to make itself more *attractive*. All these 'defence mechanisms', as the psychologists say, tend to protect the militant from the cruel solicitations of reality. It would certainly be imprudent to underestimate their efficacy and the infinite resources of self-mystification.

But precisely because history is essentially social, we must not become obsessed by the vicissitudes of Stalinist thought. All the attempts to reconstitute a communist 'good conscience' should not make us forget that the new direction is a response to social problems that have arisen in the USSR and in the world. To understand the significance of these problems, and the import of the solutions that are offered to them, is therefore the first task and the one that will enable us to determine the scope of the repercussions which may follow from the new turn in the communist world. [. . .]

### The Historical Function of Stalinism

So let us consider the new policy. It is this policy that leads us to examine the significance of the regime. It is this policy that calls into question the past and that, by claiming to distinguish what was correct from what was not, defines itself in relation to the Stalinist era. But its procedures are sufficiently odd to warn us that reality is being concealed. For all past errors are being attributed to the personality of Stalin alone. It is said that Stalin – vainly placing himself above the party, no longer tolerating critcism, endowed with a persecution complex that his dominant position transformed into a persecutor's complex – surrounded himself with intriguers of his own kind and, thanks to the incredible power at his disposal, piled up the arbitrary measures that sowed disorder and confusion through every sector of social life. It will be noticed that, in vigorously stigmatizing the cult of the personality, the new leadership does not even ask itself how it was possible for it to develop. A cult is usually the work of those who practise it, but the Stalinist cult is presented as the work of Stalin himself: *he* placed himself above the party, *he* founded his own cult. Thus one may refrain from asking how he was raised or allowed to raise himself to the summit of the state, which would be the beginning of a real analysis. Quite obviously, the present leaders, by using this mode of explanation, are not freeing themselves from the celebrated cult; they have simply passed, one might say, from the positive ritual to the negative one: the first consisting of endowing a man with every virtue, the second of endowing him with every vice, both according him the same fantastic freedom to control events at will. However, the transition to the negative ritual is peculiar in that it provokes an open rupture with Marxist ideology. Of course, the positive ritual was no more than a pathetic caricature of it, but it did not contradict it: Stalin the genius was seen as the expression of socialist society. As I have already said, the objective and subjective seemed to coincide, though mystification was everywhere. By contrast, Stalin the monster no longer corresponds to anything in society: he becomes an absurd phenomenon, deprived of all historical justification, and any recourse to Marxism becomes impossible. The good Stalinist who repeated for years that Hitler's hysterical or diabolical features could have a social function only because they were an expression of the degeneration of German capitalism finds himself alone, as it were, in face of the phenomenon of Stalin, with no other explanation than his instrinsic 'evil'.

We must therefore pose, to begin with, the characteristically Marxist question which is the taboo question *par excellence*: What was Stalin's historical function? Or, in other words, How did the role that he played relate to the exigencies of a given social situation? It goes without saying that such a question cannot be principally concerned with the personality of Stalin. It concerns his political role; it concerns the form of power which he embodied and which can be summed up in terms of the concentration of all political, economic and legal functions into a single authority, the enforced subordination of all activities to the model imposed by the leadership, the monitoring of individuals and groups, and the physical elimination of all opponents (and of all forms of opposition). It is this complex of features that is usually called dictatorial terror. As for Stalin's personality, one could say that in a certain way it expresses these features and that it is therefore *symbolic*. But it is by no means certain that it can of itself teach us anything at all.

In his *Russian Revolution*, Trotsky has admirably shown that there is a sort of historical connivance between the situation of classes and the character of their representatives, in such a way that parallels were simultaneously imposed, for example, between the situations of the French nobility and the Russian nobility on the eves of the revolutions of 1789 and 1917 respectively, and between the characters of Louis XVI and the Tsar. But this kind of account must not be given too much significance, for it makes sense only in the context of a prior interpretation of social forces. One selects certain psychological features of an individual and discovers a finality in them only because one is guided by a certain image of the social group which this individual represents. Thus, when Trotsky claims to portray Stalin in his biography of him and in *My Life*, he picks out only his intellectual mediocrity and his cunning temperament, since he is concerned above all to make this portrait coincide with his definition of the bureaucracy as a parasitical caste, as an accidental formation devoid of any historical significance. Like the image of a bureaucracy which maintains, by a series of artifices, a day-to-day existence threatened by world imperialism and by the proletariat, Stalin seems to be devoid of any understanding of history and only able to manoeuvre in order to preserve his personal position. Stalin is shown to be a false 'great man' and the party that he embodies a pseudo-party.[1] The entire construction rests on an assessment of the bureaucracy and, as we have seen, the interpretation of Stalinism governs that of Stalin. However, it would be false to conclude from this that the analysis of the historical character is ultimately without interest, since it merely repeats the social analysis while adding a psychological commentary. For the proper role of the personality is manifested not only in the fact that it fulfils a social function, but also in the way that it moves away from that function or creates a disturbance. In Stalin's case, it would be important to try to examine how his character escaped from the framework that seemed to be laid down for him by his political role, how far in particular his frenzied authoritarianism turned terror away, at a given period, from its original aim or altered its efficacy. But this kind of research is sufficient proof that one must begin by understanding the political role: Stalin can be understood only against the background of Stalinism.

There can be no question, within the limits of this essay, of providing an historical description of Stalinism; but, in so far as history is essentially part of the definition of social phenomena, we must try to understand how Stalinism differed at the outset from any previous formation. Stalinism merged together with the rise of the totalitarian party. It appeared when the party concentrated all power in its own hands, identified itself with the state and, as the state, rigorously subordinated all other institutions, freed itself from all social control, while, at the same time, within the party, the leadership was eliminating all opposition and imposing its unchallenged authority. Certainly, these features did not emerge overnight. If one wanted to trace their genesis, one would have to go back to the aftermath of the Russian Revolution and observe the party's efforts, from 1918 on, to eliminate the factory committees by integrating them into the trade unions and refusing them any real power. One would have to follow step by step the political development of Lenin and Trotsky, who always firmly declared the need for a strict centralization of all authority in the hands of the party. Above all, one would have to observe that, in the great trade-union debate of 1920, the programme of the totalitarian party had already been publicly formulated by Trotsky. We know that at this time the man who was later to be the prime enemy of party power maintained that every social group should give absolute obedience to the leadership of the party. Postulating that because of the change in ownership the state could no longer be the instrument of any kind of domination over the proletariat, he maintained that the idea of a defence of the interests of the working class against the state was absurd, and therefore he advocated the strict subordination of trade unions to the party. Furthermore, encouraged by the success of his plan to mobilize transport workers, he demanded a complete militarization of the workforce (stopping short of none of the measures of coercion that this involved). Finally, he stigmatized all forces of opposition, on the grounds that democratic principles were a form of 'fetishism' when the fate of the revolutionary society was in question.

And yet one cannot strictly speak of a pre-Stalinist Stalinism. Not only did Lenin succeed right up to his death in gaining support for the idea, if not of a control, at least of a limitation of the power of the party, recognizing the existence of an 'economic struggle' within post-revolutionary society and conceding a relative autonomy to the trade unions, but the foundations of his policy, like those of Trotsky's policy, were not those that were to be established later. For both of them, and for the overwhelming majority of leaders at that time, all 'totalitarian' measures were regarded as temporary; they seemed, to them, to be imposed by circumstances, mere devices improvised in order to maintain the existence of the USSR until the advent of the world revolution, in order to impose production discipline in a period when the economic disorganization engendered by civil war was such that democracy seemed incapable of solving it. No doubt, as we reflect on an historical experience thirty or thirty-five years after it took place, the arguments of the Bolshevik leaders cannot be accepted as they stand. Although the dictatorship of the party was reinforced under pressure of circumstances, it had already emerged, as I said, at the time of the revolution, at the expense of the power of the Soviets. Moreover, it was an extension of the activity of the Bolshevik Party before the revolution; it merely carried to extremes certain features of the strictly centralized vanguard party, a truly specialized body of professional revolutionaries which developed on the margins of the working masses. So nothing could be more artificial than to reduce the development of the party to that of a particular policy and to ignore the structural processes that conditioned that policy.

Nevertheless, it remains true that in the pre-Stalinist period a fundamental contradiction existed within the party, a contradiction that was only to be resolved with the advent of totalitarianism. Between the means adopted, which had the effect of emphasizing still further the separation between the state and the classes to which it claimed allegiance, which had the effect of increasingly freeing the state and, within the state, the Bolshevik leaders from any social control, on the one hand, and the end that was constantly being proclaimed, namely the establishment of a socialist society, on the other, there was no choice to be made. Quite obviously, the leaders did not choose: as the state concentrated all power within itself, the thesis of the withering away of the state continued to be declared as imperatively as ever. But society itself, one could say, did not choose either, in the sense that no social force was in any position to make its interests weigh decisively in the balance. The differentiation of salaries was so little marked that it produced no material social base for a new dominant stratum. Stalinism was the moment of the choice – from an ideological point of view, to begin with: the formula of socialism in one country would serve to *legitimate* the existing state of affairs, the separation of the state and the masses and the concentration of all authority in the hands of a single leadership. All the temporary features of the new society, which were fully meaningful only in terms of an overall policy orientated towards socialism, were ratified as if they constituted in themselves the essence of socialism. The double consequence of this transformation was, on the one hand, that Stalinism could be presented as the continuation of Leninism, since it was merely appropriating certain positions of the latter and treating them under a new modality – that is, by erecting into values what had been *de facto* measures – and, on the other hand, that it now abandoned any theoretical reflection on Marxism, the measures authorized by the state becoming socialist simply by virtue of being Leninist (i.e. similar to those recommended by Lenin). Whereas with Trotsky the contradiction was most acute, which may be why Trotsky felt obliged to develop his critique of democratic fetishism in the harshest terms, with Stalin the mystification was complete and the stifling of democracy did not even have to be recognized, since the Leninist precedent of the suppression of opposition sufficed to *legitimate* the socialist character of the present.

Moreover, from a 'material' point of view, Stalinism crystallized and rendered concrete a social choice. By initiating a deliberate policy of income differentiation, it emphasized considerably the existing privileges, extending and normalizing them. It transformed mere *de facto* advantages into social statuses; functions that had once been embroiled in struggles of prestige were now sustained by powerful material interests. At the same time, old conflicts of attitude were turned into social oppositions; a faction of society took root in the new soil feverishly ploughed by the party and definitively linked its very existence to the regime.[2]

In other words, Stalinist totalitarianism emerged when, after silencing the old dominant social strata, the political apparatus forged by the revolution freed itself from any control by the proletariat; *this political apparatus then directly subordinated the production apparatus to itself.*

Such a formula does not mean that an excessive role is being given to the party. If we were to adopt an economic perspective, the central phenomenon would, I believe, be the concentration of capital, the expropriation of the owners and the fusion of the monopolies in a new overall system of production, the subordination of the proletariat to a new centralized management of the economy. It would not then be difficult to show that the transformations that occurred in the USSR were merely leading to the final phase of a process that is everywhere apparent in the contemporary capitalist world and that is illustrated by the very formation of monopolies, the inter-monopolistic agreements and the growing intervention of the state in every sector of economic life, in such a way that the establishment of the new regime might seem to represent a mere transition from one type of appropriation to another within the framework of capitalist management. From such a perspective, the party would no longer appear as a *deus ex machina*; it would seem rather to be an historical instrument, an instrument of state capitalism. But, quite apart from the fact that I am trying at the moment to understand Stalinism as such and not Russian society as a whole, if we were to embrace the economic perspective alone, we would let ourselves be taken in by the image of an historical pseudo-necessity. For although the concentration of capitalism is to be observed in all contemporary societies, one cannot conclude that, by virtue of some such ideal law, it must lead necessarily to its final stage. For example, there is no reason to assume that, in the absence of a social upheaval that would sweep away the ruling capitalist stratum, a country like the United States or Britain must necessarily subordinate the monopolies to state control and eliminate private property. This assumption is all the less certain – and I shall have occasion to return to this point – in that the market and competition continue to play, in certain respects, a positive role in social life and their replacement by planning creates difficulties of a new kind for the dominant class. Even if one remains within the strictly economic context, one must ask, for example, whether the requirements of an harmonious integration of the various branches of production are not counterbalanced by the need to develop the productivity of labour by means of the relative autonomy of the capitalist firm. Nevertheless, one must accept that the tendencies of the economy, however determinant they may be, cannot be separated from social life as a whole: the 'protagonists' of capital, as Marx says, are also social groups whose very economic behaviour is influenced by their past, their way of life and their ideology. In this sense, it would be artificial to see the transformations that have occurred in the USSR since 1930 as simply the transition from one type of capitalist management to another, in other words, as the emergence of state capitalism. These transformations constitute a *social revolution*. It would be just as artificial, then, to present the party as the instrument of this state capitalism, with the suggestion that the latter, inscribed in the heaven of History, was waiting for the kind of propitious moment offered by Stalinism in order to incarnate itself. Neither demiurge nor instrument, the party must be understood as a social reality, that is, as a milieu within which the needs of a new economic management are imposed at the same time as historical solutions are actively worked out.

If the production apparatus had not allowed for, had not prepared for and had not governed its unification, the role of the political apparatus would have been inconceivable. Conversely, if the cadres of the old society had not been dismantled by the party, if a new social stratum had not been promoted to managerial functions in every sector of society, the transformation of the relations of production would have been impossible. It is observations such as these that may throw some light on the extraordinary role played by Stalinism. It was the agent, at first unconscious, then conscious and self-assured, of a tremendous social upheaval at the end of which an entirely new structure emerged. On the one hand, it conquered a new social terrain by dispossessing simultaneously the old masters of production and the proletariat of all power. On the other hand, it brought together in a new formation elements drawn from every class and ruthlessly subordinated them to the managerial task that the new economy gave them. In each case terror necessarily dominated the enterprise. However, the exercise of this terror, directed at once against private owners, against the proletariat and against the new dominant strata, seemed to confuse the situation. If we do not see that the violence had only one function, despite the many forms that it assumed, we shall try to prove, according to our preferences, that it was at the service of the proletariat or of the bourgeois counter-revolution; or alternatively one will use the fact that it decimated the ranks of the new ruling stratum to present Stalinism as a small caste, deprived of any class foundation and solely concerned to maintain its own position at the expense of the competing classes in society. From the outset, however, the development of Stalinist policy was unambiguous: terror was not a means of defence used by a handful of individuals whose privileges were threatened by existing social forces, it was constitutive of a new social force whose emergence presupposed a violent uprooting from the terrain of the old society and whose survival required the daily sacrifice of new members to the unity of the already formed organism. That Stalinism was characterized at first – before 1929, then in the period of collectivization and early industrialization – by its struggle against the private owners and the proletariat, and then by massive purges in the dominant strata, is obviously no accident. Terror followed the path of the new class, which had to secure the recognition of its existence *vis-à-vis* other classes before 'recognizing itself' in the image of its functions and multiple aspirations.

This path was also that of the bureaucratic consciousness. It could be said that only before industrialization did Stalinism represent to itself the aims that would subsequently be constituted by the formation of a new society. The fear of undertaking this industrialization, and the resistance to the Trotskyist programme that advocated it, testify to the uncertainty of Stalinism as to its own function. Stalinism was already behaving empirically according to the model that it was later to impose upon itself, feverishly strengthening the power of the state, carrying out the annihilation of the opposition, introducing, cautiously at first, a policy of income differentiation. The bureaucracy was defined by something quite other than a complex of psychological features; it was acquiring its own social existence, which differentiated it radically from the proletariat. But it still lived within the horizons of the present society. It was only when it had embarked on collectivization and state planning that new historical horizons emerged, that a proper class ideology and therefore a concerted political strategy were worked out, that the secure bases of a new material power were constituted, a power that was now creating and re-creating itself daily while siphoning off the productive forces of society as a whole. At this stage, however, new tasks were emerging and Stalinism's awareness of its historical role was then proving, in a new way, to be a decisive factor of development. For the formidable industrialization that was being carried out not only provided a basis for an already constituted bureaucracy, but it revolutionized this bureaucracy, thus giving rise – one cannot repeat it often enough –to an entirely new society. At the same time as the proletariat was being transformed, its numbers swollen in a few years by millions of peasants, new social strata were being *produced* out of the old classes and out of the traditional way of life that the old division of labour had given them. Technicians, intellectuals, bourgeois, soldiers, former feudal lords, peasants and workers were swept up into a new hierarchy whose common denominator was that it managed, controlled, and organized, at every level of its functioning, the production apparatus and the living labour power, that of the exploited classes. Even those who remained within their old professional categories saw their way of life and their outlook radically transformed, for those old professions were reorientated in order to be integrated into the new division of labour created by the Plan. Of course, the mode of labour of the new strata, the status they acquired by virtue of their dominant position in society, could not fail in the long run to produce a true class community. But, during the period in which this upheaval was taking place, the action of the party was decisive. It was the party which, by the iron discipline that it established, by the unchallenged unity that it embodied, could alone weld together these heterogeneous elements. It anticipated the future, proclaimed before all that particular interests were to be strictly subordinated to the interests of the bureaucracy as a whole.

An essential function of Stalinism, *necessary* in the context of the new society, appears here. The terror that it exercised over the dominant strata was not an accidental feature: it was inscribed in the development of the new class, whose mode of domination was no longer guaranteed by private appropriation, which was obliged to secure its privileges by the ruse of *a collective apparatus of appropriation* and whose dispersal, at the outset, could be overcome only by violence.

Of course, it may well be said that the purges carried out by Stalinism went so far as to endanger the functioning of the production apparatus. One may doubt the effectiveness of repressions that at one point wiped out half the number of working technicians. These reservations do not call into question, however, what I have called the historical function of Stalinism; they would simply enable one to discern – I have already mentioned this point – the ways in which Stalin's personal behaviour departed from the norm that dominated the conduct of the party.[3] For to say that Stalinism has a function is not to suggest that it is – from the point of view of the bureaucracy – 'useful' at all times, still less that the policy that it follows is at every moment the only possible one; in this case it is simply to maintain that, in the absence of Stalinist terror, the development of the bureaucracy was inconceivable. In other words, it is to acknowledge that, over and above the manoeuvres of Stalin, the factional struggles within the leadership and the massive purges carried out at every level of society, there was the necessity to fuse every stratum of the bureaucracy into the mould of a new ruling class. This necessity is clearly demonstrated in the behaviour of the purged elements: if the Stalinist terror was capable of developing in a society undergoing full economic expansion, if the representatives of the bureaucracy were willing to live under the permanent threat of extermination or destitution, despite their privileges, it is because, in the eyes of the victims and in the eyes of all, the ideal of social transformation embodied in the party was the overriding concern. The celebrated theme of the sacrifice of present generations to the benefit of future generations, presented by Stalinism under the travesty of a programme for the construction of socialism, acquires its real content: the party required the sacrifice of the particular and immediate interests of the rising strata to the general and historical interests of the bureaucracy as a class.

However, one cannot understand the role of Stalinism simply in terms of the bureaucracy. The terror that it exercised over an expanding proletariat presupposes that in certain respects it responded to a specific situation of the working class. Indeed it would be pointless to deny that the policy of the party, even if it met with ever stronger resistance in the ranks of the proletariat – which the labour code tied to the production process and which Stakhanovism thrust into a mad course of growth – did at the same time win allegiance for the ideal of the new regime. Ciliga has clearly shown this in his otherwise severely critical work on the USSR: on the one hand, the extreme exploitation that reigned in the factories went side by side with an enormous proletarianization of the small peasantry. For the latter, used to very harsh living conditions, this exploitation was not as noticeable as it was for the already constituted working class; indeed, in certain respects, it represented an improvement, since life in the towns and familiarity with industrial equipment and products created a genuine awakening of consciousness, a sensitivity to change and an awareness of new social needs. On the other hand, at the very heart of the proletariat, an important stratum of workers, which had been promoted to new functions by the party, the trade unions or Stakhanovism, thus found ways of evading the common condition that were unknown under the old regime. Finally and most importantly, industrialization, which brought with it thousands of modern factories, increased by tenfold the populations of the towns or built entirely new ones and dramatically increased the network of communications, seemed, in the eyes of all, to be unquestionably progressive – poverty and terror being the temporary price that had to be paid for a formidable primitive accumulation. Certainly, Stalinism built with a whip in its hand, it cynically instituted a form of social discrimination inconceivable in the post-revolutionary period, it unequivocally subordinated production to the needs of the dominant class. However, the tension created by the forces that it required in every sector, the mixing of social conditions that it brought about, the chances for promotion that it offered to individuals in all classes, the acceleration of the productive forces which it imposed as an ideal and which it achieved, all these features provided an alibi for its inordinate power and its ubiquitous policing.

## The Essential Contradiction of Stalinist Totalitarianism

If Khrushchev, an ungrateful son if ever there was one, had not been obsessed by the snubs to which Stalin had subjected him towards the end of his life, would he have been able to regard the course adopted with greater serenity? Would he not have been able to reread with equanimity the chapter in *Capital* that Marx devoted to primitive accumulation and repeat after him: 'Force is the midwife of every old society in labour. It is itself an economic power'? Would he not have been able to explain to the Twentieth Congress, in the rough language that was his: 'Stalin did the dirty work for us'? Or, in more well-chosen terms, to paraphrase Marx: 'This is what it costs to uncover the natural, eternal laws of planned production'? To read Isaac Deutscher, the well-known historian of Soviet society, such an ingratitude would seem almost distressing.[4] Not that Deutscher had any affection for Stalinism; but in his eyes, the necessities of primitive accumulation were imposed on socialism no less than on capitalism: the Stalinist purgatory was unavoidable. The trouble is that Deutscher does not see that the idea of a socialist primitive accumulation is absurd. For Marx, primitive accumulation meant the mass deportation of peasants into places of forced labour, into factories, and the extortion by every means, often illegal, of surplus value. Its purpose was to build up such a mass of means of production that by subordinating the workforce to it one could automatically reproduce it and increase it with profit. In principle and in purpose it necessarily involved the division of capital and labour: capitalism could free itself from its 'orgies', to use Marx's term, only because it was confronted by human beings who were totally dispossessed and because it was organized in such a way that their dispossession was reproduced daily at the same time as its own power was daily maintained and increased. Of course, one may question whether socialism is realizable in a society which has not yet built up an economic infrastructure, that is, which has not yet passed through a stage of accumulation; but one cannot say that socialism as such has to pass through this stage, since whatever the level of the productive forces to which it is bound, it presupposes the collective management of production, that is, the effective management of factories by committees of workers. To recognize a primitive accumulation in the USSR is to admit that relations of production of a capitalist type were still present. It is also to admit that those relations of production tend to be reproduced and to deepen the opposition that they presuppose – the building up of a stock of machinery and raw materials, on the one hand, the formation of a totally dispossessed workforce, on the other – which could have no other effect than to normalize exploitation. In this sense, Khrushchev's obstinate silence so far on the problems of primitive accumulation in the USSR seems highly reasonable. The 'original sin' in the eyes of the bourgeoisie, as Marx once again remarked, primitive accumulation is even more so in the eyes of a bureaucracy that must conceal its very existence as a class.

Moreover, it would be artificial to explain Stalinism solely on the basis of the economic difficulties that it has had to face. What I have tried to bring out is the role that it has played in the crystallization of the new class and in the revolution of society as a whole. If we want to use the Marxist term adopted by Deutscher, then we must give it a new content and speak of a 'social accumulation', meaning by this that the present features of the bureaucracy could come about only through the intervention of the party that brought them out and maintained them by violence until they were stabilized in a new historical form.

It is important to see that the bureaucracy is essentially constituted in accordance with the process I have described. For we shall then understand, by the same token, that this class conceals a permanent contradiction within itself which evolves with its history, of course, but which cannot be resolved with the liquidation of Stalinism.

The 'terrorist' dictatorship of the party is not only a sign of the immaturity of the new class, it corresponds, as I have said, to its mode of domination in society. This class is of a different nature from the bourgeoisie. It is not made up of groups that, through their ownership of the means of production and their private exploitation of labour power, each possess a share of material power and are bound together by relations based on their respective strengths. It is a collection of individuals who, through their function and the status that is associated with it, partake of a profit that is realized through the collective exploitation of labour power. The bourgeois class is constituted and developed in so far as it *results* from the activities of individual capitalists; it is underpinned by an economic determinism which provides the basis for its existence, whatever struggle the various actors may take part in and whatever political expression may, at a given time, arise from it. The intercorporate division of labour and the market render capitalists strictly dependent upon one another and collectively united in face of the labour force. On the other hand, the bureaucrats form a class only because their functions and their statuses differentiate them collectively from the exploited classes, only because these features bind them to a central administration that determines production and freely disposes of labour power. In other words, it is by virtue of the fact that there are relations of production in which the proletariat, reduced to the function of merely carrying out orders, is opposed to capital, embodied in the person of the state; hence it is by virtue of the fact that there is a class relationship here, that the bureaucrats are linked through their activities to the dominant class. Integrated into a class system, their particular functions constitute them as members of the dominant class. But, if I may be permitted to put it this way, it is not as acting individuals that they weave the networks of class relations; it is the bureaucratic class as a whole which, *a priori* — that is, by virtue of the existing structure of production – converts the particular activities of the bureaucrats (including privileged activities) into class activities. The unity of the bureaucratic class is therefore immediately derived from the collective appropriation of surplus value and immediately dependent on the collective apparatus of exploitation – the state. In other words, the bureaucratic community is not guaranteed by the mechanism of economic activities; it is established by the integration of the bureaucrats around the state, in their absolute discipline with regard to the administrative apparatus. Without this state, without this apparatus, the bureaucracy is nothing.

I do not mean that the bureaucrats as individuals do not enjoy a stable situation (though this stability was, in fact, threatened during the Stalinist era), that their status brings them only temporary advantages, in short, that their position in society remains fortuitous. There is no doubt that bureaucratic personnel are gradually consolidating their rights, acquiring with time certain traditions, a mode of life, an attitude which gives them a 'world' apart. Nor do I mean that the bureaucrats are not differentiated within their own class and do not develop among themselves severe relations of competition. All that we know about the struggle between the various clans in the administration proves, on the contrary, that this competition takes the form of a struggle of all against all, characteristic of any exploitative society. I claim merely that the bureaucracy cannot do without a cohesion of individuals and groups, each being nothing in itself, and that only the state provides the necessary social bonding. Without over-simplifying the functioning of bourgeois society one must recognize that, in spite of the ever increased extension of the functions of the state, the latter never frees itself from the conflicts engendered by the competition of private groups. Civil society cannot be absorbed into the state.[5] Even when it tends to sustain the general interest of the dominant class at the expense of competing private interests, it still expresses intercapitalist relations of power. This is because private property introduces a division in principle between capitalists and capital, each of these terms appearing successively as *reality* and excluding the other as *imaginary*. The vicissitudes of the modern bourgeois state are sufficient testimony to that *separation* about which Marx said so much: the separation between the state itself and society, and within society between the various spheres of activity. In the context of the bureaucratic regime, such a separation is abolished. The state can no longer be defined as an *expression*. It has become consubstantial with civil society, that is, with the dominant class.

But has it? It has and it has not. Paradoxically a separation is now reintroduced that in some respects is deeper than it was in any other society. The state is certainly the soul of the bureaucracy; the bureaucracy is well aware of this and knows that it is nothing without this supreme power. But the state dispossesses each bureaucrat of any effective power. It negates him *qua* individual, refuses him any creativity in his particular sphere of activity, subjects him *qua* anonymous member to the irrevocable decrees of the central authority. The bureaucratic mind hovers over bureaucrats, a divinity indifferent to particularity. Thus planning (the planning that claims to assign each individual his correct task and to harmonize him with all others) is worked out by a nucleus of leaders who decide everything; the functionaries can merely translate the ideas of the leadership into figures, deduce the consequences from the principles, transmit, apply. The class perceives in *its* state only the impenetrable secret of its own existence. Each functionary may well say: *l'État, c'est moi*, but the state is the Other and its rule dominates like an unintelligible fatality.

This infinite distance between the state and the bureaucrats has another unexpected consequence: unless they become opponents, the bureaucrats are never in a position to criticize established rule. In a formal way, this criticism is inscribed in the mode of existence of the bureaucracy: since each individual is the state, each individual is invited, by right, to direct, that is, to compare his actual activity with the socially fixed objectives. But, in reality, to criticize means to divorce oneself from the bureaucratic community. Since the bureaucrat is a member of his class only in so far as he is integrated into the policy of the state, any deviation on his part is effectively a threat to the system. Hence, throughout the whole Stalinist era, the bureaucracy indulged in an orgy of petty criticism and concealed any genuine critique. It solemnly assessed bureaucratic methods, but continued scrupulously to apply the rules which established and maintained its irresponsibility. It chattered on – and kept silent. This also explains why any serious malfunction in production was necessarily expressed by a massive purge of bureaucrats, technicians, scientists or trade-union cadres, whose deviation from the norm (whether intended or not) betrayed an opposition to the state.

So the contradiction between civil society and the state was surmounted in one form only to reappear in another, more aggravated form. During the bourgeois period, the state was linked with civil society by the same bonds that placed it at a distance from it. For capitalists, the secret of the state was an open secret in the sense that, despite every effort to embody the general will in the eyes of particular individuals, the state aligned itself with the positions of the most powerful individuals. Even if it took advantage of crises to steer between the currents, its policy still expressed a sort of natural regulation of economic forces. In bureaucratic society, on the other hand, the state has become civil society. Capital expelled the capitalists. The integration of every sphere of activity has been carried out, but society has undergone an unanticipated metamorphosis: it has produced a monster at which it gazes without recognizing its own image, a dictatorship.

This monster is called Stalin. They are trying to persuade us that he is dead. Perhaps they will leave his embalmed corpse in the mausoleum as evidence of a past that is now over. But the bureaucracy cannot hope to escape its own essence. It may bury its dead skin in the Kremlin crypt and cover its new body with alluring finery, but totalitarian it was and totalitarian it remains.

Before considering the efforts being made by the new leadership to circumvent the unavoidable difficulties to which the structure of state capitalism gives rise, we should assess the magnitude of the contradiction that lies at its heart. This contradiction concerns not only inter-bureaucratic relations, but is manifested equally strongly in the relations between the dominant class and the exploited classes.

Again a comparison between the bureaucratic regime and the bourgeois regime is apt, for the links between the dominant class and the proletariat in the USSR are of a new type. The historical origins of the bureaucracy already attest to this; for the bureaucracy was formed out of institutions – the party and the trade unions – which were forged by the proletariat in its struggle against capitalism. Of course, within the party, the proportion of intellectuals and revolutionary bourgeois elements was no doubt strong enough to have a decisive influence on the political orientation and behaviour of the organization. It would nevertheless be pointless to deny that the party was born within the working class and that, although it ended by excluding its representatives from all real power, it continued to present itself as the leadership of the proletariat. After all, the bureaucracy continues to draw on a section of the working class, to which it opens the doors of its training schools (much more widely than the bourgeoisie ever did), which it removes from the common condition by providing it with privileges and opportunities for social advancement. Moreover, the sociological definition of the proletariat, so to speak, has been transformed. In bourgeois society, an essential difference is to be found at the level of the relations of production between the owner of the means of production and the owner of labour power. Each is presented as a partner in a contract; formally, they are equals, and this equality is also recognized in the universal suffrage of a democratic regime. However, this equality seems more apparent than real: it is clear that it is not at all the same thing to be an owner of the means of production and an owner of labour power. In the first case, ownership gives the power to use others' labour in order to make a profit and this use of labour involves real freedom. In the second case, however, ownership gives the power to subject oneself in order to preserve and reproduce one's life. So the equality of the partners in the contract could only be illusory: the contract is enslavement. With state capitalism, the terms of the contract are blurred. The contract is now presented as a relationship between individuals and society. The worker does not hire out his labour power to the capitalist, he is no longer a mere commodity; he is supposed to be part of a whole that is called the productive forces of society. His new status, therefore, does not seem to be different in any way from that of the bureaucrat; he has the same relationship with society as a whole as the factory manager. Like the latter, he receives a salary as reward for a function that has been integrated into the totality of functions defined by the Plan. In reality, as we know only too well, such a status, which allows everyone to call his superior 'comrade', is the reverse side of a new subservience to capital; and this subservience is in some respects more complete, since the prohibition of strikes and collective demands, and the tying of the worker to his place of work, may follow *naturally* from it. How could the proletariat struggle against a state that represents it? When demands are made, one can always reply that they stem from a particular point of view, that the interests of the workers may well not coincide with those of society as a whole, that their immediate objectives must be placed in the context of the historical objectives of socialism. The processes of mystification at the disposal of the state are therefore more subtle and more effective in the new system. In the *social reasoning* developed by the structure through its formal articulations, essential links are concealed from the proletariat, which everywhere confronts the signs of its power while having been radically dispossessed of it.

However, the exploited classes are not alone in being mystified. By virtue of this very mystification the dominant strata are not in a position to see themselves as a class apart in society. Of course, the bureaucrats are distinguished by their privileges and their status. But this situation has to be justified in the eyes of the proletariat: the bureaucracy has a much greater need to be 'recognized' than the bourgeoisie. Thus an important part of the bureaucracy's activity (through the party and trade unions) is devoted to persuading the proletariat that the state governs society in its name. If, from one perspective, the education of the masses and socialist propaganda seem like mere instruments for the mystification of the exploited, from another perspective they attest to the illusions that the bureaucracy develops about itself. The bureaucracy cannot fully conceive of itself as a class. Prisoner of its own language, it imagines that it is not a class, that it responds to the needs of the community as a whole. Of course, this *imagination* gives way to the requirements of exploitation, that is, to the need to extort surplus value from the proletariat by the most ruthless means. As Marx said of another bureaucracy, that of the nineteenth-century Prussian state, hypocrisy gave place to conscious Jesuitry. Nevertheless, a conflict haunts the bureaucracy that never leaves it in peace and exposes it to the permanent anguish of self-justification. It has to prove to itself and to those it dominates that what it does is not contrary to what it says. During the Stalinist era, the brutal hierarchization of society, the implacable labour legislation, the frenzied pursuit of productivity at the expense of the masses, on the one hand, and the constant affirmation that socialism had been realized, on the other, form the two terms of this cruel antinomy. This antinomy serves at the same time to demystify the masses. Whereas the state calls upon the proletariat to participate actively in production, persuading it of its dominant role in society, it refuses it all responsibility and all initiative and maintains it in the position of a mere servant to the mechanization to which capitalism had assigned it since its origin. Thus the propaganda teaches, day in and day out, the opposite of what it is intended to teach.

It could be shown how the evolution of the Russian proletariat, its emancipation from the peasant yoke that still gripped it during the first five-year plans and its apprenticeship to modern technology, considerably exacerbated this contradiction of bureaucratic exploitation and played a decisive role in the recent political transformation. But here I should like to stress that this contradiction is part of the essence of the bureaucratic regime; its terms may evolve, new artifices may be invented to make them 'livable', but as long as it exists the bureaucracy cannot but be torn apart by a double demand: to integrate the proletariat into social life, to get its state 'recognized' as that of society as a whole, on the one hand, and to refuse the proletariat that integration by carrying off the fruits of its labour and by dispossessing it of any social creativity, on the other.

In other words, mystification is everywhere, but for this very reason it produces the conditions of its own reversal, it poses everywhere a threat to the regime. In certain respects, this regime has proved to be infinitely more coherent than the bourgeois system, whereas in other respects it reveals a new vulnerability.

## The Ideal of the Party and its Real Function

The problems confronted by the party in bureaucratic society take us to the heart of the contradictions mentioned above, and it is no accident that they are central, as I shall show, to the preoccupations of the Twentieth Congress.

Yet one would search in vain for an understanding of this problem among the critics of the USSR. The originality of the party is never perceived. Bourgeois thinkers are often aware of the totalitarian project incorporated in the party. They denounce the social mystique that dominates it, its attempt to integrate all activities and thereby subordinate them to a single ideal. But this idea tends to fade into the oft repeated theme of state religion. Haunted by historical precedents which prevent them from reflecting on the present as such, they compare the rules of the party with those of the great imperial regimes, its ideology with that of seventeenth-century Islam.[6] One thus ignores the essential function that it plays in modern social life, in the twentieth-century world unified by capital, dependent in its development on that of each of its sectors, both differentiated through technical specialization and rigorously centred on industry. Trotskyists, for their part, tirelessly compare the present-day Communist Party with the Bolshevik model, as if the former could be defined entirely by negative features – its distortion of socialist ideology, its lack of democracy, its counter-revolutionary conduct. Trotsky himself, as we know, hesitated a great deal before acknowledging the failure of the party in the USSR and could do no more than recommend a return to its original forms. Not only could he not admit that the features of Stalinism were foreshadowed by Bolshevism and that the course of the one was bound up with that of the other, but he absolutely rejected the idea that the party could have acquired a new function. The Bolshevik Party was the *real* party while Stalinism was something quite bizarre, a monstrous projection of that party in a world cut off from revolution.

However, one need only observe the extent of the tasks attributed to the party and the extraordinary increase in its numbers (comprising more than 7 million members in 1956) to be convinced that it plays a decisive role in society. In fact, it is something other than an apparatus of coercion, something other than a caste of bureaucrats, something other than an ideological movement destined to proclaim the sacred historical mission of the state, although it *also* connotes all those features. It is the essential agent of modern totalitarianism.

But this term must be rigorously understood. Totalitarianism is not the same thing as a dictatorial regime, as is implied whenever this term is loosely used to designate a type of absolute domination in which the separation of powers has been abolished. More specifically, it is not a political regime: it is a *form of society*, that form in which all activities are immediately linked to one another, deliberately presented as modalities of a single world; that form in which a system of values predominates absolutely, such that every individual or collective undertaking must necessarily find in it a coefficient of reality; that form in which, lastly, the dominant model exercises a total physical and spiritual constraint on the behaviour of private individuals. In this sense, totalitarianism claims to negate the separation of the various domains of social life – the political, the economic, the legal, the ideological, etc. – which is characteristic of bourgeois capitalism. It effects a permanent identification between them. It is not, therefore, so much a monstrous outgrowth of political power in society as a metamorphosis of society itself in which the political ceases to exist as a separate sphere. As I understand it, totalitarianism has nothing to do with the regime of a Franco or a Syngman Rhee, despite their dictatorships; on the other hand, it is beginning to be felt in the United States, even though democratic institutions have not ceased to operate there. This is because, at the deepest level, it is linked to the structure of modern production and to the requirements of social integration which correspond to it. The expansion of industry, the progressive invasion of every domain by its methods while increasingly isolating producers in their own particular spheres, brings about, as Marx indicated, a *socialization* of society, placing each individual in a state of dependence on all others and rendering necessary the explicit recognition of the ideal unity of society. Even if this social participation may be repressed at the same time as it is being expressed and called into being, even if the community may collapse in face of a new and implacable division between masters and slaves, even if socialization may be reduced to an inculcation of uniform beliefs and activities, collective creation reduced to passivity and conformity, even if the search for universality may sink into the monotonous affirmation of the dominant values, this immense failure should not obscure the positive demands to which totalitarianism responds. It is, one might say, the underside of communism. It is the travesty of the effective totality.

The party is the archetypal institution in which the process of socialization is both carried out and overturned. And it is no accident if, following the struggle to establish communism, it may become, without changing its form, the vehicle of totalitarianism. The party embodies in bureaucratic society an historical function of an absolutely *new* type. It is the agent of a complete penetration of civil society by the state. More precisely, it is the milieu in which the state changes itself into society or society into the state. The immense network of committees and cells that covers the entire nation sets up a new form of communication between town and country, between every branch of social activity, between all the activities of each branch. The division of labour, which tends to isolate individuals, is in a sense superseded; within the party, the engineer, the shopkeeper, the worker and the clerk are found side by side, together with the philosopher, the scientist and the artist. Everyone finds himself torn out of the narrow confines of his speciality and resituated with everyone else in the context of society as a whole and its historical horizons. The life of the state and its objectives are part of their everyday world. Thus every activity, from the most modest to the most important, is actualized and presented as a moment of a collective project. Not only do individuals seem to lose in the party the status that differentiates them in civil life, thus becoming 'comrades', social beings, but they are also called upon to share their experience, to expose their activity and that of their milieu to a collective judgement that gives them meaning. The party thus tends to abolish the mystery of the profession by introducing milieux, which are actually separated from one another, into a new circuit. It reveals that there is a way of managing a factory, of working on a production line, of caring for the sick, of writing a philosophical treatise or of practising a sport that concerns every individual because it implies a social mode of participation and, in the final analysis, is integrated into a whole whose harmony is governed by the state. In other words, the party radically transforms the meaning of the political function. A separate function in bourgeois society, where it is the privilege of a governing minority, it now becomes, through the party, diffused throughout every branch of activity.

Such is the ideal of the party. Through its *mediation*, the state tends to become immanent in society. But, by a paradox that I have already analysed at length, the party turns out *in reality* to possess a quite opposite significance. As the division of labour and capital persists and deepens, as the strict unification of capital gives effective omnipotence to a governing apparatus, subordinating all the productive forces to this apparatus, the party becomes a sham of socialization. *In reality*, it behaves like a particular group which is trying to attach itself to the groups produced by the division of labour, a group whose function it is to mask the irreducible fragmentation of activities and statuses, to represent in the imaginary dimension the continuities which reality rejects, a group whose true speciality is to have no speciality. In reality, the sharing of experiences is degraded into a supervision of those who produce, whatever their area of production, by incompetent professionals. The ideal of active participation in social activity is replaced by the blind obedience to the norm imposed by the leaders: collective creation becomes collective inhibition. Thus the penetration by the party of every domain signifies simply that each productive individual is *duplicated* by a political functionary whose role is to attribute an ideological coefficient to his activity, as if the official norm defined by the construction of socialism and the conjunctural rules that are derived from it could enable one to calculate one's departure from the real. Reduced to commentating on the actual behaviour of individuals, the party thus reintroduces a radical split within social life. Everyone has his ideological *double*. The manager or technician acts under the gaze of this double, who 'assesses' the rise or fall of production or any other result that may be quantified in terms of a fixed scale of values provided by the governing apparatus. Similarly, the writer is judged by criteria of realism laid down by the state and the biologist called upon to adhere to Lysenko's genetics. And the double need not be someone else. Everyone can play the role in relation to himself; the manager, the writer and the scientist may also be members of the party. But however close each one may seem to be to the other, the two terms nevertheless stand in permanent social contradiction. It is as if social life as a whole were dominated by a fantastic timing mechanism whose principles were worked out by the most secret research organization.

The activity of the party thus produces anew a separation of the political function, whereas it set out to abolish it; and in a sense it accentuates it still further. For the intrusion of the political is felt in every concrete sphere of production, however specialized it may be. The freedom of work everywhere comes up against the norms of the party. Everywhere the 'cell' is the foreign body; not the essential element that links the individual to the life of the organism, but the inert nucleus which drains away the productive forces of society.

Ultimately, the party itself is the principal victim of this separation. For within society, the requirements of production create, at least within certain limits, a *de facto* independence of work. The party, on the other hand, has the exclusive task of proclaiming, diffusing and imposing ideological norms. It feeds on the political. Its principal function becomes that of justifying its function, interfering in everything, denying every particular problem, constantly affirming the leitmotiv of the official ideal. As it persuades itself that its activity is essential, it finds itself excluded, on account of its behaviour, from real society. And this contradiction increases its authoritarianism, its demand for its prerogatives, its claim to universality. For it is effective where it does not know how to be, in so far as it disguises society as the state, in so far as it simulates a social and historical unity beyond the divisions and conflicts of the real world – or, as Marx would have said, it is real in so far as it is imaginary. But it is also imaginary in so far as it is real, for it is deprived of any historical efficacy where it most believes it is applying it: on the terrain of the productive life of society, which it disturbs like a constant storm.

It is hardly surprising, then, if we find within the party the defects of bureaucracy pushed to their extreme. Ideally party members might be defined as 'universal' individuals, freed from the narrow confines of a situation or a status, promoted to the task of building socialism, so many embodiments of a new humanity. In fact they are condemned to the abstraction of the dominant rule, doomed to servile obedience, fixed within the particularity of their function as a militant, drawn into a merciless struggle for the best jobs, servants to a system of self-justifying red tape, one particular group among others, determined to preserve and reproduce the conditions that legitimate its existence. However, they can no more renounce what they ought to be than they can renounce what they are. For it is by this contradiction that the party realizes the essence of totalitarianism as a centre for the 'socialization' of society and for the subordination of the productive forces to the domination of capital.

## The Reform of Totalitarianism

The Stalinist dictatorship played a determinant historical role in the building of the bureaucratic infrastructure and in the crystallization of a new dominant class. This role can be assessed precisely only when we have recognized the specific features of the bureaucracy, whose collective mode of appropriation confers on the state and on the party absolute power in every sphere of social life. The conditions that produce the system create both an identification of the state with civil society in which all distinctions between the political, the economic, the legal, the ideological, etc. tend to be abolished, and a radical divorce between society and the state that re-establishes a domination of the governing apparatus over all concrete activities and a monstrous autonomy of the political. Such are the conclusions that I have reached and that now enable me to consider the transformations of the regime made public by the Twentieth Congress, to assess the effectiveness of the historical forces that have determined them and to interpret their import. In other words, I am now in a position to ask these final questions: In what sense are the present changes integrated into the bureaucratic structure? In what respects do they respond to problems posed by the past? Does this response provide a 'solution', or does it merely change the terms of the contradictions within the regime? [. . .]

In the heroic period of the first five-year plans, Marxism, transformed by Stalinism, offered the bureaucracy a tragic vision of the world: the ideal of a new economic order, of the violent destruction of capitalists, of the historical mission which, falling upon the shoulders of the new leaders, overrides everything. For all its idealism, this vision was not incompatible with the profound cynicism of the exploiter which Trotsky denounced. But it dissimulated it. And this self-mystification was essential. One could describe the bureaucrats in the way Marx described the eighteenth-century bourgeoisie in *The Eighteenth Brumaire.* By using revolutionary terminology and draping themselves in Leninist 'costumes', they concealed from themselves the narrow and particular interests of their struggle. They succeeded in 'maintaining their passion for great historical tragedy', they 'realized the task imposed by their epoch'.[7] Like the bourgeoisie in its rise to power, the bureaucracy first raises itself above itself and is obliged to massacre its own members in order to impose the ideal of the new domination. The system consolidates itself, passion becomes excess, the exploits of the revolution lose their charm, myth tends to return to the language of everyday life. Whereas trials earlier assumed the fantastic dimensions of a Last Judgement before Humanity, the accused legitimating the cause which destroyed them, tearing out of themselves their own confessions and transforming their imaginary crime into real treason, today the court is merely the sinister executor of the despotism, the accused the simple victim of the Cheka.

The measures associated with the name of Malenkov represent a response to this evolution. A bureaucratic *habeas corpus* is formulated, a separation is re-established between the police and the system of justice, they are declared to be entirely freed from political control, citizens are thus removed from the permanent threat exercised over them by dictatorial discretion. Old trials as well as recent ones are condemned, as are the instigators of the pseudo-plot of the doctors and, retrospectively, Vichinsky, the prosecutor of the terror. Democratic rules are announced which should preside over the functioning of official institutions – the Soviets, the party and the trade unions, which had even ceased to hold their congress. At the same time, spectacular reductions in the price of consumer goods are declared and a programme for the production of goods to satisfy the new needs of the population is introduced. Finally – and this is the chief work of the Twentieth Congress – the individual who embodied the terror, Stalin himself, is sacrificed to the collectivity. We could say, once again paraphrasing Marx, that the moment of the realist spokesmen of the new class has come. They are called Malenkov and Khrushchev, Bulganin and Mikoian. They confer upon the members of their class the status that had long since been called for by their ruling function.

However, the new policy could not be interpreted solely within the framework of the evolution of the dominant group. The evolution of the exploited groups seems no less determinant, and the concessions oriented towards them are at the centre of the reform. For the methods which prevailed before the war had lost their efficacy by 1956, in a context where industrialization has greatly increased the proletariat and transformed its needs, attitudes and modes of resistance to exploitation. [. . .] New conditions of existence must be created for the proletariat which will enable it to 'participate' fully in the tasks of production. A reorganization of planning is therefore essential. Of course, it is not a matter of renouncing the traditional aim of developing heavy industry but, in order to fulfil this objective, a new interest must be taken in the production of consumer goods. More generally, it turns out that the real power of society is not defined exclusively by a certain volume of productive forces or by a certain material potential; rather, it is based on a *human* potential and this is to be measured both in terms of the technical knowledge possessed by the masses and in terms of their adherence to a certain way of life. Considerable price reductions are thus made on ordinary consumer goods and wages are increased; the working week is reduced and it is announced that reductions will soon be made in the working day; holidays with pay will be arranged in a more flexible way. These material concessions, however important they may be – and there can be no doubt that they will continue to grow – are still insufficient. Certain features of the labour legislation are being abandoned; the accusation of economic sabotage will no longer hang like a permanent threat over the head of every worker; and the worker will no longer be forced to work so long in the same factory without losing the social advantages to which he has a right. Lastly, the workers are called upon to participate more actively in the life of the party and trade unions and are offered the guarantee of a genuine democracy.

All these measures (some of which were implemented during Stalin's lifetime) have considerable significance. They reveal that a certain type of dictatorship is incompatible with the functioning of a modern society; they bring the regime of the USSR closer to that of the great industrial countries of the bourgeois world. But they take on their full meaning only if they are situated in the context of the bureaucratic structure. They do not affect the essence of totalitarianism, for this, as we have stressed, cannot be reduced to a form of government; it is bound up with a mode of economic management, with a collective class appropriation that is not for a moment being placed in question. The *new course* is presented rather as an attempt to *reform* totalitarianism, an attempt to overcome certain contradictions from the past, to invent new ways which will ensure a better functioning of society. So the problem is to investigate the nature of this reform of institutions, to determine its limits and the new problems to which it may give rise. The speeches of the Twentieth Congress provide us with an incomparable guide in our inquiry and, by following them, we can see that the dominant questions of the present for the leaders of the bureaucracy are those that we have regarded as inherent in totalitarianism. Of course, the bureaucracy wraps up its difficulties in a constant apologia for the regime. Moreover, it suggests that they are merely technical difficulties, linked to a particular set of circumstances and therefore soluble. It is not simply that the bureaucracy mystifies; it mystifies itself, because it is incapable of objectively representing to itself its own role in society, because it is condemned to envisage every problem in postulating the necessity of its own existence. Nevertheless, within the narrow horizons which are circumscribed by its interests, it is conducting a critique which is being carried as far as possible. On the state apparatus, on the party, on planning, on the functioning of industry and agriculture, the criticisms press to the heart, exposing the contradictions inherent in the totalitarian system of exploitation.

The fundamental criticisms made by Khrushchev, Bulganin and Suslov concern the split that has grown up between the state and society, between the party and productive life, between ideology and practical work, between the norms of planning and the real functioning of production. The aim, reaffirmed at each step, is the restoration of a unity which would enable the various sectors of social life to communicate effectively and which would allow the members of society to participate actively in the common task. But this aim is frustrated as soon as it is formulated. For participation and communication are subordinated to the rule imposed by the governing apparatus. Whether it is addressed to the members of the exploited class or to those of the dominant class, the appeal from the leadership may be reduced, in the final analysis, to the following formula: 'Do as if the maxim governing your action could be erected into a universal law of the bureaucratic will.' Or, in more vulgar terms: 'Desire from the depths of your heart whatever the leadership orders you to do.' Khrushchev and Bulganin declare that the bureaucracy is ready to undo itself and to provide the spectacle of incredible contortions, which would happily render it unrecognizable, without in any way altering its body. They add that the spectacle is gratuitous, but that it is in the interests of the public to believe it. [. . .]

Whether it concerns the state, the party or planning, the reforms proposed at the Twentieth Congress have in my opinion a common objective: they are aimed at *ameliorating* totalitarianism. The leaders are exposing and combating the inertia of the administrative apparatus, the impotence of the party, the degeneration of ideology, the excessive centralization of the Plan, the glaring inequalities in income. In doing so, there can be no doubt that they will succeed in eliminating *abuses*. One could hardly deny that some of these measures are progressive within the context of the system: those advocating a more judicious distribution of specialists, a reorganization of the technical and scientific institutes, the reform of the ministries or the reallocation of wages. Nor could one contest the fact that the raising of the standard of living and the elimination of police terror are having a positive effect on social life. Nevertheless, all these reforms are subordinated to one fundamental objective: to obtain new support for the regime, to awaken the creative initiative of the population, to stimulate an active 'participation' in production. Now this objective is, in the final analysis, incompatible with the structure of the system which maintains a radical division between the exploited classes and the bureaucracy, on the one hand, and which implies a strict subordination of all members of society to the state apparatus, on the other.

As far as the proletariat is concerned, it is clear that all the concessions granted by the leadership come up against the framework imposed by exploitation. The masses are called upon to join the party in larger numbers and to express their opinions there, but it goes without saying that they would not be able to challenge the validity of the official rules; lifting the norms advocated by Bulganin is the condition of participation. Similarly, the differentiation of wages is a principle that could not be questioned. Khrushchev rails and threatens the 'incorrigible braggarts' who have taken it into their heads to apply a communist policy from now on.[8] In other words, the masses are invited to act and to express themselves quite freely within the limits of the role laid down for them by the dominant group. Their own actions and claims are no more recognized today than they were recognized in the past. But, at the level of the population as a whole, the problem is still posed in the same terms. For Khruschev, the key to the struggle against bureaucratism is the supervision of each individual, good workers as well as bad. No doubt an awareness by each individual of his responsibilities is necessary, but the only way for the state to ensure that individuals are correctly aware of their role is not to take one's eyes off them. As Khrushchev says, using a formula which would be welcomed by conservatives throughout the world: 'Supervision is order.' So, after having stressed the re-establishment of socialist legality, the leader of the Congress does not hesitate to give a severe warning to all those who would expect any diminution in the powers of the Cheka; the country is swarming with spies and saboteurs and it is therefore appropriate 'to reinforce the agencies of state security'.[9] Finally, the new policy could be inscribed with this formula which Khruschev applies to literature and art: 'The party has fought and will continue to fight any representation that is not in conformity with reality', it being understood that reality, according to Khrushchev, is the bureaucratic order. In fact, for having taken the risk of presenting an image that is not in accordance with the official representation of reality, many elements have already, as we know, been severely called to order by *Pravda*. There can, therefore, be no doubt that opposition is being stifled or repressed as firmly as in the past: the regime does not tolerate it.

If one considers the new policy of the Twentieth Congress as a whole one must recognize therefore that the liberalization of the regime is only one aspect of it. This liberalization is itself a way of ameliorating totalitarianism; it is not incompatible, at the same time, with a strengthening of bureaucratic discipline. On the contrary, it calls for it, for without it the cohesion of the regime would be at risk. Whoever has read Khrushchev's speech would agree that every means is used simultaneously – both democracy and brutal constraint – to face up to the present situation. [. . .]

# 3

# What is Bureaucracy?

Although the concept of bureaucracy has entered into the sphere of the social sciences and the public domain and now enjoys widespread currency, it remains so imprecise that we can justly continue to question the identity of the phenomenon to which it claims to refer. To ask 'What is bureaucracy?' is not simply to question the dimensions, the character, the origin or the future of a social phenomenon; it is also, implicitly or explicitly, to raise the fundamental question concerning the mode of being of this phenomenon.

The diversity of responses and the persistence of uncertainty is at first somewhat astonishing. But this astonishment is merely a first impression. Bureaucracy confronts us as a phenomenon of which everyone speaks and believes to have experienced in some way, and yet this phenomenon strangely resists conceptualization. So rather than attempting straightaway to provide yet another new definition or new description, we shall begin by assessing the difficulties encountered by theory, assume that they have some significance and allow ourselves to be led by this critical reflection to the issues which lie at the origin of these difficulties and which sustain them.

## Outline of the Problem of Bureaucracy

The first representation which we shall consider is that offered by Marxist theory in the analysis of the state bureaucracy. Marx already drew attention, in his *Critique of Hegel's Philosophy of Right*, to the specific nature of the social stratum in charge of the administration of public affairs. In contrast to the corporations which were engaged in private activities and attached to particular interests, this stratum appears as the bearer of a universal interest. The development of the theory of the state, by Marx in his later works and then by Lenin in *State and Revolution*, and the application of this theory to post-revolutionary Russian society by Trotsky, go hand in hand with a reflection on the role played by the bureaucracy as a stratum essentially linked to the structure of class society. In this perspective, the bureaucracy is neither a class nor a stratum analogous to those which can be distinguished within a class (such as office workers); its existence derives from the division of society into classes and from the class struggle, since its function is to secure the general acceptance of the rules of a common order (an order which no doubt stems from the relations of production but which must be formulated in universal terms and maintained by force). The bureaucracy is 'normally' at the service of the dominant class, since the administration of public affairs in the context of a given regime always presupposes the preservation of its status. But since it is not itself a mere section of this class, it can run counter to some of its interests, assuming that an overall balance of social forces enables it to, and thus acquire a relative autonomy. The limits of its power are always circumscribed by the configuration of social relations. In short, the bureaucracy is a special body within society. It is *special* because it has the function of supporting the established structure and its disappearance would signify the end of bourgeois domination (the first revolutionary measure of the Commune, said Marx in essence, was to have suppressed the bureaucracy by lowering the salaries of functionaries to the level of the average wage of a worker). It is *within society* because it is not a basis of social structuration, because its role within society is already determined by the real historical agents: by classes in conflict.

The perspective changes as soon as one observes the growth of strata concerned with administrative tasks in the various sectors which are part of civil society. It is then tempting to look for criteria that would enable one to define a type of social organization which would take account of the features of state bureaucracy, industrial bureaucracy, party bureaucracy, trade-union bureaucracy and so on. The observation of the multiple forms of bureaucracy introduces an historical and sociological perspective. Comparison encourages one to investigate the conditions for the emergence of bureaucracies and to define a single type which gives unity to their diverse characteristics.

In this second perspective, to which Max Weber's thesis could be linked, bureaucracy still appears as a particular mode of organization, as one mode among others, which corresponds to a more or less extended sector but which is still situated *within* society. In other words, the social dynamic does not seem to be affected by the growth of bureaucracies. The mode of production, the class relations or the political regime could be studied without reference to a phenomenon which designates merely a certain type of organization.

The theory of bureaucracy thus undergoes a real transformation when it is used to describe a new class which is regarded as the dominant class in one or several countries, or which is even seen as destined to replace the bourgeoisie throughout the world. This perspective is suggested by the evolution of the Russian regime after the rise of Stalin. The disappearance of the old property owners and the liquidation of the workers' organs of power have gone hand in hand with a considerable extension of the bureaucracy of the Communist Party and of the state which has taken direct control of the management of society. But the spectacle of the social transformations which have accompanied the development of monopolistic concentration in the great industrial countries, and notably in the United States, gives rise to a parallel reflection on the growth of a bureaucratic class. This perspective does indeed mark a transformation in the theory of bureaucracy, for the bureaucracy is now understood as a stratum capable, by virtue of the role that it plays in economic and cultural life, of supplanting the traditional representatives of the bourgeoisie and monopolizing power. It is thus perceived as the basis of a new historical project, as the centre of a new social structure.

Lastly, it seems to me that a new representation emerges in opposition to the perspective just described as soon as one claims to find in the phenomenon of *bureaucratization* a gradual erosion of the old distinctions linked to the existence of private property. Bureaucratization here refers to a process which tends to impose a homogeneous social framework on work at every level, whether the work of managers or the work of those who carry out orders, in such a way that the general stability of employment, the hierarchy of salaries and functions and the structure of authority results in the formation of a single scale of social status, however differentiated this scale may be. This last thesis, like the preceding one but in contrast to the other two, attributes a social dynamic to the bureaucracy or lends it a certain finality of its own, the realization of which produces an upheaval in the traditional structure of society as a whole.

If such are the general contours of the problem of bureaucracy, we can now take up each of the theses in turn and allow ourselves to be guided by their contradictions. But I shall discuss at length only the first three, since the critique of the final thesis seems to me to follow naturally from the analysis of the others.

## The Marxist Critique of the State Bureaucracy

The Marxist representation of bureaucracy is determined, as was Hegel's, by a theory of history. When Marx criticized Hegel's philosophy of the state, his own theory was still in a state of gestation; but that did not matter greatly, for the philosophical viewpoint was of prime importance. It is nevertheless remarkable that Marx was able to sketch a description of the bureaucracy.

Hegel's mistake, according to Marx, was to have accepted the image which the bureaucracy presents of itself. It claims to embody the general interest and Hegel believes that it does. In reality, argues Marx, the general interest amounts to no more than the interest of the bureaucracy, which requires the continued existence of particular spheres of interest – the corporations and the estates – in order to present itself as an imaginary universality. The bureaucracy assigns its own aim to the state: the aim of maintaining the social division in order to confirm and sustain its own status as a particular and privileged body in society. Whereas civil society is the theatre of real activities, the bureaucracy is condemned to a kind of formalism in which it is fully preoccupied with preserving and legitimating the frameworks within which its activities are carried out. This critique uncovers a series of empirical characteristics of bureaucracy whose significance remains concealed to those who cling to appearances. In the first place, bureaucracy is marked by incompetence. As Marx observes, 'The highest point entrusts the understanding of details to the lower echelons, whereas these, on the other hand, credit the highest point with an understanding of the universal, and thus they deceive one another.'[1] But this incompetence is peculiar in the sense that it is turned into a system: 'The bureaucracy is a circle from which no one can escape.'[2] Furthermore, it lives for *secrecy*: the hierarchy guards the mysteries of the state and acts like a closed corporation with regard to the outside world. It also gives rise to a cult of authority: '*authority* is the basis of its knowledge, and the deification of authority is its *conviction*'.[3] Finally, it is open to a 'crass materialism'. The bureaucrat turns the ends of the state into his private ends: 'a pursuit of higher posts, the making of a career'.[4] Marx also shows that this materialism is accompanied by a spiritualism which is equally crass: the bureaucracy *wants to do everything*, and in the absence of a real function it is condemned to an incessant activity of justification.

Marx's analysis is applied to nineteenth-century Germany, i.e. to a backward society, but its significance is not thereby diminished. When he later observed a nation – the France of Louis Napoleon Bonaparte – where the growth of the bourgeoisie had eliminated particularities and destroyed the corporations, when he elaborated his theory of the state and treated the latter as an instrument in the service of the dominant class, he retained the idea, already developed against Hegel, that the state is an essentially parasitical body. Thus he described Bonaparte's regime as follows:

> This executive power with its enormous bureaucratic and military organisation, with its extensive and artificial state machinery, *with a host of officials numbering half a million*, besides an army of another half million, this *appalling parasitic body*, which enmeshes the body of French society like a net and chokes all its pores, sprang up in the days of the absolute monarchy, with the decay of the feudal system, which it helped to hasten.[5]

Moreover, the revolutionary measure *par excellence* of the Paris Commune was, in Marx's eyes, to have set up a government which was good value for money, that is, to have suppressed the privileges and hierarchies which were characteristic of the state bureaucracy. In *State and Revolution*, Lenin merely reiterates what Marx had said on all these points. The bureaucracy and the standing army, which he regards as the two most characteristic institutions of the state, are 'a parasite created by the internal antagonisms which rend that society, but a parasite which "chokes" all its vital pores'.[6] However, he offers some remarks which clarify the nature of this parasitical relation. On the one hand, he observes that the recruitment of the bureaucracy from the middle and lower strata detaches part of their members from the rest of the people and links their fate to that of the dominant class. On the other hand, he notes that the state bureaucracy is the site of a permanent struggle between the major parties, which haggle over administrative perks and try to appropriate, especially during a change of regime, a large enough portion of the spoils to satisfy their clientele.

What is the significance of the Marxist analysis and what difficulties does it raise? In the first place, its merit is to present the state bureaucracy, taken as an empirical phenomenon, in a light which continues to clarify this phenomenon today as it did a century ago. It is a critique which reflects the common view of bureaucracy but which gives grounds for this view. Thus it observes, for example, that the bureaucracy is a circle from which no one can escape; in the realm of the office, subordinates leave it to their superiors to take initiatives and to resolve difficulties, while the latter expect their subordinates to give, at the level of particular cases, responses which fall short of the level of generality at which they conceive of them. This collaboration in incompetence suffices to link the clerk, located at the bottom of the hierarchy, to the system of which he is part, so much so that he cannot denounce this system without simultaneously denouncing the vanity of his own function, upon which his material existence depends. The Marxist analysis also observes that the bureaucrat strives for the highest position, that the work itself is subordinated to the attainment or maintenance of a personal status, in such a way that the bureaucracy appears as a vast network of personal relationships where relations of dependence are substituted for the relations objectively defined by the division of labour, and where groupings by clans and their struggles are superimposed on the formal hierarchy and tend constantly to reshape it in terms of their own demands. The distribution of the most important positions between the major parties appears, more so today than ever before, as a sharing out of the spoils as soon as there is a change of regime: in France the period of the Liberation and the rise of Gaullism provide recent examples.

These observations deserve to be emphasized. To say simply that such characteristics are well known would be to fail to explain why they have not been examined: Marx, and after him Lenin, provide us with an explanation. Even if the latter were false, we could not avoid the task which they set themselves. In order to appreciate the importance of bureaucracy, it is necessary to go beyond a superficial account which remains at the level of its official image. In this respect, Marxism offers a freshness of approach which compares favourably with the view of certain contemporary sociologists. But as soon as Marx's description had been sketched, it was smothered by a theory. Hence the state bureaucracy was treated as a general category and no attempt was made to explain its functioning. If it is true that the bureaucracy is a circle which encloses all its members, it is nevertheless the case that it is stratified (that its very essence is stratification) and that all of its members do not participate in it in the same way. At what level is the power of bureaucrats situated? Why does the bureaucracy always grow in size? Does it serve merely as an overspill from the major political parties? Or does the very life of the bureaucratic organism contain a principle of proliferation. No doubt the state bureaucracy consists of individuals primarily drawn from the middle classes; but having become bureaucrats, do they remain members of their classes or do they change their attitudes and acquire new interests? Marxism does not answer these questions. Its conception of society as governed entirely by class struggle does not encourage one to study bureaucracy for its own sake.

Today the state is the largest capitalist entrepreneur and the largest source of investment. Beyond the sphere that it manages directly, it tends to orient its investments, at a national level, by means of its fiscal and economic policy. It is, of course, true that the state is itself the field of a struggle between the major political parties, that representatives of private capital operate within its administration and that its policy is often the outcome of forces which confront one another in society; but transposed into the sphere of the state, the struggle between groups is not the same as that which unfolds in civil society. The division of interests linked to the requirements of administering public affairs creates its own space for decision-making, a space which grows and takes shape as the state drains away more and more capital and takes over an increasing number of tasks previously left to private initiative. Moreover, the defence of the established order, which guarantees the position of dominant groups over those which are dominated, establishes and renews everyday the foundations of its sovereignty. The representation of state bureaucracy discussed above can no longer be sustained in this perspective either. In particular, the concept of parasitism which is applied to it seems insufficient, or at least indeterminate: Why does the bureaucratic mode of organization as such breed parasites? Why, for example, do ten unproductive positions grow up around one function that could be regarded as necessary in terms of the current state of the division of labour? Into the Marxist theory slips the thesis that the bureaucracy, taken as a whole, is a parasitical phenomenon. In reality, the bureaucracy is necessary in the context of capitalist society; if critique is to be effective, it must be situated at the same level as that of the capitalist organization. But would it not then appear to be the case that there is a dialectic of domination in modern society whereby a social stratum concerned with organizing and perfecting the conditions of domination *accrues* at the same time as industrial labour invades every sector of social life and as the life of the masses is subordinated to it? Would it not appear to be the case, in sum, that the process of bureaucratization, so visible in the context of the state, occurs at the same time outside of this context, at the heart of what the young Marx still called civil society?

## Bureaucracy as a Type of Organization

Let us leave these questions aside for the time being and consider a second perspective: that which uncovers the multiplicity of bureaucracies in modern society and draws attention to their common function and similarity. Here I shall refer to Max Weber's contribution, which seems to me to be exemplary, and I shall try to draw out its essential elements.

Weber lists certain features which he regards as specific to modern bureaucracy.[7]

1   The duties of the functionaries are officially fixed by laws, rules or administrative measures.
2   The functions are hierarchical and integrated into a system of command so that all lower levels of authority are controlled by higher authorities and so that it is possible for the decisions of a lower instance to be appealed to a higher instance.
3   Administrative activity is recorded in written documents.
4   Administrative functions presuppose a professional apprenticeship.
5   The work of the functionary demands complete devotion to the job.
6   Access to the profession is at the same time access to a particular technique, to jurisprudence, commercial science and administrative science.

From this analysis one can draw several conclusions concerning the position of the bureaucrat.

1 His job appears to him as the exercise of a profession which is linked to a specific body of knowledge; on the other hand, it is neither in fact nor in principle the source of fees or dividends, nor is it the object of a contract whereby the employee hires out his labour power. The particular character of the job implies that, in exchange for certain material guarantees (the guarantee of a certain standard of living), the functionary accepts a specific duty of loyalty to the job; he is at the service, not of a person, but of an objective and impersonal goal. This goal is built into the organization to which he is linked – the state, the commune, the party or the capitalist firm – and realizes certain cultural values.

2 Those who work within a public or private bureaucracy enjoy social prestige *vis-à-vis* dominated groups; this prestige is most often guaranteed by a special status which grants certain rights sanctioned by rules.

3 The functionary is normally appointed by a superior authority. Although there may be certain bureaucracies in which the members are elected, the pure type requires the principle of appointment; hierarchical discipline is undermined when the functionary draws his power from the approval of electors, that is, *from below* rather than *from above*.

4 The stability of employment is normally assured, even though a right of possession of the job is never recognized.

5 The bureaucrat normally receives remuneration in the form of a salary determined by the nature of the job and, eventually, by the years of his service in the organization.

6 Finally, corresponding to the hierarchical order of the bureaucracy, a scale of salaries is established; most functionaries want promotions to take place as mechanically as possible.

Weber also points to the role of certain factors in the absence of which bureaucracy could not fully develop. For example, its structure is definitively established only when the sectors of natural economy have been finally eliminated and capitalism dominates society. The growth of democracy, on the other hand, enables the traditional administration of notables, endowed with local authority, to be replaced by the administration of anonymous functionaries, detached from any particular social milieu and devoted to tasks of universal significance. Finally, Weber goes so far as to identify the movement of bureaucratization with the process of capitalist rationalization. For what seems to him to be determinant is not so much the quantitative development of administrative tasks but rather their qualitative change: the necessity which obliges the large organization, of whatever kind (even the state), to envisage its activities from a strictly technical point of view and to predict or calculate the results as accurately as possible. Bureaucracy in this sense is the social framework which is most adequate to the capitalist organization of production and to the organization of a society adapted to these ends. The elimination of personal relations and the subordination of all activities to the application of a norm linked to an objective goal turn bureaucracy into a model of the economic rationality established by industrial capitalism. Hence Weber does not hesitate to express a value judgement about modern bureaucracy, declaring that it is superior from a technical point of view to all other forms of organization.

However, it does not follow that the development of bureaucracies, however necessary they may seem once certain conditions are realized, must affect the nature of the political and economic system. On the contrary, Weber maintains that the numerical extent of this form of organization in no way determines its relation to power. This is demonstrated by the fact that the state bureaucracy accommodates itself to different regimes, as for example in France, where the state bureaucracy has remained remarkably stable since the first Empire. It is also demonstrated by the fact that in periods of war the bureaucratic personnel of the conquered country is naturally used by the foreign power and continues to carry out its administrative tasks. The bureaucracy is essentially indifferent to the interests and values defended by a political regime. It is an organ at the service of dominant groups, situated, as it were, between those who dominate and those who are dominated.

These analyses take on their full significance only when they are placed within a certain methodological perspective. Bureaucracy is seen by Weber as a type of social organization. In reality, bureaucracies do not necessarily attain their complete and finished form; certain empirical conditions are required for the various characteristics to be simultaneously present. But the type, once defined, renders the impure forms intelligible and enables one to discern the outlines of a form which historical conditions have not allowed to develop. Even when Weber observes that the process of bureaucratization and that of capitalist rationalization are closely linked, this observation must not be misconstrued: historical explanation is of a different order than the determination of a social type.

Thus the method determines, at least in part, its results. If bureaucracy is regarded as essentially indifferent to the nature of the economic and social systems, if it appears to have no historical goal, it is because it has been conceived by Weber as a type of organization, that is, in a purely formal way, and not as a specific social stratum which, at the same time as it establishes a certain order and style of relations between its members, produces a history of its own. As a result, the case of 'state socialism' cannot be confronted by Weber in an unprejudiced way. According to him, the bureaucracy can adapt itself more easily to state socialism than it can to bourgeois democracy; and yet the history of state socialism is not internally connected to that of the bureaucracy. The conclusions that Weber draws in this regard are curiously similar to those of certain Marxists, even though they are inspired by different principles. In the eyes of certain Marxists, the state bureaucracy is unconnected to the social dialectic which unfolds at the level of the relations of production. In Weber's eyes, a sequence of events can be reconstituted in order to render the emergence of state socialism intelligible; but bureaucratization does not generate these events, even though it may be favoured by them.

Now this thesis, preoccupied as it is with offering an empirical description, can be called into question more easily than Marx's thesis by adducing certain features of historical development. In the regime stemming from the Russian Revolution which Weber calls 'state socialism' (an expression which need not be criticized here), the bureaucracy is not *in fact* unconnected to power. The future leaders of the state are born within it: Stalin made a career in the party bureaucracy, pursued for a long time the highest position before attaining it, added to his function as secretary that of state bureaucrat before becoming the master of power. The fact that he acquired a charismatic quality during his reign does not mean that he detached himself from the bureaucracy: the latter was the permanent basis of his power. While charisma can disappear or change character with the death of a dictator, the new power will reconstitute itself on the basis of the bureaucracy. The political struggles

which take place at the highest level of the hierarchy and which concern the future direction of the state extend into broad sectors of the
upper bureaucracy; Khrushchev won out in the end only because
he was *supported* by the majority of the elements which controlled the
bureaucratic apparatus. It thus seems clear that where the state
bureaucracy has become most extensive, it has encompassed the
ultimate political and economic decisions in its sphere or, in other
words, it has become the core of a new regime. But if Weber had
acknowledged this, he would not have formulated his definition of
the bureaucratic type as he did. His account is premised on the
refusal to accept that the bureaucracy has its own dynamic and intrinsic goal; thus he fails to investigate its *constitutive* features, that is,
the ways in which it is rooted in its social being and increases its
power. The enumeration of criteria may be useful, but the phenomenon which they designate remains indeterminate so long as one has
not grasped the principle which links these criteria. It matters little
whether one adds or subtracts a criterion; the principle underlying
such an operation is not clear. Nothing enables one to decide
whether, in the absence of certain features highlighted by the
description of a type, a social complex is or is not bureaucratic. In
order to make this decision, one must move to a different level and
identify the centre of bureaucratization within this complex.

   This criticism applies not only to Weber, but to any attempt to
provide a formal definition of a similar kind. For example, Alain
Touraine writes as follows in a special issue of *Arguments* devoted to
the French working class:

> I call bureaucracy a system of organization where statuses and roles,
> rights and duties, conditions of access to a position, controls and sanc-
> tions are defined by their situation in a hierarchical order and hence
> by a certain delegation of authority. These two characteristics pre-
> suppose a third: the fundamental decisions are not taken within the
> bureaucratic organization, which is merely a system of transmission
> and execution.[8]

This definition, evidently inspired by Weber but benefiting from
conciseness, no doubt has a field of application. When Touraine
goes on to say that a government ministry is a bureaucratic organization, it is easy to agree with him. But when he adds that an industrial firm is *partially* bureaucratic, the difficulty appears. If it is
true that only the first characteristic of bureaucracy is found here,

then how can we conclude that the firm is a partial bureaucracy? Must we assume that a system of organization functioning according to fixed rules and in an impersonal way already engenders bureaucratization? If, on the other hand, we recognize that the criterion of the delegation of authority is decisive and that in fact the worker does not participate in authority, then in what sense can one speak of a 'bureaucratization of work'? This equivocation is exacerbated when, in the same issue of *Arguments*, Michel Crozier takes up Touraine's definition and remarks that 'the worker in Western countries in general, and the French worker in particular, are already well advanced along the path of bureaucracy'.[9] 'The delegation of authority,' he tells us, 'is not necessary for participation in a bureaucratic system'; it is characterized essentially by the existence of a hierarchy. Does this mean that it is possible to *belong* to the system without holding any authority? But if that were so then the problem would simply be displaced, for we would still have to define the relations within the bureaucratic system between the sector characterized by relations of authority and the sector concerned with carrying out tasks of construction and subordinated to an external authority; in other words, the problem of determining the role played by relations of authority in the constitution of the bureaucracy would remain. Even if it had to be admitted that a bureaucratic system taken as a whole did not necessarily make room for these relations and that it was characterized essentially by the existence of a hierarchy, it would still be necessary to specify what it means concretely to speak of a hierarchy of the bureaucratic type. In itself this notion is so vague that it can be applied to contexts of very different kinds: nothing is more hierarchical, for example, than the court of a hereditary monarchy. What, then, is the basis of the hierarchy in a bureaucracy? What justifies a vertical classification of functions and roles? The need to evaluate the significance of this or that criterion in terms of some conception of bureaucracy is always reintroduced.

If Weber listed a certain number of precise characteristics of bureaucracy without wishing to privilege the one characteristic among them which could alone refer to another social reality, it is because he had a strong sense of its specificity. The interest of his analysis stems from the fact that he links this sense to an awareness of the multiplicity of the forms of bureaucratic organization in modern society. Even if his analysis falls short, it has the merit of obliging us to confront his examples and the type he proposes and thus to arrive at a new representation and a new integration of the features he highlights.

Let us return again to the example of the state bureaucracy, now that we are aware of the dangers involved in treating it as essentially unconnected to political power, in order to ask which stratum of functionaries Weber wished to circumscribe. His definition certainly applies to the personnel of a ministry, at least to the functionaries whose roles involve certain responsibilities; as regards subordinate personnel who are concerned with merely carrying out orders and whose working time is rigorously specified and supervised, it cannot be said that the job implies loyalty and devotion to the goal of the organization, and a professional training which itself presupposes the possession of specialized knowledge. But does this definition, strictly speaking, apply to all functionaries holding responsible positions? For example, can it be said, adopting Weber's perspective, that secondary-school teachers are part of the bureaucracy in France? The position of the teacher corresponds exactly to that which Weber attributed to the bureaucrat. Only on one point does the definition not apply: participation in a system of authority. It could not be said that access to a certain position or to a certain level in the hierarchy gives the teacher some sort of power over subordinates. On the other hand, his position *vis-à-vis* his superiors is quite special. He is certainly subjected to an administrative power; his fate depends on decisions taken at the highest level of a government department. But for the most part he is free from this power: the content of his activity is only very partially determined by ministerial decisions. This professional activity has its own goal which should not be confused with the objective goal immanent in the ministerial organization; it is an activity oriented towards a transformation of its object and this alone can provide it with a sufficient justification. Moreover, and most importantly, the teacher is not aiming to *make a career* out of his profession. He may hope for a change, for a movement from one level of seniority to another by the most rapid route, but he does not adopt the approach which is offered to the bureaucrat: to acquire a new function which will bring with it a higher social status, greater responsibilities and increased power over dependent human beings. Finally, the secondary-school teacher remains, in certain respects, an *isolated* individual. No doubt his activity is social, since it necessarily brings him into contact with the public, but it is not socialized: the division of labour may require him to specialize in one branch of teaching and thus to link his activity to that of other teachers, but it does not generate a unified production process.

In short, if we try to apply the concept of bureaucracy in the way that Weber himself did (leaving aside the value judgements which are implicated in his description), we are led to exclude certain strata of functionaries from the framework of bureaucracy and simultaneously to revise his system of interpretation.

If it is true that Weber had not included French *lycée* teachers in his type, it follows that the characteristics which he regarded as typical and which apply to our example acquire a significance only in certain precise cases. On the other hand, there are certain features in the absence of which it seems impossible to speak of bureaucracy. In the first place, we perceive a link between a certain form of hierarchy and the existence of a system of authority (of command-subordination, as Weber says), such that progression in the hierarchy corresponds to the attainment of new statuses, of new responsibilities and of new power. In the second place, Weber's idea that the bureaucracy expects its members to identify with the organization concerned proves to have a sociological content (and not merely an apologetic function as it initially may have seemed). For such an identification presupposes a professional activity of a certain type, linked to a *role*, which is itself determined by relation to other roles within the dramatic unity of the organization. The bureaucracy expects a deputy chief clerk to say 'the Ministry' or 'the Service' instead of 'I'; and this character exists himself as a bureaucrat by this very act of identification, an act which would have no sense for all those who are rendered strictly anonymous by their work or who are individualized to such an extent that work becomes a sufficient justification of existence. In other words, what Weber calls identification with the job is something other than professional consciousness. Whereas the latter is oriented towards the act of production, the former is concerned with the exercise of responsibility: it calls for behaviour which responds to the expectations of hierarchical superiors and conforms to the interest of the bureaucracy, behaviour which should be manifested by any member of the bureaucracy placed in the same conditions. Hence the activity of the bureaucrat has two characteristics: it is technical and bureaucratic. It may lose the first but not the second. For example, the intense circulation of reports or memos in offices serves only to express the necessity for each individual to demonstrate his function to everyone else; the bureaucracy functions only by virtue of a mutual and constantly renewed recognition among its members, sustained in accordance with a specific ceremonial. As someone once remarked, the volume of paper consumed for internal use in an administration enables one to measure its coefficient of bureaucratic integration. Stripped of any malevolent intention, this observation shows that the bureaucracy can act only by constantly reflecting its activity in the mirror of its constitution. Finally – and this is the third conclusion that we can provisionally draw – Weber's analysis presupposes, by the place it gives to the system of command-subordination, that there is a geographical unity, a determinate spatial context of bureaucratic activities. Of course, all the members of a bureaucracy are not necessarily assembled in the same place, but their interrelations, the discipline which links them together and the supervision of some by others tend to circumscribe a specific office world.

A second example mentioned by Weber, that of the industrial firm, will enable us to test his ideas and to clarify ours. In the first place, we are led once again to ask whether the bureaucracy is merely an organ of transmission and execution. While recognizing that an industrial firm is never autonomous and that it must take account of the interests of the financial capital on which it depends, or of the directives of a ministry in a nationalized industry, nevertheless it remains the case that the management has considerable power for decision-making. Now these decisions as a whole are not in the hands of an individual; whatever the personality of the managing director, the decision-making power is necessarily distributed among the different departments and is actualized within each department only through a more or less collective participation in the solution of specific problems. To ask whether the management is or is not distinct from the bureaucracy is to pose a false problem. In any organization in which the hierarchy culminates in an ultimate form of decision-making, this form transcends in a certain way all those which are subordinate to it; nevertheless, if the power which it formally holds is in reality *composite*, that is, if the decisions which fall within its scope by virtue of officially fixed prerogatives are in fact elaborated, at least in part, at various lower levels, then it is itself part of the framework that it dominates.

As in the case of the state bureaucracy, however, the most important issue concerning the bureaucracy of the firm is to try to determine its boundaries. Which are the individuals who are normally *bureaucrats*, and which are those who can be regarded as falling outside this category?

It is clear that for Weber the definition of the capitalist firm as a bureaucratic organization (he goes so far as to say that it offers an unparalleled model of such organization) does not in any way determine the sector which, within the enterprise, can be described as bureaucratic. To maintain, for example – we already alluded to this argument of Crozier – that workers are part of the bureaucracy as soon as they are placed with engineers and managers on a single hierarchical scale, would no doubt have seemed rather extravagant to Weber, not because some of his criteria would have been unsatisfied but because the position of a social group cannot be established on the basis of its juridical status alone. The fact that the work of one category of workers has become assimilated to that of functionaries tells us nothing about the specific nature of the work and the relations with other social categories within a particular firm. Whether or not the firm is nationalized, whether stability of employment is guaranteed or not, whether or not workers are integrated with managerial staff in the same hierarchical system: these conditions may have important consequences in certain respects, but they do not resolve the problem of ascertaining the *real* situation of employees. In the industrial firm, the mass of workers is restricted to tasks of carrying out orders. The arrangement of workshops, the number and distribution of jobs, the rate of production and the duration and intensity of work are all fixed by an administration which operates at a distance from the shopfloor and which forms a closed and alien world with respect to it.

On the other hand, is it possible to treat all those who work in offices as part of the bureaucracy? In the first place, one must be careful to avoid confusing technical departments with those concerned with administrative and commercial tasks. They no doubt share certain common organizational norms, but the social relations differ in each case as a result of the work performed. In short, the relations of authority and the links established with the firm are not similar. In technical departments, the engineers, technicians and designers have, by virtue of their professional knowledge, a relative autonomy. The supervision of work can be effective only if the boss has a technical competence which is at least equal to that of his subordinates, that is, only if his supervision is a technically superior operation. Social supervision may be practically non-existent, for the requirements of work, within the framework of a fixed time-period, may suffice to establish a normal rate of output. Moreover, the autonomy of technicians is also indicated by their ability to move, by virtue of their skills, from one firm to another. In general terms, the job of the technician depends much more on the nature of the work he performs than on his position in the social organization of the firm.

The functioning of the administrative departments presents a very different picture. Here, at the bottom of the scale, we find clerks without real qualifications, employees whose professional training is rudimentary or non-existent. Between these employees and the managing director of the firm, the hierarchy of jobs is a hierarchy of power. The relations of dependence become determinant and to have a function is to define oneself, at each level, with regard to a superior, whether he is a branch supervisor, a departmental supervisor or a manager. In this context the double nature of work thus reappears: it both corresponds to a professional activity and constitutes itself as the expression of an established social order, an order within which the firm exists. Indeed, from the top to the bottom of the scale, the relations are such that they serve always to reinforce the authoritarian structure of the administration. But that does not mean that the individuals situated at the bottom of the scale participate in the bureaucracy in the same way as the middle or upper strata. In certain respects, clerks are like the workers who carry out orders, deprived of any authority. They often earn less than certain categories of workers who are paid by the hour. Their work could not be described as 'responsible' and it cannot be assumed that they find in their work a basis for identifying with the aims of the firm. Nevertheless, they are not unconnected to the bureaucracy: they are its *dependents*. They generally enter the firm only if they are equipped with references which testify to their 'good character'; they can obtain promotion only by giving proof of their capacity to obey and to command; they live in the hope of attaining higher status. The situation of the clerk is therefore ambiguous. He is not integrated into the bureaucratic system, he submits to it; but everything tends to make him adhere to it, and indeed he effectively does when he adopts the ideal of his superiors – promotion. Moreover, to the extent that his work is determined by the social organization of the firm, he is less able to detach himself from the bureaucratic milieu; and in drawing from this milieu the resources which are necessary for his subsistence, he perceives it as being as necessary as the organization itself.

The bureaucracy is thus a framework which goes beyond the active core of bureaucrats. The latter is constituted by the middle and upper staff which is concerned with administrative and commercial tasks; it is a hierarchy with roots which plunge into the productive sector, where supervisors and foremen monitor the activity of workers. This staff possesses effective authority. Not only do its members occupy positions which are linked, by virtue of a certain division of labour, to officially defined prerogatives, not only are they subjected, each in his place, to a certain discipline, but also their function enables them to participate in the power of the management and makes them identify with the firm as such. To say that they identify with it does not mean that they necessarily have a clear idea of the firm's interests, nor even that they are led to put the latter above their own. It means only that the horizons of the firm are completely fused, in their eyes, with the horizons of their work. The social order immanent in the firm appears to them as something which is both natural and sacred. Their own function is seen by them as something other than a source of remuneration or a type of professional activity: it is seen as the backbone of a system which needs their support in order to survive and expand.

Possessing a status which apparently differentiates his position from that of workers who merely carry out orders, enjoying a prestige which earns the others' respect, receiving a remuneration and material benefits which secure a privileged mode of existence, belonging to a world apart from which authority stems, a world where subordination is the other side of issuing commands and where opportunities for promotion are available: such are the interrelated features which define the figure of the bureaucrat.

Finally, the example of the bureaucracy of the firm dispels, better than any other, the mystification entailed by a purely formal description. The latter presupposes that the bureaucratic organization merges with the rational organization of the firm, in so far as it is rendered necessary by the technical requirements of production. Now as soon as we try to circumscribe the properly bureaucratic sector and are led to highlight a specific type of activity, we uncover a dialectic of socialization which is of a different order than the dialectic of the division of labour.

To say that it is of a different order does not mean that we could determine what an adequate social organization of the firm would be at a certain state of the division of labour, since the latter depends itself on historical conditions which include technical evolution and class conflict. It is simply to maintain that the bureaucratic organization has its own objective which cannot be deduced from the necessities imposed by the organization of production. Once it is recognized that in every large firm there are, in addition to the productive and technical sectors, various categories of tasks relating to the administration of personnel, the sale of products, the purchase of primary materials and machines, the fixing of cost price, etc. it does not follow *naturally* that the specialized departments function as they do in the actual context of the modern capitalist factory. The requirements of planning, co-ordination and information do not necessarily create a determinate social order. This order institutes itself by virtue of a particular social activity. From this point of view, it is essential to grasp the movement by which the bureaucracy creates its order. *The more that activities are fragmented, departments are diversified, specialized and compartmentalized, structural levels are multiplied and authority is delegated at each level, the more the instances of co-ordination and supervision proliferate, by virtue of this very dispersion, and the more bureaucracy flourishes.*

The status of a bureaucrat can be assessed in terms of the number of secretaries and clerks who depend on him, the number of telephones and machines in his department and, more generally, the quantity of resources which are allocated to his sphere of organization. At every favourable opportunity he seeks to extend his area of power; and he seeks always to preserve it. This tendency results in the formation of clans, in a covert war between departments which is constantly nourished by their separation, each one rushing to blame the other for errors or delays in carrying out a programme. But at the same time, since it reflects a common aspiration, this tendency always finds its path. The more bureaucrats there are and the more complicated the system of personal dependence becomes, the more the bureaucracy as a whole is constituted as a rich and differentiated milieu and acquires an existence for itself. The more established the bureaucracy becomes, the more likely it is that individuals draw from it the sense of their own objectivity. Bureaucracy loves bureaucrats, just as much as bureaucrats love bureaucracy.

The consequences of this situation may seem paradoxical. It is true, as Weber said, that the capitalist firm provides bureaucracy with a privileged context of development, that the process of economic rationalization provides a rationale for bureaucratic organization: the need to develop forms of calculation and prediction which are as rigorous as possible favours the growth of a special stratum of administrators and imposes on them a certain type of structuration. But it is no less true that this stratum plans its behaviour, actively intervenes in its structuration and, placed in historically created conditions, expands while pursuing its interest. Thus, behind the mask of rules and impersonal relations lies the proliferation of unproductive functions, the play of personal contacts and the madness of authority.

The third example which we shall consider is the mass party. This example will provide us with a kind of counter-proof, for it will confront us with a bureaucracy which appears to be as distant as possible from that we have just discussed. Once again, this is an example to which Weber referred; and that is no surprise, for Weber was aware that there is a close connection between the party bureaucracy and the state bureaucracy, and he had witnessed the emergence of a state bureaucracy in Russia out of the Communist Party. But it is surprising, in turn, that this example did not lead him to revise his definition of the bureaucratic organization. For it does not suffice to observe that the party is led by a body of 'professional' specialists in order to assimilate the latter to functionaries or to the administrators of a firm. Most of Weber's criteria are not applicable to them. In the first place, if one considers the organization of the party, it is now obvious that the bureaucracy is not merely an organ of execution and transmission: the leadership which is embodied in a politbureau or a general secretariat emerges from the bureaucracy. It hardly matters whether an individual or a handful of individuals hold all real power; they have acquired it only by rising through the hierarchy of the party and they retain it only because they are sustained by a stratum of bureaucrats who orientate the activity of the party in accordance with their directives, who justify and enact their decisions and who oust the opponents. If this stratum disintegrates, the power of the leaders collapses. In the second place, while the functions of the bureaucrats may be laid down by rules, they do not form as structured a whole as in the case of the administration of a state or a firm. There are not strict rules which determine the movement from one job to another; the hierarchy does not give rise to a differentiation and grading of salaries; bureaucrats no longer enjoy a special status, officially defined, which would distinguish them from rank and file activists; access to the highest positions does not depend on technical knowledge, itself linked to a professional training; if the principle of the appointment of officials by the organs of leadership is recognized, it co-exists with a principle of election, since these organs are themselves elected within the framework of assemblies composed of delegates mandated by rank and file activists; and finally, one need not be remunerated by the party in order to occupy an important function within it and to be placed at a high level in the hierarchy. The special character of the party bureaucracy stems from the position which it occupies in society as a whole. Its function is not determined by the division of labour; it is an institution which is based on voluntary membership and which tries to exercise an influence on power, to participate in it or to take hold of it, by assembling a mass of individuals around a programme of demands. The fact that a sector of professionals concerned to co-ordinate the activities of the party is constituted within it does not affect its formal definition; on the contrary, it confers on this sector a series of characteristics which appear to be very different from those we observed in the case of the industrial firm.

But then how can one speak of the mass party as a typical bureaucratic institution? This question brings us closer to the issue which I have tried to formulate since the beginning of this analysis: What is the social nature of the bureaucracy? Now if the mass party sheds light on this issue, it is not because we can define the party in terms of criteria which would be equally applicable to the industrial firm; more fundamentally, it is because we can distinguish a specific sector within the party where functions are ranked hierarchically by virtue of their participation in the exercise of power, where decisions are taken which affect the orientation of the party in the absence of any control from below, where responsibilities are allocated in an authoritarian way, where organizational discipline prevails over the unrestricted analysis of decisions, where a continuity of roles, activities and persons is established so that a ruling minority is rendered practically irremovable. In other words, bureaucracy appears within the party as the antithesis of democracy. But this observation becomes meaningful only if we understand how the bureaucratic organization is formed. Its genesis is all the more noticeable in that it does not depend *directly* on economic conditions. As I mentioned above, the party is based on voluntary membership which is itself motivated by ideological agreement concerning a programme. Now this characteristic, in itself, does not entail any *particular* form of organization. The technical need for an organization is only present, and is all the more determinant, when the party brings together a broad mass. But the necessity of co-ordinating the activities of small local sections, of securing the best propaganda and of properly managing the funds raised by members does not require a specific kind of social milieu. It is only by virtue of a certain *choice* that this milieu is constituted as bureaucratic. Of course, the term 'choice' must not be understood as implying that individuals decide, after careful reflection, to form a bureaucratic organization; it means only that a certain type of behaviour becomes necessary, and as a result certain demands take absolute precedence while others fade away.

Let us clarify the nature of this choice: since the party is based on voluntary membership and animated by an agreement among individuals concerning ideas, it would seem to follow that the maintenance of this membership and agreement is essential to the life of the organization. The party claims to be the expression of a collective will, the locus of co-operation: it would seem to lose its *raison d'être* if it exercised coercion over its members; and, *formally*, it cannot exercise coercion because its members are not dependent on the party for their livelihood. But on the other hand the party must act as a coherent force within society as a whole, maintaining continuity in its action, binding together in a permanent way those who lend it their support, finding a structure which guarantees its unity independently of the uncertain participation of its members.

Now if it is true that the existence of the mass party gives rise to these two alternatives, the bureaucracy is constituted by allowing the second alternative to prevail absolutely over the first and by doing this in a way which renders its own existence ever more necessary and endows its choice with an irreversible character. From the outset bureaucrats establish themselves as those whose work maintains the existence and unity of the party; and certainly their activity within the party makes them indispensable elements. But this activity has a special character which appears as soon as one compares it with the activity of ordinary militants: it is focused on the institution itself. It is what is usually called an 'organizational activity'. But this term is imprecise because it does not bring out the essential point: the activity is always concerned with directing the militants' work in a way that attests to the existence and power of the party. The fundamental aspect of this organization is the multiplication of the organs of the party: the more cells and sections there are and the more differentiated the life of the institution is, the more its power is materialized and the more numerous are the officials appointed to each sector and to the tasks of co-ordination which their separation renders necessary. The efficacy of bureaucratic work can thus be assessed in terms of the capacity of officials to preserve and extend the field of activity which they organize. But this assessment can be formulated in objective (shareable) terms only if one considers the formal aspect of the activity of the bureaucrat – the fetishism of the agenda at the regular assemblies of the party, the multiplicity of reunions, meetings, celebrations or commemorations, the existence of what could be called 'activism': a feverish and vain agitation which has become routine. The number and diversity of ceremonies from which the institution draws its daily justification goes hand in hand with the proliferation of bureaucrats. If they are entirely at the service of the party they become professionals, but they do not have to be in order to act as such. It is sufficient if their activity is precisely circumscribed, if it is concerned essentially with the preservation of the party and if it is carried out in the context of instructions issued by the leadership in order to give their function the appearance of a job.

The bureaucracy taken as a whole is this milieu for which the structure of the party is necessary, sacred and irremovable. But this milieu is itself the agent of a certain structuration. In identifying itself with the ends which justify the existence of the party, it turns the party – to paraphrase Marx – into its private property; it regards itself as necessary, sacred and irremovable. The defence of the party is the bureaucracy's self-defence. But this implies a particular interpretation of the party's aims which results in a distortion of its original vocation. For the party can intervene directly in social conflicts (as it must do if it is to conform to its basic principle) or create a broad internal space for ideological discussion only at the risk of transforming itself, or at the limit of destroying itself. The bureaucratic group thus feels that it is threatened as soon as a principle of change is introduced in the party: it is naturally conservative.

This conservatism infuses all inter-bureaucratic relations. The cult of authority, the desire to control the activity of militants at every level and the prestige accorded to functions of responsibility are so many manifestations of this conservatism, so well known that they hardly need to be emphasized. In the last instance, this aspect of the bureaucracy's behaviour has its own logic. For the party is not a purely artificial organism, born out of ideological motivations. It exists as a mass organization in the context of society as a whole; not only does it aim to seize power, but it also penetrates, in varying degrees depending on the circumstances, every sector of society. This penetration enables it to secure jobs for a significant number of its militants in departments where it controls the recruitment, either directly or through the intermediary of a friendly association. The party, which may seem like an incomplete bureaucracy if it is regarded as an isolated institution, thus displays certain material determinations of bureaucratic stability when it is placed in the context of society as a whole.

Of course, the examples that I have chosen and deliberately borrowed from Weber share certain features, but above all they encourage us to examine the phenomenon in a certain way. The bureaucracy, in my view, is a group which tends to make a certain mode of organization prevail, which develops in determinate conditions and flourishes by virtue of a certain state of the economy and of technical development, but which is what it is, in essence, only by virtue of a particular kind of social activity. Any attempt to grasp bureaucracy which does not give prominence to a specific type of behaviour thus seems to me doomed from the outset. Bureaucracy exists only through bureaucrats and through their collective intention to constitute a world set apart from dominated groups, to participate in a socialized power and to define themselves in relation to one another in terms of a hierarchy which guarantees a material status or prestige for each of them.

To emphasize the phenomenon of social behaviour is not to reduce bureaucracy to a summation of similar activities. The activity of an isolated individual is unintelligible; it becomes meaningful only when it is placed in the context of a group. The formation of bureaucracy involves an immediate socialization of activities and behaviour. Here the group is not a category of activity or of socio-economic status: it is a concrete milieu from which each individual derives his own identity. But this observation also brings out the connection between bureaucracy and the mass institution. Bureaucracy finds its appropriate form in the mass institution – the ministry, the union, the party, the industrial firm – because the unity of the context, the interconnection of tasks, the number of jobs, the proximity of individuals to the interior of each sector, the prospect of a rapid development of the institution and the amount of capital involved all contribute to circumscribing a social field of power. Hence the identification of the bureaucrat with the firm to which he is attached is a natural mediation in the consciousness which the group acquires of its own identity. But, as we have seen in each of the examples analysed above, this identification must not conceal the fact that the fate of the bureaucracy is not strictly imposed by the technical structure of the mass institution, for the bureaucracy moulds its own destiny. As the agent of a distinctive form of structuration, it multiplies jobs and departments, separates off different sectors of activity, sets up artificial forms of supervision and co-ordination and reduces an ever-growing mass of workers to the function of carrying out orders, thus subjecting these workers at every level to a form of authority seeking to attain its maximum force by creating a system of relations of dependence which is as differentiated as possible.

## Bureaucracy as Class

On the basis of these considerations, we may briefly examine the thesis that the bureaucracy can be understood as a class. There is no doubt, in my view, that a dominant class exists in the USSR. Those who persist in denying it can do no more than recite certain passages from Marx according to which the abolition of private property entails the disappearance of the dominant class, while failing to see that at a deeper level the class opposition has re-established itself in the relations of production. At this level, the form assumed by the ownership of the means of production is no longer determinant; what is determinant is the division between capital and labour. The fact that the proletariat is excluded from the management of production and reduced to functions of carrying out orders is what establishes it as an exploited class. The fact that all the decisions which determine economic life (concerning the size and distribution of investments, wages, the intensity and duration of work, etc.) are made by a particular social stratum is what establishes the position of a dominant class in relation to the proletariat. Nevertheless, my concern here is not to discuss the class nature of the USSR, but rather to make it clear at the outset that the bureaucracy can be regarded as a class only if one recognizes that it has its own dynamism, a dynamism which can be discerned initially in the context of traditional capitalist society and, in particular, in the context of the mass institutions where it develops. To define it as a parasitical organ or as a mere economic category is to disregard the ways in which it creates, by virtue of a specific mode of behaviour, a *milieu of power* and uses the circumstances in order to extend and consolidate it. On the other hand, by recognizing its distinctive historicity one is able to grasp, at the horizons of its activity, a world which it would like to mould in its image and constitute as the dominant class. The genesis of the bureaucracy in Russia is intelligible, in the last analysis, only if it is related to the genesis of a social type which is realized, in different forms, in all modern nations.

However, the analysis of the conditions in which the dominant class was formed after the Russian Revolution presents a privileged case for observing the properly social activity by which the bureaucracy constructs its power. While it may be true that this class is what it is today only by virtue of its function in the process of production, only by virtue of the planning and the nationalizations which secure its material basis, nevertheless it originated in – one can never stress this too much – a political bureaucracy whose very first weapons were not the extraction of surplus value in the context of modern industry but rather the concentration of authority in the hands of a ruling minority, the exclusion of the masses from the sphere where information circulates and decisions are taken, the hierarchical stratification of functions and the differentiation of salaries, the rigorous division of competences – in short, a scientific organization of inequality, which became the principle of a new form of class oppression. Of course, the bureaucracy of the party did not artificially create an entirely new world; and it would even be something of an understatement to say that it was aided by the circumstances. The destruction of the political and economic power of the old property owners, the taking over of large sectors of production by the state, the existence of an industry which had already attained in certain domains a high degree of concentration and hence of modern administration, the example of the large capitalist industrial countries which testified to a growing fusion of capital and the state: all these factors prepared the way for a new type of class domination. But this domination cleared its own path only by the action of the party which, through ideology, terror and privilege, fused together elements drawn from all the classes of the old Russian society.

Moreover, it is not sufficient to point out the existence of a privileged class in the USSR, nor even to trace its own genesis, in order to understand what bureaucracy actually is within the whole society that it dominates. An analysis which restricts itself to highlighting the phenomenon of exploitation at the level of the relations of production does not yet illuminate the nature of the bureaucratic class. It enables one to circumscribe a privileged stratum; but factory managers and those officials responsible for planning are not the only members of the dominant class, nor do all privileged individuals necessarily belong to it. Just as in the context of the industrial firm a mere foreman, in contrast to an engineer, can be regarded as a bureaucrat because authority has been delegated to him and he identifies with management rather than the workers, so too, at the level of society as a whole, a particular category of political or union functionaries can be placed in the bureaucracy whereas some category of technicians, although receiving higher salaries, does not belong to the dominant class, does not espouse its values and does not adhere to its ideals. The social nature of the bureaucracy cannot be deduced from its economic function; it must be observed in order to be understood. But even when observation is not possible, the question posed here has the merit of avoiding a schematic conception of history. In the USSR, as in Western countries, there is more than a single class confronting the industrial and agricultural proletariat. The bureaucracy does not consist of the working class as a whole, nor simply of several thousand or tens of thousands of leaders supported by the political police: one can define it only by describing the solidarity which unites its members and crystallizes them in the function of domination.

It is possible, nonetheless, to point to certain characteristics of this class, both by means of reflection on the principle of its constitution and by drawing on the testimonies of observers or of political leaders conscious of the difficulties that the regime must confront. I shall restrict myself to two remarks. The first is that the bureaucracy implies a model of social participation which is different from that of the bourgeoisie. Bureaucrats do not become elements of a dominant class by virtue of a professional activity which endows them with private power. If a power can be established which manages society in their name, it is not because their individual interests happen to coincide. They are first of all members of their class and their personal attributes follow from this membership; they are what they are only through their dependence on the state power which grounds and maintains the social hierarchy. In other words, political power and economic power are fused within the bureaucratic class, so that to participate in the appropriation of surplus value is at the same time to participate in a system of domination. The bureaucracy is thus the privileged terrain of totalitarianism, that is, of a regime where all social activities are measured by a single criterion of validity established by the power of the state; the plurality of systems of behaviour and value immediately pose a threat not only to the status of a ruling minority but to the dominant class itself, whose integration depends entirely on its submission to the established power.

My second remark is that, in spite of the constantly reaffirmed tendency to make a single authority prevail at every level, the bureaucracy cannot avoid conflicts which not only set clans against one another within a particular institutional context (as I have tried to show), but also set bureaucracies against one another. For if the analysis sketched above is correct, bureaucracy exists in a developed form within the limits of a mass institution – in the party, in the union, in some particular branch of production or cultural sector; in each of these contexts it seeks to expand, to take hold of an increasing share of social capital and to divide up a field of power which is as extended as possible. Bureaucracies are not attuned by virtue of a pre-established harmony. Class unity does not prevail 'naturally': it requires a constant activity of unification. The rivalry of bureaucratic apparatuses reinforced by the struggle of inter-bureaucratic clans is brought under control only by the intervention, at every level and in all sectors of social life, of a principle which is properly political. But the party which bears this principle is itself the most extensive and complete bureaucracy. If, on the one hand, class unity is inconceivable in its absence and if its mediating role 'politicizes' society as a whole and fuses the sphere of the state with that of civil society, on the other hand its presence and its natural tendency to control and subordinate everything to its own power produces the most acute tension within the dominant class. The bureaucratic system is thus engaged in an interminable trial with itself, a trial which exposes it to conflicts that are of a different kind but are no less formidable than those familiar to bourgeois regimes.

To maintain that the bureaucracy forms a dominant class in the USSR does not settle the question of its status in the large industrial nations of the West. From one point of view, the formation of a bureaucratic class seems like an extension of the bureaucratic organizations which flourish in the context of mass institutions, a process facilitated by the development of techniques which render human activities more and more dependent on one another and impose a socialization of administrative tasks comparable to that which occurs in the sphere of production. From another point of view, this class seems to require a mode of political integration, a mode of subordination to state power of such a kind that one could say that it has set up nothing less than a total system of domination. At a deeper level, these two points of view are not incompatible; they allow us to see bureaucracy – or better, bureaucracies – as a type of social behaviour whose success or failure is not given in advance but depends on a whole complex of properly historical conditions, stemming from a prior history and open to change. It is conceivable *both* that bureaucratic organizations have an affinity for a particular regime, where the definitive elimination of private property provides them with a maximum field for development and secures their integration into a new class structure, *and* that, immersed in bourgeois society and hindered in their growth by their natural conservatism as well as by the profits which they derive from the established mode of production, they prove incapable of doing more than invading bourgeois society, that is, incapable of transforming the systems of power. In other words, there are no grounds for maintaining that, in the absence of a radical social upheaval which would sweep away the established regimes (as happened in Russia by a workers' and peasants' revolution, and in the people's democracies by a war), bureaucratic organizations would naturally overcome their divisions and integrate themselves around a new state apparatus, as the elements of a dominant class.

This leads me to emphasize the *indeterminacy* of bureaucracy, which seems to me to be at the source of the difficulties encountered by the theoretical accounts. The bureaucracy is not a class so long as it is not the dominant class; and when it becomes so, it remains essentially dependent on a properly political activity of unification.

To maintain that bureaucrats already form a class within society as a whole would imply that they are differentiated by their particular interests, their style of life or the values to which they adhere. But they are in fact differentiated by their mode of group formation and by the way in which they acquire their status as members of a collectivity. These features are obviously crucial; the relations among bureaucrats within each institution correspond to a specific social model and anticipate a new overall structure. But so long as this structure is not realized, the bureaucracy does not constitute a world apart; bourgeois society assimilates it. It is not enough to point out that senior civil servants are company directors or that the upper levels of management derive part of their salary from the shares which they own, for this phenomenon of embourgeoisement can be compared to the aristocratization of the bourgeoisie, which at certain periods rushed to buy land and noble titles. What is important is that, on the one hand, the difference in the appropriation of wealth is linked neither to the nature of production nor even to the deepest relations which stem from it, while on the other hand, in the context of society as a whole, the various bureaucracies develop along the lines of traditional cleavage, thus remaining heterogeneous (despite the inter-penetration of some of them) and unaware of their identity (at least in the absence of a social crisis). Moreover, this 'polycentrism', which is part of the essence of bureaucracy, destined as it is to crystallize in particular institutions, works to prevent the formation of a class unity.

Even when this unity is attained, the bureaucracy preserves a principle of indetermination. For it does not have an objective existence rigorously separable from a social form of power; at the deepest level, it is not an economic category but is constituted through participation in a system of domination.

Hence there is a strong temptation to deny that the bureaucracy forms a class in those societies where it is seen to rule, or a specific social milieu where it is seen to multiply itself within bourgeois societies. Or if, on the contrary, one maintains that it is the dominant class in the USSR, one tends to neglect or to regard as secondary its distinctive constitution: namely, *the change in the function of politics* in bureaucratic society, the heterogeneity of organizations, the struggle between apparatuses and groups, the different ways and degrees to which the various constitutive strata are integrated into the class; above all, one tends to see in this class a model which is in the process of being realized everywhere, as if bourgeois society had to transform itself *naturally* into bureaucratic society under the pressure of the concentration of capital. One is struck by the parallel growth of economic rationalization and bureaucratization, one assumes that one is the manifestation of the other, failing to see that rationalization occurs in the context of a system based on exploitation and that bureaucratization is the reordering of a system of domination. In highlighting the phenomenon of bureaucratic parasitism, one overlooks the fact that in one and the same movement the bureaucracy establishes itself at the heart of social life and presents itself as an end, that it responds to a technical need and subordinates it to the imperative of power.

The study of bureaucracy, and the discussion that it calls for, will be fruitful only if we reject these simplifications. The important questions can then be asked; and we may hope to make some progress in answering them only if, it seems to me, we observe a few principles.

1  Attention must be given to the various specific bureaucracies instead of immediately swallowing them up in a concept which can then be applied so freely that it is stripped of all content.

2  Bureaucracy must be approached as a *social* formation, as a system of meaningful behaviour, and not simply as a formal system of organization. This perspective requires one to offer a genetic definition of the phenomenon and to see it as a human project endowed with its own goal.

3  It is essential to examine the relations that the bureaucracy maintains with other social strata and especially the relations between the bureaucratic group and other groups within the context of a specific institution.

4  From the social nature of bureaucracy (I would prefer to say its *sociality*) one cannot deduce a future course of development, for that depends on a whole complex of historical conditions in which established structures and events are determinant.

5  In raising the question of the class nature of bureaucracy, one must not allow the answer (whatever it may be) to be dictated by a comparison between the bourgeoisie and the bureaucracy. One must seek to describe the specific way in which the bureaucracy is involved in society as a whole and the connections between the *political, economic* and *cultural* determinations within it, instead of falling back on an *a priori* definition of class (which is ascribed a universal significance although in fact it pertained to the bourgeoisie in the middle of the nineteenth century) and an *a priori* account of the elements of class which are essential as distinct from those which are accidental.

6  In the context of an inquiry into a particular bureaucracy, the representation that the great bureaucrats offer of themselves must not be accepted at face value. Instead, one should try to circumscribe the milieu and to define the bureaucratic attitudes and

behaviour by listening to those who know them, those who are not easily misled by the bureaucrats and who, in being dominated by them, form the basis upon which the bureaucrats become what they are.

# 4

# Novelty and the Appeal
# of Repetition

The above essays were written before 1960 and analyse events or take stock of discussions which may seem distant from current preoccupations. For young readers – those who are most often engaged in political activity – this distance may seem all the greater in so far as the facts which nourish my reflections are not part of their memory. Those who are today between twenty and thirty years old did not experience the hold exercised by the communist parties during the lifetime of Stalin. The workers' insurrection in East Berlin in 1953 (for some, the first event to shake the image of socialism in the people's democracies), the campaign of de-Stalinization initiated by Khrushchev at the Twentieth Congress, the Hungarian and Polish uprisings – these events are merely part of the young reader's personal prehistory; they do not fit into an already formed experience which would enable them to be assimilated. The young reader will not remember the time when 'progressive' intellectuals rallied around the Stalinist banner, paying for the audacity of an independent gesture with increased fidelity, a time when leftist activities were almost entirely restricted to the Trotskyists, branching out into three or four little groups which were even weaker still, a time when communists accused the Trotskyists of being fascists and treated them as such when they had the chance, while the left-wing press was careful to avoid giving the slightest attention to their actions or their views.

Does this mean that the world of the 1950s can only awaken the interest of the historian and that what I wrote twelve or twenty years ago has merely documentary value? Does it mean that, in order to understand the present and to try to identify the lines of change, we must direct our attention to Czechoslovakia rather than Hungary, study Brezhnev's latest speech rather than Khrushchev's *Report*, challenge the Sartre who supports the *cause du peuple* rather than the one who, in 1952, offered an apologetic for communist policies in France?

If that were so, there would be no point in presenting the public with analyses which are closely linked to past events. But I believe that the questions posed then have not become outdated and that, in spite of the changes which have modified in some respects the practices and attitudes of social actors and the interpretations of ideologues, a large part of the historical context remains intact, a context within which choices and conflicts repeat themselves.

The distinction between what, at a given time, constitutes the present and the past, of what belongs to near horizons and what is lost in the distance, is more subtle than we are inclined to believe when we consider only the generation gap or call attention to the major signs of change – those signs that may effectively designate the novelty of a particular circumstance while concealing the continuity of the features of a socio-historical structure. The past is not really past until it ceases to haunt us and we have become free to rediscover it in the spirit of curiosity. But so long as the images and words continue to fill our thoughts and excite our passions, acting at a distance from people and events we have not known and experienced, they participate fully in the present – whether they serve to destroy or whether they are used by us to preserve the context of our lives.

Thus it may be that Bolshevism, or its Trotskyist variant, and the Russian Revolution no longer have any 'real' efficacy. It may be that they merely provide left-wing militants with the symbols of a struggle whose ultimate goal eludes them, with a means of identification with the imaginary community of revolutionaries, in the absence of which their opposition to established regimes would give way. It may be that the concept of revolution is being used in new ways. Perhaps the communist leaders in the USSR do not only need the phantom of Stalin but also the Bolshevik legend in order to carry out successfully the innumerable prosaic tasks of a new dominant class. What is certain is that today the evocation of heroes and the repetition of old speeches always accompany action and mobilize faith.

After twenty years the sources of inspiration have not run dry. At least for a fraction of the new generations in Western societies, they are more active than they were for their elders. And if one looks to the countries of Eastern Europe, the same points of reference support the activities of the opponents or the policies of the masters of power. Hence the attempt to destroy certain illusions, to examine the great revolutionary politics of the past and to call attention to features that are concealed (usually to protect an imitation) is even more important in current conditions than it was when it had such importance for me – when, in analysing 'The Contradiction of Trotsky', I discovered how the fetishism of the party, the fetishism of the 'socialist bases' of the state and the repression of the workers' opposition were continued in the work of someone who had once seemed to me to be the guarantor of the revolutionary attitude. At that time, we spoke for a very small group. Since then the circle has grown and the equivocal nature of the kind of militancy in which the will for emancipation is fused with a narrow subservience to tradition and a taste for the sacred has deepened. At the same time, the critique of Bolshevism and of Trotskyism has gained ground. The documents of the workers' opposition in Russia are better known, we read Volin, Arshinov and Pannekoek; the revolt of Kronstadt has at times acquired archetypical value. But is it not too easy to believe that it suffices to substitute a 'good' tradition for a 'bad' one? Are we not often content to change the symbols without renouncing the authority which we had, at one time, placed upon the pure image of a founder? Even those who see how the party separates itself from the exploited strata, detaching itself and constituting the core of a new social formation, may end up by transferring onto the Class as such the sacredness which was previously invested in an institution or in human beings. So the questions which arose when they were active in the communist party, for example, and which shattered their system of beliefs, are not extinguished by this new certainty that the evil spell stems from the organizations and by the obstinate refusal to look for the conditions of their genesis in the history of the proletariat.

Thought may well be able to free itself from certain images; but what resists this attempt is the relation that we maintain with the representation of the past, the mythical function that we make it play in order to assure ourselves of a truth which is already given and which will not betray us, in order to conjure away, in sum, the indeterminacy which constantly re-emerges in the history that we live.

It would be pointless to rely on the movement which severs us from our old beliefs. Of course, there are illusions which we are sure to have destroyed, and sometimes the benefits are not slight. But the soil in which they grow nourishes other seeds. It is perhaps when we have tasted the bitter exhilaration of overturning our original ideas that we remain most enslaved by their principles. In any case, so many desires are invested in the political sphere that the progress of knowledge merely displaces its own limits rather than eliminating them; and each time new doors open before us, we must assume that elsewhere others are closed.

We can easily see the limits in others. We are struck by their inability, when confronted by an event which troubles them, to draw the unavoidable conclusions that we have long since reached. Thus, a little while ago, communist militants reacted indignantly to the Russian intervention in Czechoslovakia; for once, they condemned the policies of the USSR and even called them imperialist. But they did so in order to denounce a 'tragic error', to proclaim that a socialist state cannot act like a great power without disavowing its principles. Their audacity was great when they rose against an authority which they saw as hitherto incontestable and when they thus risked exclusion from their party. Yet they never asked themselves whether it makes any sense to speak of socialism with regard to a state which exercises economic, political, military and cultural oppression on its neighbours. They defended the 'democratic' demands of the Czech communists, they criticized the ruling group in the USSR and the servile leaderships on which it depends in other countries. But they did so in order to contrast authoritarianism with liberalism, conservative methods with innovative methods, as if the terror of the political police was an accidental feature of the workers' state, the effect of a poor interpretation of revolutionary strategy or, at best, the sign of the ambitions of an intolerant clique. They deplored an error, but were quick to limit it to the case of Czechoslovakia. These ardent defenders of national communism, who applauded the arrival of Russian tanks in Budapest, shamelessly maintained that the Hungarian insurrection was the work of reactionaries and American agents. And there were others who said, even while condemning Moscow, that opposition to the USSR carries with it the seeds of counter-revolution. How could these people explain the supposed fact that a system of people's democracy could last for more than twenty years, almost entirely cut off from the capitalist world and fused into a bloc of socialist states, and yet preserve within itself a bourgeoisie sufficiently powerful to place the system in danger at the first failure of the leadership? At one and the same time they gave their support to Dubcek and worried about the consequences of a reform of the system; they based all their arguments on the defence of socialism – everywhere present, in their eyes, under Brezhnev, Novotny, Dubcek or Husak – and saw counter-revolution springing up everywhere, so that they did not dare to take a step in one direction without immediately beating a retreat.

But the position of certain left-wing groups also merits consideration: they too surrounded themselves with strange reservations. The Czech's taste for freedom aroused their suspicion. They were quick to see what they regarded as the most precious asset in bourgeois society – however fragile, inadequate and deformed it may be – as a sign of corruption elsewhere. They raised the spectre of anti-socialist forces, while forgetting that they did not believe at all in the reality of socialism in the people's democracies. Thus they remained prisoners of the representations from which they thought they had freed themselves. The idea that, since the Russian Revolution, the world has split into two camps is so powerful and so pervasive that they took it for granted, in spite of everything that they learned about the exploitation and oppression which prevails in the USSR. They seemed to have acknowledged the fact that the abolition of private property had resulted in the fusion of capital and the state, but then they went on repeating the claim that everything which benefits American imperialism is reactionary and that it is the relations between East and West which determine, in the last instance, the revolutionary significance of an event. Thus all the casuistry elaborated by Sartre and the 'progressive' intellectuals at the time of the Hungarian insurrection has not lost any of its efficacy. The terms have changed, the interpreters have shifted places in the ideological field, but the essential core of the old positions remains. The grip of the imaginary has not really loosened.

It is undoubtedly difficult to discover in one's own thought the forces which draw it backwards. At least with time I have acquired a certain capacity in this regard; and while no doubt I still conceal part of what guides my judgements, I feel less defenceless when confronting my earlier writings. There is no point in feigning a modesty which has no place in questions of knowledge: the essays that I wrote after having left the Trotskyist party contribute more, in my view, to clarifying the phenomenon of bureaucracy than most of the analyses which currently circulate under the label of the Revolution. What is interesting about them is that they were guided by the concern to apply to the workers' movement, or to the forces that claim to draw inspiration from it, the principles of analysis which Marxism had elaborated in the critique of bourgeois society. Of course, this was not the result of an intellectual decision. It was the experience of being a militant, over a period of several years, which taught me to examine that strange movement by which a group – however weak it may be numerically and free from economic and political constraints by virtue of the very inefficacy of its action – reintroduces into its own organization the rules, practices and specific interpersonal relations of the organizations it seeks to combat, reweaving the same kind of social fabric, cultivating the principles of division, partitioning off sectors of activity, controlling the flow of information, tending to turn its existence into an end in itself and thus giving itself a *nature* which is opaque and closed off to reflection.

This experience clarified some of the reasons why Trotskyism, in spite of all the criticisms that it levelled at communist parties, never really succeeded in distinguishing itself from them. Although in its programme it formulated different objectives, emphasizing in particular the decisive role of mass mobilization, the social relations which were in fact established within it were structured in a similar way. One remarkable consequence of this constitution was its inability to confront the key question of a sociological definition of Stalinism, that is, to examine its social bases. At best, the Trotskyists reproduced, when called upon to explain themselves, the interpretation that Lenin had given when he linked the degeneration of social democracy to the growth of a workers' aristocracy. Usually they restricted themselves to a pure and simple denunciation of ruling groups regarded as opportunistic or incompetent and attributed their prestige to that of the Russian Revolution, in the belief that the isolation of the socialist state had allowed the revolutionary project to falter and had facilitated the temporary emergence of a caste of bureaucrats. Now the failure of their account was symptomatic, for the same conception governed all the analyses of the non-Stalinist Marxist Left. Of course, this Left distinguished itself from the Trotskyists in many respects, beginning with their determination to remain in the immediate vicinity of the Communist Party; but it was Trotskyist without knowing it, by virtue of its double conviction that, on the one hand, the policies of the party were attributable to errors of method or to a distorted representation of the revolutionary task and that, on the other hand, these policies were the result of 'accidents' which occurred in the USSR after the October Revolution, that is, disturbances in the *normal* development of socialism.

Thus it is not by chance that, in a polemical exchange with Sartre, I developed an argument which, although it was seen as Trotskyist by some, was largely directed against Trotskyism. I discovered that 'progressives' and Trotskyists could not avoid meeting as soon as they applied themselves to eliminating a sector of social phenomena from Marx's critique. Marx had called attention to the gap between ideology and praxis; moreover, he knew how to turn the critique of ideologies – economic, political, religious, philosophical – into a privileged means of exposing the contradictions which operate at the level of praxis. For 'progressives' and Trotskyists, this path was lost as soon as the object of analysis was no longer the bourgeois class or the Western capitalist system. Confronted with the communist parties and the social strata from which the latter drew their strength, they restricted their critique to the level of ideas; they approached them head-on, as if they were without depth, self-sufficient, unconnected to the development of social relations. Furthermore, Marx was concerned to distinguish historical analysis from sociological analysis; his study of capitalism, however rich in references to particular events, was focused on the specific logic of a system, on the articulation of oppositions which develop once the division between labour and capital has become widespread. While concerned to describe the actions of capitalists, the remedies which they called for and the resistance which they provoked, while thus concerned to retrace certain sequences of an empirical process, he nevertheless sought to discern in apparently contingent facts the signs of a necessity which was not the conscious product of the activities of individuals but was imposed upon them in a way of which they were unaware and which was even at the expense of their immediate interests. Our epigones, by contrast, cling to the rim of historical development: faced with the USSR they could merely hang on to the chain of events, invoke the civil war, the revolutionary defeats in Europe or the capitalist blockade. It would have been scandalous, in their eyes, to have admitted that the course taken by the post-revolutionary regime was unavoidable (a limiting hypothesis whose value is merely heuristic) and that the social system which emerged had properties which had to be studied in their own right. Ultimately, these two weaknesses converged: the inability to detach themselves from an explanation in terms of events coincided with the inability to discern, beyond the representations and institutional forms, the social relations which supported them. Convinced that state ownership of the means of production and economic planning were the result of the revolution, they saw them as the bases of socialism without ever asking themselves how they modified existing relations in the process of production, what role they actually played in the socio-economic system and in which interplay of oppositions they were embedded.

No doubt I would have been unable to develop the critique of workers' organizations (based on the experience acquired as an activist in a small party) and of the mode of representation linked to them, or to take full account of the reversal of the Marxist problematic, if I had not learned to recognize in the USSR – thanks especially to the illuminating studies of Castoriadis – the features of bureaucratic capitalism. The two analyses supported one another. But in discussing ideas it is also appropriate to move beyond historical description. The important point, in my view, is that the analysis of the bureaucratic phenomenon requires a reflection on the social conditions which give rise to it. So long as these conditions remain concealed and we naively embrace the norms of our milieu, our questions will not have free reign. The analysis of the USSR, I continue to believe, is fruitful only if it is combined with an analysis of the organizations of the workers' movement in the West and of the way in which it is integrated into the capitalist system, just as the analysis of the revolutionary projects at the beginning of the century – Bolshevism in particular – presupposes that we have examined here and now the gap between practice and ideology in these organizations.

Nevertheless, however legitimate it may have been within the perspective that I was developing, the critical movement which underpins my earlier essays seems to me today to suffer from a determination to remain within the strict framework of Marxist interpretation. Fidelity becomes equivocal when it tries to find pregiven answers to new questions.

Since my only concern here is to clarify the contours of my analysis of bureaucracy, let me say to begin with that this analysis was conducted in a way which left intact the image of the proletariat as the revolutionary class, as the bearer of the universal goals of history. When I discerned in the USSR the existence of a dominant class whose power was based on the collective ownership of the means of production, believing that the whole economic system was structured in such a way as to maintain the division between a mass of people who carried out orders and a minority who monopolized the tasks of leadership, I took it for granted – without even making it an explicit hypothesis – that the new class antagonism replaced the opposition denounced by Marx in his analysis of bourgeois society. It seemed to me that the bureaucracy, while developing according to a different process, had substituted itself for the bourgeoisie. In face of the bureaucracy, the situation of the proletariat remained unchanged; but it was now in a position to discover the true nature of its objectives, hitherto concealed by the necessity of struggling against private property, and hence to recognize the foundations of socialism in the workers' management of industries and collectivities. When I imagined that in contemporary bourgeois societies the process of bureaucratization, more and more evident despite the persistence of old forms of ownership, created for the proletariat a similar awareness of its goals – an awareness which could not fail to develop as soon as workers' organizations were forced, in times of crisis, to support openly the capitalist system – I took it for granted, this time in a more general way, that the world proletariat had reached a stage where the task assigned to it by Marx could be carried out. When I linked the growth of bureaucracy, in both East and West, to transformations in the mode of industrial production – the concentration of firms, the rationalization of tasks brought about by technological change, the increasing interconnection of production and organization – I limited the effects of this evolution to the structure of the dominant class. Finally, my analysis of the ways in which bureaucracy emerges in the course of organizing the working class and institutionalizing its modes of resistance did not call into question, but on the contrary gave prominence to, the proletariat's task of establishing a society freed of all domination. This analysis persuaded me that an ordeal of alienation, carried into the very project of emancipation, was necessary before the critique of all alienations could be carried out.

In retrospect it seems to me that I lacked audacity, in the fear of admitting that the transformation of the social mode of domination implied a profound modification of the antagonistic terms described by Marx and, as a result, called for a revision of the model by which he claimed to define the ultimate reality of society.

Even with regard to the economy, I should have examined at an earlier stage the changes affecting the nature of social labour. For it seems clear that, alongside the processes of bureaucratization, there is a tendency towards the uniformization of models of action and social relations and of norms. These models, once operating only in the sector of large industry and with regard to industrial labour, are now spreading within this sector to the strata of technicians and planners, and outside this sector, not only to the state administrations on which the productive apparatus depends, not only to the service industries and the large scientific laboratories, but also into the domains which would seem naturally to resist them: public health, education, legal institutions, etc. At the same time, the worker's relation to the firm is being modified. The worker finds himself caught up in a network of obligations which go well beyond the clauses of the labour contract analysed by Marx; a considerable part of his social life is covered through institutions of social security, housing, education and leisure. Moreover, the evolution of technology (and the rationalization of tasks which accompanies it) has resulted in changes in the proportion of skilled to unskilled labour in industry, and in the proportion of tasks of production (in the old sense of the term) to tasks of organization. It would be futile to maintain, in analysing these phenomena, that the proletarianization of society is developing in accordance with the schema outlined by Marx, for the mass of people who are separated from the means of production do not resemble the image which he formed of them; within this mass, the factors of heterogeneity are as powerful as the forces of resistance. In short, it is no longer possible to group together, in the same social stratum, those who are most impoverished, those who are most exploited and those who are most frustrated in their ability to develop their creativity. Those who are most frustrated are precisely those whose capacity for knowledge and intervention in the workplace is most stimulated by their training and the quality of the tasks performed; but they do not suffer the most from exploitation, which remains the fate of factory workers, nor do they fail to benefit, sometimes substantially, from the rise in incomes. As for the most impoverished, those who are currently in unskilled jobs, they are not the most exploited in the sense that it is not from their labour that capital extracts most of the surplus value which it needs in order to reproduce itself. These observations do not imply, as some people have imprudently assumed, that the boundaries of the working class have been effaced: the specificity of industrial labour remains and the split between manual and non-manual labour is still pertinent, in spite of the modifications which have affected both (especially the latter). But equally, one cannot simply re-establish the classical antagonism at the level of an opposition between technicians and professionals, on the one hand, and administrators and technocrats on the other. This opposition certainly exists, but it does not presuppose, as Marx thought, a class which is excluded from the process of socialization instituted by capitalism, a class condemned to find itself *alien* within bourgeois society, a class which is not a class, testifying by its very existence – as soon as it escapes from the status of an economic category which defines it externally – to its calling as the agent of communism.

With the expansion of bureaucracy, several oppositions are combined. One of these is the opposition between those who give orders and those who carry them out; another is that between the strata which receive no more than the scraps of growth and those which continue to increase their share of benefits; another still is that between a minority which holds the means of knowledge and information, controlling the production and transmission of representations, and a growing mass of people who, despite their training, are deprived of these means. In addition to these oppositions within the labour process, there is another which sets collectivities, in all sectors of social life and culture, against the rules which seek to determine behaviour in every detail and to subject it to the planned circuits of the giant organizations. But this opposition develops in different directions. For it mobilizes different modes of contestation, some of which are played out within the system and are merely the effect of the bureaucratic incapacity to satisfy the needs recognized and even stimulated by the proliferation of organizational apparatuses, others of which express the desire for a collective management of resources while still others turn the fringes of the population – mainly young people – into deviants, placing them at odds with the accepted codes of behaviour and destroying the symbolic references without which the relation to reality dissolves.

In considering the ambiguous characteristics of this revolt, which strikes to the heart of the system of domination by uncovering the mechanisms that secure the combined functioning of exploitation, oppression and ideology and which, simultaneously, shakes the symbolic reference points of all socialization, we can take stock of the distance which separates us from the world analysed by Marx. In that world, the proletariat was *alien*; and it is because it was alien and at the same time the bearer of the productive forces, indeed itself the greatest productive force, that it was designated as the revolutionary class. Today, the position of the alien does not coincide with that of the producer; rather, that position is now expressed in the rejection of the models and norms of industrial society. The ways in which the key antagonisms take shape today, putting strategies into play and structuring themselves according to rationalizable aims, cannot be summed up in terms of the conflict between the owners of the means of production and the workers. Thus it becomes impossible to make everything converge towards a unique revolutionary focus, to preserve the image of a society centred on the praxis of one class, to maintain – paraphrasing Marx – that the bureaucracy trudges along to its own death as the mass of the dispossessed necessarily turns against it as a single force. The centres of conflict are multiple. The demand, revolutionary *par excellence*, for collective self-management spreads from one centre to another; but if it is more widely recognized, this demand is also cut off from the root once provided by the theory of the proletariat – the great source of Life, according to Marx, in the world of Repetition.

No doubt what we have just said applies primarily to Western capitalist societies, but it would be a mistake to imagine that, with regard to the people's democracies and the USSR, the problems arise in radically different terms. Certain indications suggest that they are merely masked by the repression which strikes down every activity of contestation. It is true that the force of this repression, the visible figure of Power in which it is concentrated, has the effect of crystallizing revolutionary energies as soon as the authority vacillates. The insurrections of East Berlin, Poland, Hungary and Czechoslovakia have provided the proof. And one may well expect that in the USSR – at some unpredictable day of reckoning – there will be a crisis of the regime, whose consequences would have unprecedented significance in Eastern Europe as well as in the Western world. But this possibility should not make us forget the complexity, the heterogeneity, of the conflicts at work in modern industrial societies – conflicts for which only the lazy imaginations of the heirs of Leninism can take pleasure in *predicting* the resolution in a 'good' dictatorship of the proletariat.

Moreover, if one wishes to study the peculiar features of the bureaucratic regime where there no longer remains anything of bourgeois institutions, then one must push the inquiry further than I have done in order to discover where the critique of totalitarianism leads. It will not suffice to identify the logic which underlies the bureaucratic organization, the new mechanisms by which the state tends to control, in every sphere of civil society and culture, the detail of productive processes, of representations and of the relations between their agents; it will not suffice to recognize in the party the opposite of what it claims to be, namely the mainspring of totalitarianism, nor will it suffice to bring out a fundamental contradiction between control and parasitism. For the critique must be pressed, in the light of this analysis, to the very core of Marxist theory.

The analysis of the regime in the USSR places in question nothing less than the definition of social reality, and with it the distinction between infrastructure and superstructure. To point out that social relations are generated at the level of production and that property relations are only a juridical expression of them – as Castoriadis has shown – is still to remain too close to the Marxist problematic. Such an approach cannot grasp that which differentiates bourgeois society from bureaucratic society; it certainly highlights a pertinent feature of the structure, but it forgets that the latter cannot be characterized by means of this feature alone. The very definition of the relations of production, reduced to the opposition between the means of production and labour power, remains abstract in so far as one does not elucidate what it presupposes, in so far as one assumes that this definition can be situated entirely within the economic sphere. It must be admitted, on the contrary, that it enables this sphere to be constituted, that it is at the origin of a system of operations which can be specified in terms of operations of production, exchange and distribution and in terms of a particular institutional context, in accordance with political and symbolic schemata in which modes of power and representation are articulated. In a sense, Marx's concept of the mode of production enables us to think about a structuration of the social field which determines the instances of the economic, the political and the system of representation as well as their articulations; but this structuration presupposes and does not itself create the referents of the economic, the political and the symbolic. One need only consider the rise of capitalism to convince oneself of the efficacy of non-economic factors. The logic of a social system, even when it is restricted to a particular sphere of economic operations governed by specific mechanisms, can be grasped only by linking together the network of relations which are instituted under the triple sign of production, power and representation. Once grasped as such, it is certainly possible to distinguish that which pertains to the infrastructure and that which pertains to the superstructure; but this distinction cannot be expressed, for example, as a distinction between the economic and the political. For it is played out at both levels, just as it is played out at the level of representation where the function of the imaginary should not be confused with that of the symbols which establish the possibility of social communication and make up the framework of the economic-political field. How else could we grasp the originality of the modern bureaucratic system? How else could we avoid the alternative presented by an impoverished sociology which sees it either as a variant of industrial society, or as a variant of a timeless formation such as Asiatic despotism? To advance the analysis we must ask how, with the destruction of the bourgeois regime, the articulations of the social field were recast at every level, how relations of power, processes of production and representations were combined in accordance with a new model of socialization. If we do not adopt this approach, preserving instead the classical Marxist conception of the state and downgrading *a priori* the political or symbolic function, then the features of totalitarianism will always seem accidental.

Such an analysis would have at least one practical consequence. For as long as one remains a prisoner of the Marxist schema, all signs of oppression – however fervently they may be denounced – are regarded as insignificant. Similarly, democratic demands are not made the object of a sociological interpretation; either they are seen as evidence of the influence of bourgeois regimes, or they are defended in the name of the timeless values of humanism. A new analysis of the social system ought to persuade us that democracy – at least if we know how to look beyond the forms that it assumes in bourgeois regimes – takes us to the heart of the fundamental processes of socialization. [. . .]

Finally, it was in re-examining my account of the processes of degeneration in workers' parties and unions that I became aware of the limits of a critique which is too faithful to the spirit of Marx. No doubt it was worthwhile to observe the structural homology between 'revolutionary' organizations and the organizations of the system that they claimed to destroy. Lenin's ideas in *What is to be Done?* remain exemplary in my view, for they explicitly attest to the transfer of norms from industry and from the militarization of work into the model of the party. But the question is not exhausted by invoking the alienation which leads exploited groups to reproduce in their own organizations the very constraints to which they are subjected in bourgeois society (or to dispossess themselves of the power to lead their emancipation after having been dispossessed of the power to manage their production), nor is it exhausted by emphasizing the role of an intelligentsia ready to transform into power the superiority that it possesses through knowledge. These answers are not false, but they leave in darkness the mechanisms which govern repetition. The adherence to the models of authority and hierarchy, the belief in the wisdom of the leader, the tenacious fidelity to a tradition, the attachment to symbols and the fetishism of the institution do not merely highlight the inability to discover one's own identity; these phenomena presuppose the investment of energy – individual and collective – in a process of socialization which Marxists prefer to ignore (although in fact they are very good at mobilizing it). The bureaucratic regime, like bourgeois regimes, would collapse in ruins if it were not nourished by identifications which conceal servitude as well as the deepness of antagonisms, and which hold the majority of people in the grip of the leaders' authority. In preferring to ignore the efficacy of the imaginary, one simply runs the risk of sustaining, under the happy banner of revolutionary optimism (which is itself both mystifying and mystified), the play of repetition.

The essays which first marked out this investigation into bureaucracy are, in my view, far from attaining their goal. My hope is that the reader will find in these essays, as I have done, the encouragement to proceed further.

# Part II

# History, Ideology and the Social Imaginary

# 5

# Marx: From One Vision of History to Another

Let us reopen the *Communist Manifesto*:

> The history of all hitherto existing society is the history of class struggles.
>
> Freeman and slave, patrician and plebeian, lord and serf, guild-master and journeyman, in a word, oppressor and oppressed, stood in constant opposition to one another, carried on an uninterrupted, now hidden, now open fight, a fight that each time ended, either in a revolutionary reconstitution of society at large, or in the common ruin of the contending classes.[1]

The thread of history may indeed be broken; it will always be restored. Even if the actors disappear, the conflict will carry on and will summon up new ones. Humanity is *one* in time. Despite pauses or regressions, there can be no doubt about the continuity of the drama. Moreover, our own society is intelligible only if we are aware of its origins: 'The modern bourgeoisie is . . . the product of a long process of development of a whole series of revolutions in the modes of production and exchange.' However, our own era is different from all others; an important change has occurred – namely, the simplification of social antagonisms – which proves that our era heralds the end of class struggle. 'Society as a whole is more and more splitting up into two great hostile camps, into two great classes directly facing each other: Bourgeoisie and Proletariat.' This simplification is accompanied by the development of the capitalist mode of production on a world scale and by the reciprocal inter-dependence of all activities within the new social formation. And in addition, it is accompanied by an entirely new rhythm of history.

Due to the rapid development of industry and world trade, the bourgeois era is the scene of a constant upheaval in its mode of production and the continual disruption of all its institutions. The past collapses, whole pieces at a time, and even the present no longer has enough time to establish a distinctive shape.

> All fixed, fast-frozen relations, with their train of ancient and venerable prejudices and opinions, are swept away, all new-formed ones become antiquated before they can ossify. All that is solid melts into air, all that is holy is profaned, and man is at last compelled to face with sober senses, his real conditions of life, and his relations with his kind.[2]

Thus, from the heart of Great History with its slow pulse – where conflicts take centuries and sometimes millennia to develop and do not necessarily resolve themselves at a certain stage by passing directly on to a higher mode of production – there emerges an accelerated history, that of a breathless world carried away by the fever of creation and destruction.

In the eyes of Marx, it is one and the same necessity which makes society simplify itself into two opposing classes and makes history break loose and explode. And it is this same necessity which dissipates the mystical haze that prevents people from perceiving their social positions and the nature of their relations. Not only do religious illusions give way, we learn, but political illusions as well. While the bourgeoisie continues to develop, the sacred, in all its forms, dissolves in the 'icy waters of egoism'; 'naked interest' is now displayed everywhere and 'modern government' becomes 'a committee for managing the common affairs of the whole bourgeoisie'.

It is useless to object to the *Manifesto* on the grounds that it is merely a political, didactic and polemical text. For the problematic of history, outlined here in general terms, is also to be found – sometimes implicity, sometimes explicitly – in Marx's great theoretical works.[3] Moreover, if the *Manifesto* could be pushed aside, then the certainty of the impending revolution would vanish with it –the certainty, that is, that this event expresses the ultimate meaning of the human adventure. The foundation of the theory of the proletariat, as the last, universal class which possesses the means to dissolve all classes, would be put into question, as would the view of communism as the 'natural' result of historical development, of a development conceived of as a prologue to the history of a fulfilled humanity or – to use a paradoxical term from the young Marx – as prehistory.

And yet, how can we be content with this part of Marx's discourse? How can we refuse to consider everything else in his work which – arising in the course of an interpretation that is constantly transformed by the very facts it seeks to embrace and the questions it raises – goes beyond, shakes up or overturns the vision of history found in the *Manifesto*? How can we do so, in any case, if we manage to resist the vertigo of ideology, if we accept to think in terms of a *divided thought*, searching within this division for an index of the reality which set this thought in motion instead of letting ourselves be fascinated by a rational order which is, after all, only the subtle equivalent of a natural order of things?

The unity of the human drama centred on class conflict, the continuity of the historical process, the formation, with the capitalist mode of production, of a society in which antagonisms are simplified, activities are made rigorously interdependent and evolution is freed of the weight of tradition, a society which thus becomes, for the first time, intelligible to itself – there is not a single feature of this account which is not contradicted by Marx himself. But there is more to it than that. For the contradiction is not introduced by means of digressions, it does not appear here and there in the margins of what might be regarded as the main discourse; rather, it is the result of a different way of perceiving history and social life.

## Precapitalist Modes of Production

Let me try to make visible one of the threads of Marx's discourse which Marxist ideology conceals. I shall take as my starting point the analysis of precapitalist modes of production. It is well known that Marx devoted a chapter of the *Grundrisse* to this subject. Now it must be acknowledged that his purpose here is not simply to identify the characteristics of each of these modes of production and to define the stages of a development of which capitalism would be the final outcome. On the contrary, he tries to bring out their kinship and to juxtapose them as a whole to the mode of production based on the division between capital and labour. It is not the continuity of the historical process, a change of forms governed by a fundamental contradiction, that he brings to light, but rather a radical discontinuity, a mutation of humanity.

The very way in which Marx begins tells us something about his approach. He begins by recalling the presuppositions of wage labour and the historical conditions of capital. It is by contrast to these definitions that the distinctive characteristics of the Asiatic, Ancient and Germanic or feudal modes of production, their structural differences, will become clear. From the outset, we see that the precapitalist forms are not simply those that the observer identifies in empirical time as prior to capitalism, but that they constitute a whole whose distinctiveness capitalism enables us to see. In other words, precapitalism is perceived, since the advent of capitalism, as its *other*.

As stated by Marx, the conditions necessary for the formation of capitalism are, on the one hand, 'free labour and the exchange of this free labour for money, in order to reproduce and to realize money', and on the other hand, 'the separation of free labour from the objective conditions of its realization – from the means of labour and the material for labour'.[4] The importance of this separation is immediately obvious, for it reveals a model of social relations in which (however diverse the variants may be) not only is labour united with its material presuppositions but also, by virtue of this fact, is not determinable as such. No doubt we could not consider this model without the concepts of labour and labourer. But their usage can be justified only in so far as the experience of our own society enables us to discern retrospectively an activity we call 'labour' and human beings we call 'labourers'.

Thus Marx does not hesitate to declare: 'The positing of the individual as a *worker*, in this nakedness, is itself a product of *history*.'[5] What were they, then, those human beings of the past who were labourers without being labourers – or who were not identified as such? Their fate was to be tied to the land, the latter constituting their 'natural laboratory'. And this was as true in the case of small holdings as in that of communal property (as true of Ancient or feudal societies as of Asiatic ones). To say that human beings do not have the status of 'labourer' is to say that they are not differentiated, in their activity, from the environment in which they work, that the land which serves as dwelling place, as raw material, and as source of implements is not external to them. They are essentially the owners of the objective conditions of their labour; by which we mean either independent private owners, as was the case in Antiquity, or co-owners when (taken as individuals or families) they are only the 'personifications of communal property'. In considering precapital-ism, Marx's analysis immediately brings to light the fact that labour is not at the origin of property. To imagine that it had this priority would be to grant a status to labour and its agent the labourer, to assign them a real identity, which they acquire only within capital-ism itself. On the contrary, it must be understood that property is the precondition of labour. It would be difficult to apply this state-ment to individuals, however, since it is meaningless to take them as a starting point; their existence is always social and, in the first instance, gregarious. Originally each individual, explains Marx, maintained with others a relationship analogous to the one which tied him to the land: in other words, the one was not external to the other. Just as the individual found himself at one with the land (a term which designates much more, of course, than just the physical environment), so too be found himself immersed in the community. So it is perhaps to the latter that property can be attributed, although this statement remains imprecise, since property belongs to the land as much as it is owned by the community.

To affirm that property is the precondition of labour implies, therefore, that human beings labour only in so far as they participate (in whatever way) in the community, in the communal property. Considering the phenomenon of the tribal community – that form which, when modified, will give rise to the Asiatic, Ancient and feudal modes of production – Marx explains: 'Each individual has the status of *proprietor* or *possessor* only as a member of the community. The *real appropriation* through the labour process happens under these presuppositions, *which are not themselves the product of labour*, but appear as its natural or divine presuppositions.'[6] And just before this, he remarked: 'the *clan community*, the natural community, appears not as a *result* of, but as a *presupposition for the communal appropriation* (tem-porary) *and utilization of the land*'.[7] But anyone who thinks that Marx is referring here only to the *representation* of the community would be on the wrong track. The community appears to human beings as it really *is*. 'Communality of blood, language, customs': such is the primordial condition of all appropriation, just as the land does not merely *seem* to be but actually 'is the great workshop, the arsenal which furnishes both means and material of labour, as well as the seat, the *base* of the community'.[8]

It is true that these remarks concern the tribal community and that Marx's intention is to describe, starting from this foundation, the genesis of complex social formations, each of which presents its own specific characteristics. However, his analysis convinces us that the 'communal character' is preserved in the passage from one form to another.

Let us recall the main lines of the argument. In the first place, the despotic, Asiatic type of formation is merely a modification of the original model. In this type of formation, small communities are subordinated to a centralizing organ which projects an image of their unity. Although the organ is separated from these communities and stands over them, this distance does not imply that it is external to them, either in representation or in reality. The power of the despot is not seen, does not see itself and does not exist *outside* of the society. Rather, what must be grasped is that, with the rise of the despot, there occurs a displacement of the communal form. No longer contained within the limits of the village community this form splits itself in two by imprinting itself on a higher, global community, ultimately embodied in the despot or in a god, an 'imagined clan-being'.[9] From this point on, we are dealing with a formation – Oriental despotism – in which communes and their members are deprived of the ownership of the land and become, along with the latter, the property of the sovereign (a figure both real and imaginary); it is a sort of generalized slavery. However, this kind of slavery must not be confused with that found in the societies of Antiquity, since the distinction between slave and freeman does not and cannot appear here. We must also recognize that, under the appearance of dispossession, communal ownership persists. Individuals remain proprietors indirectly by the double mediation of the commune to which they belong and the higher community in which the latter is included: 'Property . . . appears mediated for [the individual] through a cession by the total unity – a unity realized in the form of the despot, the father of the many communities – to the individual, through the mediation of the particular commune.'[10]

In the eyes of Marx, this model accommodates several variants, a factor which allows him to recognize in it a general type of social formation. Either 'the little communes vegetate independently alongside one another, and the individual with his family works independently on the lot assigned to them' – a part of the work being devoted to the interests of the community; or the intervention of power may bring about a transformation in the mode of labour, 'the unity may extend to the communality of labour itself, giving rise to a true system, as in Mexico, Peru especially, among the early Celts, a few clans of India'.[11] Moreover, the internal organization of the commune will display more despotic or more democratic characteristics depending on whether the authority of a tribal chief or an equality among family heads predominates. But whatever the case may be, the same pattern of ownership, with property tied to the communal form, is maintained.

When Marx goes on to analyse the second type of social formation, he separates it in the same way from the empirical configurations by which it can be perceived and interpreted. The second type of social formation, like the first, offers 'essential modifications, brought about locally, historically'. But what is much more important to notice is the fact that Marx does not establish a direct filiation from one to the other. His sole concern is to point out that it is the product of a 'more active, historic life, of the fates and modifications of the original clans'.[12] In short, the starting point of the two formations is the same. However, in the process which engenders the second, we learn that the tribal community has been modified under the combined effect of accidental events (inter-tribal wars for the preservation or occupation of a territory, migrations, etc.) and of factors promoting the independent exploitation of the soil, all of which means that geography determines, in part, the chances of historical development. 'The less it is the case that the individual's property can in fact be realized solely through communal labour – thus e.g. the aqueducts in the Orient – the more the purely naturally arisen, spontaneous character of the clan has been broken by historic movements.'[13] We have used the expression 'combined effect' because it seems that accidental events, wars and migrations tend to multiply where the necessities of labour on a large scale are less compelling if not non-existent and that, on the other hand, tribal mobility encourages the development of individual energies.[14] So it seems all the more remarkable that, in spite of these vicissitudes, the communal form is maintained within the new, so-called Ancient, mode of production.

Of course, the community no longer immediately presupposes the land, but rather the city; it does not constitute the 'substance of which the individuals are mere accidents, or of which they form purely natural component parts'.[15] The individual is a free and independent property owner linked to all others in his place of residence by a relationship of reciprocity. Unity is established *negatively*, through opposition to common enemies, whether real or potential. However, it is not the product of a coalition of property owners, nor does it appear to them as such. The status of the property owner remains conditioned by his membership in the community. The relationship of the individual to the land has not disappeared, but it is now woven into his relationship to the city or, more precisely, to the state. In other words, his independence derives from an original state of dependence which he has not produced but which attests to the power of a transcendent entity. In the words of Marx himself, 'this belonging [is] mediated by his being a member of the state, by the being of the state – hence by a *presupposition* regarded as divine'.[16]

From this point of view, the double determination of the individual, as property owner and citizen, proves to be characteristic of the Ancient mode of production, but the first term is included in the second. 'The private proprietor of land is such only as a Roman, but as a Roman he is a private proprietor of land.'[17] Or again we could say that the double determination of property, as state property (*ager publicus*) and private property, certainly exists; but the latter by itself is unable to provide its own legitimacy and finds in the former its foundation and guarantee.

The fact that the splitting of the individual or of property contains a ferment of dissolution of the mode of production is one thing; but it would be something else again to claim that the latter is racked by a contradiction whose effect would be to generate a new 'form'. The Marxist argument, it seems to me, holds that the viability of the system depends on the maintenance of the community within fixed limits. Its extension, the growth of the number of property owners, the acquisition of new territories through war, the conflicts over the distribution of land, the use of slave labour, the multiplication of needs, the development of commercial and artisan activities which create a kind of wealth different from landed property as well as a new social class in the city, constitute so many factors whose consequence is to destroy the original framework of the community, namely, the mode of ownership. We must also see that this destruction is made possible by the fact that where the status of the private property owner and that of the member of the community are dissociated without being separated, it becomes possible for the individual 'to 'lose his property' – something which could not happen within the Asiatic mode of production. Moreover, under the pressure of demographic expansion and the search for new lands, patrician power and class conflict develop in a way which undermines the foundation of the social order. Nevertheless it remains the case that the Ancient mode of production, such as it is presented to us by Marx, obeys a principle of self-preservation, even if in particular circumstances it happens to transform itself. But it leaves itself open, by virtue of its inability to stay within its limits, to the incursion of events. History, one could say, comes to it from outside.

Now this analysis is not contradicted by the consideration of the third precapitalist form, the Germanic or feudal mode of production. In the first place, Marx does not try to demonstrate here either that this mode of production is the product of a previous social formation, that is that it provides a historical solution to the contradiction of a previous formation (and indeed, how could he venture to make such a claim?). At the very most, he suggests that one mode benefits from the dissolution of the other in order to expand. But the real starting point is to be found, once again, in the tribal communities – communities whose particular characteristics are the result of factual (i.e. geographical and historical) conditions, if by that we understand conditions brought about by wars and migrations. On the other hand, the evolution of these communities, although it entails a certain dispersion – the family house, isolated and independent, becoming the basis of social organization – once again highlights the persistence of the communal form and of the relationship to the land with which it is associated. In this respect, Marx's approach is quite remarkable: he emphasizes the weakening of the commune among Germanic peoples; not only was it no longer the substance of which the individual appears as a mere accident, but it did not exist as a city either, that is, as a state-like formation 'in and of itself', independently of even the assembling of its members. What is manifested in this commune is no longer the union but rather the reunion of individuals, no longer unity but unification. In order for it to exist, the commune must be actualized in an assembly of landowners. Although private property is still distinguished from communal property, the latter (the *ager publicus*) does not constitute, as in Antiquity, the economic existence of the state; it is merely a complement to individual property, a form in which a common identity is represented in the face of enemy peoples. And yet, it would be futile to attempt to reduce this representation to the reciprocal relationship between individuals, for it is detached from them and, in the last analysis, confers on its terms their own particular identity: 'individual property, as basis of the commune, has no other existence for itself except within the assembly of the members of the commune and their coming-together for common purposes'.[18]

There can be no doubt, then, about the kinship of the three forms analysed. It is expressly underlined by Marx:

> In all these forms . . . there is to be found: (1) Appropriation not through labour, but presupposed to labour; appropriation of the natural conditions of labour, of the *earth* as the original instrument of labour as well as its workshop and repository of raw materials. The individual relates simply to the objective conditions of labour as being his; [relates] to them as the inorganic nature of his subjectivity . . . (2) but this *relation* to land and soil, to the earth, as the property of the labouring individual . . . is instantly mediated by the naturally arisen, spontaneous, more or less historically developed and modified presence of the individual as *member of a commune* . . . An isolated individual could no more have property in land and soil than he could speak.[19]

Now what does it mean to say that the appropriation of land is not the result but the precondition of labour, if not that the individual *is one with the land* and that only because of this is he able to act as shepherd or farmer? And what does it mean to say that the community mediates the individual's relationship to the land, if not that it divides up the land and moulds it into a human, subjective form? This communal form cannot be confused with the determinate reality of a given community – such as that which came about, for example, in India, Peru, Rome, or feudal Europe. Nor could it be reduced to a structure, that of a mode of production which would be exemplified by real communities as variants of the same social model. The communal form is at one and the same time a primordial form, a natural form, and a form of representation. And what the study of pre-capitalism enables us to discern is a whole range of variations in space and modifications in time and, simultaneously, the permanent efficacy of this form.

Thus, two schemata of interpretation can be distinguished which sometimes exclude one another and sometimes come together. On the one hand, Marx sketches an evolutionary history; on the other, a repetitive history. The former seems to be governed, in various texts, by the development of productive forces which come up against the limits of the relations of production and, in the long run, dissolve them. Nevertheless, already from this point of view, the autonomy granted to this factor – even though it is supposed to include demographic expansion – seems to contradict the key idea that production remains subordinate to socio-natural conditions, to the existence of the community which mediates the relationship to the land; or, to express the same point more clearly, it seems to contradict the idea that the consequences of production are conditioned by the communal form: ' *The original conditions of production* (or, what is the same, the reproduction of a growing number of human beings through the natural process between the sexes . . .) *cannot themselves* originally *be products* – results of production.'[20] Now these 'original' conditions, such as they have been defined, do not cease to be determinant while the development of the productive forces continues. What this development modifies, let us repeat, is the particular arrangement of social relations, not the communal form. Is it this difficulty which induces Marx to put forward another factor of change? Whatever the reason may be, he gives a preponderant role at times to migration and war. The latter are events which acquire, in Marx's interpretation, a symbolic function, in the sense that they signify the instability of human beings, a trait as primordial as their rootedness in the community and the land.

In a manner which seems significant to me, Marx considers that the pastoral state and migration constitute the first mode of existence, while at the same time specifying that pastoral peoples 'relate to the earth as their property, although they never give it a fixed status'.[21] In Marx's imagination, the nomadic theme combines the idea of the land primordially imprinted in the communal form with the idea of the land primordially apprehended as a 'limitless element'. In fact, there is no room for doubt here: his general argument constantly exploits the double image of the establishment of humanity within limits and the inevitable dissolution of all limits.

As for war, it seems to be no less decisive a factor of change for sedentary peoples. Thus Marx goes so far as to assert:

> The only barrier which the community can encounter in relating to the natural conditions of production – the earth – as to *its own property* . . . is

*another community*, which already claims it as its own inorganic body. *Warfare* is therefore one of the earliest occupations of each of these naturally arisen communities, both for the defence of their property and for obtaining new property.[22]

However, this kind of language does not resolve the difficulty. The idea that a community perceives and deals with the enemy as if it were its own inorganic body implies that, in spite of the results of conquests and of new conflicts liable to break up an existing structure, history continues to play itself out on the same symbolic level.

Marx describes this symbolic level so forcefully that the distinction he makes between the two kinds of history – evolutionary and repetitive – ends up coinciding with the distinction between precapitalism and capitalism. It is at this point that the two patterns of interpretation come together; it must be added, however, that they come together only in the sense that they both prove to be secretly governed by the necessity of bringing to light a completely new type of social development. It is pointless, we are told in so many words, to inquire about the origin of the relationship to the land and to the mediating community, for this relationship is primordial.

> It is not the *unity* of living and active humanity with the natural, inorganic conditions of their metabolic exchange with nature, and hence their appropriation of nature, which requires explanation or is the result of a historic process, but rather the *separation* between these inorganic conditions of human existence and this active existence, a separation which is completely posited only in the relation of wage labour and capital.[23]

And again we read:

> In the relations of slavery and serfdom this separation does not take place; rather, one part of society is treated by the other as itself merely an *inorganic and natural* condition of its own reproduction.[24]

The importance of this last sentence should be carefully weighed: the opposition of classes – presented in the *Manifesto* as the mainspring of universal history – does not call into question, until the rise of capitalism, the unity of humanity–land, in whatever forms it might appear. Freeman–slave, patrician–plebeian, lord–serf, guildmaster–journeyman, these figures of social division in whose succession we were supposed to read the movement of universal history, are not ordered as such on account of a progressive separation of humanity from the inorganic conditions of its existence. Of course, Marx never abandons the idea that the dissolution of the ties between human beings and the land, and those between one human being and another, constitutes the last stage of a process as ancient as humanity itself. But the idea of an inevitable breaking up of the 'restricted relationships' established here and there, within such and such a mode of production which has come about and as a function of particular circumstances – this idea, we must repeat, belongs to a different schema than the idea of *separation*, of the break which sets free a cumulative history or, if you prefer, institutes a principle of social self-transformation.

In examining precapitalism, we see that evolution is governed by the destruction – at times slow, at times accelerated – of the human order; but this destruction is only the sign of an inevitable contradiction between the relationship of human beings to their *finite* humanity – anchored in the land, of which we can say that they both possess it and belong to it – and their relationship to their *infinite* humanity, which goes beyond any particular determination in reality and is associated with the 'limitless element of the land'. Irrespective of the way in which the destruction of the human order is carried out – by the erosion of institutions, as a consequence of the emergence of new factors of internal differentiation or as a result of aggression by foreign communities – the form of human existence is not altered. The infinite is signified only by the immediate negation of the finite, the limitless only by the immediate negation of the limit. The change does not entail that human beings will perceive themselves as separate from the land and from each other (even when they oppose each other as masters and slaves). In sum, what Marx is calling attention to, with his emphasis on the constancy of what he calls the communal character, is *an image of the body* which eliminates the dimension of externality. Between the individual, the community, the land as dwelling place, as raw material or as supply of tools, there is a play of reciprocal embodiments, and this is so whatever the degree of differentiation of individuals (the latter identifying themselves, for example, as independent private property owners) or the degree of communal differentiation (for example, one community placing itself above a multiplicity of others and claiming to be the organizing principle of social life). And this image seems so resistant to all structural modifications that the enigma of history comes to be concentrated in the moment of its decomposition.

## The Asiatic Mode of Production

Nevertheless, we must note that, among the precapitalist formations, there is one in particular which creates a problem for Marx and induces him to develop as far as he can the schema of a repetitive history. In fact, the Asiatic or Oriental mode of production subverts not only the idea of a continuity in the historical process on the level of humanity, but even the idea of the inevitability of social change which conforms to the schema of evolutionary history.

The originality of this type of formation lies in the fact that individuals within it prove to be entirely dependent on their communities. Not only is their relationship to the land mediated by the communal relationship, but they do not own the land they cultivate; they are merely the possessors of it. In comparing this situation to that with which the Romans were familiar, Marx observed, let us recall, that the possibility of change was implicit in the Ancient mode of production, for there individuals could 'lose their property'. In India, on the other hand, they seemed welded to their community. Now this feature is linked with another which Marx constantly underlines: since the commune behaves like a total organism whose members and activities are rigorously interwoven, there is no distinction within it between agriculture and manufacture, a distinction which elsewhere generates social division. Its autarchy shields it from the disturbing effects of exchange, the latter being limited in this case to the surplus capable of satisfying collective needs. The risk of change found within the Asiatic mode of production is thereby set aside:

> In the oriental form the *loss* [of property] is hardly possible, except by means of altogether external influences, since the individual member of the commune never enters into the relation of freedom towards it in which he could lose his (objective, economic) bond with it. He is rooted to the spot, ingrown. This also has to do with the combination of manufacture and agriculture, of town (village) and countryside.[25]

Marx is talking here about the basic commune, but the quasi-corporeal nature of the social relation found within it is not at all destroyed by the formation of the despotic state. Whatever the nature of the 'objective' constraints which determine the birth of the latter may be, the corporeal image is maintained; the basis of property ownership is merely transferred to the state or, more specifically, to the person who incarnates the state, to the body of the despot. Moreover, the basic social organization is unchanged; the appropriation by the state of the surplus labour requires only the action of a small bureaucracy grafted onto the productive organism.

We know that Marx takes up this analysis again in *Capital* and clarifies it by using the example of Indian communities. After having described their mode of production and distribution, the narrowly limited function of exchange, and the role of the agents of the state, all of which are examined one by one, he concludes:

> The simplicity of the productive organism in these self-sufficing communities which constantly reproduce themselves in the same form and, when accidentally destroyed, spring up again on the same spot and with the same name – this simplicity supplies the key to the riddle of the unchangeability of Asiatic societies, which is in such striking contrast with the constant dissolution and refounding of Asiatic states, and their never-ceasing changes of dynasty. The structure of the fundamental economic elements of society remains untouched by the storms which blow up in the cloudy regions of politics. [26]

It is true that this appraisal is meant to clarify the general phenomenon of the division of labour in society and manufacture (such is the heading of the fourth section of the chapter). However, its importance far exceeds the limits of the argument. Let us note in passing that the opposition formulated in the last instance between the structure of fundamental economic elements and the 'region of politics' is not consistent with the interpretation Marx sketches of the primitive commune; for the organization of the latter, he suggests, is no less political than economic. Or, to put it more rigorously, these two determining factors cannot be dissociated. What is expressed in terms of property can just as well be spoken of in terms of power: it is one and the same thing to say that individuals are not property owners and to say that they are not free. But the essential point lies in the distinction between two histories – the history which occurs at the level of fortuitous events and the one which restores not only the communal form (in the sense that we have given to this term) but also a particular type of organization – and in the assertion that the first kind of history is neutralized

by the second. Marx clearly recognizes that, in the case under consideration, the process of *dissolution* of the human order – a process on
which he confers, moreover, a universal efficacy – comes up against
the almost unbreachable resistance of a social structure. He imagines
an endogenous historical time, the time of a reproduction of social
relations moulded into their form, to which he opposes an exogenous
time, the time of the sudden emergence of events which would necessarily sweep away every established edifice; and it is to the first of these
that he gives priority. In short, Asiatic societies seem to secrete their
own history. What retains one's attention here is not only that, as
Marx notes, the communes are sheltered from all the torments of the
political domain, but also that a given mode of communal existence
proves to be shielded from *outside* attacks. Neither wars nor variations in the population, the latter being the result of a growth in the
birth rate or of epidemics, are liable to alter it. And moreover, we
are forced to go even further: neither the constraints which weigh
on the mode of production of the communes, nor the tendency for
the productive forces to develop – a tendency generally considered to
be inherent in the (social) nature of human beings – have this power.

Indeed, rather than be surprised by the maintenance of the communal model despite the vicissitudes of the state, we should instead
regard the very rise of the state as a strange phenomenon. Marx suggests that it is the product of 'objective' necessities – the conveying of
water being among the first of these (a hypothesis amply developed
by Wittfogel) – but this argument only makes more striking his conception of the state as an 'imaginary community' in which the principle of property ownership and control becomes embedded. If the
state comes to exercise a function that the communes are incapable
of fulfilling, due to their limited expanse and their scattered nature,
and if it makes possible certain kinds of labour requiring a co-
operation which the communes are unable to initiate, how can one
explain the fact that technical and economic innovation has no effect
on the basic social organization? It seems clear that the interpretation of these phenomena contradicts the schema of evolutionary
history. It implies both that there is and that there is not change with
the formation of the state. Of course, Marx does not go quite as far
as to draw this conclusion: he plays with the idea of the 'un-
changeability of Asiatic societies', sharply distinguishing between
the economic structure and the political domain, as if the latter had
no consistency of its own. Nevertheless, his analysis of despotism

makes it quite clear that despotism itself possesses, as a model, a stability which outlasts the shock of its emergence.

Now it would be of no use to put aside the phenomenon of despotic societies under the pretext that they constitute a limiting case. In taking up this phenomenon,[27] Marx is led to a line of reflection on history which breaks with the idea of a development strictly governed by the unfolding of productive forces, as well as with the idea of the inevitable dissolution of every social structure. The limiting case is methodologically crucial. It enables one to decipher the signs of a mechanism of self-preservation, the signs of a history guided by repetition, to which the whole range of precapitalist societies bears testimony.

## Genesis of the Capitalist Mode of Production

It is in relation to capitalism, we have remarked, that all other social formations reveal their kinship. With capitalism, a cumulative history is inaugurated, whose conditions are the double separation of free labour and money, on the one hand, and labour and the means of production, on the other. It is significant, however, that the analysis of the genesis of the capitalist mode of production reintroduces a distinction between two types of history.

Indeed, one has only to refer to the three chapters in volume one of *Capital* devoted to co-operation, manufacture and large-scale industry. Marx identifies the moment of the great mutation in the co-operation established by the production workshops at the end of the Middle Ages: 'A large number of workers working together, at the same time, in one place (or, if you like, in the same field of labour), in order to produce the same sort of commodity under the command of the same capitalist, constitutes the starting-point of capitalist production.'[28] This starting point located within the history of humanity is also the starting point of a completely new history. From now on, we have to deal with a revolutionary mode of production, in contrast to all the previous modes of production, which were conservative. Of course, Marx observes that, in the first instance, the difference introduced by co-operation is purely quantitative. But he is quick to point to a sequence of consequences which make the difference qualitative. Let us recall the basic argument: co-operation requires the mobilization of a quantity of capital in order to exploit a mass of labour power associated with a quantity of means of production. In other words, the double separation located at the origin of capitalism proves to be methodically reproduced and deepened until it becomes both the cause and the goal of the social system. In addition, co-operation tends to eliminate the qualitative differences between individual forms of labour and to institute an average social labour which is a necessary condition for the universalization of the market (all commodities finding themselves reduced in principle to a common denominator). So here, it seems, is the definitive dissolution of the communal social form, within which relationships of dependence were established and workers remained united with their means of production.

Capitalist co-operation differs, Marx explains, from all the old forms of co-operation, such as the types of production based on small independent property ownership: capitalist co-operation marks a radical change in the history of humanity.

> Co-operation in the labour process, such as we find it at the beginning of human civilization, among hunting peoples or, say, as a predominant feature of the agriculture of Indian communities, is based on the one hand on the common ownership of the conditions of production, and on the other hand on the fact that in those cases the individual has as little torn himself free from the umbilical cord of his tribe or community as a bee has from his hive. Both of those characteristics distinguish this form of co-operation from capitalist co-operation. The sporadic application of co-operation on a large scale in ancient times, in the Middle Ages, and in modern colonies, rests on direct relations of domination and servitude, in most cases on slavery. As against this, the capitalist form presupposes from the outset the free wage-labourer who sells his labour-power to capital. Historically, however, this form is developed in opposition to peasant agriculture and independent handicrafts, whether in guilds or not.[29]

In very few places does Marx express himself with such conciseness and rigour. Even more remarkable is the way that his argument is modified when he examines manufacturing. It is no longer the phenomenon of co-operation which appears decisive here, but that of the division of labour. The idea of a rupture between pre-capitalism and capitalism, and of the irreversibility of the historical process thus established, acquires a new meaning.

It is not necessary to go into all the details of the analysis which brings to light two ways in which handicrafts are transformed by manufacturing:

> On the one hand it arises from the combination of various independent trades, which lose that independence and become specialized to such an extent that they are reduced to merely supplementary and partial operations in the production of one particular commodity. On the other hand, it arises from the co-operation of craftsmen in one particular handicraft; it splits up that handicraft into its various detailed operations, isolating these operations and developing their mutual independence to the point where each becomes the exclusive function of a particular worker.[30]

In both cases, we are witnessing a process of the decomposition of human labour: a phenomenon which does not correspond simply to an historical evolution in the division of labour, but which is considered to be radically new.

Let us note: this phenomenon designates much more than a separation of the labourer and his means of production; it is the separation of the labourer from himself, or his dissolution within the *collective labourer*. There appears for the first time 'a productive organism whose parts are human beings'.[31]

Only this event – the existence of capital, not only as money or as a mass of means of production, but as 'the collective working organism . . . which is made up of numerous individual specialized workers'[32] – enables us to interpret the mutation of which simple co-operation constituted only a condition of possibility. 'While simple co-operation leaves the mode of the individual's labour for the most part unchanged, manufacture thoroughly revolutionizes it.' And Marx goes on: 'Not only is the specialized work distributed among the different individuals, but the individual himself is divided up, and transformed into the automatic motor of a detail operation, thus realizing the absurd fable of Menenius Agrippa, which presents man as a mere fragment of his own body.'[33]

However, the metaphor of the body, which Marx exploits on several occasions in order to describe the new mode of production, merits a closer examination, for it is ambiguous. This body, monstrous or absurd, emerged from the ruins of individual or communal bodies; but it would be a mistake to think that it retained nothing of their character. In fact, in manufacturing, the production organism 'whose parts are human beings' is still constructed, we discover, according to the model of the corporeal constitution of the labourer.

> The analysis of a process of production into its particular phases here coincides completely with the decomposition of a handicraft into its different partial operations. Whether complex or simple, each operation has to be done by hand, retains the character of a handicraft, and is therefore dependent on the strength, skill, quickness and sureness with which the individual worker manipulates his tools. Handicraft remains the basis, a technically narrow basis which excludes a really scientific division of the production process into its component parts.[34]

Now this representation of the production organism, of the body of labour, modifies our appreciation of manufacturing in that the latter ceases to appear as a radically new institution which would contain the principle of a continuous revolution. Not only does Marx point out its dependence on the crafts of the Middle Ages and link its tendency to convert 'a partial task into the life-long destiny of a man' to the model of older societies,[35] but he shows that beyond a certain degree of development, manufacturing has no end other than its own preservation.

> The history of manufacture proper shows how the division of labour which is peculiar to it acquires the most appropriate form at first by experience, as it were behind the backs of the actors, and then, like the guild handicrafts, strives to hold fast to that form when once it has been found, and here and there succeeds in keeping it for centuries.[36]

Of course, one could deny that there is any ambiguity in the Marxist interpretation. It could be said that simple co-operation, manufacturing based on the division of labour and large-scale industry are stages. That is what Marx says, I admit. Each stage presupposes a previous technological foundation which is only gradually overturned, in such a way that one discovers antagonistic aspects within it. But such an account would retain only the descriptive dimension of the genesis of capitalism. Now Marx goes well beyond mere description; he pursues the idea of a difference of form on both the socio-economic and historical levels. And it is important to identify the displacement of that instance where the difference is manifested, because it makes visible a tension between two schemata of thought which, I believe, was never dissipated. From this point of view, the analysis of manufacturing seems to me exemplary, in so far as it shows how the movement, which for the first time 'profoundly revolutionizes the mode of individual labour', does not free itself from the phantom of the body and, as a result, tends to re-establish a congealed structure.

The analysis of large-scale industry fully confirms this interpretation, concerned as it is with linking the *objective, impersonal, inhuman* character of the mode of production to its revolutionary character.

Of what does the radical newness of the era of large-scale industry consist? From now on, the production process becomes autonomous; the mode of the division of labour obeys the technical necessities of mechanical fabrication such as they are made known by the natural sciences, instead of remaining bound to the range of individual aptitudes. In the language of Marx, the subjective principle of the division of labour is replaced by an objective principle. In manufacturing, the worker certainly had to adapt himself to a specific operation before entering into the production process; but the operation was accommodated in advance to the worker. In other words, the organic constitution of the worker determined the division and combination of gestures required for a given production process. A corporeal schema continued to determine how the workshop was structured. In mechanical production, by contrast, the principle of the division of labour ceases to be subjective.

> It becomes objective, that is, emancipated from the individual faculties of the worker: the total process is viewed in and for itself, and analyzed into its constitutive phases. The problem of how to execute each particular process, and to bind the different partial processes together into a whole, is solved by the aid of machines, chemistry, etc.[37]

From now on, 'a production organism, completely objective or impersonal', separates itself not only from the individual workers, who were already deprived of the control of their own bodies in manufacturing, but also from the collective being in which they were amassed.

The process of socialization of labour breaks with the communal reality and representation which survived in the collective labourer.

Such is the observation on which the theory of *reification* is based. It is not necessary here to dwell on this aspect of the analysis. Let me simply call attention to the function of the metaphor of the automaton, which emerges in this context to echo the metaphor of the body. Marx speaks at one point of 'a mechanical monster whose body fills whole factories, and whose demonic power, at first hidden by the slow and measured motions of its gigantic members, finally bursts forth in the fast and feverish whirl of its countless working organs'.[38] Elsewhere he takes the metaphor of the automaton from Ure and alters it in order to apply it to capitalism: 'the automaton itself is the subject, and the workers are merely conscious organs, coordinated with the unconscious organs of the automaton, and together with the latter subordinated to the central moving force'.[39] However, if the form of the collective body turns out to be replaced by another form which, while resulting from the destruction of the first form, still remains in complicity with it, the logic of the destruction of all fixed limits implies that the apparatus of the automaton will itself be dismantled.

In fact, the objective principle of the division of labour generates both a continued transformation of the mode of production and a more and more intimate connection between all the activities which establish and make apparent the unity of social labour. In contrast to the past when, within the boundaries of each guild, a particular mode of the division of labour tended to become rigidly fixed, when production procedures were appropriated by each guild to the point of becoming trade secrets and when, because of the partition of activities and groups, a relation to society as a whole was rendered impossible, the emancipation from the subjective point of view created the conditions for a universal communication among human beings and a homogenization of the field of their activities. The rootedness in a particular mode of existence and the private appropriation of techniques gives way to the growing mobility of labourers and the growing transparency of their activities and their relations.

This description of the mode of production based on large-scale industry is best summarized in the penultimate section of chapter XV of *Capital*. After having recalled that 'one of the most characteristic facts is that right down to the eighteenth century, the different trades were called "mysteries", into whose secrets none but those initiated by their profession and their practical experience could penetrate', Marx comments:

> Large-scale industry tore aside the veil that concealed from men their own social process of production and turned the various spontaneously divided branches of production into riddles, not only to outsiders but even to the initiated. Its principle, which is to view each process of production in and for itself, and to resolve it into its constituent elements without looking first at the ability of the human hand to perform the new processes, brought into existence the whole of the modern science of technology.[40]

And, finally, the difference between two historical schemata is emphasized in a general way:

> Modern industry never views or treats the existing form of a production process as the definitive one. Its technical basis is therefore revolutionary, whereas all earlier modes of production were essentially conservative.[41]

The dissolution of particular contexts of activity, freedom from the hold of the past, demystification of the relationship to reality, continuous revolution of the mode of production: these phenomena prove to be rigorously linked with one another in Marx's interpretation. And this mode of production, as the remainder of the chapter makes immediately clear, includes not only the system of production itself but also the whole of the social system which is linked to it. Indeed, the explicit reference to the *Manifesto* is hardly necessary in this context; the judgement brought to bear on industrial capitalism in volume one of *Capital* rejoins, in its main lines, the judgement formulated by Marx in 1848.

## A Contradictory Image of Bourgeois Society

Nevertheless, can one stop at the conclusion that the representation of a history governed by the logic of revolution is based on different premises in the *Grundrisse* and *Capital* than in the *Manifesto*? Can one be satisfied with demonstrating the discovery of a radical discontinuity between the capitalist era and all the previous ones, the sign of which would finally be provided by the emergence of large-scale industry?

Of course, it must be conceded that Marx never drew all the consequences of this discovery, that he never abandoned the belief in an evolution from simple forms to more and more complex ones. We should not neglect the theoretical compromises to which he devoted himself, and especially the famous text of 1857 (now the 'Introduction' to the *Grundrisse*), in which he rejects and re-establishes the evolutionist schema. He asserts, on the one hand, that bourgeois society allows us to decipher the structure of all previous societies, that it gives us the key to them, just as human anatomy enables us to understand the anatomy of the ape; and, on the other hand, he asserts that the categories which come to light as a result are 'fully valid' only within the limits of bourgeois society.[42] But the fact remains that the principle of a division between two types of historical development was formulated by Marx and that it contradicts his conception of the history of humanity. The conclusion to be drawn from this would not be insignificant.

But this conclusion still leaves intact the coherence of his representation of bourgeois society. For we have taken into account up till now only a simplified version of its structure and history.

Indeed, how can we be content with this combination of features which seems to characterize bourgeois society: dissolution of particular contexts of activity, freedom from the hold of the past, demystification of the relationship to reality, continuous revolution of the mode of production and of all the institutions? The truth is that, from the works of his youth through *Capital*, Marx formulates a contradictory image of bourgeois society. The latter appears as that altogether unique society in which various conditions co-exist: the conditions of an interdependence of all activities and a communication among all social agents, as well as the conditions of a reciprocal externalization of all activities and a reciprocal alienation of all agents. Thus, while a purely economic order of relationships emerges as a distinct and autonomous domain, another sphere is separated off in a parallel way – the sphere of the political, the religious, the legal, and scientific, the educational, the aesthetic.[43] And, as Engels saw very well, in spite of his mechanistic tendencies, each sector of the economy and each sector of social activity is the scene of its own history, even though the latter takes place under conditions determined by the structure of the mode of production.[44] Bourgeois society experiences a dissolution of all the traditional forms of production and representation, but simultaneously dissimulates its own history, even eludes it by taking refuge in models of the past or by succumbing to the spell of spirits of the dead. It is not of medieval or archaic societies but of the society of the capitalist era that Marx is thinking when he declares in *The Eighteenth Brumaire* that the 'tradition of all the dead generations weighs like a nightmare on the brain of the living', adding that just when men

> seem engaged in revolutionising themselves and things, in creating something that has never yet existed, precisely in such periods of revolutionary crisis they anxiously conjure up the spirits of the past to their service and borrow from them names, battle-cries and costumes in order to present the new scene of world history in this time-honoured disguise and this borrowed language.[45]

And it would be quite insufficient to say simply that, in bourgeois society, a path is opened to the material basis of social life; for this would take no account of the Marxist analysis of ideology, which originates in the splitting of the mode of production, in the unbearable ordeal of social division, and which fulfils a new function (irreducible to that of religion or myths in previous societies): that of substantiating the illusion of rationality and universality. It would be quite insufficient to sum up the history of bourgeois society in terms of the feverish movement of destruction–creation, since Marx uncovers, beneath the triple effect of the autonomization of each sector of production, the disguising of the present in the past and the obscuring of reality by ideology, a principle of social petrification.

Let us return once again to *Capital*. Its aim, of course, is to reveal the internal logic of a mode of production whose categories are not natural but social and historical, having come into existence and being destined to disappear – categories which support particular interests and class relations; in addition, the laws of its development are presented as those of its collapse. But what fantastic world is described for us there, a world where classes are merely 'personifications' of economic categories; where, in each phase of social life, entities acquire an existence independent of individuals; where real relationships – in the fragmentation and division brought about by the process of production – become established as illusory ones; where, lastly, it is increasingly the 'dead labour which dominates men and pumps the living substance from them'. As Harold Rosenberg so aptly remarked, in order to understand this world, 'one must return to witches, to the Shakespeare of Hamlet or

Macbeth'.[46] The history which there unfolds under the sign of the unleashing of productive forces is still interwoven with a history governed by repetition.

It is hardly necessary to evoke the famous analysis of commodity fetishism. But it is worth recalling that, in this case, illusion and reality are not dissociated by Marx. If he observes that 'it is nothing but the definite social relations between men themselves which assumes here, for them, the fantastic form of a relation between things', he adds almost immediately that this relation between things effectively constitutes the reality of their social relation:

> The labour of the private individual manifests itself as an element of the total labour of society only through the relations which the act of exchange establishes between the products, and, through their mediation, between the producers. To the producers, therefore, the social relations between their private labours appears as what they are, i.e. they do not appear as direct social relations between persons and their work, but rather as material [*dinglich*] relations between persons and social relations between things.[47]

It is more important to recall the description of the social process of production found in the last part of the third volume of *Capital*. There, Marx is not content to denounce the mystification which makes production relations appear as 'things' in all societies reaching the stage of commodity production; and he is not content to stress that it is only within developed capitalism that 'this enchanted and perverted world develops still more'.[48] He finds the roots of this mystification in the movement of capital formation, he shows how it originates and thickens in each moment of this movement, in such a way that the history or genesis of social relations is completely obscured and these relations are, in their very reality, detached from living human beings, no longer their product but a mechanism which dominates them and which possesses the principle of its own repetition.

'Capital–profit (profit of enterprise plus interest), land–ground-rent, labour–wages, this is the trinity formula which comprises all the secrets of the social production process.'[49] Capital seems and, in a sense, is separated from land and labour. 'Thus, capital appears to the capitalist, land to the landlord, and labour power, or rather labour itself, to the labourer . . . as three different sources of their specific revenues, namely, profit, ground-rent and wages.' And, adds Marx immediately thereafter,

> They are really so in the sense that capital is a perennial pumping-machine of surplus-labour for the capitalist, land a perennial magnet for the landlord, attracting a portion of the surplus-value pumped out by capital, and finally labour the constantly self-renewing condition and every self-renewing means of acquiring under the title of wages a portion of the value created by the labourer.[50]

According to Marx's interpretation, this separation of economic categories – in representation and reality – results from the transformation of the total value into these categories, where the total value is simply materialized social labour. Now the *totality* is invisible and cannot be otherwise from the moment that the living labour force is separated from the means of production monopolized by one section of society. Or we could say that what is invisible is the capitalist system which, as a result of this first split, brings to light and into existence, as independent of one another, capital, land, labour. The latter are *phantom-like* entities. 'Capital is not a thing', says Marx, and in particular, 'it is not the sum of material and fabricated means of production'. It is 'a social system of production'. Moreover, one cannot limit oneself to saying that these means of production acquire an independent existence *vis-à-vis* the producers. Such an opposition presupposes another: social relations rise up before the means of production and tower over them as the dominant force. Nevertheless, converted into a thing, capital appears to be endowed with its own movement; it produces itself. Here is the image of the world turned upside down.

It is not important to follow in all its detail the analysis of company profit and its dissimulation under the features of the salaried labour of the capitalist (or entrepreneur). The analysis leads to the conclusion that, while this part of the profit is detached completely from the relations of capitalist exploitation, the other part, interest, is detached from the salaried labour of workers and capitalists 'as if capital were its particular and autonomous source'. This elicits the following commentary: 'If capital originally appeared on the surface of circulation as a fetishism of capital, as a value-creating value, so it now appears again in the form of interest bearing capital, as in its *most estranged and characteristic form.*'[51]

Now, following the same logic, land and labour detach themselves as abstractions. Of labour, last term of the 'trinity', Marx says that it is a 'pure phantom'. He explains that 'taken in itself', as 'the' labour, it is 'nonexistent' or the mark of such a general relation of organic exchanges with nature that it does not even presuppose the social condition of human beings. Yet it is to the 'phantom', to this 'nonexistent entity', that social existence is fantastically bound. But it is the relation between capital and land which reveals most profoundly the mechanism concealing the foundations of social life.

> Since here a part of the surplus-value seems to be bound up directly with a natural element, the land, rather than with social relations, the form of mutual estrangement and ossification of the various parts of surplus-value is completed, the inner connection completely disrupted, and its source entirely buried, precisely because the relations of production, which are bound to the various material elements of the production process, have been rendered mutually independent.[52]

If we recall the analysis of precapitalism, in which the land was presented as the 'natural laboratory of man', we may acquire a new perspective on the historical rupture that capitalism introduced. We may agree that capitalism generates a new kind of history, as well as a socialization process freed from the 'natural' limits found in the 'communal form' – a form in which the relationships of human beings to one another and to the land were established. But at the same time, 'natural' determination reappears, this time in a purely social space (structured around a purely social division), as the imaginary determination *par excellence*, under whose effect the capitalist envelope is sealed and the connections of living labour become impossible to read. The land itself becomes an independent power, coupled with capital (and caught up in the capitalist mode of production), pumping out the living force of labourers. It is no longer *the element* of social life, the Mother-Earth, subsisting in spite of all changes; it is the Dead-Earth.

The universe of bourgeois society, of 'historical' society, of the society which sets itself up within purely social horizons by the continuous destruction of every fixed order and which becomes intelligible to itself, turns out in a contradictory way to be 'an enchanted, perverted, topsy-turvy world in which *Monsieur le Capital* and *Madame la Terre*, who are social characters as well as mere things, do their *danse macabre*'.[53] This *danse macabre* was already that of the 'mechanical monster', of the great automaton: the feverish and dizzy dance of its organs. But how much more complicated and strange it appears, when we see the gigantic limbs of the monster fill up with, not merely 'whole factories', but society as a whole, when unconscious and conscious organs are no longer machines and individuals, but social relations transformed into things.

The dance in which a 'demonic force' is set free – whether it is perceived on the stage of large-scale industry or on the general stage of society – is capitalist history, whose figures are arranged according to the law of repetition. How can one doubt this vision? It reiterates the idea of progress – or better yet, of the birth of communism in the pain of the organic transformation of bourgeois society – in the same way that the vision of the communal form, written into all the old modes of production and resistant to evolution, reiterated the idea of a universal history. It is true that the analysis of precapitalism and that of capitalism imply a different 'splitting' of representation. The material taken up by thought 're-works' the representation. In both cases, a life principle and a death principle were apparent to Marx. But in the first case, life is associated as much with the movement of conservation of the communal form as with that of evolution; life is manifest in the link between the organic and the inorganic, just as it is manifest in the differentiation of the social fabric engendered by evolution: death, associated with the moment of inexorable dissolution of every finite form, still appears to be serving the interests of life. In the case of capitalism, by contrast, life and death split apart. And for Marx, all history organizes itself in a contradictory way around the poles of life and death. On the one hand, 'the dead seizes the living'; on the other, productive forces accumulate, converge to give force to the pure living entity, the proletariat, the universal class, in which the mortal determination of finitude is abolished.

### A *Danse Macabre*

This last contradiction, the signs of which we found in *Capital*, is not less evident when Marx claims to decipher the history of bourgeois society in a sequence of events. *The Eighteenth Brumaire*, if one read it with the *Manifesto* in mind (a comparison which is all the more instructive since the two texts belong to the same period), would leave no illusion about the coherence of Marxist theory. In fact, the *Manifesto* presents bourgeois history like a grandiose epic and *The Eighteenth Brumaire* represents it like a *danse macabre*.

What does Marx discover upon examining French society from February 1848 to the *coup d'état* of 1851? Does he discover the simplification of social antagonisms, the division of society into two camps, of which the *Manifesto* speaks so eloquently? In a sense, yes: the June Days make this division appear in a dazzling light. But only for a moment. What Marx describes, in fact, is much more the growing complexity of social antagonisms and, as a consequence, the intertwining of multiple histories, each of which is anchored in a particular class. But this last term is still ambiguous. For what are these classes? It may be a class in the process of becoming, which is condemned to impotence because of its immaturity: such is the proletariat. Or it may be a class opposed to itself, which comes together intermittently for fear of its enemy, but which flees before the image of its own identity: such is the bourgeoisie. Or it may be an intermediate class within which 'the interests of opposing classes are blunted', such as the petite bourgeoisie. Or it may be a class which is a non-class, 'a simple addition of homologous magnitudes' forming a class 'much as potatoes in a sack form a sack of potatoes'.[54] Or again, it may be a class regarded as the rubbish, the refuse of society – the lumpenproletariat. And even this schema does not fully do justice to the complexity of the situation. The faction of pure Republicans which formed the official opposition under Louis-Philippe and later dominated the Constituent National Assembly was certainly bourgeois, but it 'was not a faction of the bourgeoisie held together by great common interests and marked off by specific conditions of production'.[55] As for the bureaucracy and the army, that dreadful parasitical body which 'enmeshes the body of French society like a net and chokes all its pores', how can it be characterized? It was the instrument of the dominant class during the Restoration and under Louis-Philippe, but it seems to have become completely independent under the second Bonaparte, to the point where only its development renders intelligible the great event that Marx wants to explain; and, more than that, only its development makes the future course of history understandable, since the fantastic elevation of the state above society proves to be, according to Marx, the condition of the revolution.[56]

So there we have the strange historical actors whose conflicts produced the Bonapartist *coup d'état*. But is it a question of actors? And do their conflicts produce *events*? 'The period that we have before us', declares Marx, 'comprises the most motley mixture of crying contradictions';[57] these contradictions are sterile: 'passions without truth, truths without passion; heroes without heroic deeds, history without events; development, whose sole driving force seems to be the calendar, made wearisome through constant repetition of the same tensions and relaxations'. And to finish: 'the official collective genius of France brought to naught by the artful stupidity of a single individual'.[58]

In short: 'If any section of history has been painted grey on grey, it is this. Men and events appear as inverted Schlemihls, as shadows that have lost their bodies.'[59] Do we not recognize here, transferred to the register of political history, the twin representations of machinery and phantasmagoria which we noted in *Capital*?

Marx's vision seems to me all the more remarkable in that it is contradicted at several points in his analysis. The analysis clearly demonstrates that an historical issue breaks into the February Revolution: namely, the issue of whether the bourgeoisie is able to secure political domination, the necessary condition for its unification as a class. It shows that the struggle around this issue determines the rise and fall of the pure Republicans, and then the rise and fall of the Party of Order; that this struggle is profoundly disturbed by the arrival of the proletariat on the social scene; and finally, that the rise of Louis Napoleon Bonaparte constitutes much more than a minor and meaningless episode, since the division of state and civil society creates an entirely new situation. The last chapter even goes as far as to invert radically the first perspective. Events are no longer phantom-like, their sequence governed by the sole force of the calendar; history is no longer phantasmagorical nor mechanical: it is the revolution which 'does its work methodically', pursues its objectives. It is the revolution which, in the first instance, 'perfected the parliamentary power, in order to be able to overthrow it. Now that it has attained this, it perfects the *executive power* . . . in order to concentrate all its forces of destruction against it'.[60] However, Marx is not at all sensitive to this contradiction. Once again, he juxtaposes two representations of history. And, under the circumstances, how can it be denied that one of them predominates? In fact, he hardly speaks of the proletariat. He ridicules the bourgeoisie's plan for political domination. As for the revolution, invisible and sure of itself, it is evoked in a few lines. It seems that what interests him is to take apart a political intrigue, to make us aware of its complexity and to denounce its vanity.

He claims, of course, to reduce the intrigue to the effects of economically determined social conditions, turning our attention away from the surface and back to the foundation of things. Thus, speaking of the conflict between Democratic Republicans and Royalists, he invites us to shed our fondness for 'this superficial appearance, which veils the *class struggle*'.[61] Analysing the opposition of Legitimists and Orleanists, he asserts that they are not divided by 'so-called principles', but by their material conditions of existence, linked to two kinds of property: one landed, the other capitalist. In this way we find ourselves sent from the vanity of manifest conflicts back to the reality of antagonisms whose rigid form makes historical development impossible. However, even this intention does not explain the central function that Marx assigns to 'illusions', to 'idle dreams', and in a decisive way, to the disguising of the present in the past, in the interests of a history 'without events', repetitive, even regressive. Ultimately, it is not the logic of interests which underlies the sequence of events, but rather the logic of their misrecognition – class interests are written into a social structure whose division prevents every actor from grasping its form and its dynamic. At the end of the analysis, Bonapartist power appears as an imaginary product, a product of combined myths, a product of a society which can only face the problem of its unity – or better, of its identity – through the mode of illusion.

So strong and constant is the power of the imaginary in Marx's eyes that he discovers it at the very origin of bourgeois society. We must not let ourselves be dazzled by the judgement which opens *The Eighteenth Brumaire*: 'Hegel remarks somewhere that all facts and personages of great importance in world history occur, as it were, twice. He forgot to add: the first time as tragedy, the second as farce.'[62] It is not the universal phenomenon of the return of things which matters. The examples prove that the author is thinking only of the modern era. He suggests that, in the latter, individuals are confronted with what is *new*, but they are unable to conceive of it. At the very moment when they are involved in a creative process of becoming, which forces them to undertake unprecedented tasks, they evoke the dead, disguise the present in the past, dress up as Romans. At the moment when the continuity of time is broken in reality, they *invent* a past. In other words, the past *surges up* in the representation. This representation defends them against the feeling of vertigo engendered by their own action, an action whose particular, historical character signifies to them that they are themselves particular, historical, mortal actors. The image of the Romans is constitutive of the bourgeois revolution, because the bourgeoisie can conflate the representation of itself with that of society as such only if it can dissimulate its class character *within* society; and it can conflate its own development with history as such only if it can dissimulate the contingency of the present. In this sense, the opening lines of *The Eighteenth Brumaire* on the double repetition and the passage from tragedy to farce is much more than mere rhetoric. In a society which has been formed in the misrecognition of its reality, a situation could not arise in which the social order (and, at the same time, the nature of the social) were put into question, unless there were a return to the inaugural moment of the repetition and, once the founding moment has past, unless this repetition were simple parody. The mechanism of repetition can be brought to a halt only through the intervention of an actor whose existence and interests show themselves to be in contradiction with the nature of the social system: only the proletariat can free itself from the dead and carry out a revolution which, as Marx says, draws its poetry not from the past but from the future.

As a historian, Marx can very well lay the blame for the failure of the republic on the immaturity of industrial capitalism; his vision of bourgeois society implies that it cannot generate real events. Thus, in his eyes, the February Days constitute a revolution (immediately aborted) only in so far as the workers took part in them. Brought back to its causes, its objectives and its result, it was 'a surprise attack, a *taking* of the old society unawares',[63] 'a simple superficial shake-up, a prologue of the revolution'.[64] And such is its historical *insignificance* that the sequence of subsequent events, in which Marx nevertheless reveals the logic of a counter-revolution, appears, in the last analysis, like the episodes of a comedy.

Comedy? Masquerade, we should say. And if we follow Marx to the very basis of things, how can the order of material reality be distinguished from that of phantasmagoria?

From 1848 to 1851 only the ghost of the old revolution walked about ... An entire people, which had imagined that by means of a revolution it had imparted to itself an accelerated power of motion, suddenly finds itself set back into a defunct epoch and, in order that no

doubt as to the relapse may be possible, the old dates again arise, the
old chronology, the old names, the old edicts, which had long become
a subject of antiquarian erudition . . . The nation feels like that mad
Englishman in Bedlam who fancies that he lives in the times of the
ancient Pharaohs.[65]

And what about the proletariat itself? It was, of course, the author
of the June insurrection, 'the most colossal event in the history of
European civil wars'.[66] Vanquished, at least 'it succumbs with the
honours of the great, world-historic struggle'.[67] But before that? Its
representatives found a place in the February government where
'nothing and nobody ventured to lay claim to the right of existence
and of real action'.[68] It 'revelled in grandiose perspectives',
unaware of its enemies and of those who ought to have been its
allies: the peasants and the petite bourgeoisie. And then? It drew
closer to social classes which, one after another, transmitted their
weakness to it, and it suffered the burden of their defeat.

> In part it throws itself into doctrinaire experiments, exchange banks
> and workers' associations, hence into a movement in which it re-
> nounces the revolutionising of the old world by means of the latter's
> own great, combined resources, and seeks, rather, to achieve its
> salvation behind society's back.[69]

By passively accepting the law of 31 May 1850, which abolished
universal suffrage, it allowed itself to be excluded from the political
battlefield and renounced 'the honour of being a conquering class'.

And what about the petite bourgeoisie and its democratic
spokesmen? There is no point in lingering here over Marx's well-
known analysis. He shows that it was a class and a party condemned
to illusion by their situation. They imagined themselves to be above
social antagonisms and they took themselves for The People: a fic-
tional being.

How can the politics of the dominant class and its representatives
be explained? It is in wrestling with this problem that Marx claims
to discover, beneath the conflicts of representation and the phraseology of the parties, the determining role of interests. But, far from
coming down to this conclusion, the description of the divisions between the two factions allied in the Party of Order brings out clearly
the inability of the bourgeoisie to act in accordance with its own interest and the tribute that it pays to its idle dreams.

Legitimists and Orleanists wave *fleur-de-lys* and the tricolor flag and seem to fight for their respective dynasties. Illusion without unity, Marx declares in the first instance: the division between them is rooted in the mode of property ownership. Some of them defended '*large landed property* which, under the Bourbons, had governed with its priests and lackeys'; others defended 'high finance, large-scale industry, large-scale trade, that is, *capital*, with its retinue of lawyers, professors and smooth-tongued orators'.[70] It is impossible for them really to unite, since monarchy for some meant 'the political expression of the hereditary rule of the lords of the soil', whereas for others it was 'the political expression of the usurped rule of the bourgeois *parvenus*'. From such a perspective, their alliance inside the Party of Order seems to be a product of circumstances. They had to borrow the Republican language in the wake of the February Revolution and they joined together after June to oppose any current which was liable to upset the system of domination. But the picture is immediately modified: 'We speak of two interests of the bourgeoisie', Marx explains, 'for large landed property, despite its feudal coquetry and pride of race, has been rendered thoroughly bourgeois by the development of modern society.'[71] Let us weigh these terms carefully: Legitimists and Orleanists are both divided and united by their material conditions of existence – and divided, in the last analysis, because they belong to the capitalist system which splits surplus-value between land rent and profit (industrial, commercial and financial). They do not express the aspirations of two kinds of social organization, one persisting – though belonging to the past – inside the other, which is in the process of developing. It is the very structure of bourgeois society that entails an opposition of the dominant class to itself. No doubt Marx regards Royalist illusions to be even more inconsistent when he demonstrates the common interest of the two factions. To listen to him, it would seem that it is only 'behind the scenes' that their representatives 'donned their old Orleanist and Legitimist liveries again and once more engaged in their old tourneys'. On the other hand: 'on the public stage, in their grand performances of state, as a great parliamentary party, they put off their respective royal houses with mere obeisances and adjourned the restoration of the monarchy *ad infinitum*. They did their real business as the *Party of Order*.'[72]

At this point, however, his argument allows us to catch a glimpse of the mainspring of repetitive history – by this I mean a history which, instead of creating new political forms, takes the actors back along the paths of the past. Tempted to exercise a political domination which suits their common interests – and for a moment they did exercise a 'more unrestricted and sterner domination over the other classes of society than ever previously under the Restoration or under the July Monarchy'[73] – hence tempted to play to the utmost the game of the parliamentary Republic, which provides the only possible expression of the dominant class, the bourgeois members of both factions draw back from this enterprise out of fear of appearing on the social scene with their true faces exposed.

> Instinct taught them that the republic, true enough, makes their political rule complete, but at the same time undermines its social foundation, since they must now confront the subjugated classes and contend against them without mediation, without the concealment afforded by the crown, without being able to divert the national interest by their subordinate struggles among themselves and with the monarchy. It was a feeling of weakness that caused them to recoil from the pure conditions of their own class rule and to yearn for the former more incomplete, more undeveloped and precisely on that account less dangerous forms of this rule.[74]

In short, far from finding itself endowed with an immediate efficacy, the particular interest (lodged in landed property or in purely capitalist activity) seems finally to be mobilized in the movement of withdrawal which accompanies the rise of the bourgeoisie.

This particular interest blossoms only in a process of regression, when *representation* comes to mask the imperatives of the present. The conflict between the two interests of the bourgeoisie is actualized by virtue of a defence mechanism, itself triggered off by the anxiety surrounding an historical undertaking which is liable to expose the contingency of domination.

I speak of *regression*. The 'analytic' resonance of the term is welcome, for what Marx describes at one point, as a function of an inability to overcome the contradiction in reality, is both a process of breaking up the bourgeoisie and the resurgence of the phantasized past.

The contradiction comes to a head in 1850, Marx notes, when the question of the revision of the Constitution is raised before Parliament. Let us recall that the question concerns the status of the President of the Republic, Louis Napoleon, elected on 10 December

1848, to whom it was forbidden to request a new mandate; but that on this occasion, since the two possible alternatives proved, according to our author, to be impracticable for the Party of Order, the conflict revived the illusion of a monarchist solution and the dynastic quarrel. Multiple illusions: Legitimists and Orleanists dream, each in their own camp, of realizing the political unification of the bourgeoisie under a monarch who would merely 'personify' one of its interests, whereas in fact the bourgeoisie could only subsist within a parliamentary Republic. The Fusionists (partisans of a dynastic compromise), who give the impression of being realistic politicians, sink still deeper into a dream world, for they do not see that the antagonism of interests between the two bourgeois groups is only made more acute when it takes the form of family interests. In short, they imagine a solution at the level where the terms are solidified under the most singular traits of personal passion. Finally,

> the disintegration of the Party of Order did not stop at its original elements. Each of the two great factions, in its turn, underwent decomposition anew. It was as if all the old nuances that had formerly fought and jostled one another within each of the two circles, whether Orleanist or Legitimist, had thawed out again like dry infusoria on contact with water, as if they had acquired anew sufficient vital energy to form groups of their own and independent antagonisms.[75]

Marx sketches here an astonishing analysis of the social imaginary. It is formed in the movement of decomposition of the bourgeois party, it takes on substance in the new groupings and engenders new antagonisms; the present flows back toward the past and the past invests itself in the present.

Let us consider, finally, the peasantry, that social force which Marx sees as providing, in the last analysis, the real foundation of Bonapartist power. I briefly mentioned earlier that it is and is not a class:

> The small-holding peasants form a vast mass, the members of which live in similar conditions but without entering into manifold relations with one another. Their mode of production isolates them from one another instead of bringing them into mutual intercourse. . . . A small holding, the peasant and his family; alongside them another small holding, another peasant and another family . . . In this way, the great mass of the French nation is formed by simple addition of

homologous magnitudes, much as potatoes in a sack form a sack of potatoes. Insofar as millions of families live under economic conditions of existence that separate their mode of life, their interests and their culture from those of the other classes, and put them in hostile opposition to the latter, they form a class. Insofar as there is merely a local interconnection among these small-holding peasants, and the identity of their interests begets no community, no national bond and no political organization among them, they do not form a class.[76]

Now it is not as a class but as a non-class that the peasantry proves to be the foundation of Bonapartism. For the condition of its members is such that:

They cannot represent themselves, they must be represented. Their representative must at the same time appear as their master, as an authority over them, as an unlimited governmental power that protects them against the other classes and sends them rain and sunshine from above. The political influence of the small-holding peasants, therefore, finds its final expression in the executive power subordinating society to itself.[77]

In other words, the peasants dream of a power which would respond to the image of their dispersion, bring them unity from outside and turn the whole of society into a mass of atomized elements analogous to their own.

Marx abundantly underlines the fact that the characteristics of the French peasantry can be explained only in terms of the economic development of bourgeois society. He shows that the proliferation of small holdings was a direct result of the great Revolution and of the first Bonapartist regime, as well as being the condition of their success.

Under Napoleon, the fragmentation of the land in the countryside supplemented free competition and the beginning of big industry in the towns. Even the advantages given to the peasant class were in the interest of the new bourgeois order. . . . The peasant class was the ubiquitous protest against the landed aristocracy which had just been overthrown.[78]

In fact, it is only with Napoleon that a regime was established in which the peasants could recognize their power, since the latter must be separated from them in order to conform to their state of mutual separation. Such is the subsequent development of capitalism that the exploitation of the peasant is re-established under new forms and by new mechanisms. The feudal lord is succeeded by the city usurer; bourgeois capital replaces large landed property; the small holding, which had initially provided the bourgeoisie with some protection against the return of the *ancien régime*, is no more than 'the pretext that allows the capitalist to draw profits, interest and rent from the soil, while leaving it to the tiller of the soil himself to see how he can extract his wages'.[79] But this picture does not say everything. The worsening of the peasants' circumstances should induce them to become aware of the new situation created for them under the capitalist system – and indeed, notes Marx, they adopted a revolutionary attitude at several points, notably under the parliamentary Republic. Moreover, their political adherence to the second Bonapartist regime is not determined, in the last analysis, by interest, but by illusion. Misrecognizing the real conditions of their misery, which should lead them to join the proletariat in its struggle, they are moved by the 'phantoms of the empire'. 'Superstitious faith', 'prejudice' and the 'past' bind them to the Bonaparte dynasty. And their illusions weigh so heavily that it is the most revolutionary elements of one moment which turn out to be the most conservative; it is precisely in the 'reddest' regions that the peasant population votes finally for Bonaparte.

Once again, Marx interweaves an analysis of socio-economic conditions with an analysis of the social imaginary. It is impossible, we discover, to stop at the first. The constitution of the class which is a non-class does not suffice to explain the rise of the second Bonaparte. At the very most, it reveals an affinity between a certain type of social relations and a certain type of power. Actual history remains unintelligible if we do not take account of 'historical tradition'. The latter 'gave rise to the belief of the French peasants in the miracle that a man named Napoleon would bring all the glory back to them'.[80] It matters very little that the individual is *grotesque*, for it is a 'legend' which he embodies. It is the *idée fixe* of a class which converts into reality the *idée fixe* of an impostor. Once again, the interest of a class proves to be effective only when changed into representation, thus becoming the interest of the small holding of the past. The *idées napoléoniennes* are 'only the hallucinations of its death struggle, words that are transformed into phrases, spirits transformed into ghosts'.[81]

Now Marx extends this last analysis to the investigation of the army and the state bureaucracy. It is pointless to try to evaluate the function of the army within the limits of the present. It can be understood only by studying the 'real' conditions of historical development, but the latter cannot be dissociated from the imaginary depths of the peasantry. It is not enough to recall the role played by the army in the birth of the new society during the Revolution.

> The army was the *point d'honneur* of the small-holding peasants, it was they themselves transformed into heroes, defending their new possessions against the outer world, glorifying their recently won nationhood, plundering and revolutionising the world. The uniform was their own state dress; war was their poetry; the small holding, extended and rounded off in imagination, was their fatherland, and patriotism the ideal form of their sense of property.[82]

And that poetry arose, even though it was deprived of its inspiration, even though in fact the enemies of the peasants were no longer the Cossacks but the bailiffs and the tax collectors and even though the small holding was lodged no longer in the fatherland but in the register of mortgages.

As for the state bureaucracy, at best it forces us to recognize the ambiguity of bourgeois history. We must see within it the social force which Louis Napoleon needed in order to rise above all the classes. 'And an enormous bureaucracy, well-braided and well-fed, is the "*idée napoléonienne*" which is most congenial of all to the second Bonaparte.'[83] Of course, this idea, too, has its roots in reality. The immense bureaucratic and military organization began to be set up at the time of the absolute monarchy, during the struggle against feudalism. It was developed by the Revolution, whose task was to destroy all independent bases of power and local characteristics in order to create the bourgeois unity of the nation. Finally, Napoleon continued to perfect the mechanisms of state power: the Legitimate Monarchy and the July Monarchy did no more than extend to this sphere the division of labour which held sway in civil society. So the bureaucracy is certainly not an idle dream; it is an instrument of the political centralization necessary for bourgeois domination. Nevertheless, the process which tends to turn it into an independent power can only be partially explained in terms of its instrumental function. For the structure of capitalism is such that the general interest can never be established except in an illusory form at some distance from real society. Thus Marx says that 'Every *common* interest was straightway severed from society, counterposed to it as a higher, *general* interest, snatched from the activity of society's members themselves and made an object of government activity.'[84] In this severing off of state power, we see the outlines of the inversion carried out by Bonapartism, an inversion in which the product appears, and presents itself, as the author and master of civil society. While only outlined in *The Eighteenth Brumaire*, this analysis – which we know to have been fully developed, starting from other premises, in the *Critique of Hegel's Philosophy of Right* – suggests that the phantasm of Louis Napoleon is grafted onto a phantasm materialized in the political institution.

Who would think of denying the fact that Marx had sought to grasp the history of humanity and deliver the key to its development? We have not let this fact be forgotten in the course of these pages. But this ambition cannot account for the actual movement of his interpretation; to believe that it could is the illusion, maintained most often by posterity, that we wanted to dissipate.

The Marxist vision of history splits apart when one examines precapitalism, and splits apart again when it confronts the difference between precapitalism and capitalism; and most remarkably, this splitting is reproduced in the crucial case of the analysis of capitalism itself. Marx continuously and persistently tried to bring out, from a range of social transformations and a confusing mass of events, that which was properly historical – that is, which was able to produce a meaning in which the destiny of humanity was at stake. But he also tried always to describe the forces that were mobilized in order to defuse the effects of what is new. The moment when he recognized the definitive dislocation of all communal forms seems to me to be decisive: at that point, the labourer is no longer one with the means of labour; more importantly, he is separated from his own body, so that the present is no longer one with the past. Now this moment is precisely the one in which phantoms are set free, in which imaginary forces materialized in institutions dominate human beings, in which the past severed off from the present – as capital is from living labour – acquires an independent movement, both in representation and in reality.

Marx says that the tribal being, as represented in a god or a despot, embodies an imaginary community, over and above the multiplicity of actual communities, but he does not call this tribal being a phantom. The arrival of phantoms on the scene coincides with the emergence of a society without a body, a society devoid of substance. From then on, phantoms are within society, within history; they are, for example, the personifications of economic conditions, or they are the Roman heroes for the bourgeois of the French Revolution, or the eighteenth-century heroes for the bourgeois of 1848. Society as such, history as such, become themselves phantom-like entities, while nature is reabsorbed into the social and the historical.

And finally, how can one not see that, from this vision of history as well as from the vision of the irresistible movement of productive forces set loose by capitalism, there arises the image of this strange being, the proletariat: at once purely social, purely historical, and, as it were, outside society and history – a class which ceases to be one, since the dissolution of all classes takes place within it, and the only class which can act in a way which is free from the poetry of the past; a strange being who fulfils the destiny of humanity, but abolishes all tradition – an heir without a heritage. Should we say that it is the destroyer of the social imaginary or the last product of Marx's imagination?

# 6

# Outline of the Genesis of
# Ideology in Modern Societies

To outline an analysis of ideology is to spare oneself the work that would be required by a thorough critique of the ideological formations which can be discerned in determinate historical conditions. If such a critique were carried out, it is by no means clear that the outline would hold up in the actual circumstances, or that it would retain its original value. Indeed, its limitations are only too obvious. To present a *profile* of 'bourgeois ideology', without reference to dates or places, is to ignore many of the features which should be taken into consideration – for example, the relationship that the dominant discourses maintain, in differing circumstances, with the course of class conflict, the political regime, national tradition and cultural heritage. In re-examining these articulations, several forms might come to light where previously only one was discerned, and thus the assumed perspective would not be left intact. The suspicion which looms over the analysis of totalitarianism is no less serious. This analysis does not set Stalinism apart from Nazism or fascism, although it does not suggest that there are no differences between them. Moreover, nothing is said about the ideological transformations which have occurred since the 1950s in the USSR and in Eastern Europe, nor about that very unusual variant of totalitarianism which may be found in China. As for that ideology which, for lack of a better term, I describe as 'invisible' (not because it actually is, but because it seems to be organized in such a way as to blur the oppositions characteristic of the previous ideology): this ideology, which currently prevails in the Western democracies, is merely indicated rather than described in detail. No doubt many careful investigations would be necessary to uncover the discursive connections suggested here: from the nature of the organization to that of education; from the nature of the media to that of, for example, social psychology; or investigations of literary, philosophical and artistic expression. This latter shortcoming is all the more noticeable in that I seek to discover, by reflecting on this third form, the general properties of ideology and the principle of its transformation. Nevertheless, the presentation of my views in the form of an outline can be explained, if not justified, by the concern to reinitiate as quickly as possible a form of critique whose foundations are currently buried beneath the rubble of Marxism.

Indeed, how can we avoid mentioning the debasement of the concept of ideology in the use which is made of it both by sociologists or historians, who invoke the authority of science, and by revolutionary militants? Some have proclaimed 'the end of ideology' (a formula which was very popular at the beginning of the sixties and which has recently been revived), convinced that the imperatives of industrial society demand a gradual adaptation to reality and that the great doctrines no longer mobilize the masses. Others are content to denounce the decomposition of bourgeois ideology by calling attention to the powerlessness of dominant groups to defend the system of values which, from the industrial firm to the family, once governed the functioning of institutions to the advantage of dominant groups. Still others, from a different point of view, situate all thought at the level of ideology; indeed, faced with their adversaries, they do not hesitate to lay claim to a proletarian ideology, as if each class interest, determinate in itself, found direct and coherent expression in language.

In the first case, ideology is reduced to the *manifestation* of a global project of social transformation – that is, in fact, to the explicit discourse of a party, whether communist or fascist (or one of its variants); but the question of how it arose from the crisis of bourgeois ideology, and why the latter can manage without a general thesis on the organization of society, is effaced. In the second case, the ideology which is currently dominant is identified with bourgeois ideology, defined by the features that were formerly attributed to it by the Marxist movement, in such a way that one cannot, in principle, see the signs of a transformation in the decomposition of bourgeois ideology; and hence one succumbs either to the myth of a revolution in progress, at the point of bursting out, or to the myth of an unrestrained domination and exploitation, which are incapable from now on of recognizing, and securing the recognition of, their legitimacy. Finally, in the third case, the concept of ideology preserves no trace of the initial meaning from which it derived its critical force: ideology is reduced to the ideas that one 'defends' in order to assure the victory of a class, to a good or a bad 'cause', whose nature one knows or could know, and whose agent one knows or could know oneself to be.

In one way or another, the split between an order of practice and an order of representation – that split which Marx obliges us to examine – is ignored; or perhaps it would be better to say that it is 'dissimulated', in order to emphasize the fact that it is not a matter of the modification of a concept, but rather that it signals, in the misrecognition of the problem of ideology, an ideological blindness. It is similar to the way in which the misrecognition of the problem of the unconscious would not be a matter of an error in the reading of Freud, but rather would attest to a new resistance to a discovery which would endanger the certitudes of the subject.

Thus, by means of a remarkable ruse, ideology has come to designate almost the contrary of what it originally meant. Once referring to the logic of dominant ideas, removed from the knowledge of social actors and only revealing itself through interpretation, through the critique of utterances and their manifest connections, it has today been reduced to a corpus of theses, to the system of beliefs that provides the visible framework of a collective practice, identified with liberal-democratic discourse for some, with Leninist or Stalinist (indeed Maoist or Trotskyist) discourse for others, or even with fascist discourse; and it is identified with these discourses *in the very form in which they present themselves.*

To reopen the path to a critique of ideology, and to the examination of the present, is not, however, to return to the original purity of Marx's theory. Such a return would be doubly illusory, both because there is not, strictly speaking, a theory of ideologies in Marx's work – his analyses are ambiguous and one cannot make use of his work without interpreting it – and because the present can be deciphered only by drawing from it the resources that enable one to call into question the principles which govern its intelligibility. Moreover, to rejoin Marx's project can only mean that one reproduces his approach *at a distance* and includes, in the examination of ideology, an examination of thought about ideology. The distance certainly proves to be considerable, for Marx could conceive of ideology only with regard to 'bourgeois ideology' and it is incumbent upon us to recognize it in other forms and, moreover, to grasp the principle of its transformation. Nevertheless, we must stress the fact that Marx did not treat bourgeois ideology as a product of the bourgeoisie; rather, he leads us to relate it to social division and to link its origin to that of a particular historical formation, which he describes as the capitalist mode of production and which he regards as different from all previous formations, themselves grouped together under the category of precapitalism.

My outline begins from the following conception: it restricts ideology to a particular type of society, and thus formally challenges the application of the term to a feudal, despotic, or stateless structure in which the dominant discourse still draws its legitimacy from the reference to a transcendent order and leaves no room for the notion of a social reality intelligible in itself, nor, by the same token, for the notion of a history or a nature intelligible in itself. On the other hand, we clearly break with Marx's conception in so far as we do not treat ideology as a reflection, but seek to uncover its processes and to think of formation and transformation together, that is, to attribute to it the ability to articulate and rearticulate itself, not only in response to the supposed 'real', but in face of the effects of its own dissimulation of the real. So this break, it should be stressed, concerns not only the conception of ideology, but also the conception of the mode of production, or the Marxist definition of the locus of reality.

The society whose specificity Marx conceives of by contrast to all previous formations comes into being with the split between capital and labour. Class oppositions are condensed in the antagonism between bourgeoisie and proletariat. The separation between the state and civil society corresponds to the need for a power which represents the law in everyone's eyes and which possesses the means of generalized constraint; detached from the dominant class, the state is capable of making its general interests prevail over the particular interests of one faction or another and of maintaining the obedience of dominated groups. At the same time, the fragmentation of sectors of activity, tending to organize each under the image of its autonomy, arises as a consequence of the growing division of labour and the need for specialists to take charge of the social needs of bourgeois domination (the political splits off from the economic at the same time as the legal, scientific, educational, aesthetic and other sectors are delimited). In this society, the conditions for the unity of the process of socialization are already set out; capital already embodies, without individuals knowing it, materialized social power, whereas with the increasing abstraction of labour, a class arises which is more and more homogeneous and which tends to absorb all the exploited strata. However, this latent unity can become effective only by the negation of the division, a negation whose driving force lies in the revolutionary class, in a praxis in which its productive force and its struggle against exploitation are articulated. The contradictions which stem from the accumulation of capital and from the separation of the various sectors of activity within the overall structure, the gap between them, their unequal development, social struggles (above all class struggles, but also those between groups linked to specific interests and practices): all these make capitalist society an essentially *historical* society, that is, a society destined to undergo a process of continuous institutional upheaval, destined to give birth to new social forms and explicitly to experience the real as history.

In the context of such a description, ideology is specified in turn as a separate domain; it constitutes a world of ideas in which an essence of the social is represented: oppositions of every kind are changed into determinations of the universal, domination is converted into an expression of the law. The affinity between the political and the ideological is evident: just as power splits off from a thoroughly divided society in order to embody the generality of the law and to exercise physical constraint (simultaneously transposing and distinguishing the domination of a class), so too ideological discourse splits off from all forms of social practice in order to embody the generality of knowledge and to exercise the force of persuasion (simultaneously transposing and disguising, in the form of an idea, the fact of domination). Indeed, in the final analysis, the political and the ideological are intelligible only if one recognizes both the fact that the process of socialization has not been completed, and the fact that the possibility of this completion is inscribed *in reality*, a possibility to which communism will give effective expression. But whereas the political is still determined within the limits of the process of socialization, ideology realizes in an imaginary way that unity which only a real movement – namely, the negativity of labour and of proletarian praxis – will bring about.

Fruitful as it may be, this analysis (which certainly does not summarize all of Marx's thought) misrepresents the symbolic dimension of the social domain. It is impossible, in my view, to deduce the order of law, of power or of knowledge from the relations of production; it is also impossible to reduce the language in which social practice is articulated to the effects of the labour–capital division. These relations are organized, and these effects develop, only as a function of *conditions* that we cannot situate at the level of the real; on the contrary, such conditions become accessible to us, are organized and become intelligible, only when the reference points of a new experience of law, power and knowledge are established, only when a mode of discourse is developed in which certain oppositions and certain practices actually *take hold* – that is, relate to one another and potentially contain a universal sense, in allowing for a regulated exchange between action and thought.

At the origin of capitalism may be found, according to Marx, the development of exchange relations and the progressive establishment of a market; but, despite its considerable expansion and the maturity of its techniques, commercial activity came up against limits within other social formations (for example, in China) which prevented it from spreading. These obstacles formed part of the symbolic system, that is, of a configuration of the signifiers of law, power and knowledge which did not permit the dismantling of the social relations of personal dependence. At the origin of the accumulation of capital could be found, as well, the naked violence of dominant groups, who tore peasants away from their means of production and reduced them to the status of pure labour power. But what Marx calls the original sin of capitalism was also the original sin of his theory, for the violence which 'gave birth' to the new mode of production was not silent. It was sustained by a representation of cause and effect, whose articulation was meaningless in other social conditions; it was inscribed in a discourse which could find the criterion of its coherence within its own limits, and which could become the basis for an articulation of the law and the real.

No description of the changes that have occurred in production, exchange and ownership could enable us to understand what is brought into play with the formation of the modern state. It is the very *stage* of the social which *appears* at that point when political power is circumscribed *within* society, as the instrument which confers unity upon it, at that point when this power is supposed to originate from the very domain supposedly produced by its action. It is the institution of the social which is represented on this stage; and it is in the events that are acted out there, in the relations that are formed between individuals and groups, that the web of the 'real' may be found.

Although power is brought within the boundaries of the space and time where social relations are articulated and is thereby disconnected from the law that it represents, this does not mean that it becomes *de facto* power. If it were to appear as such, the reference points of social identity would be destroyed. However, it is true that power is exposed to this threat as soon as its representation is caught up in the institution of the social; and not only in so far as it appears to be generated within society, but also in so far as it appears as founder, since it is henceforth deprived of the signs of its own foundation, cut off from the order of the world from which it drew the assurance of its function. Thus it can be established under the sign of the law only if it always re-establishes itself through the deployment of a *discourse* – where the difference between the self and the other, and the difference between saying and what is said, are related to the identity of the social subject. This discourse is itself ambiguous, for it cannot appear as the product of power without falling, in turn, into the realm of fact, nor can it refer to a transcendent guarantee without losing its properties. Hence it is concerned to produce its own 'truth' in the course of being uttered, to affirm its *discursive power*, in such a way that its determination as the discourse of power is negated. This ambiguity is such that power proves for the first time to be simultaneously localized and non-localizable. It is non-localizable in so far as it arises at the intersection of two movements which refer back to one another, in so far as it is produced by the society that it produces; but it is necessarily localized in so far as it is tied down to the social field.

The disentangling of the social order and the order of the world goes together with the disentangling of the political and the mythical-religious; but, by the same necessity, it also goes together with the disentangling of the political and the non-political *within* the social order. Only under these conditions can one make sense of the differentiation of economic, legal, educational, scientific, aesthetic and other practices, which exist, not simply as given practices (in the pores of society, to use the Marxist metaphor), but as practices in which the reality of the social as such is put into play. And, simultaneously, this differentiation is a differentiation of social discourses, of 'particular' discourses, but ones which are concerned to claim universal truth. The oscillation indicated between the discourse of power and the power of discourse contains the possibility of a disjunction between power and discourse. In other words, each particular discourse exercises its power, not only at a distance from institutionalized political power, but in contradiction with the determination of power represented in itself, in so far as it is articulated with a particular practice which is characterized by social division. Thus each discourse tends to set off in search of its own foundation; in its very deployment each discourse forms a relation to knowledge, the limits of which are not strictly determined in the sense that there is no general knowledge of the order of the world and of the social order in conjunction with the power of the state. The fact that the various discourses are interrelated in no way means that they can be condensed into one, for the truth is not simply that they are simultaneously instituted as a function of the same experience; they take part in the institution of the social and decipher it through the disarticulation of power and the law and through their own differentiation, each referring back to itself in elaborating its difference.

With such a process, it is not a question of attributing the *cause* to the *fact* of the modern state. To do that would be to succumb to the same illusion that I denounced in Marx's work; it would merely transfer to another level the determinism that Marx was tempted to locate at the level of the relations of production. Furthermore, we could say that the characteristics of the modern state are determined only in a system in which knowledge bears the mark of its differentiation, in which discourse bears within itself the mark of otherness (instead of speech being organized around the external pole of the Other), events whose beginnings were laid down by the humanism of the Renaissance. If, however, I use the term 'political' to describe the 'form' in which the symbolic dimension of the social is revealed, it is not in order to give priority to relations of power at the expense of others; rather, it is in order to make it clear that power is not 'a thing', empirically determined, but is inseparable from its representation, and that the excercise of it – being simultaneously the exercise of knowledge, the mode of articulation of social discourse – is constitutive of social identity.

From this point of view, the break with Marx goes so far as to touch upon what is for him the ultimate question: the future unity of the process of socialization *in reality*. The question of unity cancels out the question of social identity. The latter question could not arise

illusions of bourgeois economics and of the phantasmagoria of the market provides the basis for the discovery of the unity of social labour and the process of value formation. Nor should we underestimate, by virtue of having become all too familiar with his method, the audacity of his attempt to discern the signs of a logic of dissimulation in all dominant modes of representation, and especially in those philosophical discourses which claim to offer a radical critique of established ideas. Finally, we should not fail to observe that the distinction between reality and ideology is immediately articulated in his work with the implicit distinction between knowledge and ideology, and that the latter distinction prevents the terms of the former from being situated at the level of objective knowledge. In fact, it is when he dismantles, in his *Critique of Hegel's Philosophy of Right*, the mechanism of Hegel's philosophical system, of its 'folly', that Marx acquires for the first time an understanding of the ideological phenomenon. What he reveals is not merely the attempt to substitute an ideal genesis of the state for its real genesis (a process of inverting reality); it is not merely the transposition of contingent socio-historical determinations into the space of theory and the imaginary solution of existing contradictions (a process of idealization). He also reveals a movement of knowledge that closes in on itself, simulating the mastery of the totality and dissimulating from itself the fact of its own production, thereby effacing the division between thought and being. We must recognize that in ideology (and it is of little importance that the concept has not yet been strictly defined, for the outline of its constituent features has been brought to light) a triple denial is effected: the denial of class division, articulated with the division of social labour; the denial of temporal division, the destruction–production of forms of social relations; and, finally, the denial of the division between knowledge and the practice that it reflects, and on the basis of which it is instituted as such. Moreover, when Marx analyses the state and the bureaucracy (and no longer the Hegelian representation of them), and when, later, forgetting the 'folly' of the philosophical system, he concerns himself only with understanding the 'folly' of the capitalist system, it is in order to bring to light the same process. The discourse inscribed in the institution sustains the illusion of an essence of society; it staves off the double threat which weighs upon the established order by virtue of the fact that it is divided and the fact that it is historical; it imposes itself as a discourse rational in itself, a closed discourse which, while masking the conditions of its own production, claims to reveal that of empirical social reality.

My aim is not to analyse Marx's thought. If that were the case, it would have to be acknowledged straightaway that his distinction between knowledge and ideology contains only the beginnings of the critique of any discourse claiming to stand over reality while mis-recognizing the conditions which secure its position of externality. It would also have to be acknowledged that he himself yielded to the temptation to occupy this position of externality by investing the positive sciences with the certainty which he had stripped away from philosophy. Nevertheless, it is important to reformulate briefly Marx's problem, to prise it apart from the dogmatic commentaries which have obscured it, in order to assess the theoretical demands that he has imposed upon us as well as the limits which must be overcome if we wish to take up his interpretation again in examining contemporary societies.

This problem is posed in terms which preclude the reduction of ideology to the discourse of the bourgeoisie, and hence which prevent one from retaining only its function of mystification, justification and conservation in the interests of one class. Of course, this func-tion was amply emphasized by Marx, notably in *The German Ideology*, but is intelligible only if ideology is first considered in relation to its primary focus: social division. Marx implies that a society can relate to itself, can exist as a human society, only on the condition that it forges a representation of its unity – a unity which, in reality, both attests to the relation of reciprocal dependence of social agents and is concealed by the separation of their activities. Although social divi-sion is not determined by the universal division between classes (the division between the bourgeoisie and the proletariat), the existence of 'restricted social relations' entails the projection of an imaginary community, under the cover of which 'real' distinctions are deter-mined as 'natural', the particular is disguised beneath the features of the universal and the historical is effaced in the atemporality of essence. The representation in which the social relation is embedded marks in itself the place of power, since the imaginary community rules over individuals or separate groups and imposes behavioural norms upon them. In this sense, the universal assumes the task of inserting those who are dominated into their condition of domi-nation and providing those who dominate with the assurance of their own position.

Nonetheless, the viewpoint of class domination and the viewpoint of 'representation', however closely linked they may be, do not coincide. Analysing Asiatic depotism, Marx observes that the prince embodies the imaginary community which stands above the dispersed rural communities. The 'real' power – which can be located, in practice, by the signs of command (control of a bureaucratic apparatus), of constraint (recruiting peasant labour for war or for state objectives) and of exploitation (extraction of surplus value from agricultural production) – this empirically determinable power is framed in a representation which both reflects social division (the absolute distance between the master and the enslaved people symbolically transposes the brute separation of rural communities) and conceals that division. Still, it is true that this is a limiting case, since the bureaucracy exists as a class only through the mediation of the despot; it is also true that the discourse of the despot (be he a god, a demi-god or a divine representative) tends to be confused with the discourse of the universal. The indications Marx gives concerning the formation of classes in *The German Ideology* are even more suggestive. He brings to light a division between individuals such as they are determined in a collective relation, in terms of their common interests *vis-à-vis* a third party, and these same individuals defined as members of a class, receiving their identity as 'average individuals' and finding themselves related to a 'community' which is detached from the actual movement of the division of labour, hovering over the individuals and representing, by effacing the third party, the essence of the social. From this point of view, the class itself – unlike the economic category on to which it is grafted – proves to be caught up in the ideological process. The analysis in *The Eighteenth Brumaire* reveals, moreover, that its formation as the dominant political class implies a denial of temporal difference, the misrecognition of the present; the disguising of the present beneath the features of the Roman past proves to be a necessary condition for the revolutionary action of the bourgeoisie.

## Social Division is not in Society

If this is the path that Marx seems to open up, there can be no doubt that he also closes it off. Indeed, he could not follow this path while claiming, at the same time, to determine the nature of the social by means of the positive sciences, thus succumbing to the fiction of an intrinsic development accessible to the observer, and while reasoning in terms of a crude opposition between *production* and *representation*. Of course, it must be recognized that the concept of production has a very broad sense in Marx's work. He observes that human beings produce not only the tools necessary to meet their needs, and, having satisfied these needs, produce not only new needs; they also produce their social relations. It could even be said that language falls within the sphere of production, since Marx acknowledges that it appears with the necessity for commerce among human beings and since, in sum, he envisages its development by relating it to the model of a communication between individuals or groups, which is one aspect of the social relation. Nevertheless, the usage of the concept of production, however broad it may be, continues to serve as a guarantee of the natural evolution of humanity. It is true that human beings produce both their instruments of production and their social relations; and what is produced is, in turn, a productive force, in such a way that human beings are also produced by what they produce; but the idea that production is self-production does not eliminate the mechanistic character of Marx's construction. The social state of affairs turns out, in the last analysis, to be a combination of terms whose identity – whether it be a matter of the needs, instruments, linguistic signs or labour of an individual or collective agent – is never called into question. From such a viewpoint, the concept of the division of labour itself refers to a brute fact, to a fact of evolution, of course, but to a fact which is situated in a field secretly laid out in advance, in such a way as to give the impression that the elements are naturally determined.

Nothing could be more significant in this regard than Marx's attempt, in *The German Ideology*, to return to the origins of the division of labour and his assertion that originally it was nothing other than the division of labour in the sexual act. There, unequivocally, Marx's positivism is revealed. His thesis presupposes precisely that which is not explained: a division of the sexes in such a way that the partners would naturally identify themselves as different, and hence would naturally come to reflect upon this difference and to represent themselves as man and woman. It is clear that this is no mere deviation in the interpretation, for, in the same section of *The German Ideology*, while Marx is enumerating the three fundamental conditions of the history of humanity, procreation is presented as the act of production of the family, of the double relation man–woman and parent–child. Just as copulation is thought to provide the original model of co-operation and social division, procreation is supposed to provide the model of the historical production of humanity. In both cases, what is negated is the articulation of the division – between the sexes or the generations – with the 'thought' of the division, a thought which cannot be deduced from the division since it is implicated in the definition of its terms. What is negated is the symbolic order, the idea of a system of oppositions by virtue of which social forms can be identified and articulated with one another; what is negated is the relation between the division of social agents and representation. In other words, Marx refuses to recognize that social division is also, in a primordial way, the division between the process of socialization and the discourse which describes it.

To criticize Marx does not at all imply that we must assert the primacy of representation and fall back into the illusion, which he denounced, of an independent logic of ideas; nor does it lead us away from the task of discovering the mechanisms which tend to secure the representation of an imaginary essence of the community. On the contrary, I wish to conceptualize these mechanisms, but without succumbing to the naturalist fiction. Such an attempt presupposes that we no longer confuse social division with the empirical distribution of individuals in the process of production. We cannot determine it any more than we could determine the division of the sexes in an objective space that supposedly preexisted it; we cannot relate it to positive terms, even though they emerge as such in its very movement. We must appreciate that it is the social space which is instituted with the division, and it is instituted only in so far as it appears to itself. Its differentiation through relations of kinship or class, through the relation between state and civil society, is inseparable from the deployment of a discourse at a distance from the supposed real, a discourse which enunciates the order of the world. Hence it would be impossible to take up a position which would enable one to grasp the totality of social relations and the interplay of their articulations. Similarly, it would be impossible to grasp the totality of historical development, to establish a beginning and an end of social division, since we would then be concealing from ourselves our own insertion in the domain of discourse which is already implicated in the division, and this oversight would lead us to regard our representation as real in itself.

At this point, what seems to me to define the limits of Marx's thought is the fact that he treats the process of representation as if it were produced by the activities of co-operation and division, as if this reality were determined at the natural level of labour. Thus he could not avoid the risk of confusing the order of the ideological with the order of the symbolic, of reducing mythological, religious, political, legal and other discourses to the projection of 'real' conflicts into the imaginary, of demoting the indices of law and power to the empirical level, thereby transforming them into social 'products'.

## The Imaginary and 'Historical Society'

This critique must be pressed further. To say that the institution of the social is simultaneously the appearance-to-itself of the social lends itself to misunderstanding. For one is once again tempted to think of the emergence of the discourse on the social in terms of the emergence of the social space, and thus to reconstitute a version – albeit a more sophisticated one – of sociologism. In fact, the misunderstanding is already present when we speak of the 'discourse on the social', as if it were possible to grasp it as such, to include within it the discourse which enunciates the order of the world as well as the discourse which enunciates the order of the body; as if the question of social division, even freed from empiricism, included in itself the question of the division between human beings and the world, as well as the question of the divisions between the sexes and the generations; as if, in particular, the question of where human beings come from and the question of birth could be reduced to the question of origin as it is inscribed in society through myth or religion. In each period, the discourse of human beings is governed by a meta-sociological and meta-psychological question. We misunderstand it when we believe that we can enclose it within certain limits; but we misunderstand it more seriously still when we forget, as a result, that the discourse on the social does not coincide with itself in the social space where it is deployed and which it simultaneously institutes. We misunderstand it when we forget, finally, that what it articulates presupposes the fact of its own articulation, or, in other words, that the processes of division and institution are 'older' than those of social division and social institution. The limits of Marx's thought are thus most clearly revealed by the attempt to conceive of the social from within the boundaries of the social, history from within the boundaries of history, human beings in terms of, and with a view to, human beings. Hence Marx fails to address, not the relations between human beings and 'nature' (for he speaks of this constantly in order to assure himself of an objective determination of human beings within a naturalist perspective), but rather the relation of human beings, the social and history to what is in principle beyond their reach, on the basis of which this relation is produced and which remains implicit in it.

It is in becoming aware of these limits that we are led to reformulate the conditions of an analysis of ideology. We cannot, as previously noted, undertake to delimit ideology with reference to a reality whose features would be derived from positive knowledge, without thereby losing a sense of the operation of the constitution of reality and without placing ourselves in the illusory position of claiming to have an overview of Being. On the other hand, we can attempt to understand how, in a given period, the dominant discourse is organized in such a way as to dissimulate the process of social division, or what we could now just as well call the process of generating the social space – or indeed, of generating the *historical*, in order to make it clear that social division and temporality are two aspects of the same institution. No doubt it will have to be admitted that such a discourse, in so far as it is embedded in the division, can only remain, in the course of describing the social space, opaque to itself. But it is an altogether different matter to say that it embodies a form of knowledge whose principle is hidden from it and that it is organized in accordance with the need to dissimulate the traces of social division, that is, the need to represent an order which would seem to secure the natural determination of its articulation and, with this, the articulation of social relations *here* and *now*. Discourse *qua* instituting is deprived of any knowledge of the institution; but in so far as it is concerned with staving off the threat which weighs upon it as a consequence of this task, the threat of the manifestation of a gap between being and discourse, it is actively engaged in negating the institution of the social. It is the discourse of occultation in which symbolic reference points are transformed into natural determinations, in which the enunciation of the social law, the law of the world and the law of the body come to mask the unthinkable connection between the law and the enunciation, the dependence of the law on the person who utters it and the dependence of speech on the law.

Nevertheless, we must immediately reflect on the condition under which it is possible to grasp this distinction. It presupposes that the institution of the social space has become perceptible to itself, in such a way that the instituting discourse cannot efface its traces through the operation of the imaginary. In other words, it presupposes that social division and historicity have come to prevail in such a way that the work of occultation remains subject to their effects, in such a way that, through the failures of occultation, in the continual attempt to correct them, through its discordances, it allows what we can now justly call the *real* to appear, the latter term indicating that here it is a question of that which marks the impossibility of achieving concealment. In this sense, the examination of ideology confronts us with the determination of a type of society in which a specific regime of the imaginary can be identified.

Although Marx, as we have just pointed out, was tempted to transform social division into the empirical division of classes and succumbed to the illusion of a determinism which would govern the sequence of modes of production, it is still to him that we owe this idea of the modification of the regime of the imaginary. In opposing the capitalist mode of production to all previous ones, he glimpsed the peculiarity of a mode of institution of the social in which the effects of division and historicity can no longer be neutralized under the sign of representation. In seeking to define Asiatic despotism (to which we have already alluded), he actually undermines his own account, since he asserts that this social formation tends to reproduce itself as such, independently of all events, wars, migrations and changes of dynasty; that the economic and social organization is as if petrified by the absolute separation of the imaginary community and the rural communities. In so doing, he encourages one to call into question the respective functions of production and representation, by allowing it to be assumed that the first is subordinate to the second. Although he refrains from presenting despotism as an imaginary formation which is grafted on to the reality of the division of labour, he cannot avoid, at the same time, recognizing that it has a symbolic efficacy (which is attested to by the very characterization of the mode of production in non-economic terms); but above all, by examining a limiting case, he clarifies a distinctive feature of all precapitalist formations. The assertion that their mode of production remains essentially conservative in spite of all the historical differences, that the division of labour and social relations always tend to crystallize there and to resist the forces of change, is in fact intelligible only if one recognizes the full efficacy of the symbolic device which, by virtue of the separation of two places – that of the law, of the discourse on the social and of the power which both supports and guarantees this discourse, on the one hand, and the place of actual social relations, on the other – renders possible the inscription of the established order of social groups and agents in the order of the world, and thus defuses the effects of social division. This device has the peculiar characteristic of being able to secure the conditions of occultation without allowing the question of an opposition between the imaginary and the real to arise. Indeed, the real turns out to be determinable only in so far as it is assumed to be already determined, by virtue of an utterance which, mythical or religious, attests to a knowledge whose basis cannot be brought into play by the actual process of knowledge, by technical inventiveness or by the interpretation of the *visible*. Discourse is indeed instituting: it governs the possibility of an articulation of the social. But it defines oppositions as 'natural', and thus stabilizes the status of the dominant and dominated groups in relations of kinship and class, by means of the dissimulation of social division in the representation of a division which is massively affirmed – in the representation, that is, of another world, of a materialized invisibility. We can only grasp the full significance of this operation if we appreciate that, in a sense, it realizes a possibility implicit in the institution of the social; for it makes it seem that this institution is not in itself a social fact, that the question of the social space is, from the outset, a question of its limits or its 'outside' (just as the question of the body is that of its origin and its death), that discourse is not only the product of individuals but that they are articulated in it. In rejecting the idea that myths and religions are mere human inventions, we are once again transgressing the boundaries of Marxism, but only in order to follow in its wake and to attempt to formulate a model in which the symbolic device is such that the dissimulation of social division coincides with the actual power to check its effects, and in which the dissimulation of the historical coincides with the actual power to block the path of change or to contain its development.

If I were to try to conceptualize the genesis of the different types of social formation, I would have to refine these statements considerably. The differences between the structures of a primitive society, of Asiatic despotism, of the ancient city-state and of European feudalism are so great that it may seem somewhat arbitrary to treat them as variants of a single model. From the perspective that I have developed, I am obliged, in particular, to overlook an essential articulation – that of power with the discourse on the social – which alone can reveal the movement in which the pole of enunciation is dissociated from the pole of the law and where the contingency of the utterance and its function of occultation run the risk of being disclosed. It must be acknowledged that, when the place of power is kept 'empty' and social relations are organized in terms of its neutralization (as in certain primitive societies), there is no criterion which would mark the distinction between the imaginary and the real, whereas when power is linked to the action of individuals and disconnected from the law, the possibility of this distinction is already present. Nevertheless, it turns out in every case that the origin of the discourse about the order of the world and the order of the social is conceived of from *elsewhere*.

Marx himself is able to develop this model (irrespective of his claim to produce a theory of the evolution of humanity) only on the basis of his analysis of the capitalist mode of production. It is in discovering that the latter is essentially 'revolutionary' – that is, not subject to haphazard occurrences but in itself productive of events that continually modify established relations – that Marx is led to draw a general contrast between two types of social formations.

Let us briefly recall the two features which, in Marx's view, characterize modern society: on the one hand, the unification of the social domain through the generalization of exchange and the reduction of all concrete labour to abstract labour; and on the other hand, the split between capital and labour, the concentration of the means of production and the formation of an ever-increasing mass of social agents reduced to the mere deployment of their labour power. These two features are inseparably linked: society becomes increasingly inter-connected in all its parts – or, in the language of the young Marx, the 'reciprocal dependence' of all social agents becomes increasingly achieved – to the extent that, for the first time, a split occurs between two antagonistic poles whose relation to one another affects the identity of the whole. Thus the social space tends to appear within its own limits (and not with reference to another place from where it would be visible) as soon as all divisions are subordinated to a general division, as soon as kinship and territorial relations and, more generally, relations of personal dependence, are dissolved and as soon as each of the two terms of the division, by the negation of its opposite, refers to the unity of the social. Of course, these operations are not symmetrical. The mass of workers carries out the negation by creating the image of the collective producer (who recognizes itself only in the abolition of the division), whereas capital, the embodiment of social power, realizes itself only by deepening the division and by creating the image of a class locked in the phantasy of being the universal class while remaining a *particular* class. Within this process lies the origin of ideology, as the attempt to represent the universal from the particular point of view of the dominant class. The uniqueness of this attempt consists in the fact that it is rooted in the social division, that it stems, as it were, directly from it. As I have already said, this attempt cannot be interpreted in terms of collective psychology; it must be seen, instead, as the sign of a logic which is built into the institution of the social from the moment that division no longer finds its expression in the division between the world of production and the world of representation, but rather is represented within the world of production itself, that is, is concealed by the image of a rationality immanent in the real. In this sense, the uniqueness of the attempt also lies in the fact that it occurs together with the movement which frees capital from all the limitations imposed by restricted social relations and which invests in it, as a socialized system of exploitation, an unlimited power for objectification and for the rationalization of production. The ideological process is different from the religious process not only because it tends to develop within the limits of the social space, but also because, in so doing, it becomes intricately linked with 'scientific' knowledge, a knowledge which claims to be the self-deciphering of reality. But, equally importantly, the ideological process is distinguished by the fact that it is subject to the effects of the incessant social upheaval generated by capitalism, in which institutions, attitudes and collective forms of behaviour are modified, in which the centres of power are shifted, in which the bourgeois strata, which draw their income and power from different sources, enter into opposition; by the fact, therefore, that it must carry out its task of concealing the division by modifying its own statements or by having recourse simultaneously to a multiplicity of representations in order to seal the cracks which change opens up in the 'rationality of the real'.

At this point we can see the unique relation between ideology and 'historical society'. The imaginary is no longer part of a symbolic device which tends to define the institution of the social by referring the detail of social organization to a discourse which is split off from it. Rather, in so far as the question of the genesis of the social is raised from the sphere of the social itself (the mastery of this genesis, the means of denying and containing it remaining hidden), a new type of discourse comes into being, concerned with defusing the oppositions and ruptures on the twin levels of time and space. In other words, ideology is the sequence of representations which have the function of re-establishing the dimension of society 'without history' at the very heart of historical society.

If we exploit once again the full sense of Marx's words, we see that the idea of 'conservation' fulfils a strategic function in his interpretation. In all precapitalist formations, it is the mode of production which is conservative; in capitalism, it is the ideology which is conservative and which is assigned the task of concealing the revolution that resides in the mode of production. Marx undoubtedly sensed that, in this latter case, the imaginary has become one sphere within the institution of the social, as a result of the manifest breakdown of every symbolic system capable of mastering this institution. Marx may indeed, like Feuerbach, continue to treat religion as a typical expression of ideology; but, in demonstrating that religion has emigrated into social relations, he glimpses the specificity of ideology: the tacit recognition of historicity and of division, and indeed the recognition of the implication of representation in that which it represents. He glimpses the fact that in modern societies the process of the imaginary goes hand in hand with an unprecedented experience of the 'real' as such. By reflecting on this emergent distinction between the real and the imaginary, he acquires the ability to apply it to social formations within which it would be indecipherable. But this ability is sustained by an illusion which lies at the heart of modern society: namely, that the institution of the social can account for itself. Marx grasps the principle of ideology as a specific mode of the imaginary, but he continues to suppose that it can be reduced to the dissimulation of *something*: class division, the division between capital and labour, between the state and civil society, between the historical present and its tasks. He does so without ever going so far as to consider that if it effectively ensures this dissimulation, it is governed and sustained by a principle of occultation which has been substituted for the one that governed the symbolic system of all precapitalist formations. The impossibility of a discourse on the social which is generated from its own place is no less radical than the impossibility of a discourse which is generated from elsewhere.

We must not confuse ideology with the misrecognition of this impossibility which, regarded more generally, is the same one that is confronted by every discourse in modern societies, in that every discourse is in search of its own foundation. Moreover, we should not say today that Marx's thought is ideological, any more than we should say the same of any other work to which we attribute an innovatory power in modern times. Again, social discourse, and not only the discourse which is expressed in theoretical works, cannot be considered as ideological on the sole grounds that it is developed in relation to such an impossibility. Furthermore, I consider the argument that discredits the principles of democratic discourse by reducing them to statements of bourgeois democracy to be false, although I do recognize therein the impossible attempt to lodge the instituting moment within the instituted. It is under the reign of such confusions that a critique by part of the *intelligentsia* is developing at the present time. It sees the signs of ideology everywhere, it proliferates condemnations of political discourse as such, of economic, legal, philosophical or educational discourse, without being able to assess what was involved in each particular case, and what is still involved each time that the attempt is made, on the basis of instituted knowledge, to bring thought into contact with the instituting moment. Such an attempt, by virtue of its very inability to succeed, turns discourse into a place of labour whose effect is to keep open the questioning which lies at its source, in spite of all the arguments that are asserted and affirmed. And in this sense (the paradox is only apparent), this mode of discourse attests, in the very movement which condemns it to a certain blindness, to that which is beyond the grasp of acting and knowing, a relation to the enigma of the institution. If we were to regard as ideology the discourse which confronts the impossibility of its self-genesis, this would mean that we would be converting this impossibility into a positive fact, we would believe in the possibility of mastering it; we would once again be placing ourselves in the illusory position of looking down at every discourse in order to 'see' the division from which it emerges, whereas discourse can only reveal this in itself. My view is altogether different. I maintain that ideology is organized by a principle of occultation which does not derive from its activity: it marks a folding over of social discourse on to itself, thereby suppressing all the signs which could destroy the sense of certainty concerning the nature of the social: signs of historical creativity, of that which has no name, of what is hidden from the action of power, of what breaks apart through the dispersed effects of socialization – signs of what makes a society, or humanity as such, alien to itself.

Such is the nature of ideological discourse, already glimpsed by Marx, I suggested, but deceptively related to a hidden reality (the state of the division of labour determined by that of the productive forces); it is a secondary discourse which follows the lines of the instituting discourse, which does not know itself and, under the latter's influence, attempts to simulate a general knowledge of the real as such. Hence it is a discourse which develops in the affirmative mode, the mode of determination, of generalization, of the reduction of differences, of externality with regard to its object and, as such, it always implies a viewpoint of power. It is a discourse which carries the guarantee of an actual or virtual order and which tends to become anonymous in order to attest to a truth imprinted in things. This second discourse draws nothing from its own depths; and it is this fact which justifies Marx's comment that ideology has no history. But it would be a mistake to conclude that it is linked to a determinate body of statements. We can already see that its dependence on the instituting discourse has several effects. In the first place, it tends to take hold of the signs of the new in order to incorporate them into its work of dissimulating the historical, in such a way that the representation of the 'modern' – we shall come back to this – is extremely effective in masking temporal difference. Second, it tends to carry out its project of homogenizing the field by dealing with, in order to defuse, the questions which arise as a consequence of the differentiation of the social space and the conflicts between classes or groups. It is in this way that the delimitation of a political practice, which we have no right to call ideological as such, gives rise to a particular discourse which actively elaborates the image of an essence of the political (whether this is to affirm its rationality or its ultimate irrationality is not important). This operation is repeated, beginning with the delimitation of a legal, aesthetic and educational practice; its efficacy consists in the fact that the same schemata govern each discourse, so that each one refers to the others and constitutes a link in the general discourse on the social. But it is equally true that the different strata come to speak – each in accordance with the conditions in which it is placed and its particular aspirations – a language at the service of 'rationality' and the 'real', of the dissimulation of any temporal or spatial break; and the effect of this is to ensure the complementarity of the representations in a particular period. Third, the attempt to fill in the lacunae of the general discourse, always subjected to the ordeal of the impossible mastery of the instituting moment, imposes a successive recourse to disparate schemes of explanation, schemes which are logically incompatible, although one model evidently predominates. The task of ideological discourse is distributed not only among different social agents; this discourse is obliged to displace its references in order to nourish its justification – references, for example, to the past and the future, to ethics and technical rationality, to the individual and the community. It is condemned, in this sense, to make the most of what it has, to adapt itself to heterogeneous versions in order to preserve the effectiveness of its general response.

Nevertheless, these remarks are not sufficient. Even when corrected in this way, the proposition that ideology has no history might well be misleading, for it masks the contradiction in which ideology is ensnared and which governs its transformations. Moreover, it may conceal from us the logic of the social imaginary in historical society. We can find the driving force of ideological changes not only in 'real' history, as Marx believed; to some extent, the necessity for its reorganization is determined by the failure of the process of dissimulation of the institution of the social. Ideology cannot operate without disclosing itself, that is, without revealing itself as a discourse, without letting a gap appear between this discourse and that about which it speaks, and hence it entails a development which reflects the impossibility of effacing its traces.

Bourgeois ideology, which Marxists persist in confusing with ideology as such (prisoners that they are of an empiricist schema that reduces it to a determinate state of class division) only constitutes one instance of ideology. It is by examining the signs of its failure that the genesis of totalitarian ideology is brought to light. And in uncovering the limits of the latter, we may gain some understanding of the mechanisms which govern the social imaginary in contemporary Western societies and whose efficacy presupposes both the exploitation and the neutralization of the totalitarian enterprise.

## So-called 'Bourgeois' Ideology

Everything that I have said concerning the general properties of ideology applies to bourgeois ideology. One can discern, at its peak in the nineteenth century, a social discourse which is external to the social, a discourse governed by the illusion of an interpretation of the real from within the real and which tends to present itself as an anonymous discourse in which the universal speaks of itself. Whatever support it may draw from religion during certain periods and for certain strata of the dominant class, this discourse is subject to the ideal of positive knowledge and thrives on challenging, explicitly or implicitly, any reference to an 'elsewhere' from which knowledge about the social order and the order of the world might be gathered. But we must not overlook the uniqueness of the mechanism by means of which ideological discourse attempts to fulfil its function. It is organized in terms of a split between *ideas* and the supposed *real*. The external character of the 'elsewhere', linked to religious or mythical knowledge, is effaced, but the discourse refers back to itself only via the detour of the transcendence of ideas. The text of ideology is written in capital letters, whether it is a question of Humanity, Progress, Nature, Life, or of the key principles of bourgeois democracy inscribed on the pediment of the Republic, or even of Science and Art, but also of Property, Family, Order, Society, Nation; it may be a conservative or progressive version of bourgeois discourse, or a socialist or anarchist version of anti-bourgeois discourse. This text bears the constant signs of a truth which establishes the origins of facts, which encloses them in a representation and governs the structure of the argument. The determination of an order of appearances is asserted or assumed by virtue of the transcendence of the idea; or, more generally, the possibility of an objectification of the social is opened up, no matter what point of view is adopted.

The double nature of the idea as both representation and norm cannot be over-emphasized; nor can the double character of the argumentation, which attests to a truth inscribed in the real and to the conditions of acting in accordance with the nature of things. Moreover, an essential articulation of ideological discourse is indicated by the function explicitly attributed to the rule. Once again, the same model applies across the whole range, from conservatism to anarchism: a set of prescriptions is established, whose application is the condition of knowledge and action. From political or economic discourse to educational discourse, the power of the rule is confirmed; in every case and no matter how it is interpreted, the rule provides the assurance of the real and the intelligible. In this sense, the discourse on the social can maintain its position of being external to its object only by presenting itself as the guarantor of the rule which attests, by its very existence, to the embodiment of the idea in the social relation. The position of the guarantor is itself explicit. It is inscribed in the representation; a whole panoply of images is unfolded, in which the features of the bourgeois, the boss, the minister, the family man, the educator, the militant, etc. appear. It is no doubt true that, at one pole of ideological discourse, authority tends to be hidden behind the power of the idea; but then it is also true that this power becomes excessive, that science is brandished beneath its sign with much more vigour and that, if the particular determinations of social agents are sometimes engulfed by it, the image of man as universal man comes effectively to support, in both socialism and anarchism, the truth of the rule.

It should be noted that the representations of the idea, of the intelligible sequence of facts, of the rule, of the master holding the principle of action and of knowledge, presuppose a unique type of discourse destined to display itself as such. The discourse on the social asserts itself as discourse; it is based very significantly on the pedagogical model. This feature helps to clarify the distance, which is also represented, between the speaker, wherever he may be situated, and the *other*. I do not mean to say that the discourse emanates from a particular agent, or from a series of agents who would simply be representatives of the dominant class. In so far as it is presented as a discourse on the social, extricating itself from the social, ideological discourse develops in an impersonal way; it conveys a knowledge which is supposed to arise from the order of things. But it is essential for it to bring out the distinction, at every level, between the subject, who establishes himself by his articulation with the rule and expresses himself in expressing the rule, and the *other*, who, not having access to the rule, does not have the status of subject. The representation of the rule goes hand in hand with the representation of nature; and this opposition is converted into a series of manifest terms: for example, the 'worker' is represented in opposition to the bourgeois, the uneducated in opposition to the cultured man, the uncivilized in opposition to the civilized, the mad in opposition to the sane, the child in opposition to the adult. Thus there emerges, through all these substitutions, a natural being whose image sustains the affirmation of society as a world above nature. Such is the artifice by means of which social division is dissimulated: the positing of reference points which enable a difference to be established between the social and the sub-social, order and disorder, the world and the underworld (a difference which has no status in 'precapitalism', where the social is conceived of from another place, from an order which goes beyond it), in such a way that what reality conceals from discourse can be identified and mastered. Thus discourse can cover up the question of its genesis – or, what amounts to the same thing, the question of the institution of the social – by rearranging the boundaries of that which has no genesis, of that which is not an institution, by identifying a disturbing growth of irrational facts whose development must be arrested. Of course, it must be said once again that this representation is challenged in anti-bourgeois discourse, but the latter shares, and even deepens, the pedagogical aim. It tends to enclose itself within a counter-discourse which offers a fixed image of the irrationality of the present and reduces the *other* to the malevolent figure of the dominator; it is no less haunted by the fiction of a society which is, in principle, transparent to itself.

As I have already suggested in calling to mind Marx's analysis, the strength of ideology in the model that I am broadly sketching stems from the fact that the discourses, whose homology I have pointed out, remain disjointed. Ideology, I said, follows the lines of the institution of the social; if it provides a general 'response', the latter does not reside in one place alone. It proliferates in accordance with a differentiation whose principle Marx vainly attributed to the division of labour – vainly, because the latter cannot be treated in itself as the driving force of change. This principle would have to be related instead to the split between political power and the law and, as a result, to the process by which institutions, and the social discourses which underlie them, are segregated. Thus ideological discourse falls back on the situation constituted by the delimitation of the state, the firm, the school, the asylum, modern institutions in general; it falls back on the trace of determinate spaces in which measurable relations between definite agents are organized. On the basis of an articulation which has emerged historically, it gives rise, here and there, to the image of an essential necessity. No doubt each of these attempts is possible only because it draws on all the others.

There is a constant criss-crossing between the processes of legitimation and dissimulation which are put into play. But it remains the case that 'knowledge' is not concentrated at a single pole, and in this sense a gap between power and discourse is always and everywhere preserved. The task of homogenizing and unifying the social domain remains implicit. And for this very reason, there is always the possibility of a displacement and even an overturning of statements – or, in other words, of contradictory versions which, in spite of the conflict, secure a point of reference for social agents.

However, the conditions which ensure the efficacy of bourgeois ideology also contain the possibility of its failure. Of course, in order to explain its breakdown, we would have to go beyond its limits and examine the course of history; but I propose only to highlight the internal contradictions of ideology which compel it to modify itself in order to continue to carry out its function in historical society.

According to a well-known Marxist argument, the breakdown supposedly results from the fundamental contradiction between ideological discourse and *real* practice, which is becoming more and more apparent to the dominated class. This thesis is too familiar to require elaboration here; and it is also well known that it found a privileged point of support in the Leninist critique of 'formal democracy', whose mystification is gradually discovered by the masses through oppression. While one must grant a certain truth to this thesis, one may justly ask how reality comes to appear, whether it is sufficient to refer to the lived experience of a class in order to conceptualize the formation of a social discourse which would gradually weaken the hold of ideology. This question is all the more pressing when we consider the societies in which formal democracy has collapsed; for we must acknowledge that it gives way, not to *real* democracy, but to totalitarianism.

The Marxist interpretation seems to me to be more fruitful when it emphasizes the internal contradictions of ideological discourse. The need to state propositions of universal value and, at the same time, to provide a representation of the established order which justifies class domination would have the effect of destroying its apparent rationality and would prevent it from ever fully realizing what it claims, in such a way that, in its very exercise, it would give rise to criticism, to a counter-discourse on each of its levels. It will be recalled that Marx suggests, in *The Eighteenth Brumaire*, that bourgeois discourse concurs in its own way with the division of labour. The intelligentsia specializes in the cult of abstract truths; it maintains the illusion of an essence of humanity which does not allow for the image of particular interests; it speaks the language of poetry, while the political representatives of the bourgeoisie speak the language of prose. According to this account, as soon as order is threatened, the latter remain alone on the stage. Although he sees them as the realistic spokesmen of the dominant class, his analysis makes room for the view that their discourse is embedded in ideology. Although they take measures that unequivocally manifest the defence of class interests, they will make use of a language which claims to explain the facts, to state the law of reality and the reality of the law. The concept of property, the state, labour or the family is no less ideological than those of the humanist intelligentsia. Moreover, if one or another of the intelligentsia's concepts, such as that of equality, finds itself relegated to a particular set of circumstances because it might give rise to revolutionary demands, the prose could never break completely with the poetry; the discourse on liberty always comes back to support the discourse on property, just as the discourse on justice comes back to support the discourse on order. Furthermore one could, without touching on the conflicts which tear apart the agents of ideological discourse, deal with the latter in a general way with a view to analysing its oppositions and demonstrating that there is not a single idea that could be formulated, not a single argument that could be developed for its purposes, whose assertion would not require an idea or an argument that contradicted them. The discourse harbours incompatible representations; it lives on the 'horrible *mélange*' of the image of an unconditioned individual placed side by side with that of an unconditioned society, the image of an artificialist and mechanistic thought allied with one that is substantialist and organicist. And since it is essential for it to make itself explicit as discourse on the social, since it constantly designates things, it unwittingly creates, by the effect of its internal discordances, a gap between discourse and the social.

However, if we want to determine the full extent of the contradiction, without forgetting that it is rooted in the impossible project of a discourse which claims to represent the transparency of the social and to be, *qua* social discourse, discourse on the social, we must examine that unique property of bourgeois ideology of realizing itself by procedures such as the enunciation which is almost perceptible to itself, the statement which is almost determinate, the image of the speaker who is almost visible, whereas, at the same time, everything is supposed to dissolve into the quasi-appearance of the social to itself. For, in itself, the internal contradiction does not destroy the discourse; as I have pointed out, it also gives the discourse its strength. It produces an articulation between opposing terms; it secures the possibility of saying everything, or, in other words, of 'saving' everything, even the most subversive. On the other hand, ideology is undermined by its need to produce ideas which are visible to all and which present themselves as transcendent in relation to reality at the very moment that they determine it or seem only to express it. Nothing is more remarkable than this operation: the idea of property or of the family falls back on to the fact of property or of the family. It is not that the latter is silent; there is no institution which is not organized within a linguistic activity. But we are dealing here with a second-order language which seeks to distance itself from the first-order language and tries to stave off the danger which lies within it, a danger stemming from the fact that, in the latter, speech circulates and differentiates agents at the same time as it relates them to one another, looping back on itself only by virtue of a movement in which the possibility and limits of exchange are brought into play – an activity whose conditions and effects escape the institution. The idea of the family encompasses the fact of the institution and implies the belief that its conditions of possibility and its limits are conceivable from within it. It is as a consequence of the representation, therefore, that the question of the family arises. It does not arise from the simple fact that there exists a determinate kinship network; as Lévi-Strauss rightly observes, the latter presupposes speech, knowledge, sometimes highly developed reflection on its principles of organization, but not a *view of* the institution which circumscribes it as such, which delimits it within the social domain and at a distance from others. The differentiation of functions and roles, the hierarchy of rights, in no way presupposes that there is a *view of* the father, mother, child or, as I would say, a development of the representation which allows an essence to emerge – or, what amounts to the same thing in this case, which allows an imaginary construction of the social relation to emerge.

It would perhaps be a commonplace to say that the idea of the family is formed in response to the fact that the contingency of the institution has become almost perceptible. However, it is less banal to observe that this contingency is not abolished but displaced by the idea; that the idea, whose function is to conceal the contingency, is immediately marked by it; and that, finally, a limitless movement of interconnected ideas is initiated in order to efface the contingency effects of the enunciation. This is the activity of argumentation and justification which, as we have already observed, is itself represented in ideology; it projects the image of rationality extricating itself from the real (the fact that this leads to the conclusion that human nature is irrational is, it should be said, of little importance). The only check on this activity is its sudden abolition in the return to the blunt statement of the idea, that is, to the assertion that the institution is sacred: the family, the social cell, lying at the foundation of society. The idea, then, is realized as pure transcendence; and we know that this realization corresponds to a potentiality implicit in ideological discourse, wherever it is expressed. The latter tends to retreat towards a point of certainty where the necessity to speak is cancelled out. It is haunted by tautology. The words 'family', 'property' and 'society', but also 'freedom', 'equality', 'progress' or 'science', crystallize a knowledge which dispenses with all justification. But the point of certainty is untenable, the transcendence of the idea is vain. For that which is sought but cannot be attained is something which lies beyond the social, a certainty about the social as such, a referent whose very loss is at the origin of ideology. Hence this referent could not be brought into relation with the statement of ideas; it could not develop, in accordance with the latter, a discourse on the social, envisaged as a determinate space. The idea could not, therefore, fall back on itself without giving rise again to the need to produce its own foundation by taking hold of signs which, in the supposed reality, attest to it. And this operation implies, it may be noted, a recognition of the difference between what is and what is said. In this sense, the discourse recognizes itself as discourse and is content to represent itself as such. For, in so doing, it maintains the illusion of a mastery of its origin and of its own space. Paradoxically, it is the ostentation of the verb which enables it to dissimulate the enigma of its genesis, or what I have called the question of social division. Yet the consequence of this phenomenon is no less remarkable: if ostentation gives rise to fascination, it is equally true that discourse reveals itself and finds itself threatened with being perceived as *de facto* discourse.

An analogous contradiction may be discerned in the status conferred upon the rule and upon the authority that is supposed to support it. The social world, it must be remembered, is a world of rules; and there are no rules which, even in the absence of repressive apparatuses designed to ensure that they are respected, do not imply a knowledge of what is prohibited or prescribed. But in ideology, the representation of the rule is split off from the effective operation of it. Certainly, this split is accompanied by profound modifications in the relations actually maintained between social agents, but let us set aside this difficult problem in order to consider only the phenomenon of representation. Perhaps this phenomenon can best be observed, as I have already suggested, within the pedagogical context, and particularly in the context of learning a language. According to the dominant myth, language can be mastered by going back to the principles of its construction, as defined by grammar. The rule is thus extracted from the experience of language; it is circumscribed, made fully visible and assumed to govern the conditions of possibility of this experience. The enigma of language – namely, that it is both internal and external to the speaking subject, that there is an articulation of the self with others which marks the emergence of the self and which the self does not control – is concealed by the representation of a place 'outside' language, from which it could be generated. In its original state, this fiction was carried to an extreme when Jesuit education prohibited the use of one's first language at school and imposed an artificial Latin in order to develop a means of persuading one that speech is generated from the rule. Even though this fiction cannot stand up to the demands of a child's socialization in historical society, it brings to light the whole logic behind a representation of education which claims to overcome the insurmountable difference between the institution of knowledge and the knowledge of the institution. Once again, we encounter the ambiguity of the representation as soon as the rule is stated; for its very exhibition undermines the power that the rule claims to introduce into practice. This exorbitant power must, in fact, be shown, and at the same time it must owe nothing to the movement which makes it appear. To be true to its image, the rule must be abstracted from any question concerning its origin; thus, it goes beyond the operations that it controls. Its virtue is to confer upon the subject a right to speak, to know, to be the master of his action; whereas without the rule, the subject is not only deprived of the means of expression or knowledge, but literally dismissed, that is, thrown outside the network of the institution. But to be true to its image, the rule must also prove its validity through usage; it is constantly subject to the demonstration of its effectiveness, and is thus contradictorily represented as a convention. Only the authority of the master allows the contradiction to be concealed, but he is himself an object of representation; presented as possessor of the knowledge of the rule, he allows the contradiction to appear through himself. On the one hand, he embodies an authority which does not have to account for itself or, as they say, for divine right; while on the other hand, he lavishly displays the signs of his competence.

The configuration which is particularly evident in education can be discerned in all sectors of the social domain. Not only the representation of education, but also that of literature, painting or philosophy implies the same set of contradictions. Let me repeat, in passing, in order to counter the misunderstanding which is so widespread today (and which is embedded in a new form of ideology): we could not have a *view* on the historicity of education, philosophy, literature or painting which would free us from the questions brought into play in their institution; we can only speak of the representation which in each case comes to overlap the institution in order to try to cancel out its effects and to simulate a domination of the socialization process by means of a determination of the rule and of the master. But we should not hesitate to extend this analysis. Even in the context of the industrial firm one can see the separation of the institution and the representation, of the social discourse implicated in practice and the discourse on the social which claims to establish its principles by presenting the image of the leader who possesses, on the one hand, an authority of divine right and, on the other, a specific competence; and also by presenting the image of rules, a prescriptive body in which an unconditioned knowledge of the industrial organization and of the mundane conditions of the productivity of human labour is expressed.

The ideological discourse that we are examining has no safety catch; it is rendered vulnerable by its attempt to make visible the place from which the social relation would be conceivable (both thinkable and creatable), by its inability to define this place without letting its contingency appear, without condemning itself to slide from one position to another, without thereby making apparent the instability of an order that it is intended to raise to the status of essence. We are perhaps now in a better position to understand why this discourse, in its aim to extract itself from the social and to affirm itself as discourse, can only remain scattered, and why its task of the implicit generalization of knowledge and the implicit homogenization of experience could fall apart in face of the unbearable ordeal of the collapse of certainty, of the vacillation of the representations of discourse and, as a result, of the splitting of the subject. Claiming its discursive power, it never coincides with the discourse of power; it manifests in itself the position of power. However, whether the latter is the power of the actual or potential government or one of its countless substitutes, this discourse represents it, displays it to the eye of the other; but this discourse is not structured or unified around a principle which would condense the multiplicity of statements into the same assertion and relate them to the same guarantor. I have just said that this ideological discourse has no safety catch: in other words, it is constructed in such a way that it is marked by the absence of a guarantee of its origin. The answer to the question of origin governs its development, but it transforms itself, displaces itself within its limits; and this is the cost at which power is exercised in actual social relations.

### Totalitarianism and the Crisis of Bourgeois Ideology

The phenomenon of totalitarianism enables us to decipher the specific features of bourgeois ideology, for the contradiction of the latter is reflected in it. To some, it may seem scandalous to treat fascism and Nazism, as well as what is called 'communism' (even though, in fact, it constitutes merely the discourse of a bureaucratic society), as variants of the same model. Nevertheless, I shall speak of totalitarianism without taking into consideration the differences of regime, which in other respects are highly significant, because my sole concern is to clarify a general aspect of the genesis of ideology.

In totalitarianism, the process of occultation of the institution of the social seeks to complete itself. With Nazism, it is not essentially a matter of resurrecting a system of values which derive from precapitalism and which were challenged by bourgeois society, even though there is evidently an attempt to return to the representation of a communal order, based on a relation to the earth, blood ties and personal dependence, and even though this representation has continued to survive on the margins of bourgeois ideology in all the forms of conservatism. With communism, it is not essentially a matter of attempting to turn the universalist values of bourgeois society into reality by destroying the idea of private interest at all levels of social activity, even though this concern is effectively part of its project and is rooted in the history of the revolutionary struggles of the proletariat within the capitalist world. The formation of totalitarianism is intelligible only if one takes account of the 'response' which is offered to the problem of the division between ideological discourse and the socialization process of society, or of what I shall call 'the historicity of the social'. The fiction stems from a social discourse which, implicated as it is in practice, seeks to invest in itself a general knowledge – that knowledge which was always maintained by bourgeois ideology in an external dimension – and seeks, wherever it operates, to radiate the signs of its unity and hence of the homogeneity of the objective domain. Thus the boundaries of sectors which formerly were explicitly recognized, such as the economic, political, legal, educational, aesthetic and even scientific sectors, are obliterated. The affirmation of the identity of the real as it appears seeks to find expression in every particular statement; it nourishes a passion for tautology and, simultaneously, the quest for an explicit totalization is substituted for the labour of occulation of bourgeois discourse, whose peculiar characteristic was to allow the generalization to remain latent. Whereas the latter tends to render its discursive essence perceptible to itself and, as such, remains disjointed with respect to power, totalitarian discourse is deployed in the conviction of being imprinted on reality and of embodying the potentiality of a continued and general mastery of its articulations. In this sense, it is political discourse through and through; but at the same time it denies the particular fact of the political and tries to dissolve the political into the pure generality of the social.

More precisely, totalitarian discourse denies all the oppositions that bourgeois ideology dealt with in a representation which was constructed in each case in order to defuse their effects and which threatened the foundations of each term by exposing it to the necessity of accounting for itself. Above all else, totalitarian discourse effaces the opposition between the state and civil society; it seeks to make the presence of the state manifest throughout the social space, that is, to convey, through a series of representatives, the principle of power which informs the diversity of activities and incorporates them in the model of a common allegiance. Yet we must not lose sight of the fact that the discourse carries out this operation, not by means of a commentary which would exploit its distance with regard to the real in order to designate it in its truth, but rather by diffusing itself throughout the circuits of socialization, by elaborating systems of signs whose *representative* function is no longer identifiable, by taking hold of actors in order to insert them within these systems, in such a way that the discourse speaks (almost) through them and abolishes (almost) the space, which is indeed indeterminate but always preserved in bourgeois ideology, between the enunciation and that which is enunciated.

The mass party is the instrument *par excellence* of totalitarianism, through which the consubstantiality of the state and civil society is manifested. In every forum, it embodies the principle of power; it diffuses the general norm which provides the assurance of a sort of reflection of the society on itself and, with the polarization of society towards a goal, delivers it from the silent threat of the inertia of the instituted, making it possible to grasp its identity under the imperative of activism. But the practice and structure of the party cannot be distinguished from the discourse of which it is, or seeks to be, the centre (other than by showing at every level the contradictions within which this discourse operates and which it dissimulates). Just like all those agents which fulfil the same function at a more specific level (unions, associations for young people, women, intellectuals, etc.), this representative acts in practice precisely in accordance with the demands of the representation; it projects into its own internal relations the very unity which it guarantees for the whole of society. It is in itself a system of signs which allows a hierarchy to be formed, which enables a split to be produced between the apparatus and the base, between the leaders and the followers, which enables sectors of activity to be partitioned off; and these operations are carried out while simulating a self-transparency of the institution, a reciprocity of decisions and a homogeneity of the body politic.

The ideological discourse, in this sense, tends to become the discourse of the party – the discourse *on* the party being only a detached part of the latter, although it is absolutely essential to it and marks a limit of the enterprise to which we shall return. Nothing better clarifies this phenomenon than the moulding of a new type of social agent – the militant – a figure in which we can see the inscription of the subject within the discourse that he is supposed to speak. The militant is not in the party as if in a determinate milieu with visible borders; he is in himself a representative of it. He draws from it the possibility of freeing himself from the conflicts to which he is exposed by his participation in various institutions governed by specific imperatives of socialization, the possibility of embodying in

his person the generality of the social. As bearer of the representation, the militant carries out his function by constantly reflecting
that which is organized independently of him in the supposed social
system. At the same time, he establishes himself as the possessor of
power and knowledge. He monitors the worker, the peasant the
engineer, the teacher, the writer; he proffers the norm, crystallizes
the virtues of *activism* and finds the vocabulary and syntax of his
discourse imprinted in himself in such a way that he constitutes
himself in the operation of ideology.

In addition to the task of gathering social discourse into itself,
beyond every division, of welding together the scattered images of
man in bourgeois society, of grasping the key which unlocks all the
doors of the social order and leaves all the forms of economic,
political and aesthetic activity open to view, of taking possession of a
general knowledge and of linking all these experiences to a single
pole of truth, discourse is faced with the task of effacing itself before
the anonymity of the idea, of argumentation, of the rule and of the
supreme authority, all of which are, as it were, welded together. The
militant merely brings to its full expression the attempt to efface
the difference between the individual and society, between the particular and the general, between the private and the public. The initial image is that of the man without specific features, who acquires
his definition as fascist or communist man; a pure social agent whose
adherence to a class provides only an accidental modality of his insertion into society as a whole, or may even be expressly challenged
in the pure denial of any internal schism in this society. There can be
no doubt that, in this respect, 'communist' totalitarianism succeeds
in exploiting most effectively the mechanisms of ideology. For it does
not merely reject class determination; it goes so far as to give form to
social relations in which the features of the dominant class become
less and less distinguishable, eventually dissolving into the image of
a purely functional hierarchy, each member of which would be
gradually tied in to the central focus of socialization, to the lines of
division between the dominant and dominated groups. Yet whether
it is a matter of fascism or communism, one can see at work a logic of
identification whose aim is to cancel out the conflicts which
developed as a result of the oppositions peculiar to bourgeois society.
Whereas in the latter, the power of the representation is maintained
by a constant displacement of the 'solution', a deferring of the contradiction by virtue of a gap between the agencies of discourse, in

totalitarianism there is a brute affirmation of the identity of the representation and the real, a condensation of the terms of the contradiction in images which reflect one other. In the first, discourse is organized in terms of constant compromises between the principal antagonists, whereas in the second, it looks for its efficacy in a general response which would exclude the traces of the question. But the success of the latter would be unintelligible if it were not able to make the signs of the totality manifest in the detail of social life. Indeed, the mechanism of identification operates in a modern society which, at every level of its activity, bears the mark of differentiation, internal opposition and change; not only must the effects of the division of labour be dealt with, but also those of the segregation of socio-cultural spaces. The very attempt to efface the opposition between the state and civil society and to render perceptible the unity of the political and the non-political presupposes that the logic of the norm appears within the form of social relations, here and now, that is, that a system of articulations is deployed by virtue of which power can be diffused without running the risk of being divided.

By subjecting all spheres of society to the imperative of the organization, ideological discourse, be it fascist or communist, is able to master the oppositions which develop within and between these spheres and it is able to reduce the gap between itself and its object. Indeed, the representation of the organization allows the difference between the subject and the law to be concealed, a difference which is created in the very movement of the institution and which implies the impossibility of relating the latter either to human action (whether focused on the individual or the group) or to a transcendent principle. In a sense, the organization eliminates the traces of the social subject, irrespective of the modality of its appearance; it does not eliminate the positivity of an empirically determined subject, whether it be the dominant class, the dominated class, or the producing individual, but it does conceal the question of the subject as such, a question in which the relation between the self and the other, as well as between the self and the law, is brought into play. Thus the organization, in representing a system of operations which would assign definitions to agents and their relations, renders invisible the general antagonism between the dominator and the dominated, an antagonism which emerged in bourgeois society within the context of production. But, simultaneously, this system appears as a pure construction, as an overall, self-sustaining operation – and, in this sense, as a pure manifestation of the human Logos, a pure manifestation of the prevailing socialization – of an institution in action, having to deal only with itself and polarized towards the totality. The representation of the organization tends to be carried out within the very context of the organization, because the latter is organized through the fiction of a knowledge of the social which is manifest in the network of operations to which the agent belongs.

The dependence of totalitarian ideology on bourgeois ideology is once again shown by the fact that it takes hold of the two principles which remain juxtaposed in bourgeois ideology, a radical artificialism and a radical substantialism, and welds them together in the affirmation of a society which seems to be thoroughly active, concerned with assuring its *functioning* – a human factory, and, as such, closed in on itself, in possession of its foundation. Totalitarianism obviously draws its faith in the organization from capitalism; but while it found itself thwarted by the need to represent the differences of the social domain, this faith overflows in response to the threat of the disintegration of this domain and turns the organization into the essence of the social. But it must be emphasized that the new ideology implies the vision of a *centre*, from which social life is organized; a centre which shifts from one sector of civil society to another but which, at the heart of the state apparatus, possesses power and knowledge. The discourse of the organization, arranged in such a way that anonymous knowledge governs the thought and practice of its agents, is thus only supported by constant reference to the authority in which the decision is concentrated. It is on this double condition that the contradiction of bourgeois ideology is 'overcome' by the concept of the total state. The network of the organization makes it clear that nothing is lost in the movement of socialization which involves the externalization of social discourses and practices; the self-identity of power expressed in the substitution of leaders renders manifest the origin of the norm.

Fascism and communism, let me repeat, fall within the domain of a meta-sociological interpretation. Any attempt to analyse them as empirical, socio-historical formations will be limited, however rich the documentation may be, for such an attempt will fail to see that it is the question of the existence of the social, of the historical as such, which is brought into play in totalitarianism. The latter is neither an accidental deviation in the development of industrial capitalism, nor an aberration for which psychology can provide the key; it realizes a potentiality which is implicit in the social from the moment that its institution can no longer be conceived or contained by a discourse that seeks its origin elsewhere, in another place. Moreover, the greatest error is to regard it as merely a variant of despotism. Even though Stalin's power, like Hitler's, resembles that of a despot – and indeed, even though both draw on the archaic sources of Germanic culture and the Asiatic world – nevertheless it is a unique history which is inaugurated with totalitarianism. It is not the resurrection of an old political system which is grafted on to industrial society, but rather the attempt to close the social space in on itself from the imaginary centre of its institution, to make being and appearance coincide here and now. The despot and his bureaucracy govern society, but their power is the sign of a transcendent power, a sign of that which lies *outside* humanity. Totalitarian power, Nazi or Stalinist, is diffused in the representation of the organization, and it exercises the fascination and the terror of representing precisely the social as a whole, the non-division, the inhuman discourse *qua* absolutely human.

Such, at least, is the pole towards which totalitarian ideology tends, but in overcoming the contradictions of bourgeois ideology, it constantly comes up against the impossibility of fully realizing itself; it lives, in turn, under the threat of the effects of social division, as my description has already suggested. The ideal of the bureaucracy is the anonymity of social discourse, the manifestation of rationality in the organization, the insertion of the subject in the logic of fascism or in the logic of communism, such that his speech cannot attest to a gap without lapsing into nonsense. But equally essential to it is the representation of the centre of decision-making, a power that asserts itself in full positivity, beyond all contestation. The two representations can be conjoined only by disregarding the power oppositions within the bureaucracy and excluding the mass of those without power from the ruling apparatus. The strength, as well as the weakness, of bourgeois ideology consisted in the fact that the discourse on the social, in its always perceptible articulation with a real or potential position of power, did not coincide with social discourse, nor with the discourse of power, and hence that it could pass through different centres and be opposed to itself without destroying itself. Totalitarian discourse, by contrast, has no room to manoeuvre; it does not tolerate a separation of subject and discourse and it necessitates its identification with power and with those who hold it at the highest echelons of the state. Of course, this analysis is an extreme one; there are no circumstances, even at the apogee of totalitarianism, in which the abolition of the subject in the discourse, or a complete identification with the master, can be carried out. Even a *parallel* exchange of words conveys the signs of distance and difference. But the fact remains that the oppositions cannot be transcribed symbolically: they must be absolutely rejected or, failing that, terror is substituted for discourse.

In general terms, the contradiction of totalitarianism stems from the fact that, on the one hand, power is doubly masked therein, as representative of the society without division and as agent of the rationality of the organization, whereas, on the other hand, power appears there, as in no other society, as an apparatus of coercion, the bearer of naked violence. This contradiction is not that between the representation and the fact. And even my formula must be corrected: terror is not simply substituted for discourse. For it is spoken, as we know; it sweeps along a fantastic argumentation whose effect is to fill in the intolerable gap between subject and discourse. Moreover, it must be added that this enterprise cannot be interpreted as a mere response to events which would disrupt the established order. As the history of Stalinism clearly shows, the image of power as terrorist power, as an exorbitant power, has a necessary function. For it is also through this image that individuals demonstrate their dissolution in the general element of the social, that is, the contingency of any particular determination with regard to the law proferred by the master – the absolute master of the state, but also his representatives at all levels of the hierarchy and in all sectors of activity. However, with the slipping from one position of power to another, a principle of instability is introduced which could make the mechanism of domination visible. If the danger in bourgeois ideology is that power is exposed to derision, in totalitarian ideology it runs the greater risk of arousing horror.

It is true that, as the effects of the contradiction develop, means of defence are set up in an attempt to reinforce the cohesion of ideological discourse. Thus, after Stalin's death, his example is used in order to represent and denounce the fact that power has exceeded rationality (such is the function of the personality cult), whereas at the same time the example of the petty bureaucrat is used to represent and denounce the fact that irresponsibility has prevailed over the just impersonality of decisions. But these defences testify to the latent crisis in the system of bureaucratic representations. It is no less instructive to observe its vulnerability in the face of all kinds of events, from both the economic and cultural orders, which elude the prediction of the leaders and which are capable of manifesting, here and now, a breakdown of the general norm, a 'failure' in the functioning of the organization. In a sense, the resources of discourse are inexhaustible in face of the event. The articulation of discourse with power and with the law is such that the 'real' cannot arise as a question; access to it is strictly governed by the representation. But this representation requires signs of the effectiveness of the organization. Power is not mirrored in the hierarchy, but in structures in which social action and social aims must be exemplified, in which, at a deeper level, individuals must discover their common existence in the pure dimension of social action orientated towards a social goal. Thus, for example, the indices of production, feverishly displayed, are thought to provide the continuing proof of the validity in reality of the dominant discourse. In sum, a double necessity is imposed: to include absolutely and to exclude absolutely the event, to build it into the logic of the organization and to deny it absolutely as a force of disorder. The magnitude of this contradiction can be appreciated only if it is remembered that totalitarian ideology is engendered in 'historical society', that is, let me repeat, in a society which cannot be anchored in a representation of its limits, which is, in principle, open to the question of its origin, destined to face excessiveness and conflict, which, in each of its parts, experiences the effects of changes in the others, a society where the internal differentiation, the gaps between practices and between representations, go hand in hand with its history. The bureaucratic phantasy is to abolish the historical in History; to restore the logic of a 'society without history'; to identify the instituting moment with the instituted; to deny the unpredictable, the unknowable, the continual loss of the past, under the illusion of a social action, transparent to itself, which would monitor its effects in advance and which would maintain continuity with its origin.

However strong the illusion, it is apt to be denied. And no doubt the denial is, in turn, concealed; the failures of planning, for example, are attributed to bureaucratism, to the residual inertia of the social body, to the mania for regulations. Again one must convince onself that the representation of bureaucratism is no less ideological than the representation of social action; it is an essential component of the system, whose function is to underline the virtues of the rule in its coincidence with power and to attribute any perversion of the rule to the presence of parasitic elements. But, apart from the rule appearing excessive at the very point where rationality is supposed to show itself, the whole logic of the organization 'may' appear as a logic of the absurd. It is true that the ideology has means of defence far more effective than that of denouncing bureaucratism which it can employ in order to resist the backlash from the decisions taken by those in power, or, more generally, to resist the effects of the real. The attempt to ensure its mastery of the social space is supported by the representation of the enemy: an enemy who cannot be presented as an opponent, but whose existence strikes at the integrity of the social body. Moreover, the enemy does much more than personify adversity or, as it is often observed, serve as a scapegoat. In a society which does not tolerate the image of an internal social division, which claims that it is homogeneous despite all the differences which exist in fact, it is the other as such who acquires the fantastic features of the destroyer; the other, however he is defined, to whatever group he belongs, is the representative of the *outside*. Whereas in bourgeois ideology, the essence of man is affirmed with regard to a sub-humanity (even though the latter is relegated to the lower regions of society and is never plunged so far down into 'nature' that it does not pose the problem of how to manage it, for it is perceived as *in* society), totalitarian ideology is maintained by the exclusion of an evil agent, a representative of the anti-social. But the effectiveness of the representation should not lead one to forget that it does not have complete control over its effects. It tends to circumscribe the place of the other, but it succeeds in doing so only by means of a generalized denial – as I have amply underlined – of the difference between the subject and social discourse. Any sign of this difference is susceptible of denouncing the subject as the enemy. Otherness cannot be encircled; the image of the concentration camp is not enough to disarm it. The individual himself, wherever he must enter the discourse of power, is exposed to the possibility of exclusion, in so far as he is capable of speaking and is revealed as potentially guilty. In this sense, the bureaucratic world continues to be haunted by insecurity, even though it is wholly organized to represent a bastion of security, a community infused with the certitude of its cohesion. The affirmation of the social totality does not dispense with the self-devouring phantasy.

Totalitarian discourse eliminates the externality of the idea. The discourse on the social tends to be reabsorbed into social discourse, effacing the externality of power. The state tends to carry out its fusion with civil society, effacing the externality of the rule. The organization tends to suffice as a conveyor of rationality, effacing the externality of the other. Social division is dissimulated. But externality returns; discourse runs the risk of appearing as a generalized lie, as discourse in the service of power, the mere mask of oppression.

## The Invisible Ideology

Totalitarian ideology prevails in a large part of the world; a rigorous analysis would have to take account of the specific features that it reveals in certain countries, particularly in China. It would also have to consider the modifications which have occurred in the USSR and in Eastern Europe since the late 1950s. To my mind, the observable differences in time and space do not call into question the coherence of the system. An understanding of this system, I suggested, enables us to discern in retrospect the features which constitute the specificity of bourgeois ideology. It must now be added that it also illuminates the formation of the new ideological discourse in the Western democracies of our time.

My conviction is that this new discourse continues to exploit a system of representations which reached its full efficacy in the second half of the nineteenth century, but that this system is no longer at the centre of the social imaginary. This hypothesis makes no claim to originality; an already extensive critical sociology – associated with the names of Marcuse, Whyte, Roszak and Baudrillard – has brought to light the function currently fulfilled by the themes of the organization, of social communication, group membership, consumption, etc. Since these ideas are no doubt familiar to the reader, I need not elaborate them here. But what does deserve to be emphasized is the relation that contemporary discourse maintains both with totalitarianism and with bourgeois ideology, the way in which it is situated within the general genesis of ideology. Although occasionally the totalitarian aim of this discourse has been justly stressed, it has hardly been perceived that its formation attests to a 'reflection' of the contradictions which haunt totalitarianism, to an attempt to stave off the threat that weighs upon social existence – that it attests, in other words, to the project of making explicit the representation of an homogenization and unification of the social. This project, I emphasized, went together with its opposite; that of eliminating the distance between the discourse on the social and social discourse, inserting the first into the second. Now it is this latter enterprise which is repeated in the new ideology, but it is dissociated from the affirmation of the totality, put back into a latent state and, in this sense, reconnected to the principle of the system of bourgeois ideology, in which the displacement of imaginary formations was required, their conflict tolerated and compromises constantly worked out. Concealing the distance between the representation and the real, which jeopardizes bourgeois ideology, renouncing the realization of the representation in the form of the totalization of the real, which jeopardizes totalitarian ideology: such, in my view, is the double principle which organizes a new logic of dissimulation.

If the affirmation of the totality, notably in communism, is carried out under the exigency of rejoining the state and civil society, of discarding the image of a dispersion of power and its fall into the realm of fact, it implies, I observed, that the discourse of ideology is transformed into the discourse of power; this affirmation exposes it dangerously by revealing the separated agencies of decision and coercion and the various features of the master, not only at the summit of the state but also through its many 'representatives'. A new strategy is developed in order to represent a society sheltered from this danger. Admittedly, the use of the term 'strategy' suggests the action of a subject who would enjoy the freedom to define the best means of dissimulation. But I have said often enough that the old ideology was not that of the bourgeoisie; and hence I would obviously reject the idea that the old ideology has turned into the ideology of a new class (for example, the technocracy), as some commentators like to claim. The strategy of which I am speaking refers to the ruses of the imaginary, a process which, although unconscious and 'without history' in the sense intended by Marx, nonetheless takes into account the effects of knowledge and history and moulds them into new configurations in the service of a task which always remains the same.

Thus the 'group', set up as a positive entity and treated as both the expression and the objective of social communication, becomes a screen which obscures the separation of the apparatus of domination from the mass of those without power. The representation of a structure of the group, indifferent to the conditions which dictate the status of its members, tends to exclude from its domain the question of the origin, the legitimacy and rationality of the oppositions and hierarchies instituted in each sector. A new faith is invested in this representation: the faith in a 'mastery' of the social in the very experience of socialization *here and now*, that is, within the perceptible boundaries of each institution, in each situation where the individual finds himself situated by virtue of the 'natural' necessity of production or of economic activity more generally, but also of education or leisure, of political, trade union or religious practice. So many analyses have been devoted to the phenomenon of human relations in industry, to the spread of group techniques in a wide variety of organizations, to the practice of seminars and information sessions, to the application of social psychology in firms, schools and hospitals, that it would be useful to dwell for a while on the ideology of social communication. But no less instructive is the role played in this regard by the great instruments at the service of this ideology: radio and television. Without them, the new system of representation would certainly not be viable; for it is in propagating itself, not only from one particular milieu to another, but each time from an apparently circumscribed focus to an apparently indeterminate one, it is through its indefinitely multiplied transmission from the private pole of the institution to the public pole of information, that ideological discourse attains the generality necessary for its task of homogenizing the social field in an implicit way. With the constant staging of public discussions turned into spectacles, encompassing all aspects of economic, political and cultural life, ridiculing everything from the most trivial to the most revered, an image of reciprocity is imposed as the very image of social relations. The image is doubly effective, for communication is extolled independently of its agents and its content at the same time as the *presence* of individuals is simulated: a head of state confides his difficulties to a conversational partner who knows how to listen, or this listener, drawn from the masses but duly installed, probes a minister or questions an expert who knows how to respond, and so on. This performance goes so far as to make the identities of the actors apparent. Here we no doubt have one of the most remarkable movements of the imaginary: to absorb the personal element into the impersonal discourse which presents the essence of social relations, while substantiating the fiction of a living speech, the speech of a subject, when in fact the latter is dissolved into the ceremony of communication. It is a fiction because the limits of discussion are determined outside of its visible domain; the neutrality of the chairperson dissimulates the principle of its organization and, in the end, those who hold the power are presented on the same level as those whose fate they decide behind the scenes.

We would still not take into account the full extent of the phenomenon if we were to become obsessed by the manifestly political aspects of social communication. The effectiveness of discourse such as that transmitted by radio and television lies in the fact that it is only partially manifested as political discourse – and it is precisely because of this that it acquires a general political significance. It is the things of everyday life, questions of science and culture, which support the representation of a realized democracy where speech seems to circulate without obstruction. The signs of this circulation are produced ostentatiously, whereas the statutes remain crystallized according to oppositions of power. In no other period has so much been said: the discourse on the social, facilitated by modern means of transmission, natters on; it is overcome by a dizzying infatuation with itself. Nothing escapes the agenda of conferences, interviews and televised discussions, from the generation gap to traffic flow, from sexuality to modern music, from space exploration to education. This narcissism is not that of bourgeois ideology, since the new discourse is not spoken from above. It does without capital letters; it pretends to propagate information, pretends even to question and to probe. It does not hold the other at a distance, but includes its 'representative' in itself; it presents itself as an incessant dialogue and thus takes hold of the gap between the *self* and the *other* in order to make room for them both within itself. In this way, the subject finds himself (almost) lodged in the system of representation, in an altogether different way than in totalitarian ideology, since he is now invited to incorporate the terms of every opposition. And at the same time, he is lodged in the group – an imaginary group in the sense that individuals are deprived of the power to grasp the actual movement of the institution by taking part in it, by confronting the fact of their differentiated relation to one another.

This clarifies the remark I made about the implication of the personal in the impersonal, an event which once again marks the distance from totalitarian discourse. The latter tends to dissolve the personal element, because it does not tolerate the image of a dispersal of the centres of socialization, nor does it take the risk of allowing the subject to have a particular experience in a particular place which would elude the general norm. But this dispersal ceases to strike at the integrity of the representation of the social from the moment that the subject finds himself captured by his own image in the network of socialization. Thus the television screen simply materializes an impalpable screen on which a social relation is projected, a relation which is self-sufficient in so far as it condenses the double representation of a relation to itself and a relation between people. It is in this light that one may assess, for example, the efficacy of a mechanism which, from commercials to programmes on politics or culture, provides the constant illusion of a *between-us*, an *entre-nous*.

The informant's speech presents itself as anonymous and netural; as such, it diffuses an objective knowledge (whatever its nature), but at the same time it makes itself unique, mimics living speech, assumes personal attributes in order to ensure its links with those addressed who, in spite of their mass, their separation and their ig-norance of one other, will find themselves personally contacted and silently brought together by virtue of their common proximity to the one who speaks. In this sense, the most banal programme is an in-cantation of *familiarity*; it installs within mass society the limits of a 'little world' where everything happens as if each person were already turned towards the other. It provokes a hallucination of *nearness* which abolishes a sense of distance, strangeness, imperceptibility, the signs of the outside, of adversity, of otherness. Let me note in passing that one is sometimes surprised to see people strolling down the street or sunbathing on the beach with transistor radios stuck to their ears, or to see homes in which televisions or radios are on con-stantly, even in the absence of those who turned them on; no other phenomenon better illuminates the imaginary dimension of com-munication. For the latter provides the assurance of the social bond, well removed from any test of its reality; it provides a background, an accompaniment – just like the music which is rightly called by the same name, although it is only a variant of the generalized com-munication – and this background is the foundation, this accom-paniment is the lining continuously spun from the intolerable fact of social division. The certainty of the communication may, ultimately, be sufficient in itself; for, while taking his leave in fact, the subject continues to be lodged in its network. It hardly matters whether he stops watching with his eyes or listening with his ears; his personal phantom is installed, once and for all, in the place of the *entre-nous*.

What appears in this *entre-nous* – a deodorant, an increase in prices, a death on the road – is not of great significance; more important is the power to imply a primordial relationship which could not be brought into play in the operation of discourse and the possible oppositions of its agents. The faith in social communication and in *belonging* to a group still leaves room for the idea of social division, even when the latter is camouflaged, that is, passed off as a flaw in the dialogue between individuals or classes, or as a rupture in cohesion. On the other hand, the representation of the social relationship is unconscious, the *entre-nous* assures both the implementation of the communication and the implication of the subject in the group. This implication requires neither the conceptualization of the actual group as the 'right' group, nor the identification with a power which is supposed to represent its unity. At the level of the *entre-nous*, the *nous* is not asserted but presupposed, destined to the factual invulnerability of remaining invisible. No doubt political leaders are led to proclaim 'we liberals', 'we men of progress', or 'we socialists', just as those who speak on the air do not hesitate to proclaim, outside any political context, 'we French'. But this 'we', however efficacious it may be, is secondary; for, prior to its utterance, the conditions of a network are established in which agents are linked together by being deprived of any mark of their opposition to one another, as well as any criterion of discourse as discourse.

Only these conditions allow ideological discourse to be constantly buried in the socialization process, and at the same time create the illusion that, in principle, nothing is removed from the sphere of communication. All contestation is focused on ideas, on particular agents – that is, precisely, on what appears, on what remains of bourgeois ideology, on its ineradicable residue which is, nonetheless, absolutely necessary for sustaining the dialogue and for the representation of oppositions. Yet what escapes, or tends to escape, contestation is the phantasmagoria of reciprocity, according to which everything is in principle sayable, visible, intelligible, for such is indeed the ultimate effect of the occultation of division: the image of an unlimited discourse in which everything would become transparent. One can understand, therefore, why this discourse pretends to ignore prohibitions; since it invades the social field, it abolishes all the distances which are carefully maintained by the discourse of bourgeois ideology. It introduces sexuality, violence and madness into the *entre-nous*; it effaces the division between the social world and its lowest depths; it ignores the danger of nature. This feature also distinguishes it from communist discourse which, forever haunted by the representation of a social whole, of a flawless body, does not tolerate any attachment to signs that seem to strike at its integrity and sustains itself by multiplying taboos about subjects which evade social control. And it is also distinguished by its propensity for letting its agents speak instead of restricting the right to speak, defending itself against the violation of its space by simulating within itself a place for the contradictor.

The effectiveness of the system also presupposes the representation of the scientificity of discourse. In a sense, this representation was at the heart of bourgeois ideology; but, with the latter, science still figures as a visible pole. There was a discourse on science as well as an exploitation of science in order to produce a discourse on the social. In the context of industrial production itself, a knowledge of the rationality of work was elaborated, a knowledge which was displayed but which was also circumscribed within the limits of a ruling apparatus. Taylorism, as is well known, eventually gave it full expression. Now, once again, we must certainly recognize the persistence of the old ideology, but, even more, we must assess the extent of the modifications which have occurred. Let us consider, to begin with, the industrial firm, not in order to specify the features of its actual transformation, but in order to examine the representation. This representation is that of the organization, of an organization which is not a product, a mere application of science, but one which embodies it and whose formula is not the property of the manager, but is inscribed in reality. This representation no longer tolerates the division between managers and those who carry out their directives, nor the division between human labour and the means of production; it links together all the terms by eliminating their subordination in order to articulate them within a structure which seems to function in itself, in response to rational imperatives, independently of the desires and choices of human beings. The image of the agency of decision and constraint and the image of the rule are concealed by the law of the organization. This law coincides with the discourse of the organization; it is hidden from the subjects' view, even though these subjects occasionally demonstrate its absurdity in the details of programmed operations. Its efficacy lies in the fact that it is not perceived as external, just as the efficacy of the discourse which conveys it lies in the fact that it is not obliged to appear as a discourse on the organization, or that the latter, in coming to be expressed, appears only as a part of the former and leaves its validity and legitimacy implicit. This consequence of the law and the discourse is possible only because the agents find in them the form of their established relation, because their action and co-operation are supposed to be pre-figured in the model of the organization. But it would be a mistake to think that the relation between individuals is reified, to use the Marxist term; the model tends to convert the subject into the 'organization man', as Whyte indicates. In other words, the reference points of the real become those of the organization, signs of a self-rationalization of the social; and the reference points of the subject's own identity are provided by a supposed knowledge that the organization possesses *about him*.

Again, it must be emphasized that this representation is not restricted to the industrial firm. It is disseminated in all the major social establishments, in commercial enterprises, in public and private administrations, in the universities, the hospitals and so on.

The discourse of the organization does not fulfil itself in the totalitarian phantasy. We have already indicated its limits. But it is important to point out that it receives support from the diffusion of the representation of science outside the context I have just mentioned. This representation cannot be localized; invested in it is a generalized belief in the self-intelligibility of reality and the self-intelligibility of human beings. In other words, at the level of objectivity, the distinctions essential to bourgeois ideology – those between nature, the psyche and society – tend to be effaced. In particular, it is impossible to appreciate the significance of the discourse of the organization, and how it is kept implicit, without considering the work carried out by the human sciences. As Marcuse rightly noted, the official discourse of psychology and sociology is governed by artificialism, operationalism and formalism. The psyche, society and culture are commonly defined as systems; hence the human sciences are governed by the general model of an organization, of the functioning of the personality, by the concepts of social integration, communication, tension and regulation, in the most simplistic or most sophisticated versions.

If we wished to develop the analysis of the various forms of the new ideology, we would have to examine the unique contribution of literature and literary theory, of philosophy or aesthetics (even more so in that they are most often presented as anti-ideological critiques). The pursuit of a language which raises the question of its genesis, which no longer accepts the self-assurance of the narrative, the novel, the image, the theory, the self-assurance of a natural distance between a supposed subject and a supposed object, which bids farewell to the established forms of reading and writing, of the viewer and the visible, of the author and the other, which welcomes the flight of meaning, the explosion of the origin (to borrow an apt expression from Merleau-Ponty), which is applied to deciphering the unconscious structures in which desiring and thinking are at work before any thought or desire appears as such – in short, everything that gives strength to the instituting discourse finds itself concealed beneath the new fiction of a machinery of the text, of thought, of desire, the fiction of an internal play of difference, of the 'real' suppression of the subject, of meaning, of origin, of history. It is a fiction which establishes new reference points, which is sustained by eluding the ordeal of the uncontrollable division between the self and the other, between sense and nonsense, between the space of the work and that of the world, between what is embedded within and what appears outside, a fiction which culminates, in all modes of writing, in a technique of illegibility that tends, very significantly, to defuse the danger of interpretation, providing its just response to the process of occultation which governs the discourse of the organization.

Since I can do no more here than offer a few sketchy remarks, let me emphasize the role of psychology, for it operates, not at the periphery, but at the centre of the new ideology. Indeed, how can one fail to see that it is psychology which provides the organization with the representation of a knowledge about the subject, which nourishes the phantasy of an evaluation of the agent, not only of his aptitude but of his personality. It materializes this phantasy in a battery of tests, questionnaires and interviewing manuals, in an apparatus claimed to be scientific, whose triple function is to establish the image of the 'organization man', to make him appear to himself under the knowledge of the other, and to dissimulate the image of those in power by generating the illusion of an impersonal norm.

Of course, one could rightly observe that the entire system of education, and not only psychology, is organized according to a capacity to measure knowledge and imposes the self-image of an evaluated individual. Is it necessary to add in passing that one of the dominant themes in modern education, self-assessment, is among the most effective for obliterating the presence of the teacher and rendering invisible the discourse of power? In any case, the cult of the qualification – even independently of the efforts of the educational system to procure 'socially necessary' agents for the world of the organization – generates throughout society the identification of the individual with the agent of knowledge.

Although it is more specific, the action of psychology is no less decisive, for it is through its activities that the imaginary of the 'personality' arises: a system which is decipherable for the other, or, since the other takes refuge behind science, one which is accessible to the understanding of the organization. Indeed, one could not give too much attention to the role of the psychologist in the educational system. Even very young children are subjected to testing; already at this age the psychologist's knowledge takes hold of them and marks them with the sign of inaptitude or deviance. Gradually, the psychologist is substituted for the teacher in order to displace the relation to the law, to ward off the visible blow of authority and to relate the sanction to the decree of a neutral and anonymous power.

Moreover, it is impossible not to examine the great show of scientificity developed by the radio, the television and the press. The incantation of social communication is complemented by an incantation of information. We must not underestimate the hold of the expert's knowledge, or of the functionaries engaged in scientific popularization, who, day after day, dispense the truth about child rearing, for example, about the couple, sexuality, the secrets of the organism or of space. It is not only the magic of the *entre-nous* which renders everything sayable; it is also the magic of objectivity. One feature of the system which must not escape our attention indicates once again the distance taken with regard to totalitarian ideology. The closure of knowledge is not represented, nor does it have to be. If everything can be said, that which is said will be marked by indeterminacy; hence its perpetual novelty. Whereas totalitarianism ensures itself against the risk of the fracturing of time by brutally asserting an historical truth which turns future progress into a development of the present (in such a way that only certain things can be said within the boundaries of the established order, and that the unknown is domesticated, circumscribed in the sphere of what is known), the new ideological discourse takes hold of the signs of the new, cultivates them in order to efface the threat of the historical. Just as social communication is content to be realized here and now, knowledge is exhibited here and now, bearing the solution to the secret of nature and the secret of man, giving rise to the fascination with the present. Thus, not knowing means not coinciding with the time, not coinciding with the being of the social as it manifests itself. Not knowing means incurring the tacit sanction of society, excluding oneself from the legitimate social bond.

The 'new', then, is nothing more than the materialized proof of temporal difference, of the historical, and hence of its concealment beneath the illusion of a difference in time, of a controllable distance between the present and the past, of a controllable relation to the present as such. Invisible once again is the operation which defuses the effects of the institution of the social, which attempts to prohibit the question of the sense of the established order, the question of the *possible*. Whereas the possible is linked to desire, bringing into play the rejection of what is accepted, newness blocks the view. It is the rattle that an infantilized group tries to grasp or catch, always a step behind the movement which reveals the object to be known. And once again we must not neglect to associate the mania for newness inside organizations with the mania manifested – especially in France, which is exemplary in this respect – in the circles of the intelligentsia, devoured as they are by the fear of not producing or not grasping the latest little thing which guarantees the death of the past and the fullness or splendour of the present.

Finally, from this point of view one could interpret the function of the ideology of consumption. Many analyses of the practice of consumption, conducted in the context of a critical sociology, could not avoid giving rise to ambiguities. I suspect that this practice would have to be analysed in relation to the genesis of historical society. Perhaps we could do no better than interpret in this phenomenon the signs of the institution of the social, of which no one is the instigator, nor do better than see therein a world in which our own identity is given to us. On the other hand, the representation which haunts the practice of consumption is open to criticism precisely in so far as it arises from the institution's attempts to dissimulate it, precisely in so far as it elaborates a 'response' which seeks to ward off the insecurity engendered by differentiation and by the non-knowledge of differentiation in time and space.

Baudrillard has shown in depth that the consumer product, whatever its nature, does not become attractive by virtue of responding to some need whose origin can be located in the individual or group. It is the representative of a 'system of objects' in which demand and satisfaction are conjoined and the articulation of signs between them is governed, in such a way that it closes in on itself and presents the illusion of the social as such. In this sense, the discourse of consumption condenses the representation of the organization and that of communication. It introduces one to a world in which the difference between producer and product is effaced through the appearance of an independent network of objects, and in which the difference between one subject and another is simultaneously effaced through the appearance of a common belonging to the same world. But it should also be noted that what is consumed is constantly new, the representative of a difference in time which nourishes desire by simulating the indefinite return of the object desired, at the very moment when the latter is ensnared in the representation. This simulation indicates, once again, the attempt to represent the historical, to make change invisible by establishing the visible reference point, by thrusting forth the new.

However, by restricting ourselves to these observations, we might miss the essential ideological function of the discourse of consumption. For the fiction it substantiates is that of a world in which human beings perceive only the signs of human beings. It is a world whose space is open to any path, where everything is graspable, however modest one's means may be; it is a world in which vision, the manipulation of objects and movement are magnified without limit and fitted to an all-visible, all-manipulable, all-explorable world. We need only consider the little advertising fable which presents us with the house of our dreams, completed and ready to welcome us, the key in the door; it sums up a very long discourse on the social, teaching us that the things of outside are there, within, that the universe is arranged for man, that nature is his environment. There, ideology completes its task, it brings about the great closure; but it makes it invisible, for it has no need of statements about the total man and the total society.

But although it completes its task, does that mean that its contradictions have been resolved? How could they be if it is true that historical society is that society which undermines every representation of its institution?

The more the discourse on the social seeks to coincide with social discourse, the more it seeks to control the uncontrollable movement of the institution, to take hold of the signs of the instituting moment,

# Part III

# Democracy and Totalitarianism

# 7

# Politics and Human Rights

Not long ago, the review *Esprit* organized a conference around the theme, 'Do human rights constitute a form of politics?'. It is a question worth asking. But, in my view, it calls for a second question: Do human rights belong to the sphere of the political? Moreover, should one not relate both questions to a third which is logically prior to both: Are we justified in speaking of human rights, and what do we mean by the term? If we believe that there are rights inherent in human nature, can we do without a definition of what is characteristically human? It is true that to confront this or the first question head on would be somewhat foolhardy. Not only would we run the risk of getting caught up in a reflection which would obscure our initial purpose, but the answer would no doubt remain elusive. The fact is that one of the most penetrating thinkers of our time, Leo Strauss, prepared the way for such a reflection without going so far as to reach a conclusion. We can learn from his book, *Natural Right and History*, that the question of human nature was in no way settled by the abandonment of the premises of classical thought, that it has continued to haunt modern thought and has become more complicated as a result of the contradictions engendered by positive science and historicism. Such a lesson is certainly not insignificant, but it does leave a great deal of uncertainty. And yet if we have to abandon a set of questions on the grounds of their difficulty, there is a danger that we will cut ourselves off from them entirely. The question that concerns us would be debased; we would continue to ask ourselves only if we could avail ourselves of the idea of human rights, of the demands that are inspired by them, with a view to mobilizing collective energies and converting them into a force capable of standing up to other forces in what is called the political arena. We would argue in terms of utility, even though we would invoke the noble motive of resistance to oppression.

How, then, can we avoid the facilities of pragmatism, without giving way to the vertigo of philosophical doubt? It seems to me that the best way of approaching the matter is to begin with the second question. In fact, this question serves as a hinge for the other two. Nothing rigorous can be said about a politics of human rights until one has examined whether these rights have a properly political significance; and nothing can be said about the nature of the political that does not involve an idea of human existence or, what amounts to the same thing, of human co-existence.

Moreover, it should be pointed out that this question arises in the specific historical conditions in which we find ourselves; it testifies to a new sensitivity to issues of politics and rights. It is a question which must be confronted by all those who are no longer satisfied with an analysis in terms of relations of production, still less in terms of ownership, and for whom the abandonment of the perspective of communism has in no way led to a withdrawal into a religious or moral vision of the world, but has led, on the contrary, to the search for new modes of thought and action.

The spread of Marxism throughout the whole of the French Left has long gone hand in hand with a devaluation of rights in general and with the vehement, ironic or 'scientific' condemnation of the bourgeois notion of human rights. And we should note in passing, before coming back to this point, that, for once, Marxism was not unfaithful to the inspiration of its founder; Marx's famous critique of the 'rights of man' in *On the Jewish Question*, though a product of his youth, was not contradicted by his later works, nor by the contributions of his heirs. Quite recently, Marxism has begun to change its tone; it has taken on a liberal phraseology, while a small number of ideologues, who previously presented themselves as the intransigent guardians of the doctrine, have turned against it. We all know where the shock came from. The discovery of the extent of the system of concentration camps in the Soviet Union, through the flood of information diffused by the victims of the Gulag, with Solzhenitsyn foremost among them, followed by the efforts of dissidents throughout the socialist states, availing themselves of the Helsinki Agreements in order to demand respect for human rights, have had a most disturbing effect on many minds. These rights no longer seem to be formal, intended to conceal a system of domination; they are now seen to embody a real struggle against oppression. From now on, those who disapprove or condemn repression in the countries of the East feel obliged to recognize that these rights have a value here, in the context of so-called bourgeois democracy, and to declare that the establishment of socialism would have to safeguard them.

Yet what do we hear in the new declarations in favour of human rights? Either they are defined as the indispensable complement of a good regime, a complement which is still lacking in socialism but which will be added at some future date, or they provide proof of an independence of mind or heart in face of the sinister constraints of politics. While some dream only of remodelling socialism so that it may acquire a 'human face', others are content to invoke the humanity of man in order to defend it against the aggression of the state – an evil state, whatever its nature. It is as if, on the Marxist side, human rights have made it possible to rediscover the virtues of the '*supplément d'âme*' and, on the side of the destroyers of socialist idols, they have led to the re-establishment of the opposition between the individual and society, or that between the inner man and the man enslaved in the city.

The action of the dissidents has certainly given rise to a revaluation of human rights, but few attempts have been made to assess its significance. Most of the dissidents, it is true, declared that they had no wish to 'get involved in politics'; this made it all the easier for those in the West who did not wish to hear. But what did those declarations mean? It is true that they had no political ambitions, that they were not seeking to overthrow the established power, to propose a new programme for the government, to create an opposition party, or to develop some new doctrine in opposition to Marxism. They demanded no more than the guarantees in force in the democratic nations, without which there was neither liberty nor security for the citizen. However, there is no need to attribute hidden intentions to them in order to discover the political sense of their action. For as soon as the rights that they are demanding become incompatible with the totalitarian system, it is only too clear that they are involved in politics, even though they have no political aim, programme or doctrine; and it becomes equally clear that these rights turn out, in practice, to be bound up with a general conception of society – of what was once called the *polis* or city – which totalitarianism directly negates. What is new in recent years, in the Soviet Union and Eastern Europe as well as in China, is not, I would suggest, that individuals are protesting against the arbitrary action of the police, denouncing the subjection of the courts to the state and demanding specific liberties, but rather that they are now placing their action under the sign of the defence of human rights; and what is also new is not, of course, that they are persecuted for their opinions and condemned without being able to defend themselves, but rather that human rights have become, through them, the enemy of power. A fundamental opposition is thus emerging – beyond the fact, which has long been established, of the coercion exercised on individuals and groups – between a totalitarian model of society (whatever its many variants may be, Stalinist or neo-Stalinist, Maoist or neo-Maoist) and a model which implies the recognition of rights.

This opposition is not one which has exercised the minds of what is called the Left in France. On several occasions, the Communist Party, notably through its general secretary, Georges Marchais, has protested against the arrest and imprisonment of dissidents. His recent statements on the Prague trials were particularly strongly worded. But when he declares that one cannot prosecute individuals for having the wrong opinions, who bothers to ask him if the defence of human rights is the expression of an opinion? And when he claims his allegiance to those rights, who bothers to ask him what their political implications might be? Before the break-up of the Union of the Left in France, the socialists were happy to exploit the protestations of the Communist Party in the interests of their electoral strategy, delighted at being able to present their ally as a party that had been won over to the cause of democracy. But was this mere opportunism? It is worth asking the question. For I believe that their attitude testifies just as much to their inability to conceive of human rights as anything other than the rights of the individual. They share this conception with the majority of the French Left, whether actually Marxist or merely imbued with Marxism. In fact, the non-communist members of the Left wish to be both liberal and socialist. As liberal, they readily invoke the principles of 1789 (which does not prevent them, in all likelihood, from adoring Robespierre) and are content to imagine a happy *mélange* of socialism and freedom. Their blindness with regard to totalitarianism finds an explanation here. When they read the ever-increasing mass of documented evidence, they are certainly capable of discovering all the signs of a new system of domination; but they go no further than to conclude that bureaucratic power is distressingly arbitrary. And although they condemn the vices of this system, they continue to regard the regimes of the Soviet Union, Eastern Europe, China or Vietnam as socialist (only the case of Cambodia leaves them perplexed). Beneath all these judgements lies the tenacious idea that reality is to be defined at the level of the relations of property and relations of power; as for the issue of rights, when it is seen as anything more than a rationalization of these relations, it is installed in the sanctuary of morality, a sanctuary that each individual carries within himself.

So we should not be surprised by the ease with which the communists combine criticism of the trials of the Soviet dissidents with defence of a regime presented as 'positive in an overall sense'. They have room to manoeuvre, for they are borrowing a logic which is not their own but which they turn skilfully to their advantage. But it is still not enough to observe how this logic governs the thinking of the Left; we must also see how it operates outside its frontiers. Modern conservative thinking does not doubt that relations of property and relations of power constitute the essence of politics, however keen it is to extol the values of democracy. Of course, it regards individual liberties and the guarantees accorded to the security of citizens as sacred. But it scrupulously distinguishes between what falls within the domain of morality and what falls within the domain of politics, where the latter concerns the competition for power and the necessites of preserving the established order or the *raison d'état*.

Hence there is a general indifference with regard to the violations of rights committed by political figures: it is accepted that every means will be used to defend their position, just as it seems to go without saying that relations between states are determined by interest or by the imperatives of power. This would explain, for example, the cynical reactions of many people when the scandal of the Watergate Affair burst in the United States some years ago.

The Communist Party is thus protected from the criticisms which would penetrate most deeply. When it reproves the methods of Stalinist repression or what is left of them, some are amazed at what they hear; others attack it for speaking out too late, too timidly, too seldom. Its enemies, who regard the Party's statements as hypocritical, are worried about their positive effect on liberal voters. But no one comes forward to say whether or not the Soviet state's aggression against rights is an aggression against the social body. The question is not asked, because it would imply the idea that rights are constitutive of politics. Yet, without such an idea, it may be noted in passing, one cannot even say that the defence in principle of individual liberties is incompatible with the justification of Stalinism. One is content to reduce human rights to those of individuals in order to bring out, at a distance from the latter, an order of reality *sui generis*. Henceforth the only relevant problem is whether, in given historical conditions, the preservation of the state could, or can at present, accommodate itself, and to what degree, to the exercise of such rights. From now on, the facts decide what is right. In other words, it is a question of examining whether certain coercive methods of government were deduced, or are being deduced, from the need to preserve a political system – socialism – or whether they were and still are going beyond such needs. In this context, the communists may quite safely concede to their liberal interlocutors that arbitrary arrests for holding the wrong views, let alone the concentration camps, are to be condemned, but this condemnation is carefully adapted to the criterion of realism, in accordance with the convention, *accepted on both sides*, that the violation of human rights is a violation of individual rights, of rights which are not political. Thus they are able to demonstrate that errors of government, of which individuals (even if they amount to millions) were victims, do not allow us to call into question the nature of the state, since the latter is distinct from the nature of individuals, since the state obeys laws and is subject to constraints which are specific to it. And they can still declare that the definition of Stalinism as a historically determinate form of socialism cannot be placed in question by the investigation of what are called its 'excesses', since these excesses are merely the by-products of an intitial excess of political authority, which is itself unassailable since it was required by the imperatives of social cohesion. But irrespective of the way that the communists defend their point of view, their defence is always effective, for they speak the same language as their non-communist partners or their enemies.

Now those who resolutely break with political realism and take up unconditionally the defence of human rights do not free themselves from this language, for this break is accompanied by a pure and simple refusal to think about politics. They elaborate a religion of resistance to all power and turn the dissidents into modern martyrs. But by anchoring human rights in the individual, they are unable to conceive of the difference between totalitarianism and democracy, except in terms of a difference in degree of oppression; and, by the same token, they give new credit to the Marxist view, which, in its initial state, rightly denounced the fiction of 'abstract man' and exposed its function in the context of bourgeois society.

We must extricate ourselves from Marx's framework if we are to give the notion of human rights its full meaning. But, in doing so, we must not fall short of his thought; on the contrary, we must return to his critique of human rights, which was not at all pointless, in order to uncover the error or illusion which underlies his argument and which links it so closely to those of his present-day adversaries.

## Marx's Critique of Human Rights

It was, I said, in *On the Jewish Question* that Marx presented the central themes of his interpretation of human rights; let us therefore examine this work. Marx's interpretation stems from the conviction that the representation of these rights in the late eighteenth century, first in the United States and then in France, served only to provide a cover for the dissociation of individuals in society and a separation between this atomized society and the political community. 'Who is *homme* as distinct from *citoyen?*' Marx asks. 'None other than the *member of civil society*. Why is the member of civil society called "man", simply man? Why are his rights called the *rights of man*? How is this fact to be explained? From the relationship between the political state and civil society, from the nature of political emancipation.' And he goes on to observe: 'The so-called *rights of man*, the *droits de l'homme* as distinct from the *droits du citoyen*, are nothing but the rights of a *member of civil society*, i.e., the rights of egoistic man, of man separated from other men and from the community.'[1] Marx derives from these propositions a series of consequences concerning the status of opinion, in particular religious opinion, liberty, equality, property and security. What does he have to say about opinion? In sum, that it is recognized as legitimate at the moment when it seems to be a spiritual equivalent of private property. On liberty? That, defined as the individual's 'right to do everything that harms no one else', it presupposes that each individual is 'an isolated monad, withdrawn into himself'. On property? That, defined legally as each citizen's right 'to enjoy and to dispose as he wishes of his property, his income, the fruit of his labour and industry', it makes every man see in other men 'not the *realization* of his own freedom, but the *barrier* to it'. On equality? That it simply offers a new version of the theory of the monad. And, lastly, on security? That it is 'the highest social concept of civil society, the concept of *police*, expressing the fact that the whole of society exists in order to guarantee to each of its members the preservation of his person, his rights, and his property'. It is, in short, the '*insurance* of his egoism'.[2]

Now the experience of totalitarianism throws a sinister light on the weaknesses of this interpretation. Totalitarianism is built on the ruin of the rights of man. However, under this regime, man is dissociated from man and separated from the community, as he never was in the past. But this is not because he is supposed to represent the natural individual; no, it is because he is supposed to represent communist man, because his individuality must be dissolved in a good body politic, the Soviet people or the party. This dissolution is at one and the same time the dissolution of the difference between man and man and of the difference between man and the collectivity. It is not because he is assigned to the limits of a private life, to the status of the monad, because he enjoys the right to have opinions, freedoms, property and security, but because this enjoyment is forbidden. Lastly it is not because civil society is supposed to be dissociated from the state, but because the state is supposed to hold the principle of all forms of socialization and all modes of activity.

It is true that Marx's interpretation claims to account for a great historical event, the transition from feudalism to bourgeois society. For him, feudalism designates a type of society in which all of the elements – material and spiritual – had a political character, in which they were incorporated into organically linked wholes, the seigneuries, the estates, the corporations, the guilds. In putting an end to this system, he observes,

> the political revolution thereby *abolished* the *political character of civil society*. It broke up civil society into its simple component parts; on the one hand, the individuals, on the other hand, the *material* and *spiritual elements* constituting the content of the life and social position of these individuals. It set free the political spirit, which had been, as it were, split up, partitioned and dispersed in the various blind alleys of feudal society. It gathered the dispersed parts of the political spirit, freed it from its intermixture with civil life, and established it as the sphere of the community, the *general* concern of the nation, ideally independent of those *particular* elements of civil life.[3]

However, the historical analysis of the transition from the feudal to the bourgeois world is framed within a theory of human emancipation that determines its meaning. The entire work which we are considering, and in particular its conclusion, is convincing on this point. Marx retains from the bourgeois revolution what he calls 'political emancipation', that is, the delimitation of a sphere of politics as a sphere of the universal, at a distance from society, leaving society reduced to a combination of particular interests and individual existences, broken down into its component parts. He regards this political emancipation as a necessary and transitory phase in the process of human emancipation. And since this phase is conceived of by the bourgeoisie as the very realization of human emancipation, he sees it as the moment of the 'political illusion' *par excellence*. In this sense, political 'emancipation' and political 'illusion' turn out for him to be indissociable. And since, simultaneously, the particular elements of civil society are detached from one another as if they were independent, the political illusion coincides according to him with the illusion of the independence of these elements, or with the illusory representation of the rights of man whose aim it is to maintain it. In other words, politics and the rights of man constitute the two poles of the same illusion.

If this is the theoretical structure of the analysis of the bourgeois democratic revolution, we are entitled to ask whether it can support an analysis of the totalitarian revolution. Now it may well be necessary to reverse most of the terms in order to account for the latter. Indeed, totalitarianism tends to abolish all the signs of the autonomy of civil society, to negate the particular determinations that might compose it. Apparently, the *political spirit* is then propagated throughout the social sphere. The party, as the representative of the political spirit, undertakes to form an alliance between the state, which is supposed to embody the people in general, and all the institutions of civil society. However, no one who reads Marx in good faith will conclude that totalitarianism provides the formula for what he called 'human emancipation'. Among all the reasons that make such a conclusion impossible, let me mention only one: the process of the destruction of civil society entails a formidable extension of the political sphere, but certainly not its disappearance. In other words, the propagation of the political spirit goes together with the strengthening of the power which is supposed to represent the community and to decide 'what is of concern to the people in general'. In the light of Marx's account, totalitarianism appears as that regime in which the 'political illusion' is at its peak, in which it is materialized in a state that possesses all power (or at least tries to do so). At that point, the rights of man are destroyed; the relationship between 'politics' and the 'rights of man', which Marx saw as the two poles of the same illusion, disappears. Hence we must make a preliminary observation: Marx's framework has been undermined by the events of our time. But this leads to a second observation: his critique of the rights of man, situated as it is in the context of an analysis of the bourgeois democratic revolution, was already ill-founded. This does not necessarily undermine the whole of his critique. To rush to this conclusion would be to ignore one rather remarkable fact: on many occasions, Marx confined himself to commenting on, sometimes even paraphrasing, extracts from the American Constitution, or from the Declarations of 1791 or 1793. We must, therefore, force a certain moderation upon Marx's detractors, who claim to champion the rights of man but who prefer to ignore the ambiguities in these rights, to retain nothing of the formulations that lent themselves and still lend themselves to objections, not only from Marx or Marxists, but from those who are not content to accept egoism as the rule of conduct of individuals in society. Many of those formulations, in the Declaration of 1791, which served as a model in Europe, certainly give substance to the image of a sovereign individual, whose power to act or to possess, to speak or to write, is limited only by the power of other individuals to do likewise. Moreover, it is not arbitrary to regard the right to property, stated in the last article, as the only right which can be characterized as sacred and as the one on which all the others are based. So it is not so much what Marx sees in the rights of man that ought to elicit our criticism as what he is unable to find in them. Indeed Marx falls into and draws us into a trap, which, on other occasions and for other purposes, he was very skilful in dismantling: that of ideology. He allows himself to become the prisoner of the ideological version of rights, without examining what they mean in practice, what profound changes they bring to social life. And, as a result, he becomes blind to what, in the very text of the Declaration, appears on the margins of ideology.

Let us now return to this text. Consider Marx's response to the article on liberty, which stipulates that: 'Liberty consists of being able to do everything which does not harm others'. Marx's comment is that this right turns man into a 'monad' and that it is based not on the association of man with man, but, on the contrary, on the separation of man from man: 'It is the *right* of this separation, the right of the *restricted* individual, withdrawn into himself.'[4] Thus he circumscribes the negative function of 'not harming' by subordinating it to the positive function of 'being able to do everything which . . .', without taking into consideration the fact that any human action in the public sphere, however society may be constituted, necessarily links the subject to other subjects. Since this link is a primary given, which has nothing to do with particular political or institutional mechanisms (or, what amounts to the same thing, since the isolation, the monadism of the individual is strictly unthinkable), since even when he is in fact separated from his fellow men, this separation is still a modality of his relation to others, the only question ought to be the following: What, in this or that society, in this or that social formation, are the limits imposed upon the action of its members, the restrictions laid down on where they live, their movements, their ability to visit certain places, to pursue certain careers, to change their conditions of life, or on their mode of expression and communication? Instead of posing this question, Marx strangely ignores the lifting of the many restrictions which weighed upon human action under the *ancien régime*, before the democratic revolution; he ignores the practical significance of the Declaration of Rights, captivated as he is by the image of a power anchored in the individual and capable of being exercised only up to the point at which it encounters the power of others. Of course, he did not invent this image. It emerges in the article on liberty, it is true; but it is no less true that it disguises a new mode of access to the public sphere. However, much more significant is Marx's reluctance to appreciate the two articles concerning the freedom of opinion, the second of which is nevertheless as precise as it could be. In fact, he does not even comment on them in the passage devoted to the examination of the rights of man, and this omission is in itself worthy of note, for it reveals his prejudice. But the argument of *On the Jewish Question* is essentially intended to demonstrate, against Bauer's thesis, that the right to express one's religious convictions – even those of the Jews, who imagine themselves to belong to a people apart and whose beliefs apparently contradict their membership of a political community – this right merely testifies to the split that has occurred and has been sanctified by the rights of man between the individual, particular, private element, which constitutes civil society, on the one hand,

and the life of the state, on the other, between the member of bourgeois society and the citizen. Certainly it would be wrong to deduce
from this argument that Marx is against religious freedom, or even,
as some imprudent or foolish individuals have maintained, that he
shows himself to be anti-semitic. But one must admit that freedom of
conscience is for him merely the most eloquent expression of the
democratic fiction – a fiction that marks, let me repeat, a necessary,
but transitory, phase of human emancipation.

Now what exactly is said in the articles that Marx passes over in
silence? Article 10 declares: 'No one may be challenged in his right
to hold opinions, even religious opinions, provided that their expression does not disturb the public order established by law.' Article 11
states: 'The free communication of thoughts and opinions is one of
the most precious rights of man, every citizen may therefore speak,
write and freely print, unless what he does constitutes an abuse of
that liberty in the particular cases laid down by law.' Was Marx so
obsessed by his schema of the bourgeois revolution that he could not
see that freedom of opinion is a freedom of relationships, just as it is
said in this case to be a freedom of communication? Of course, in
other writings of his youth he defended the freedom of the press. But
my purpose here is not to examine the variations in his thought; all
that matters is the coherence of a line of argument whose effects can
still be seen, in our time, among those who certainly do not possess
the generous intentions of the founder. Now the object of Marx's
critique is the bourgeois representation of a society made up of
individuals; it is aimed at the representation of opinion as the private
property of the individual, understood as the thinking individual.
This representation can indeed be discerned; but it is not adequate
to the sense of the transformation which has taken place. It cannot
even be translated into the language of the Declaration without
being contradicted. Even supposing that the first of the two articles
mentioned does not go beyond the metaphor of property, the second
clearly implies that it is man's right, one of his most precious rights,
to step out of himself and to make contact with others, through
speech, writing and thought. Moreover, it suggests that man cannot
be legitimately assigned to the limits of his private world, that he has
a right to public speech and thought. Or, better still, for these last
formulas run the risk of reducing communication to the operations
of its agents, individuals, defined one by one as instances of man in
himself, let us say that the article suggests that there is a communi-

cation, a circulation of thoughts and opinions, speech and writing which in principle falls outside the authority of political power, except in cases specified by law. It is the independence of thought and opinion with regard to power, the separation between power and knowledge, that is at stake in the affirmation of the rights of man, and not only or not essentially the split between the bourgeois and the citizen, between private property and politics. Why did Marx not see this? Why did he see the defence of opinion as merely the sign of a fiction which converts man into a monad? Why did he hold this view when he knew better than many others that, in reality, society was not reducible to a juxtaposition of individuals and when he was, therefore, quite capable of understanding that the rights imputed to individuals were embedded in a social context which bourgeois discourse could not dispose of as it wished? Let us leave the question unanswered for a moment in order to take up the contemporary debate on the freedom of opinion.

In the socialist states, it is not individual rights that are violated when people are condemned for holding the wrong opinions. And it is not a matter of errors or mistakes, of accidental infractions of legality which have to do with a defective exercise of power. Such events attest to a particular mode of constituting society, to the specificity of its political system. For the ambition of totalitarian power is to reduce public thought and speech to its pole; to encircle the public sphere – an objective, of course, that is impossible to attain and towards which it only tends – in order to convert it into its private sphere, a sphere which would ideally coincide with the 'body' of the Soviet people and properly belong to it, while at the same time defining its law of organization. Thus, one might reverse the common argument: when, for once, the Soviet bureaucrats allow the publication of accounts written by former prisoners of the Gulag or allow Sakharov to speak in front of foreign journalists, it is then that there is a violation of principle, the totalitarian principle, and there is perhaps an error or mistake, in any case a cruel compromise with the reality principle. But when human rights are violated, the violation exists only in the eyes of the victims; the state is acting in accordance with the nature of the regime. It does not give in to the arbitrary, it is not undergoing some return to the Stalinist fever, it is not giving a lesson to its opponents; it is not a fear of the people that is at work, since it is in the nature of tyrants to instill fear in the people – no, it is simply that the logic of the system prevents it from accepting any opinion which may be seen as a sign that social life is external to power, that there is an otherness in the social sphere.

But to return to Marx – Marx, who had only bourgeois society to observe, who put all his energy into conceiving of 'human emancipation' and whom I would not dream of accusing of foolishness or hypocrisy. Why is he so blind to the questions of the rights of man? Why is he captivated by the bourgeois ideology of the rights of man? Let us look more closely at this blindness. He comments ironically on security, basing his case on an article in the Constitution of 1795: '*Security* is the highest social concept of civil society, the concept of *police*, expressing the fact that the whole of society exists only in order to guarantee to each of its members the preservation of his person, his rights, and his property.'[5] In fact, the commentary alters the sense of the text; for the latter stipulates that security consists in the protection afforded by society to each of its members for the preservation of his person, etc. No less remarkable is the neglect of the Declaration of 1791, which, in other respects, he exploits abundantly, and the articles of which are more precise. For instance, article 7 states: 'No man may be accused, arrested, or detained except in cases laid down by the law and in accordance with prescribed forms. Those who elicit, expedite, carry out or have carried out arbitrary orders must be punished; but any citizen called upon or seized by virtue of the law must obey instantly; resistance will be construed as guilt.' Article 8: 'The law must lay down only those penalties that are strictly and obviously necessary; and nobody may be punished except under a law established and promulgated prior to the offence and legally applied.' Article 9: 'Any man being presumed innocent until he has been found guilty, if it is considered indispensable to arrest him, any harshness that is not necessary to secure his person must be severely punished by the law.'

I hope I will be forgiven for reminding the reader of such well-known texts, but it is useful to compare them with Marx's interpretation. Marx is not concerned to demonstrate that the principles expressed are transgressed in practice, or even that their expression may permit their transgression – in short, he does not draw a distinction between their form and their content, as he was to do, for example, in *The Eighteenth Brumaire* when analysing the Constitution of 1848. He ignores the recognized function of the written law, the status that it acquires in its separation from the sphere of power, a status that protects it from the circumstantial exploitation by legislators subject to government pressure and confers upon it the necessary authority for it to be applied even to those in government and to their agents. He brings law down to the level of empirical reality, this being conceived as the reality of individual relationships, and thus turns it into a device intended to preserve those relationships. But, it will be said, Marx denounces the utilitarian definition of the law, which is based on the idea of the egoistic individual. That is certainly true, but at the same time he exploits it, basing his own critique on the idea of generic life or the generic being. Far from merely rejecting a bourgeois interpretation of the law, he effaces the dimension of the law as such. The law, to which the Declaration refers, has no other meaning for him than that which he assigns it in the bourgeois representation. We hardly need to be reminded that Marx is not trying to defend the prerogatives of power, to free power from all constraints and to place individuals at its mercy; he is trying to conceive of a society delivered from the oppression and exploitation of human beings by one another. But, within that society, he does not envisage any particular institution and he does not make room for human rights because individuals seem to him at that point to be immediately immersed in social life, in a fully human life, or because they seem to him to breathe the same air of freedom. Such a vision prevents Marx, for example, from considering the formula 'Each man being innocent until he has been found guilty . . .' and from seeing in it an irreversible acquisition of political thought. He ignores it because this formula presupposes that there are innocent individuals and guilty individuals and third parties, the latter capable of arbitrarily confusing the innocent and the guilty or indeed of correctly distinguishing between them; he ignores it because it presupposes distinctions which are not of the order of life, but which are symbolic. Much more striking to Marx, almost to the point of blinding him, than the guarantee given to the innocent was the notion of guilt, the image of a position from which the true and the false, the just and the unjust, are enunciated, a position which reveals power and justice both in conjunction and disjunction.

So let us not be misled by the critique of bourgeois society as a society of egoism. It is true that Marx's critique of the rights of man is guided by the idea of a decomposition of society into individuals, a decomposition which seems to be the result of the unleashing of private interests, of the dissolution of bonds of dependence which were economic, social and political and which formed quasi-organic wholes. But Marx shares this idea with a great many of his contemporaries; it is at the heart of conservative, anti-individualistic and anti-bourgeois discourse; it is even to be found in the writings of liberals. Finally, we know the extent to which it was developed in Hegel, to whom Marx explicitly refers in *On the Jewish Question*. Little would be served here by pointing out what distinguishes Marx from Burke or de Bonald, de Maistre or Guizot, Hegel or de Tocqueville, and what they have in common. In my view, what is specific to Marx – and what, paradoxically, may have enabled him to decipher a reality that the others ignored or merely glimpsed, that of the relations of production and class relations – is his rejection of the political, which is very evident even before he has fully defined his field of interpretation. The critique of the individual is carried out as soon as one adopts a theory of society in which the dimension of power, and with it the dimensions of law and knowledge (giving this term its widest sense, to include opinions, beliefs and scientific knowledge) are abolished. Such a theory does not allow one to grasp the meaning of the historical mutation in which power is assigned limits and right is fully recognized as existing outside power: this double movement becomes unintelligible, a mere sign of illusion.

However, the illusion does not exist within the society where Marx lodges it; it exists in his own mind and it forces him to give an imaginary reconstruction of the formation of the modern state. He sees this state, it should be remembered, as the complement of bourgeois society, contrasting the new system with that of feudalism. Now it is certainly his refusal to think in political terms that prevents him from examining a development which should be analysed – namely, the development of the monarchical state, a state that long before the French Revolution had established itself by destroying both the organization and the spirit of feudalism. Had he done so, Marx would never have said that the advent of the democratic state marked the moment of the institution of an 'ideal community'. He would have had to agree that the figure of the Nation, of the People, of the agency that serves as guarantee of its unity, began to emerge in the fourteenth century, that the split of which he speaks between the universal and the particular took place for the first time in Europe as a result of the formation of the monarchy, based on a theory of sovereignty, and not as a result of the fragmentation of private interests. He would have had to agree that, far from the state arising out of the emancipation of bourgeois society, shaking itself free of the feudal world, it was much more the case that the establishment of territorial kingdoms, unified by the common allegiance of subjects to the monarch and gradually levelled down by state power, created the conditions for the expansion of the bourgeoisie. And he would have been led, in the wake of Hegel, to investigate the modality of the state–society division, as well as that of the class division and that of the articulation of power and right. The fact is that, as soon as one engages in such an investigation, the first development of the democratic state and the establishment of human rights appear in a new light. For if they mark a mutation of the political, this mutation occurs on the boundaries of a unique history, the history of the emergence of that state which embodies right, the *état de droit*. How can we forget that this state was instituted, on the one hand, as the result of a secularization of Christian values – and, in its earliest stage, as the result of the transfer of the representation of Christ the mediator between God and man to that of the king, mediator between the political community and its subjects – and, on the other hand, as the result of a religious reworking of the Roman legacy, its transcription into a problematic of transcendence, and of the mediation of juridico-rational values, which already sustained a definition of the sovereignty of the people, of the citizen, of the distinction between public and private, etc. What, with regard to this history, does the modern 'political revolution' signify? Not the separation of power and right, for such a separation was essential to the monarchical state. Rather, it signifies a phenomenon of disincorporation of power and disincorporation of right which accompanies the disappearance of 'the king's body', in which the community was embodied and justice mediated; and, by the same token, it signifies a phenomenon of disincorporation of society whose identity, though already figured in the nation, had not yet been separated from the person of the monarch.

Instead of speaking of 'political emancipation' as though it were a moment of political illusion, it would be better to examine the unprecedented event constituted by the separation of power and right – or, if we have fully appreciated what is involved in right, the simultaneous separation of the principle of power, the principle of law and the principle of knowledge. Separation, here, does not mean complete break; or, if the term break is suitable, it is only on condition that it does not efface the mode of articulation which is instituted by the break itself. Power does not become alien to right; on the contrary, its legitimacy is more than ever affirmed, it becomes more than ever the object of juridical discourse and, similarly, its rationality is more than ever examined. But the notion of human rights now points towards a sphere that cannot be controlled; right comes to represent something which is ineffaceably external to power. No doubt the prince, in the Christian monarchical state, had to respect rights, the many specific rights that had been acquired over the centuries (for example, those of the clergy, the nobility, the cities, estates and corporations); they were rights which were rooted in a past whose memory could not be erased, rights which belonged to a kind of pact. But those rights and that pact were supposed to constitute the monarchy itself, in such a way that the prince was subjected to them only because he conformed to its nature, as if it were an exercise of his own freedom, as if he bore the rights in himself, as if he had contracted the pact with himself. Though limited, the power of the prince was nevertheless unlimited in fact, to the extent that right seemed consubstantial with his own person. Subjected to right, in the sense that the origin of this right was to be found in God or in Justice, his power extended nevertheless beyond all limits, to the degree that he dealt only with himself in the relation that he formed with his subjects. Hence a quite different mode of externality in relation to power is established as soon as right is deprived of a fixed point.

This last statement may seem somewhat excessive. For surely a new point is fixed: man. And what is more, it is fixed by virtue of a written constitution: right is categorically established in the nature of man, a nature present in each individual. But what kind of anchor point is this? As soon as we ask the question, we are confronted by a triple paradox. The first form of the paradox is this: society is now conceived as a society of free and equal individuals, a society which is ideally one, in this sense, and homogeneous. However, as we have said, beyond the declaration of natural rights, and even in their very declaration, an essential mutation is apparent, for this society now turns out to be uncircumscribable, by virtue of the fact that it cannot be related to itself in all its elements and represent itself as a single body, deprived as it has now become of the mediation of an incorporated power. In other words, modes of existence, modes of activity and modes of communication, whose effects are indeterminate and which, for that very reason, move out of the orbit of power, are now recognized. The second form of the paradox is this: the rights of man are declared, and they are declared as rights that belong to man; but, at the same time, man appears through his representatives as the being whose essence it is to declare his rights. It is impossible to detach the statement from the utterance as soon as nobody is able to occupy the place, at a distance from all others, from which he would have authority to grant or ratify rights. Thus rights are not simply the object of a declaration, it is their essence to be declared. The third form of the paradox is this: the rights of man appear as those of individuals, individuals appear as so many little independent sovereigns, each reigning over his private world, like so many microentities separated off from the social whole. But this representation destroys another: that of a totality which transcends its parts. It discloses a transversal dimension of social relations, relations of which individuals are the terms but which confer on those individuals their identity, just as much as they are produced by them. For instance, the right of one individual to speak, to write, to print freely implies the right of another to hear, to read, to keep and pass on the material printed. By virtue of the establishment of these relations, a situation is constituted in which expression is encouraged, in which the duality of speaking and hearing in the public sphere is multiplied instead of being frozen in the relation of authority, or being confined in privileged spaces. One has only to consider the guarantees concerning the principle of security to realize that one cannot restrict oneself to the idea of protection of the individual. Once again, it must be said that what is called into question here is the notion of a society which would embrace, or rather include, individuals as its members and the notion of an organ which would decide their movements. It is the image of the engulfing of the particular within the social space which is destroyed.

Let us draw the consequences from these paradoxes. Once the rights of man are declared, there arises, so it is said, the fiction of man without determination. The entire critique of Marxist inspiration, but also the conservative critique, rushes into that fragile citadel and demolishes it. Thus Joseph de Maistre declared: 'I have met Italians, Russians, Spaniards, Englishmen, Frenchmen, but I do not know man'; and Marx thought that there were only concrete individuals, historically and socially determined, shaped by their class condition. With less talent, a number of our contemporaries continue to sneer at abstract humanism. Now the idea of man without determination cannot be dissociated from the idea of the *indeter-*

*minable.* The rights of man reduce right to a basis which, despite its name, is without shape, is given as interior to itself and, for this reason, eludes all power which would claim to take hold of it – whether religious or mythical, monarchical or popular. Consequently, these rights go beyond any particular formulation which has been given of them; and this means that their formulation contains the demand for their reformulation, or that acquired rights are not necessarily called upon to support new rights. Lastly, for the same reason, they cannot be assigned to a particular period, as if their meaning were exhausted by the historical function they were called upon to fulfil in the service of the rising bourgeoisie, and they cannot be circumscribed *within* society, as if their effects could be localized and controlled.

From the moment when the rights of man are posited as the ultimate reference, established right is open to question. It becomes still more so as the collective wills or, one might prefer to say, social agents bearing new demands mobilize a force in opposition to the one that tends to contain the effects of the recognized rights. Now, where right is in question, society – that is, the established order – is in question. While a class may have effective means at its disposal to exploit for its own ends and to deny others the guarantees of rights, and while power may have effective means to subordinate the administration of justice or subject laws to the imperative of domination, nevertheless these means remain exposed to an opposition in terms of right, an *opposition de droit.* This term, it seems to me, should be weighed carefully. The *état de droit* has always implied the possibility of an opposition to power based on right – an opposition like the remonstrances to the king or the refusal to comply with taxes in unjustifiable circumstances, even the recourse to insurrection against an illegitimate government. But the democratic state goes beyond the limits traditionally assigned to the *état de droit.* It tests out rights which have not yet been incorporated in it, it is the theatre of a contestation, whose object cannot be reduced to the preservation of a tacitly established pact but which takes form in centres that power cannot entirely master. From the legal recognition of strikes or trade unions, to rights relative to work or to social security, there has developed on the basis of the rights of man a whole history that transgressed the boundaries within which the state claimed to define itself, a history that remains open.

I hope it is clear that these remarks are not intended to call into question the justified criticisms brought against the actual application of human rights, or more generally against the actual formulation of the laws that are supposed to be based on them, or even against the representation that they substantiate of a liberty and an equality which would be valid for all, over and above the contingencies of social life. As long as they are made at the factual level, these criticisms are valid, whether they denounce the vices of legislation in this or that domain or the iniquities in the system of justice by attacking the interests and passions that govern them, or whether they dismantle the mechanisms by which opinion is manipulated or fabricated, or whether they show how the sacralization of property serves to mask the opposition between capital and labour. My main purpose was to bring out the symbolic dimension of human rights and to show that it has become a constitutive element of political society. It seems to me that if one ignores this dimension, considers only the subordination of juridical practice to the preservation of a system of domination and exploitation, or confuses the symbolic and the ideological, one can no longer see the damage to the social tissue that results from the denial of the principle of human rights in totalitarianism.

## Human Rights and Democratic Politics

I shall now venture to raise again the question with which I began. But perhaps it would be wise to reformulate it more prudently: Does the struggle for human rights make possible a new relation to politics? I would prefer to put it like that in order to suggest that it is not simply a question of examining the conditions of a particular political thought or action that has broken with ideology.

It seems that one must give a positive answer to this question and sustain it unhesitatingly with regard to the democratic societies in which we live. Indeed, it is impossible to confine the argument to the observation of totalitarianism, as I seemed at first to be doing. Under totalitarianism it is clear that human rights are annulled and that by struggling to get them recognized the dissidents are attacking the political foundation of the system. But it would still be misleading to declare simply: here, in our societies, these rights exist. For just as one has reason to say that the essence of totalitarianism is to reject them, so one must refrain from granting them a *reality* in our own society. These rights are one of the generative principles of democracy. Such principles do not exist in the same way as positive institutions, whose actual elements can be listed, even though it is certainly true that they animate institutions. Their effectiveness stems from the allegiance that is given them, and this allegiance is bound up with a way of being in society, which cannot be measured by the mere preservation of acquired benefits. In short, rights cannot be dissociated from the awareness of rights: this is my first observation. But it is no less true that this awareness of rights is all the more widespread when they are declared, when power is said to guarantee them, when liberties are made visible by laws. Thus the awareness of right and its institutionalization are ambiguously related. On the one hand, this institutionalization involves, with the development of a body of law and a caste of specialists, the possibility of a concealment of the mechanisms indispensable to the effective exercise of rights by the interested parties; on the other hand, it provides the necessary support for an awareness of rights. Furthermore, one sees, even under totalitarian domination, especially in the Soviet Union, what use the dissidents have been able to make of the established laws of the constitution, for all their vices. This remark would merit a whole examination to itself, for it shows that in a modern society, when the religious foundations of right are destroyed, power may deny right, but it is incapable of depriving itself of its reference to it. However, since we are speaking of democratic society, it should be observed that the symbolic dimension of right is manifested both in the irreducibility of the awareness of right to all legal objectification, which would signify its petrification in a corpus of laws, and in the establishment of a public register in which the writing of the laws – like any writing without an author – has no other guide than the continuous imperative of a deciphering of society by itself.

From such a point of view, to reduce the problem of right to the terms of the Marxist critique, to oppose form and content, to denounce the language that transposes and disguises the bourgeois relations and the economic reality on which those relations are supposed to rest, is, by ignoring this symbolic dimension, to deprive oneself of the means to understand the meaning of the demands whose aim is the inscription of new rights, as well as the changes that occur in society as a result of the dissemination of those demands and, no less, in the social representation of the difference between legitimate ways of life; lastly, it is to maintain intact the image of state power, in the tenacious conviction that only its conquest would make possible the development of something new. We can already assess the extent of this blindness, and also the extent of the tasks of a politics of human rights, by considering either the transformations that affected French society, or the forms of contestation that it has seen emerge, since the last war and still more since 1968. The inability to conceive of them politically, not so much provoked as masked by a fear of allowing the regime to take credit for them, has had strange consequences: whether they concern the family, women, children, or sexuality, whether they concern justice, the function of the magistrates or the condition of prisoners, whether they concern employment, the management of enterprises, the status of farmers or the defence of peasant property against the intrusion of the state, or whether they concern the protection of nature, we have seen either changes in legislation or the rise of new demands that, despite their failure, testify to new collective needs and, judging by the positive response that they have received, to a new social sensibility to these needs. And yet the parties or small vanguards of the Left have been able to do no more than feverishly exploit the signs of these transformations and these needs in the interests of their own strategy, introducing them as so many ingredients in their traditional programme, without ceasing to proclaim that socialism alone is able to change life.

Now is it not in the name of their rights that workers or employees challenge the right of a management to deprive them of work, that they press their claims to the point of taking over the management themselves, as happened at the Lip factory, that they rebel, here and there, against the working conditions that they have to endure, that they demand new measures for their safety? Is it not in the name of their rights that peasants, like those in the Larzac, resist the expropriation which is regarded as indispensable by the state? Is it not again in the name of their rights that women claim recognition of their equality with men, that homosexuals rise up against the prohibitions and repression to which they are subjected, that consumers band together or that city-dwellers and country people oppose the devastation of the natural environment? Are these various rights not affirmed by virtue of an awareness of right, without objective guarantee, and equally with reference to publicly recognized principles which are partly embodied in laws and which must be mobilized in order to destroy the legal limits that restrict them? And, lastly, can one not see that under the thrust of these rights, the web of political society either tends to change, or appears more and more susceptible to change?

If we wish to conceive of a new relationship to the political, we should begin by recognizing that it is beginning to take shape before our eyes. So our first task is not to invent; it is to interpret, to raise to the level of reflection a practice which is not silent, of course, but which, being necessarily diffuse, is unaware of its significance in society at large and which cannot be truthfully expressed by their political formations, for the latter are concerned merely to make use of these practices and, partly and not without some success, to disarm them. What is new in the character and style of these demands? In the first place, they are not looking for an overall solution to conflicts through the conquest or destruction of established power. Their ultimate objective is not that famous inversion which would place the dominated in the position of the dominators and pave the way for the dissolution of the state. I do not mean that the existence of state power is ignored. But in a sense, it is the opposite pole of this power which must be recognized. If one considers, for instance, the turn that the struggle against redundancies has recently taken, it would be a mistake to try to reduce this struggle to its economic significance; it appeals to a social right to work, the notion of which is actually very ancient, but which acquires new vigour in opposition to the power acquired by the state. The state is less and less able to leave entirely to individuals, however powerful they may be, the right to decide on their strategy, at the whim of circumstances and power relationships. It is too involved in the management of national production, directly as an entrepreneur and indirectly as regulator of the economic system and stabilizer of social conflicts, and too dependent on the constraints of all kinds which stem from its involvement in the world. Thus one sees the formation of a *social power* in which a multiplicity of elements, apparently distinct, and less and less formally independent, combine around political power.

Now it is this social power that is shattered by the right to work, as it is articulated in the various demands coming from one branch of production, one region, one locality or some enterprise determined to rid itself of its surplus workers. The legality of actions taken by employers or bureaucrats, whose exercise, according to the conventional image, the state is supposed to guarantee, as if it existed above the parties concerned, is opposed by a new idea of what is socially legitimate: an idea of such force that it sometimes gives protest a character close on rebellion, while the symbols of authority are singled out as its targets (this is evident in the occupation of the 'sacred' space of the management's offices in a factory or the sequestration of its representatives). The way in which legality is challenged in the course of demonstrations is an indication of the contestation of established legitimacy; it tends to reveal the presence of social power in places where it had been practically invisible. And, by the same token, it tends to bring out a pole of right from which power runs the risk of being dissociated. No doubt the state may always prevail by virtue of its monopoly of legitimate violence and make recourse to its traditional means of coercion. It does this, from time to time, when the danger seems to be sufficiently circumscribed. But the concessions granted by the government are remarkable; this is because the legitimate foundation of violence seems more and more threatened, the risk involved in using violence ever greater, when the state penetrates more into the detail of social life. A violence that was exercised only at the edge of legality would undermine the foundations of the regime. This example gives us some idea of the extent of the contradictions inherent in the democracy of our time and allows us to assess the opportunities for change that it offers. It is undeniable that there has been an accentuation of the constraints exercised from above on ordinary social activities and relations. But, at the same time, demands are propagated, transversely, so to speak, which are not simply *de facto* signs of resistance to these constraints, but which testify to a vague sense of justice and reciprocity, or of injustice and the breakdown of social obligation. Thus exclusion from the sphere of work appears to individuals as much more than an injury, much more than a sign of the arbitrary power of the employers: it is like a denial of right, of a social right.

One would search in vain among the struggles brought about by the crisis in the steel industry, for instance – and earlier by that in the watchmaking or textile industries – for the first signs of a revolutionary situation or even a political upheaval that might bring to power the parties claiming allegiance to socialism. Although these parties might derive some benefit from them (and we have seen from the failure of the Union of the Left how precarious this very hypothesis is), there is every reason to believe that, if successful, these parties would be confronted by the same difficulties as those faced by previous governments, or even that they would give rise, with new hopes, to more intense demands. Such demands are rooted in the awareness of right. However substantial they may be, and whatever changes they might introduce into the system of managing enterprises and into every sphere of administration, they do not seek to be resolved by the action of state power. They stem from a domain that the state cannot occupy. The are constantly aroused by the need for the aspirations of minorities or particular sections of the population to be socially recognized. These minorities, it should be said, may be the product of circumstances; whether they are made up of workers made redundant in a firm, inhabitants of a region threatened with the loss of their main source of subsistence through the disappearance of an industry, farmers struck by a disastrous harvest or fishermen and shopkeepers affected by an oil slick: these minorities and categories may discover their own identity, whether it is of an ethnic order or based on a cultural affinity or a similarity of situation, or they may group together around some project of general importance (consumer protection, defence of the environment, etc.). So varied are their motives and modes of formation that at first sight one would think they had nothing in common. At one end of the spectrum, we have seen conscientious objectors who demanded exemption from a specific national obligation and claimed a particular status, or homosexuals who wanted no more than to have a particular way of life respected: what brings these instances together is the fact of being different in some way. At the other end of the spectrum, we have seen the protests of those suddenly deprived of the normal means of subsistence: their concern is, in a sense, to re-establish themselves as similar to others. Considering the heterogeneity of the forms of protest and demand, one hardly dares speak of a spectrum. But despite this variety, the initiatives of the minorities are linked together by virtue of the fact that they combine, in a way that seems paradoxical, the idea of legitimacy and the representation of a particularity. This conjunction, whatever the motives, whatever the circumstances that trigger it off, attests to the symbolic efficacy of the notion of rights. Claims based on interest are of a different order: these conflict with one another and are regulated by means of a power relationship. State power is based on interests; indeed, it affirms itself by exploiting their divisions, by taking advantage of the benefits obtained and the injuries inflicted, each one always relative to the other, in order to enlarge the circle of its autonomy. On the other hand, faced with the demand for or defence of a right, it has to respond according to its principles, according to the criteria of the just and the unjust and not only of the permitted and the forbidden. In the absence of such a response, the law runs the risk of being reduced to the level of constraint; and, while it loses its transcendence, the power that seems to apply it runs the risk of falling into triviality. Let me stress once again that the right affirmed against the claims of state power to decide, according to its own imperatives and its own expansion, does not attack it head on, but obliquely; by circumventing it, as it were, it touches the centre from which it draws the justification of its own right to demand the allegiance and obedience of all.

What we have to examine, then, is the meaning of conflicts which presuppose both the fact of power and the attempt to gain respect for different rights. These conflicts are becoming more and more characteristic of modern democratic societies. The agency of state power, and its ever more extensive intervention, is an ineffaceable aspect of these societies. It would be naive or insincere to imagine that an abolition of power would be possible or even that the tendency for the state apparatus to become more powerful could be reversed by substituting others for those who exercise authority. On the contrary, one is tempted to believe that under the cover of socialism the concentration of the means of production, information, regulation and control of social activities, the use of all the instruments capable of bringing about the unity of the people, would increase. If the development of this tendency can be stemmed, this counter-tendency will not emerge from the place of the state. As soon as that place was fully fixed, separating itself from the meta-social 'other place' for which religion once provided the reference, the possibility arose of an objectification of the social space, a complete determination of the relations between its elements. Moreover, this process was not the result of a seizure of power by the aspirants to despotism: the delimitation of a properly social space, perceptible as such, intelligible as their space, constitutive of a common identity for the groups which inhabit it and relate to one another, without supernatural disguise, goes hand in hand with the reference to a power which, at one and the same time, emerges from it and becomes, as if at a distance, its guarantor. So we must recognize equally that the project which now haunts power, and which is now able to take advantage of the hitherto unknown and unimagined resources of science and technology, can no longer be imputed to a category of individuals or to some instinct for domination. Rather we must recognize that this project mobilizes the energies and moulds the attitudes of those who are in a position to carry it out. However, this conclusion merely confirms my conviction that it is at the heart of civil society, in the name of an indefinite need for a mutual recognition of liberties, a mutual protection of the ability to exercise them, that one may discern a movement antagonistic to that which is propelling state power towards its goal.

This brings us to the second feature of the struggles inspired by the notion of rights: emerging or developing in various centres, sometimes as a result of temporary conflicts, those struggles do not tend to fuse together. Whatever their affinities and convergences, they are not dominated by the image of an agent of history, a People-as-One, and they reject the hypothesis that right will be achieved in reality. So we must resolve to abandon the idea of a politics that would compress collective aspirations in the model of an alternative society, or, what amounts to the same thing, the idea of a politics that would stand over the world in which we live and allow it to be struck by the thunderbolts of the Last Judgement. No doubt it may seem difficult to reconcile ourselves to this abandonment, for the faith in a future freed from the ties to the present is deeply rooted in the minds of those who are convinced that reformism is a trick. But we ought to examine this faith and ask ourselves whether revolutionism is not nourished by illusions identical to those of reformism. For both avoid, each in its own way, the question of social division as it is posed in modern society, the question of the origin of the state and its symbolic function, the question of the nature of the opposition between dominators and dominated which is at work throughout the entire width and depth of the social sphere. Reformism suggests that the state, by its own activity, or as a result of the growth of popular demands (in both cases thanks to the increase in production, wealth and education), may become the agent of social change and the promoter of an increasingly egalitarian system. Revolutionism suggests that the conquest of the state apparatus by dominated groups or by a particular party that guides them, and the use of its resources for their own advantage, creates the conditions for the abolition of domination. Both seem unable to conceive, at one and the same time, of two movements that are nevertheless inseparable: the movement by which society is circumscribed, brought together, endowed with a definite identity by virtue of an internal split that establishes the pole of power as a pole above, a pole more or less separated from the whole, and the movement by which, beginning from this pole and as a result of this quasi-separation, the means of every kind of domination (material resources, skills, decision-making) are accumulated in the interests of those who possess authority and seek to consolidate their own position. Reformists and revolutionaries are blind to the symbolic function of power and obsessed by the appropriation of its *de facto* function, that of control over the functioning of social organization. This blindness and this obsession have not only the same causes, but the same effects: the struggles that are developing in various domains of civil society are assessed only in terms of the opportunities they offer, in short or long term, of altering or overthrowing the power relations between political groups and the organization of the state. Now it is these struggles, I believe, that must be freed from the mortgage imposed on them by the parties whose ambition is power; and this we may do by bringing out the idea of a transformation of society by movements which are wedded to their autonomy.

Of course, autonomy is a resounding word and it requires some elucidation if we are not to fall victim to the fictions that at present disarm rather than mobilize energies. Autonomy, it has to be said at once, can only be relative. But we must recognize that it is also pointless to wish to fix or to efface its limits in empirical reality. These two temptations can be observed in the debate on workers' self-management, a concept that does not have the same value as that of autonomy, but which has won considerable support in a society dominated by the fact of production, and even more by that of organization. Either one denounces as inconsistent the idea of a society entirely governed by the principle of self-management, or one is not afraid to regard any resistance or criticism that it may elicit as stemming from a desire to preserve old structures of domination. The arguments that are put forward in this regard have the effect of concealing the question of the political. Those invoked in the name of realism are well known; there is no need to develop them further. The imperatives of production and of modern organization more generally would make the participation of everyone in public responsibilities unviable; they would impose a schema of division of labour that would reinforce hierarchies based on competence and would increasingly treat the latter as the basis of authority. More-over, the sheer size of our societies, the complexity of the tasks required to mobilize resources for aims that are in the general interest, the co-ordination of sectors of activity, the satisfaction of social needs of all kinds, the protection of public order and national defence: these considerations could be accommodated only through a process of centralized decision-making, combined at best with an increase in the number of representative bodies, kept strictly apart from the unstable mass of their constituents. If one takes these necessities into account, the idea of a self-management realized within the boundaries of innumerable social cells would seem some-what fanciful.

Such arguments are neither weak nor always hypocritical, as is sometimes all too readily said. They derive simply from an analysis of the social structure such as it has come to be and they grasp that structure as something natural. This being so, they confuse notions which ought to be distinguished if we wish to go beyond the limited horizons of our social life. In particular, they confuse the exercise of power with the exercise of competence. There is no reason to deny that competence confers authority; but the idea that competence secretes power is applicable only to a society in which a general apparatus of power has emerged as a distinct entity and in which, such power being accorded or itself assuming a position of knowledge or control of society as a whole, there is the possibility that individuals possessing competence and authority will successively identify with power (from the latter's point of view, that is). This objection is not a purely formal one; it makes it possible to bring out what very often remains hidden by the realist argument, namely, that there is a dif-ference between the exercise of competence and the exercise of power. It is the image of power that mobilizes for its purposes the image of competence; and it does that at a time, of course, when technological and scientific developments are increasing the impor-tance of competence. How, for example, can one say that, in reality, individuals who have a technological or scientific training, or who possess a capital of skills in whatever sphere which distinguishes them from the majority, benefit proportionately from a degree of freedom and decision-making that involves them in a system of pol-itical power? One has to say that they are more likely to be buried in the shadowy regions of the organization. What is true, but quite different, is that competence (real or simulated) provides the criterion for a hierarchy of rewards and that this constitutes a solid support for the preservation of the socio-political structure. But it should be noted that the arrangement of this hierarchy cannot be deduced from the principle of distinction based on competence; it stems from an interpretation which is, in the widest sense, political. Finally, the same realist subjection to the conditions of the established order prevents one from imagining a society whose functioning would not be governed by an ultra-centralized state apparatus; it forgets, to a large extent, that causes are also effects, that the choices of technologies, energy resources, favoured forms of production, systems of information, modes of transport, ways of stimulating industrial development, town-planning programmes, etc. also trigger off the social processes of a mass society as well as the processes of administrative centralization and the concentration of power. By the same token, the critique of the ideal of self-management leads one to ignore all the possibilities for collective initiatives to be found in those spaces which are governable by those who inhabit them, possibilities for new models of political representation, as well as possibilities for new channels of information that would change the terms of participation in public decisions.

On the other hand, one remains surprised at the poverty of the theory of self-management as soon as it claims to apply its aims in reality. The argument of the adversary is turned against him, the limits of autonomy disappear. It is as if the idea of being together, producing together, deciding and obeying together, communicating fully, satisfying the same needs, both here and there and everywhere simultaneously, became possible as soon as the alienation which ties the dominated to the dominator is removed; it is as if only some evil and complicit servitude had for centuries or millennia concealed from people the quite simple truth that they were the authors of their own institutions and, what is more, of their choice of society. If this is believed, there is no need to confront the problems posed on the frontiers of the history that we are living through. Paradoxically, the idea that any established system is capable of being called into question collapses into these claims: that there is no other weight of the past than *de facto* weight, that humanity has always found itself, as it finds itself today, faced with a radical possibility – and this is a way of saying that there is no history. Nor is there any more concern to examine the question of equality and inequality. The plausible idea that inequality is expressed in reality only at the price of a certain social and political compensation collapses into the claim that it is merely a false scent serving to sustain the project of domination.

There would be no mystery in obedience to power, as it is embodied in material institutions, as it is represented by human beings, as something merely likeable or detestable, if *loftiness* were only a trap; if it did not testify to a general movement of elevation as well as a general movement of lowering; if it did not capture something of the institution of the social at the same time as it folded back upon itself, responding, through an increase of its strength and a growth in its mass, to the necessity of disposing of the social. In particular, there would not be that astonishing reversal of liberty into servitude, no enigma of voluntary servitude (to borrow the forceful expression of La Boetie), of a servitude which is opposed to the desire for liberty without being alien to it, if the sign of that which falls from above did not have some relationship with an aspiration.

To think about the limits of autonomy in this way is not to take up again the question of the political in terms of the general relationship between society and power. I am not substituting the idea of an ambiguous power for the idea of an evil or benevolent power. I am trying to catch a glimpse of a dimension of the social space which is generally obscured. Why is it obscured, if not, paradoxically, because of a phantasized attraction for the One and an irresistible temptation to project it into the real. Whoever dreams of an abolition of power secretly cherishes the reference to the One and the reference to the Same: he imagines a society which would accord spontaneously with itself, a multiplicity of activities which would be transparent to one another and which would unfold in a homogeneous time and space, a way of producing, living together, communicating, associating, thinking, feeling, teaching which would express a single way of being. Now what is that point of view on everything and everybody, that loving grip of the good society, if not an equivalent of the phantasy of omnipotence that the actual exercise of power tends to produce? What is the imaginary realm of autonomy, if not a realm governed by a despotic thought? This is what we should be thinking about. This does not prevent us from seeing that the wise reformers, predicting the advent of a rational power which would be able to circumscribe the experiences of autonomy within just limits, to combine, as is sometimes said, the authority of the plan with the virtues of self-management, have decided to assess the value of collective initiatives by the criterion of their conformity with the decisions of the state; they wish to leave to the tenants of the socialist edifice only the freedom to be heard in order to obey the instructions of the landlord.

To free oneself from revolutionism is not to rejoin reformism; I am simply saying that nothing is served by ignoring the attraction for the One, by denying the distinction between the high and the low. I am saying that we would do better to strive to resist the illusion of a power which would really coincide with the position that is represented of it and that it seeks to occupy, as well as the illusion of a unity which would be perceptible, real and which would dissolve all differences within it. As soon as one confuses the symbolic and the real one falls into this double illusion, the consequence of which is to obscure in one way or another the plurality, fragmentation and heterogeneity of the process of socialization, and also the transversal development of practices and representations, the mutual recognition of rights. What defies the realist imagination is the fact that society organizes itself in terms of a quest for unity, that it testifies to a latent common identity, that it relates to itself through the mediation of a power which goes beyond it and that, simultaneously, there are many different forms of sociability, forms which are not determinable, not totalizable. I am not surprised by this; the imagination to which such noisy homage is paid in our time is powerless to make us confront the contradiction, the true contradiction, I would say, the one that obstinately resists its resolution, because it is an indication of the questioning that lies within the institution of the social. And let me note in passing that it must always betray the mark of what it repressed: the imagination of the One secretly conveys the representation of power (the Other by whom the One is named), a sign of social division; the imagination of the free development and free flowering of collective energies secretly conveys the representation of the Same, a sign of non-division.

In the final analysis, what eludes the imagination, although it finds unknown resources therein, is democracy. Its emergence was accompanied by the appearance, for the first time or in an altogether new light, of the state, society, the people, the nation. And one would like to conceive of each of these forms in the singular, to defend it against the threat of division, to reject anything that flaws it as a symptom of decomposition and destruction, and, since the work of division seems to be unleashed in democracy, one would like either to suppress it or to get rid of it. But state, society, people and nation are indefinable entities in democracy. They bear the imprint of an idea of the human being that undermines their affirmation, an idea which seems derisory in face of the antagonisms that tear apart the world, but without which democracy would disappear; and they remain in perpetual dependence upon the expression of rights which resist the *raison d'état* and the sacralized interest of society, people and nation. So we should not assume that the desire for revolution, understood as the advent of communism, and the desire for a good society frees us from the imaginary figures which haunt democracy. Such desires modify them, but they reinforce at the level of phantasy the belief on which they are nourished; they serve the cult of unity, the cult of an identity found at last in the singular, and it is not by accident, but following its own logic, that it abolishes the idea of right. We should consent, instead, to think and act within the horizons of a world which offers the possibility of freeing oneself from the attraction of Power and of the One, a world in which the continuous critique of illusion and political invention are carried out in the context of an indetermination of the social and the historical.

A politics of human rights and a democratic politics are thus two ways of responding to the same need: to exploit the resources of freedom and creativity which are drawn upon by an experience that accommodates the effects of division; to resist the temptation to exchange the present for the future; to make an effort, on the contrary, to discern in the present the signs of possible change which are suggested by the defence of acquired rights and the demand for new rights, while learning to distinguish them from what is merely the satisfaction of interests. And who could say that such a politics lacks audacity, when one looks towards the Soviets, towards the Poles, the Hungarians or the Czechs or towards the Chinese in revolt against totalitarianism: it is they who can teach us to decipher the meaning of political practice.

# 8

# The Logic of Totalitarianism

Italian fascism was the first movement to pride itself on constructing a totalitarian state, *uno stato totalitario*. It is to that movement that we owe the invention of a formula that was to be echoed, some years later, in Germany, that of the *totale Staat*. One might be tempted to think, therefore, that the critique of totalitarianism came as a response to its apologia. But without wishing to deny this particular form of its expression, I doubt whether it is able to throw much light on the fortune of the concept.

Between the two wars, socialists and liberals who denounced the regimes of Hitler and Mussolini saw their struggle in terms of anti-fascism. Whatever attention they gave to the totalitarian theme could be revealed only by meticulous research, but it was not, to my knowledge, an important aspect of their work. On the other hand, one must admit that this theme inspired right-wing ideologists, who condemned at one and the same time fascism, national socialism and Bolshevism. Significantly, the *Petit Robert* dictionary illustrates its definition of the French word *totalitaire* with a quotation taken from a book on Germany by Jacques Bainville, published in 1933:

> Henceforth a single party has the right to exist in Germany. It goes without saying that it is the National-Socialist Party. The same holds for fascism in Italy and bolshevism in Moscow. It is a new form of political society. The God-State does not tolerate dissidence, for it is represented by a minority that possesses all power, the rest of the population consisting of passive citizens. Indeed the totalitarian conception culminates in a process of purging.

Jacques Bainville was a conservative nationalist thinker, one of the founders of *Action française*. His was not an isolated judgement, although it is true that a large section of the Right had praised the

wonders of fascism, before rallying to it under the authority of
Pétain. However, even more instructive, it seems to me, was the
growth in the critique of totalitarianism after the Second World
War. Of course, during the war, the propaganda of the allies was
not slow to point out the totalitarian nature of its enemies. But it was
only later, during the period when the ideological conflict between
the Western powers and the USSR was unleashed – what is called
the cold war – that the denunciation of totalitarianism acquired new
force and mobilized a broad current of liberal opinion. From then
on, communism was defined as a totalitarian system, the most
highly developed and perfected example of that system, one which
had withstood the destruction of fascism and national socialism, but
which proceeded from the same causes and pursued similar ends.
The critics of totalitarianism were not merely transferring to communism certain features which had once been imputed to fascism. In
my opinion, a new political category was being formed; the transition from an epithet applied to enemy states to a noun created in
order to designate a new socio-historical type took place when, and
only when, Soviet communism seemed to threaten the existence of
the democracies.

   If there is any point in examining the conditions in which the
representation of totalitarianism originally emerged and then
developed during the course of several decades, it is because those
conditions throw some light on the resistance of left-wing opinion.
The new concept was regarded as a concept of the Right, forged to
serve reactionary purposes. The struggle against totalitarianism
seemed like a diversion whose aim was to obscure the reality of
Western imperialism and to disarm the critique of the capitalist
system. But we still have to ask why the non-communist Left, Marxist
or quasi-Marxist, had left the initiative for formulating the totalitarian problem to conservatives or liberals, why analyses like those
of Hannah Arendt found so little support. Indeed, we should not
forget that, from the 1930s onward and to an even greater extent
after the war, the Soviet regime was the object of many critiques by
isolated individuals or small revolutionary groups, who were aware
of the formation of a bureaucratic stratum, the growth of social inequalities, the perfecting of the police system, the existence of the
concentration camps and the cult of Stalin. No doubt the most
astonishing thing is that the mass of evidence, documentation and
judgements that no longer seem open to question today did not

shake the majority of left-wing opinion, which was still able to divide the world up into two camps, one profoundly evil, despite the advantages that it gave the socialist movement, the other profoundly good, despite the vices of Stalinism. However, it is equally surprising and, for my purposes, even more instructive that, even among those who were dismantling the mystification of Soviet communism, most of them could not bring themselves to compare Stalinism and fascism and avoided speaking of a totalitarian state in the USSR. They were accumulating material for such an interpretation, but they shied away from the necessity for a new conceptualization.

The case of the Trotskyists in this respect is exemplary. However small they were numerically, there can be no doubt that they exercised considerable influence in Western Europe on left-wing intellectuals. And they never varied in their judgement: fascism, for them, was and remains a means adopted by large capital, in a particular set of historical conditions, to reaffirm its domination over the proletariat, while Stalinism seemed to them and still seems to them to be the monstrous product of a situation in which the failure of world revolution had dissociated a bureaucratic superstructure from a socialist infrastructure, in which a parasitical caste had grafted itself on to the proletarian state. This case certainly deserves our attention, for the master-thinker, the guide from whom all the arguments were borrowed, had, at the end of his life, indicated his own willingness to reassess the Soviet system as a totalitarian system. In the very last lines of his work on Stalin, which was interrupted by his death, Trotsky dared to write:

'L'État, c'est moi' [I am the State] is almost a liberal formula by comparison with the actualities of Stalin's totalitarian regime. Louis XIV identified himself only with the State. The Popes of Rome identified themselves with both the State and the Church – but only during the epoch of temporal power. The totalitarian state goes far beyond Caesaro-Papism, for it has encompassed the entire economy of the country as well. Stalin can justly say, unlike the Sun King, '*La Société, c'est moi*' [I am Society].[1]

Paradoxically, it is on the side of the theoretician of the distorted, but still living, revolution of the workers' state – degenerate, but always ready to be restored – that one can find the beginnings of an analysis of totalitarianism. It is little more than a beginning and one may doubt whether it would have been pursued in view of the role that he played in the formation of the Bolshevik dictatorship. Nevertheless it says a great deal in a few words. Observing that the state embraces the economy, Trotsky suggests that the distinction between the political and the economic has vanished; imputing to Stalin the formula *La Société, c'est moi,* he points to the specificity of totalitarianism with regard to absolutism and the force of the mechanism of identification which imply that nothing, from now on, escapes state power. And yet it is as if, for his own followers, Trotsky had said nothing.

To find a new way of considering the nature of the USSR, the Marxist or quasi-Marxist Left would have had to abandon the vision of social reality that sustains all its analyses – whether they are reformist or revolutionary in inspiration. This vision, let us recall, was formed in opposition to that of liberalism, in a world overturned by the expansion of capitalism. Liberalism had forged the fiction of a society that was spontaneously organized as a result of free competition between independent owners and in which the state confined itself to ensuring that the rules of the game were respected and to protecting persons and property. In denouncing this fiction by exposing the polarization of society into antagonistic classes, by showing that it was conditioned by property relations and by bringing all its criticism to bear on the irrationality of the capitalist system, socialist thought has not freed itself from the problematic in which the theory of liberalism developed. It demonstrated that the actual dynamics of the market contradicted the laws of classical political economy, that the crises were not accidental but structural and that there was no harmony between capital and labour, but rather a radical opposition of interest between those who possessed the means of production and those who did not. However, in arguing in this way, it in no way abandoned the idea that reality was to be disclosed at the level of the economy. The fiction of an organization of production under the management of associated workers, that is, in fact, of their representatives, was substituted for that of a market that seemed to harmonize interest and satisfy needs by self-regulation. Thus, the liberal denial of the antagonism of classes in the actual reality of capitalism was complemented by the illusion of an abolition of this antagonism in a more or less near future, thanks to a revolution or to the gradual abolition of private property. The repression of the question of the political was carried as far as it would go. Whereas economic liberalism at least claimed to be combined with a political liberalism, even if it sometimes encouraged the latter to seek its own foundation within itself (in France, the work of Benjamin Constant, Guizot or de Tocqueville testify to this concern at the beginning of the nineteenth century), the socialists, however ardent they may have been in defence of liberty, equality and justice, deprived themselves of the means of understanding the dangers hidden in a state which would become master of the economy, as well as depriving themselves of the means of grasping the roots of democracy. This did not, of course, prevent them from appreciating the threat posed by fascism. They resisted fascism all the more resolutely in that it overtly contradicted their humanist ideas and seemed to them to be a product of capitalism. But it is one thing to mobilize against an intolerable enemy because it exalts the values of nationalism, even of racism, because it openly practises the cult of power and the cult of the leader; it is quite a different thing to be able to raise the principles of its criticism to the level of reflection. This is apparent in the inability of socialists to conceptualize the nature of the Soviet regime. As soon as they saw private property abolished, as soon as class antagonism could no longer be deciphered in the known context of capitalism, their thinking was disarmed. They were quite capable of concluding that the Soviet state was loaded with vices; but they could identify nothing more than vices, whose origins were imputed to accidents of history. The Left lacked a theory of the state, or more profoundly still, a conception of political society. And, by the same token – a fact too seldom noticed – it proved to be incapable of interpreting the evident signs of the exploitation of workers and peasants, the signs of class division, which were being produced by new relations of production. Because they had circumscribed the sphere of reality within the limits of the economy, they were blind to the structure of a system of production which was explicitly embedded in the political system.

Why, I asked, was the Left reluctant to employ the concept of totalitarianism? At first I replied: because it had been invented by the Right. That is true. But, I went on to ask, why did it allow itself to be outstripped by its adversaries? I would now dare to say: because this concept is *political* and the Left does not think in political terms. This proposition seems paradoxical. Socialists are determined advocates of state intervention in every domain of social life in order to diminish or suppress the inequalities that arise in the context of civil society, to attenuate the effects of the appropriation of wealth by a minority or to make it impossible. It is to them that one must attribute, over the last hundred years, all the efforts that have been made for a less inequitable distribution of taxes, all the most effective proposals or measures to defend wage earners against the arbitrary actions of their employers, to ensure stability in employment, to improve working conditions and security. It is to them that we owe the most radical initiatives in education, public health, housing or leisure. In a word, although the idea of progress was not born with the socialist movement, although it was first mobilized in a liberal, humanitarian current, it found its firmest expression within the socialist movement, in association with the idea of state intervention. Unlike the communist project, which sees an entire restructuring of the state apparatus as a condition for social change, the notion of a political struggle has always been at the heart of the programme of the socialist Left. However, we must not confuse a capacity to act politically, with a view to the formation of a reforming or revolutionary state, with the capacity to conceive of society as a political society.

Such a conception would require a reflection on the nature of the division that has been established between civil society and the state; it would require a reflection on the implications of the distinction that has emerged historically between, on the one hand, political power, whose boundaries were delimited and whose formation, exercise and renewal were subjected to democratic rules and, on the other hand, administrative power, whose sphere of competence was equally restricted in principle but always more extended in fact, by virtue of its responsibility for the needs of the population and its ever more regular, ever more detailed control of social life. But as long as one is content to define the state as a mere organ of society, which is differentiated from it in order to exercise functions of general interest, one is forced to choose between the following two accounts. According to the first, the state is only partly detached from society, its power is entirely dependent on the dominant class, its only task is to secure the conditions for the functioning of an economic system which obeys its own logic, while substantiating the image of a common collective identity and disguising, in the cloak of the general interest, the particular interests of those strata that benefit from capitalism. According to the second, the state may, with the support of popular forces, rise above private individuals and thus make itself more and more consubstantial with society, truly representative of a general interest in which private interests are dissolved; it then appears as the great organ that decides all the movements of the social body and simultaneously is one with it.

These two accounts, that of the bourgeois state and that of the socialist state, do not enable us to discern the nature of political power and the peculiar dynamics of the state bureaucracy. In the first place, one misunderstands the meaning of a mutation which lies at the origin of modern democracy: the establishment of a power of limited right, of such a kind that outside the political sphere (in the narrow, conventional sense of the term), economic, legal, cultural, scientific and aesthetic spheres are circumscribed, each of which obeys its own norms. The ultimate consequence of this event is nothing less than the separation of civil society from the state. Now, to appreciate this fully one would have to reject the thesis which governs the Marxist interpretation and admit that the modern state, far from being a product of capitalism, created its conditions of development by ensuring the possibility of relatively autonomous relations of production and exchange. Above all one would have to recognize the symbolic character of power instead of reducing it to the function of an organ, an instrument, at the service of social forces which allegedly exist prior to it. In the absence of such a perspective, one does not see that the delimitation of a properly political sphere is accompanied by a new form of legitimation, not only of power, but of social relations as such. The legitimacy of power is based on the people; but the image of popular sovereignty is linked to the image of an empty place, impossible to occupy, such that those who exercise public authority can never claim to appropriate it. Democracy combines these two apparently contradictory principles: on the one hand, power emanates from the people; on the other, it is the power of nobody. And democracy thrives on this contradiction. Whenever the latter risks being resolved or is resolved, democracy is either close to destruction or already destroyed. If the place of power appears, no longer as symbolically, but as *really* empty, then those who exercise it are perceived as mere ordinary individuals, as forming a faction at the service of private interests and, by the same token, legitimacy collapses throughout society. The privatization of groups, of individuals and of each sector of activity increases: each strives to make its individual or corporatist interest prevail. Carried to an extreme, there is no longer a *civil* society. But if the image of the people is actualized, if a party claims to identify with it and to appropriate power under the cover of this identification, then it is the very principle of the distinction between the state and society, the principle of the difference between the norms that govern the various types of relations between individuals, ways of life, beliefs and opinions, which is denied; and, at a deeper level, it is the very principle of a distinction between what belongs to the order of power, to the order of law and to the order of knowledge which is negated. The economic, legal and cultural dimensions are, as it were, interwoven into the political. This phenomenon is characteristic of totalitarianism.

The same considerations explain why the socialist Left misunderstands the dynamics of state bureaucracy. This bureaucracy remains invisible as long as the state seems to spring from society, as the organ in which the will and power of the dominant strata, or the will and power of the people, are condensed. History shows, however, that the modern state, *qua* centre of decision, regulation and control, tends increasingly to subordinate the detail of social life to itself. But the meaning of this process is misunderstood when it is imputed to the perversity of the individuals who run the state bureaucracies. In a society in which homogeneity is increasing as a result of the dissolution of the old 'natural' hierarchies, which is more and more concerned with the problem of its organization, which no longer has recourse to a transcendent guarantee of its order, which no longer finds in the language of religion a justification for its inequalities: in such a society, the state alone appears to all and represents itself to itself as the sole instituting principle, as the great actor that possesses the means of social transformation and the knowledge of all things. It is the emergence of this 'point of view of the state' – of a state potentially at the centre of power and knowledge – that makes possible the formidable expansion of bureaucracies, whose members may cultivate their own interests and derive as much power and advantage as possible from it, on the alleged basis of their sovereign distance from those who are administrated. Now, blind to this evolution and to its causes, won over to the idea that the expansion of the state is good in itself, the socialist Left is unaware that it is working, under the appearance of noble motives, for an ever-increasing separation between the administrative, regulatory and policing power, on the one hand, and the society thus taken into control, on the other; it is unaware that it is precipitating the formation of a bureaucratic stratum, which, despite its internal differences and conflicts, is separating itself off from the rest of the population. As a result, the totalitarian phenomenon eludes the socialist Left once again, for it is essentially linked to the idea of a state that aspires to be omnipresent through its bureaucratic network.

I am in no way suggesting that the socialist movement bears the seeds of totalitarianism within itself. How could one claim such a thing? It is only too clear that totalitarianism implies the destruction of this movement. I am simply trying to understand why this movement, despite its *de facto* attachment to democratic institutions, to public liberties and human rights, remains incapable of conceptualizing the nature of the new social system of which the USSR has created the model. Why has it continued to maintain a shady relationship with the communist movement, notably in France, Italy and Spain, and why, even when it is in open conflict with it, does its theoretical analysis fall short? Why, for example (to refer to a recent event which is fading but which is not yet forgotten), was it sufficient to disseminate a new phraseology concerning 'Euro-communism' for socialist leaders and militants to pin their hopes on Berlinguer, Carillo and Marchais, as if their organizations had suddenly changed their character? It may be said that in several countries the communists are deeply rooted in the working class and, more widely, in the wage-earning strata, that they are engaged in struggles (how and to what end is a different matter) whose immediate objectives coincide with those of the socialists. I do not deny this fact, but it in no way explains the failure to develop a critique of totalitarianism. It would be extravagant to suppose that this critique remains unformulated for mere tactical reasons. The truth is more simply that it would require a new conceptualization, a political conceptualization, which would shake the very foundations of socialist thought.

Since I have made use several times of the term 'political' without defining it, it is time to try to clarify its meaning. I suggested that the Left did not think in political terms, because it misunderstood the symbolic nature of power in democratic society and the symbolic nature of the modern state. However I also suggested that this misunderstanding extended to the structure of society, that is, to the division between the state and society as a whole, and to the internal division between, as well as the relationship maintained by, a certain articulation of power, law and knowledge with the ordering of social relations (beginning with those that are formed in the context of production). In doing so I was laying a stepping stone. In my view, the phenomenon of power lies at the centre of political analysis, but this is not because the power relationship is autonomous (reduced to its simplest expression, as the domination of a single individual or group over a collectivity, this relationship tells us nothing); it is because the existence of a power capable of obtaining generalized obedience and allegiance implies a certain type of social division and articulation, as well as a certain type of representation, to some extent explicit, to a larger extent implicit, concerning the legitimacy of the social order. I am not even content to say that there is no power that does not require procedures of legitimation, for that would create the illusion of a naked power that would have to produce images or ideas capable of concealing it and of making it seem necessary and desirable. This work of legitimation does take place: it is carried out by those who hold power and by their religious or legal agents. But before assessing it, one must decipher the conditions that made it possible; one must ask oneself, in each given case, What change in the principles of legitimacy, what reshaping of the system of beliefs, in the way of apprehending reality, enabled such a representation of power to emerge? And I say 'representation' to suggest that it is of the essence of power to present and make visible a model of social organization.

In this sense, nothing is more instructive than to examine the formation of the totalitarian state in the USSR. Now, it is certainly necessary to examine the political events (in the narrow sense of 'political') that account for it. Indeed, as everyone knows, but as is all too often forgotten, the upheaval in the economy did not take place until the years 1929–30; it was preceded by the establishment of a new system of domination, sketched out immediately after the Revolution, while Lenin was still alive. However, it is not sufficient to note the signs of the conquest of power and its appropriation by the Bolshevik Party, or even the signs of a bureaucratization in the many institutions that sprang from the Revolution, whose effect was to crystallize around the party a stratum of cadres who were indispensable to the transformation of the state. It is no doubt right that the strategy of the party should hold our attention: it eliminated all rival political formations, then subordinated, when it did not actually suppress, all the revolutionary organs – soviets, factory committees, district committees, soldiers' committees, workers' militias, the young Red Guard – to the point of concentrating in its own hands, or rather in the hands of its leadership, all the means of decision and coercion. No doubt it is also important to observe, in the post-revolutionary context of disorder and penury, a sort of spontaneous selection, within the population, of leaders who, by consolidating their functions and deriving material advantages from them, created new interdependencies, from one institution to another, and attached themselves to the firmest pole of authority. As Marc Ferro has shown in a masterly analysis, the process of bureaucratization from below complemented that of a bureaucratization from above and facilitated the formation of a new dictatorial state apparatus.[2] But these phenomena, however important they may be, do not convey the full meaning of the situation. In fact, the Bolshevik Party, as Ferro observes, was not the only party to combine manoeuvring with demagogy, to manipulate meetings and exclude adversaries from key positions, just as it was not the only party able to win over to its cause elements seeking to make a career for themselves in a society freed from anarchy. What we must understand is that its force of attraction bore little relation to its real force. What distinguishes it and explains its success was its ability to identify with the Revolution as an irreversible movement, as a power capable of carrying out a radical break with the past and providing the radical foundation of a new world; its ability to fuse together the demand for social transformation with the claim to have an absolute knowledge of history and society; lastly, its ability to conceive of itself and to appear as the depository of socialist legitimacy and truth. These closely related features gave it a unique image and account for its hold over members who lacked political training and education and over an intelligentsia which was inexperienced in organizational and economic matters. The party embodied the centre of knowledge and action; it attracted to itself those who could only theorize, because it *was* theory, and those who could only practise, because it *was* practice.

It turned rough, uneducated men into the guardians of grand theory; it turned intellectuals (those it did not destroy) into militants, organizers, guardians of revolutionary praxis. And even when it still left some room for internal debate and navigated its way through compromises with one group or another, in short, even when it was still neither a monolithic party nor a single party, it potentially combined these two characteristics because it represented the Party-as-One, not one party among others (the strongest, most daring among them), but that party whose aim was to act under the impulse of a single will and to leave nothing outside its orbit, in other words, to merge with the state and society.

In short, a political analysis would remain inadequate if it were to consider only the conquest of power, the modalities of its exercise and the establishment of a hierarchy of bureaucrats capable of sustaining it and diffusing its norms and decrees. A political analysis requires us to examine the mutation that occurred with the emergence of a new type of party. This mutation is of a symbolic order. It cannot be identified at the level of events; it testifies to a new system of representations that determines the very course of events.

This system, it is true, was only beginning to emerge in Lenin's time. In order to grasp its logic, one must consider the period in which the new power was stabilized, the new bureaucracy was fully constituted and the material foundations of the regime had been laid, thanks to the abolition of the private ownership of the means of production, collectivization and the development of the instruments of state intervention, that is, of planning.

Why, then, are we justified in speaking of totalitarianism? Not because dictatorship has attained its greatest strength, because it is able to exercise its constraint over every category of the population and to issue instructions which have the status of norms in every sphere of social life. Of course, it does all these things. But to stop short at the features of dictatorship is to remain at the level of empirical description. What is being created is the model of a society which seems to institute itself without divisions, which seems to have mastery of its own organization, a society in which each part seems to be related to every other and imbued by one and the same project of building socialism.

It is hardly possible to distinguish between cause and effect in the sequence of relations that tend to efface the traces of social division. In the first place, power is declared to be *social power*; it represents, as it were, society itself *qua* conscious, acting power: the dividing line between the state and civil society has become invisible. And, by the same token, the dividing line between political power and administrative power also disappears: the state apparatus loses all independence from the communist party and its leadership. Paradoxically, as Hannah Arendt has very well shown, the various state bureaucracies lose the boundaries that make each of them, in modern society, a distinct world, whose prerogatives and attitudes are fixed; and at the same time their members cease to be located within regularly constituted hierarchies. Political power circulates through its agents – the functionaries of the party and the secret police – in every sphere of the bureaucracy, tending to dissolve particular relationships, based on the division of labour and clan solidarities, leaving only a general relationship between the directing organ (and the supreme leader) and those who carry out its orders, who, as individuals, possess a status and existence without guarantee. Simultaneously, at the summit of party and state, power merges with the position of the individual or individuals who possess authority. This merging is not accidental, it is not the outcome of the behaviour of the leader or leaders. It is the same necessity which requires the state to fuse with society, political power with the state apparatus and the leaders with one another. In other words, by a reversal of the democratic logic mentioned above, power ceases to designate an empty place: it is materialized in an organ (or, in extreme cases, an individual) which is supposed to be capable of concentrating in itself all the forces of society.

A second feature is that the principle of a division internal to society is denied. All the signs of such a division, which have in no sense disappeared, are attributed to the existence of social strata (kulaks, bourgeois) deriving from the old order or to elements accused of working for foreign imperialism. The new society is thought to make the formation of classes or groups with antagonistic interests impossible. However the affirmation of totality requires no less urgently the denial of difference between the norms according to which each mode of activity and each institution is defined. At its extreme, the production enterprise, the administration, the school, the hospital and the legal institution appear merely as special organizations, subordinated to the ends of the great socialist organization. At its extreme, the work of the engineer, the civil servant, the teacher, the lawyer and the doctor is no longer his own responsibility and is subjected to political authority. Finally, it is the very notion of social heterogeneity which is rejected, the notion of a variety of modes of life, behaviour, belief and opinion, in so far as this notion radically contradicts the image of a society in harmony with itself. And the project of mastery, of normalization, of uniformization is carried furthest at the point where the most secret, the most spontaneous, the most ungraspable element of social life is to be found: in customs, in tastes and in ideas.

Let us now consider these two moments of the totalitarian project, two moments which are, in fact, inseparable: the abolition of the signs of division between state and society and the signs of internal social division. They imply a de-differentiation of the agencies that govern the constitution of a political society. There are no longer ultimate criteria of law or of knowledge which are beyond the reach of power. This observation best enables us to identify the uniqueness of totalitarianism. For, without even speaking of European absolute monarchy, which quite clearly always involved a limit on the power of the prince – a limit bound up with the recognition of rights acquired by the nobility and by the cities, but even more fundamentally governed by the image of a Justice of divine origin – despotism (that celebrated oriental despotism which some commentators were fond of seeing as a prefiguration of the Stalinist regime) never appeared as a power that drew from itself the principle of law and the principle of knowledge. For such an event to take place, all reference to super-natural powers or to an order of the world would have to be abolished and power would have to be disguised as purely social power.

Totalitarianism presupposes the conception of a society which is sufficient unto itself and, since the society is signified in power, the conception of a power which is sufficient unto itself. In short, it is when the action and knowledge of the leader are measured only by the criterion of *organization*, when the cohesion or integrity of the social body turns out to depend exclusively on the action and knowledge of the leader, that we leave the traditional frameworks of absolutism, despotism and tyranny. The process of identification between power and society, the process of homogenizing the social space, the process of enclosing both society and power are linked together to constitute the totalitarian system. With the constitution of this system the representation of a 'natural' order is re-established, but this order is supposed to be social-rational and does not tolerate apparent divisions or hierarchies.

At the basis of such a system, we must identify certain key representations which make up its ideological matrix. In a sense, they are not new, they derive from an experience of the world that modern democracy has initiated; but they cease to be latent, they acquire a power to affirm the existence of the social that gives them a quite new efficacy as well as a new destiny.

Indeed, it is remarkable how each of these representations is split in the process of its actualization. What appears, in the first instance, is the image of the People-as-One. It does not matter that, for a while, the people is confused with the proletariat: the latter is then conceived mythically as the universal class into which all elements working for the construction of socialism are absorbed; it is no longer, strictly speaking, a class within a stratified society, it has become the people in its essence and notably includes the bureaucracy. This image is combined with that of a Power-as-One, power concentrated within the limits of the ruling apparatus and, ultimately, in an individual who embodies the unity and will of the people. These are two versions of the same phantasy. For the People-as-One can be both represented and affirmed only by a great Other; in the initial period, it can be so only by that great individual whom Solzhenitsyn has so aptly called the *Egocrat*. But the same image is also combined with the image of the element alien to the people, with the image of its enemy. This latter, it must be understood, is not secondary. The definition of the enemy is constitutive of the identity of the people. And, from this point of view, the metaphor of the *body*, which was current even in the time of Lenin, demands attention. The campaign against the enemies of the people is seen as a form of social prophylaxis: the integrity of the body depends on the elimination of its *parasites*.

No less determinant, it seems to me, is the representation of the organization. It is not sufficient merely to observe that organizations proliferate throughout the social sphere. What is new is that society is perceived in its entirety as a vast organization comprising a network of micro-organizations. Now this representation also splits in two. While the image is imposed of this general organization, in which individuals are inscribed and in which they find their status and function predetermined, while the notion prevails of a rationality immanent in the social, simultaneously society turns out to be amorphous matter to be organized, something which is organizable and which lends itself to the constant intervention of the engineer, the builder of communism. In this sense, the structure of each particular organization and the place and function of each of its agents are never established or certain. Finally, just as the identity of the people and the integrity of the body depend on a constant struggle against alien or parasitical elements, the virtue of the organization presupposes the idea of disorganization, of an ever-threatening chaos, of elements likely to disturb or sabotage the laws of socialism. If we examine these two representations, we can already assess the contradiction that haunts the militant or leader in a totalitarian society. On the one hand, he is merged with the people, the proletariat, the party, he is incorporated in it, dissolved *qua* individual in a communist 'us', or he is a part or a driving-belt in the organization, in the machine; and, on the other hand, he occupies the position of master, he who sees and names everything, or that of the organizer, the activist, the mobilizer of the masses.

We must consider two other representations which, however close they may be to the previous ones, are nevertheless distinct from them. The first is that of social-historical creation, the other that of society's transparency to itself. The first is underpinned by the myth of a social raw material offered to the power of the organizer, but it has deeper roots; for, even before the model of bureaucratic (industrial) rationalization was formed during the period of the French Revolution, the idea of the creation of an altogether new society, of a new man, had been born, as if it were possible and necessary to build on a *tabula rasa*. Hence, today, a faith in the permanent construction of socialism, the vision of a 'radiant future', is affirmed, a faith which justifies all present actions and especially the sacrifices imposed on the generations of the transitional period. Nor must the counterpoint of this idealization elude us. The idea of the creation, or rather the self-creation of society is accompanied by a prodigious refusal of any innovation that might transgress the limits of an already known future, a reality that in principle is already mastered. In this sense, the image of a history which is being made at every moment proves to be absolutely contradicted by the image of a fixed history. The unknown, the unpredictable, the indeterminable are avatars of the enemy.

The last representation again emerges from the depths of modern democracy; but more remarkable is its transformation in the context of totalitarianism. As soon as the state tends to merge with society, there is no longer merely the presumption of a rational viewpoint on the whole complex of activities: this viewpoint becomes that of a power which, through the intervention of its political agents, police and planners, possesses total knowledge of the detail of social reality. And, simultaneously, this knowledge aspires to be society's knowledge of itself. Thus an intense activity develops which is intended to make clear the objectives and results of the socialist project. The best testimony to this project is the phantasmagoria of the Plan. It is as if power had the capacity to exhibit the collective social labour, or as if, through it, society exhibited itself to itself. However, the aim of transparency turns out to be in contradiction with that of opacity. For the 'whole' does not allow itself to be expressed through articulations, each of which would know its function. The 'whole' must remain outside its articulations and therefore a secret. Referring to Hannah Arendt's fine analysis, I noted the insecurity – I would now say uncertainty – which is associated with the position of the militant, the bureaucrat in the administration, the engineer or manager in industry: a radical uncertainty for each individual, whatever his rank, as to the reasons for the decisions taken at the top and as to the limits of his own authority. Now this phenomenon is not merely the indication of a tyrannical power which is to be feared all the more in that no one knows or can predict its intentions. The truth is that a society which would ensure the greatest intelligibility of social action would be one in which there would be, in each domain, a testing of reality, a knowledge of the possible and the impossible, a taking into account of the resistance of men and things and, consequently, a grasping of the particular conditions of the various forms of relationship and work. Such a society would in principle be resistant to the totalitarian project. Totalitarianism can develop only by seeking to destroy any guarantee of competence in the very sphere of the bureaucracy, by tangling the skein of responsibilities, while keeping the centre of omniscient power hidden. Thus the ideal of secrecy turns out to be complementary to the ideal of knowledge (and, one should add, that the ideal of the secret police goes hand in hand with a political exhibition of everything that has been accomplished).

In order to appreciate the efficacy of the system of representation outlined above, we would have to leave the level of abstraction at which we have been operating and take into consideration all the points of contact which enable it to be embedded in social life. The first of these points is obviously the party. After having been the mould of the totalitarian project, it becomes, once the regime has been established, the privileged agent of the process of identification between the power and the people, and of the process of homogenization of the social field. But it carried out these functions only by combining itself with innumerable mass organisms. Thus, while on the one hand it penetrates into every part of the state edifice, to the point of dislocating its conventional articulations and using it as a mere facade for political power, on the other hand it produces dozens or hundreds of micro-bodies, whose essence is that their nature seems to be distinct from its own, in such a way as to simulate the specificity and autonomy of purely social, that is, non-political relations, but which are in fact consubstantial with it. Trade unions of all kinds, mutual aid groups, cultural groups for workers of various categories, organizations for youth, for children, for women, circles of writers, artists, scientists, academics, a whole network of 'collectives'is set up in which communist norms circulate. In each of these collectives the image of a common social identity and a leadership that is its depositary, the image of the good organization and the activist-organizer, is re-created; in each, the mechanism of eliminating parasites, saboteurs and deviants is redeployed. Each collective combines the imperative of innovation with that of the strictest conservatism; it combines the imperative of exhibiting objectives and results with that of concealing the decision-making centres. And, by this fact, any social relation, any exchange, any communication, any reaction that might express individual, unexpected, unknown initiatives, situated outside the domesticated space of the collective, becomes a target. The work of *incorporation* of individuals into the legitimate groups corresponds to the work of breaking down freely established relations; the work of an artificial socialization corresponds to the destruction of the forms of natural sociability.

Anyone who does not pay attention to the immense apparatus constructed to dissolve the subject, wherever it can express itself, into an 'us', to agglomerate, to melt these various forms of 'us' into the great communist 'us', to produce the People-as-One, will fail to understand how the logic of totalitarianism operates. He may well denounce the excesses of dictatorial power, the expansion of the bureaucracy, the proliferation of apparatuses by means of which those who are supposed to participate in the life of the institutions are reduced to the function of carrying out orders, but he would fail to see that dictatorship, bureaucracy and apparatuses need a new corporeal system.

Perhaps we are touching here on the deepest cause of the blindness of the Left when faced with the communist variant of totalitarianism. Whereas the Left feels nothing but disgust for all the forms of organization created by fascism, which it sees as attempts to militarize and mystify the population, because the cult of the leader and of discipline is overtly practised in fascist regimes, the Left most often remains bemused by the process of association, mobilization and mass organization, because it apparently occurs in the name of *real democracy*. Since the ideal of real democracy is its own, the Left restricts itself to deploring the fact that it is distorted in practice by the action of manipulators. Curiously enough, it is quite happy to apply the accusation of parasitism or sabotage to bureaucrats, without ever wondering whether the idea of the 'collective' good is to be found in the totalitarian system of representations. Paralysed by the justified critique of bourgeois individualism and of the fragmentation of roles and activities produced by capitalism, it is unable to develop a critique in the opposite direction: to dismantle the fiction of the unity, the identity, the substance of the social and to show that it leads to the isolation of individuals carried to its highest degree, to the dissolution of the subject, to the furious destruction of human sociability. And such is its inability to develop this critique that it is disarmed when new-wave communists, notably the Italians, proclaim the merits of 'mass democracy', as if this concept were not perfectly constructed to conceal the invasion of every sector of culture – before those of the economy – by groups dedicated to cohesion, devoted to conformism and held together by the hatred of deviants.

To try to discern the main features of the totalitarian project is one thing. It would be quite another to ask oneself what its effects are in reality. One would have to observe the disorder that lies beneath the order; the corruption beyond the imagery of the healthy body; the struggle for survival or for careers on the way to the 'radiant future'; the virulence of the bureaucratic antagonisms under the rule of power. This has not been my task. But let the reader be in no doubt: the totalitarian system is not achieving its ends. More than any other system it is contradicted by experience, which makes it all the more important to appreciate its coherence at the level of phantasy.

# 9

# The Image of the Body
# and Totalitarianism

The problem of totalitarianism has long occupied a central position in my thinking and requires, I believe, a new approach to politics. This term has enjoyed a rise in its fortunes recently, at least as applied to regimes described as 'socialist'. It is true that Hannah Arendt, Raymond Aron and a few, very few others, including myself, made use of it twenty or twenty-five years ago, taking it in its widest sense, to describe its socialist as well as fascist variants. Each of us was following his or her own course; for my part, I did not know the work of Hannah Arendt when, after devoting a number of studies to the critique of bureaucracy (the first being published in 1948), I began to work out a more clearly political conceptualization in an essay entitled 'Totalitarianism without Stalin', which dates from 1956. To speak of totalitarianism in relation to the Soviet Union was regarded as scandalous at the time and continued to be so until fairly recently. Today the term surprises no one. I would even say that it has become worn out before becoming meaningful. What does it signify? It signifies a regime in which state violence is practised on society as a whole, a system of generalized, detailed coercion – scarcely more than that. It is now becoming the foundation of a new kind of political thinking, a new interpretation of the history of modern societies or of history in general. So I am a little afraid of adding my voice to the concert of those known as 'new philosophers'. But I have regarded totalitarianism for too long as the major fact of our time, posing an enigma that calls for a re-examination of the genesis of political societies, to give into the fear that I might be following fashion.

Having referred to my earliest work on bureaucracy, I should also indicate or remind the reader that my thinking was carried out at first within the horizons of Marxism. In close collaboration with Castoriadis, who had at an early stage identified the features of a new social formation in the USSR, I set out to demonstrate the class division that had grown up after the Russian Revolution and the specific character of a state with which the dominant class, the bureaucracy, had become interlocked. The bureaucracy did not find the basis of its power in private property, but collectively, inter-dependently, in its dependence on state power, the party-state, which possessed all the means of production. This bureaucratic stratum displayed a strength and stability that Trotskyist thought was incapable of grasping; for the Trotskyists continued to imagine that a mere caste, parasitical and transitory, had superimposed itself on a socialist infrastructure and they failed to realize that a new form of domination and exploitation had been established at the expense of the peasantry, the proletariat and the overwhelming majority of the population.

Comparing the bourgeoisie and the bureaucracy, I observed that the latter offered a remarkable contrast between the strength of its constitution as a class and the fragility of the position of its members, who were constantly threatened with annihilation, whatever their rank and authority, on account of their subjection to political power. The great Stalinist purges showed that the bureaucracy was ideally everything and the bureaucrats nothing; the periodic eviction of thousands or tens of thousands of bureaucrats, far from being con-trary to the interests of the bureaucracy, seemed to me to be proof of its power, beyond the fate of individuals. I developed these analyses under the aegis of what seemed to me to be authentic Marxism, the Marxism of Marx, which I regarded as having been completely distorted in all the versions of so-called orthodox Marxism. This being the case, I firmly believed, at the time, in the role of the proletariat. It was, in my view, the privileged agent of history. I thought, in short, that the bureaucracy, although it had taken advantage of the modern conditions of industrial society, had been able to constitute itself and develop as a historical force only because the working class had been divided, opposed to itself, during its century-long struggles to organize and emancipate itself; because it had given rise to a dominant stratum, it had become alienated from itself in the figure of a Leader, a power that turned out to be an alien force working for its own gain. By virtue of a dialectic, whose resources we know only too well, I concluded that this alienation of the proletariat from itself, this ultimate form of alienation, was necessary, that the proletariat had to go through this experience at the end of which a bureaucracy separated itself off from it and turned against it, so that the need for an abolition of all social division, and not only of private property, would be fully affirmed. Thus the representation of a society delivered from division governed my thinking.

But there are two reasons, it now seems to me, which contradicted that Marxist perspective and prevented me from fully accepting a conception that reduced the creativity of history to that of the proletariat. These two reasons apparently belong to quite different orders. In the first place, at the very moment when I imagined an abolition of social division and found in the proletariat the true agent of history, I was reading Marx in a way which encouraged and facilitated questioning. In terms of my background, I am neither a sociologist nor a political scientist. My training is philosophical, and I acquired it, while still on the lycée benches, from Merleau-Ponty, a thinker who had a gift for breaking certainties, introducing complications where one sought simplification, who refused the distinction between the subject and the object, taught that the true questions were not to be exhausted in the answers, that they come not only from us, but are the sign of our interaction with the world, with others, with being itself. So drawn to, indeed enchanted by Marx, I nevertheless could not read him without satisfying the high standards laid down by the philosophy of Merleau-Ponty. I developed a relation to Marx's work in and through my questioning of it. No doubt what I found there responded to a desire within me whose origin I could not identify, but that is of little significance. The fact is that what attracted me in Marx was the ambiguity of his thinking and, more than that, his opposition to himself, the way in which his thought escapes from itself in the best of his works and from one work to another, the indetermination that undermined what was presented as a system, that undermined the commentary which he himself sometimes gave on his work in order to bring it together in the form of theses.

For instance, I very soon became aware of an opposition in Marx between the notions of continuity and discontinuity in history: the idea of an ineluctable movement governed by the growth of productive forces, moving from one mode of production to another, on the one hand, and the idea of a radical break between all precapitalist modes of production and modern capitalism, on the other; or in other words, an opposition between the idea of a dissolution of all restricted social relations and the idea of a force of conservation, of mechanisms of repetition which, even in capitalism, seemed to ensure the permanence of a structure. Similarly, I was very aware of the vacillation of an interpretation that sometimes was concerned solely to discover the material foundations of social life and its evolution, while at others revealed the full weight of the social imaginary, the function of the phantoms that haunt the present or the function of fetishism – an interpretation that was sometimes Darwinian, sometimes Shakespearean in inspiration. In short, while being drawn to the theory of the proletariat or of a classless society, I was no less attracted by the elusive elements in Marx's work. Thus, unknown to myself, the ideal of a complete determination of social reality, of the essence of history, was in contradiction with the discovery of an indetermination proper to thought, of a movement that removed statements from any univocal determination. If I have taken the liberty of referring to this relation to Marx's work, it is in order to make it clear that there could be no full adherence to his thought, no question of resting firmly on his theory, as soon it became apparent that, at one and the same time and somewhat paradoxically, the proletariat provided me with the guarantee of social practice and history while the guarantee of this guarantee – namely, Marx's thought – was the object of my questioning. It was inevitable that the moment would come when my earlier certainties would crumble.

The second reason I referred to concerns my experience, while still very young, as a militant in a small political group. I think a brief mention of this will throw light on what I have to say. I joined the Trotskyist party before the end of the war and remained in it for about four years. This group originated, as is well known, in the condemnation of Stalinism. It presented itself as the legitimate heir of Marxism–Leninism, claimed to be taking up the task initiated by the Russian Revolution and prefigured in the Paris Commune; it denounced the counter-revolutionary role of the communist parties, seeing them as carrying out, *mutatis mutandis*, the same role once played by the social democrats. Whereas the Third International had condemned the betrayal of the interests of the proletariat by the Second International, the Fourth now condemned the Third International and, in short, demanded a return to primal sources. The

Trotskyist party claimed allegiance to a founding hero, Trotsky, a hero who was both dead and immortal, and claimed allegiance more generally to a dynasty; immortality was embodied in the crown that had been worn successively by Marx, Engels, Lenin and Trotsky. And that crown guaranteed the immortality of the 'body' of the revolutionaries. Stalin, on the other hand, was represented as the usurper that the body of the revolutionaries would expel. Now it gradually occurred to me that the Trotskyist party functioned like a micro-bureaucracy, despite the rules of so-called democratic central-ism which allowed a conflict of tendencies – a conflict that was intense at times. The power of the apparatus, the division between leaders and followers, the manipulation of meetings, the withholding of information, the separation of activities, the stereotyped character of the dominant discourse in its various forms, the imperviousness to events that might challenge the correctness of practice and theory: innumerable such signs convinced me that, despite the enormous gulf between our group and the Communist Party, one could find in the former a tiny replica of the latter. What concerned me was that this micro-bureaucracy had no basis of a material kind. The positions of power occupied by a small number of militants was ultimately based on the possession of a certain knowledge, a skill in speaking and, to be more precise, the ability to inscribe every internal or external fact in a mytho-history. Russia provided the privileged context for this. It would be impossible here to enumerate all the sacred episodes that, from the formation of Bolshevism to the Stalin-ist betrayals, made up the register on which the present acquired its meaning. The function of this mytho-history, of the discourse that found its referent there, profoundly disturbed me. After all, this was precisely how I exercised whatever power I had in the party.

It seems to me that not only are we confronted by the problem of bureaucracy, but that certain elements of totalitarianism are to be found here. I don't mean, of course, that I regard the small party to which I belonged as a totalitarian embryo. That is certainly not the case. Indeed it did not have the means of being so. But what strikes me, and already struck me then, was the closed nature of the party, supported by a discourse that was supposedly scientific, declaring the rationality of the real and governed throughout by the representation of what had taken place, of the already-done, the already-thought, the already-seen. This discourse is fundamentally invulnerable; it is subject to error and rectification in fact, but not in principle. It imprints the signs of the real in a text – that of the great authors, but more usually that of a founding past – and it constantly nourishes the reading of the great text with these signs. And what strikes me no less is that the closed nature of this discourse derives from the fact that it is the discourse of no one person: it is the discourse of the party, the ideal body of the revolutionary, which traverses each of its members. Each individual sees himself caught up in an *us*, a *nous*, which imposes a break with the outside; the things of the world, which everybody talks about so much, can be grasped only by being carried back to the imaginary enclosure of history, of which the party is the trustee. And while the militant is incorporated, the supposed real is destined to be assimilated.

The two experiences that I have described are not unrelated. The first cannot be confined to the sphere of theory, the second to the sphere of practice. Being a militant presupposes a certain relationship to knowledge. Every communist is a person of knowledge, his identity is bound up with a body of knowledge that enables him to apprehend texts and things. The adventure of interpretation, on the other hand, implies a relation to power. To read a work, and I have experienced this even more in connection with Machiavelli than with Marx, is to allow yourself to lose the bearings which assured you of your sovereign distance from the other, which assured you of the distinction between subject and object, active and passive, speaking and hearing (to interpret is to convert reading into writing), the difference between one time and another, between past and present (the latter can neither be suppressed nor ignored), lastly it is to lose your sense of the division between the space of the work and the world on to which it opens. Thus by different paths, which cross and recross, I was gradually led to carry my questioning to the very centre of Marxist certainty.

I have now come to the question that I wanted to pose, after giving a brief indication of how I arrived at it. Why is totalitarianism a major event in our time, why does it require us to probe the nature of modern society? At the foundation of totalitarianism lies the representation of the People-as-One. It is denied that division is constitutive of society. In the so-called socialist world, there can be no other division than that between the people and its enemies: a division between inside and outside, no internal division. After the revolution, socialism is not only supposed to prepare the way for the emergence of a classless society, it must already manifest that society which bears within itself the principle of homogeneity and self-transparency. The paradox is the following: division is denied – I say denied, since a new dominant stratum is actively distinguishing itself from the rest of society, since a state apparatus is separating itself off from society – and, at the same time as this denial, a division is being affirmed, on the level of phantasy, between the People-as-One and the Other. This Other is the other of the outside. It is a term to be taken literally: the Other is the representative of the forces deriving from the old society (kulaks, bourgeoisie) and the emissary of the foreigner, the imperialist world. Indeed these two representations converge, for it is always imagined that the representatives of the old society are linked up with foreign centres. So it is understandable that the constitution of the People-as-One requires the incessant production of enemies. It is not only necessary to convert, at the level of phantasy, real adversaries of the regime or real opponents into the figures of the evil Other: it is also necessary to invent them. However, this interpretation can be carried further. The campaigns of exclusion, persecution and, for quite awhile, terror reveal a new image of the social body. The enemy of the people is regarded as a parasite or a waste product to be eliminated. The documents assembled by Solzhenitsyn, some of which have been known for a very long time, are highly instructive in this regard. The pursuit of the enemies of the people is carried out in the name of an ideal of social prophylaxis, and this has been the case since Lenin's time. What is at stake is always the integrity of the body. It is as if the body had to assure itself of its own identity by expelling its waste matter, or as if it had to close in upon itself by withdrawing from the outside, by averting the threat of an intrusion by alien elements. So there must be no failures in the functioning of institutions, failures that might suggest a relaxation in the monitoring of the mechanism of elimination or an attack from disruptive agents. The campaign against the enemy is feverish; fever is good, it is a signal, within society, that there is some evil to combat.

It should also be observed that in totalitarian ideology, the representation of the People-as-One is in no way contradictory with that of the party. The party does not appear as distinct from the people or from the proletariat, which is the quintessence of it. It does not have a specific reality *within* society. The party *is* the proletariat in the sense that it is identical with it. At the same time, it is the guide or, as Lenin put it, the consciousness of the proletariat; or, as I would say, using an old political metaphor, to which I shall come back, it is its head. And, similarly, the representation of the People-as-One is not in contradiction with that of an omnipotent, omniscient power, with, in the last analysis, that of the *Egocrat* (to use Solzhenitsyn's term), the ultimate figure of that power. Such a power, detached from the social whole, towering over everything, merges with the party, with the people, with the proletariat. It merges with the body as a whole, while at the same time it is its head. A whole sequence of representations is to be found here, the logic of which should not escape us. Identification of the people with the proletariat, of the proletariat with the party, of the party with the leadership, of the leadership with the Egocrat. On each occasion, an organ is both the whole and the detached part that makes the whole, that institutes it. This logic of identification, secretly governed by the image of the body, accounts in turn for the condensation that takes place between the principle of power, the principle of law and the principle of knowledge. The denial of social division goes hand in hand with the denial of a symbolic distinction which is constitutive of society. The attempt to incorporate power in society, society in the state, implies that there is nothing, in a sense, that can indicate an externality to the social and to the organ that represents it by detaching itself from it. The dimension of law and the dimension of knowledge tend to be effaced, in so far as they do not, as we know very well, belong to the order of things which are socially (or indeed psychologically) conceivable, in so far as they cannot be located in empirical social life, in so far as they establish the very condition of human sociability. A kind of positivisation of the manifest law takes place through intense legislative, legal activity, at the service of the totalitarian state; and a sort of positivisation of manifest knowledge takes place through intense ideological activity – ideology becoming that enterprise of phantasy which tends to produce and to fix the ultimate foundations of knowledge in every sphere. In fact, what one sees is the attempt by power to appropriate the law and the knowledge of the principles and ultimate goals of social life. But this language is still inadequate, for it would be wrong to attribute power with unbridled freedom; to do so would be to confuse, once again, arbitrary power with totalitarian power. Of course, it is true that in innumerable ways power manipulates and subjugates legal rules and 'ideas'. But one must also see that it is caught up in ideology: the power of discourse is fully affirmed, while the true discourse becomes a discourse of power.

And we must also see that the law, positivized and reduced to the law of socialism, regulates power and renders it opaque to itself, more opaque than it ever was before.

This very sketchy interpretation is concerned only, I should like to stress, with the aim of totalitarianism. It is not my purpose here to inquire into the facts of social development and change. Were this the case, I would have to try to analyse all the forms of resistance to the totalitarian project – and I am not speaking here of conscious, political resistance, but of the social relations that elude the grip of power. I would also have to try to analyse all the pathological processes of the bureaucratic world, for the perversion of the function of power, of law and of knowledge has effects on the whole of social life – let us be in no doubt – even when there is not, or no longer, any support for the regime. Among others, Alexander Zinoviev is one of the most severe analysts of this pathology.

My purpose is rather to bring out, and to submit to the reader's questioning, the image of the political body in totalitarianism. It is an image which, on the one hand, requires the exclusion of the male-volent Other and which, simultaneously, breaks down into the image of a whole and a part that stands for the whole, of a part that paradoxically reintroduces the figure of the other, the omniscient, omnipotent, benevolent other, the militant, the leader, the Egocrat. This other offers his own body – individual, mortal, endowed with all the virtues – whether he is called Stalin or Mao or Fidel. A mortal body which is perceived as invulnerable, which condenses in itself all strengths, all talents, and defies the laws of nature by his super-male energy.

Of course, I am aware that I am drawing on only one thread of the interpretation. I cannot develop this remark here, but I should like to suggest that we ought to examine another pole of the totalitarian representation – that of the organization. Or, to use another term which is more likely to convey the discordance within the totalitarian representation, I would say that the image of the body is combined with that of the machine. The scientifico-technical model and the model of the production enterprise, governed by the rational division of labour, have not only been imported from Western capitalism, but have in a sense taken hold of the whole society. Socialism seems to be linked, at least in an ideal way, with the formula of a harmoni-ous society, in touch with itself through all its parts, delivered from the dysfunctions of a system in which the various sectors of activity each obeyed specific norms and in which their interdependence remained at the mercy of the vicissitudes of the market. The new society is presented as a single organization comprising a network of micro-organizations; furthermore, it is presented paradoxically as that 'great automaton' which Marx claimed to uncover in the capitalist mode of production. It is worth pointing out that such a representation is split in two: the social, in its essence, is defined as organization and as the organizable. From the first point of view, socialist man is the man of the organization, imprinted in it; from the second point of view, he is the constantly working organizer, the social engineer. But it is important above all to note the articulation of the two key-images, that of the body and that of the machine. In a sense, they are convergent: they involve an ambiguity of the same kind. In the first case, the political agent is dissolved in an *us* that speaks, hears, reads reality through him, thus identifying himself with the party, the body of the people and, at the same time, representing himself, through the same identification, as the head of that body, attributing consciousness to himself. In the second case, the same agent proves to be a part of the machine, or one of its organs, or a driving belt – a frequently used metaphor – and at the same time an activist-machinist who makes decisions concerning the functioning and production of society. However, the two images do not fully merge; the image of the body is altered when it comes into contact with that of the machine. The latter contradicts the logic of identification; the communist 'us' is itself dissolved. The notion of the organization, even though it gives rise to that of the organizer, poses a threat to the substance of the body politic, making the social appear at the boundaries of the inorganic.

I shall now dare to ask the question, From where does the totalitarian adventure arise? It is not born out of nothing. It is the sign of a political mutation. But what is that mutation? It seems to me that it would be futile to try to analyse it at the level of the mode of production, as the consequence of a final concentration of capital; but it would be equally futile to treat it, as some have been content to do, as the product of the phantasies of revolutionary intellectuals, seeking to complete the work of the Jacobins of 1793 in order to reconstruct the world on a *tabula rasa*. In my view, totalitarianism can be clarified only by grasping its relationship with democracy. It is from democracy that it arises, even though it has taken root initially, at least in its socialist version, in countries where the democratic transformation was only just beginning. It overturns that transformation, while at the same time taking over some of its features and extending them at the level of phantasy.

In what characteristics can we discern this process? I believe that my brief comments on the image of the body politic indicate the lines of a response. For modern democracy is that regime in which such an image tends to vanish. I say *regime* advisedly. Taken in its conventional sense, this term is inadequate. Beyond a historically determined system of political institutions, I wish to call attention to a long-term process, what de Tocqueville called the democratic revolution, which he saw coming to birth in France under the *ancien régime* and which, since his time, has continued to develop. As we know, this revolution found its motive force in the equalization of *conditions*. However important this phenomenon may be, it does not shed enough light for my purpose and it leaves an essential mutation in the shadows: the society of the *ancien régime* represented its unity and its identity to itself as that of a body – a body which found its figuration in the body of the king, or rather which identified itself with the king's body, while at the same time it attached itself to it as its head. As Ernst Kantorowicz has shown in a masterly fashion, such a symbolism was elaborated in the Middle Ages and is of theologico-political origin. The image of the king's body as a double body, both mortal and immortal, individual and collective, was initially underpinned by the body of Christ. The important point for my purpose – it would be quite outside the scope of this essay to analyse the many displacements of this representation in the course of history – is that, long after the features of liturgical royalty had died away, the king still possessed the power to incarnate in his body the community of the kingdom, now invested with the sacred, a political community, a national community, a mystical body. I am not unaware of the fact that in the eighteenth century this representation was largely undermined, that new models of sociability emerged as a result of the growth of individualism, progress in the equalization of conditions of which de Tocqueville spoke and the development of the state administration, which tended to make the latter appear as an independent, impersonal entity. But the changes that occurred did not entirely eliminate the notion of the kingdom as a unity which was both organic and mystical, of which the monarch was at the same time the body and the head. It can also be seen that, paradoxically, the growth of social mobility and the increasing uniformity of behaviour, customs, opinions and rules had the effect of strengthening rather than weakening the traditional symbolism. The *ancien régime* was made up of an infinite number of small bodies which gave individuals their distinctive marks. And these small bodies fitted together within a great imaginary body for which the body of the king provided the model and the guarantee of its integrity. The democratic revolution, for so long subterranean, burst out when the body of the king was destroyed, when the body politic was decapitated and when, at the same time, the corporeality of the social was dissolved. There then occurred what I would call a 'disincorporation' of individuals. This was an extraordinary phenomenon, the consequences of which seemed, in the first half of the nineteenth century, absurd, even monstrous, not only to conservatives, but to many liberals. For these individuals might become entities that would have to be counted in a universal suffrage that would take the place of the universal invested in the body politic. The relentless struggle to combat the idea of universal suffrage is not only the indication of a class struggle. The inability to conceive of this suffrage as anything other than a dissolution of the social is extremely instructive. The danger of numbers is greater than the danger of an intervention by the masses on the political scene; the idea of number as such is opposed to the idea of the substance of society. Number breaks down unity, destroys identity.

But if we must speak of a disincorporation of the individual, we must also analyse the disengagement of civil society from a state, itself hitherto consubstantial with the body of the king. Or, to put it another way, we must examine the emergence of social relations, not only economic ones, but legal, educational and scientific relations which have their own dynamic; and, more specifically, we must examine the disentangling of the spheres of power, law and knowledge that takes place when the identity of the body politic disappears. The modern democratic revolution is best recognized in this mutation: there is no power linked to a body. Power appears as an empty place and those who exercise it as mere mortals who occupy it only temporarily or who could install themselves in it only by force or cunning. There is no law that can be fixed, whose articles cannot be contested, whose foundations are not susceptible of being called into question. Lastly, there is no representation of a centre and of the contours of society: unity cannot now efface social division. Democracy inaugurates the experience of an ungraspable, uncontrollable society in which the people will be said to be sovereign, of course, but whose identity will constantly be open to question, whose identity will remain latent.

I referred to the experience of an ungraspable society. It is true that this society gives rise to a multi-layered discourse which tries to grasp it; and in this sense it emerges as an object, by the very fact that it is no longer imprinted in the order of nature or in some supernatural order. But it seems remarkable to me that the discourse that may be imputed to bourgeois ideology was maintained in the early days of democracy under the threat of a breakup of society as such. The institutions and values proclaimed – Property, the Family, the State, Authority, the Nation, Culture – were presented as bastions against barbarism, against the unknown forces from without that could destroy society and civilization. The attempt to sacralize institutions through discourse is directly related to the loss of the substance of society, to the disintegration of the body. The bourgeois cult of order which is sustained by the affirmation of authority, in its many forms, by the declaration of the rules and the proper distances between those who occupy the position of master, owner, cultivated man, civilized man, normal man, adult and those who are placed in the position of the *other*, this whole cult testifies to a certain vertigo in face of the void created by an indeterminate society.

However, as I have just suggested, we must be attentive to another aspect of the mutation. What emerges with democracy is the image of society as such, society as purely human but, at the same time, society *sui generis*, whose own nature requires objective knowledge. It is the image of a society which is homogeneous in principle, capable of being subsumed to the overview of knowledge and power, arising through the dissolution of the monarchical focus of legitimacy and the destruction of the architecture of bodies. It is the image of the omniscient, omnipotent state, of a state both anonymous and, as de Tocqueville puts it, tutelary. It is also, in so far as inequality exists within the boundaries of the equality of conditions, the image of a mass that passes the last judgement on good and evil, the true and the false, the normal and the abnormal, the image of sovereign opinion. Lastly, what emerges is the image of the people, which, as I observed, remains indeterminate, but which nevertheless is susceptible of being determined, of being actualized on the level of phantasy as an image of the People-as-One.

From this point of view, may not totalitarianism be conceived as a response to the questions raised by democracy, as an attempt to resolve its paradoxes? Modern democratic society seems to me, in fact, like a society in which power, law and knowledge are exposed to a radical indetermination, a society that has become the theatre of an uncontrollable adventure, so that what is instituted never becomes established, the known remains undermined by the unknown, the present proves to be undefinable, covering many different social times which are staggered in relation to one another within simultaneity – or definable only in terms of some fictitious future; an adventure such that the quest for identity cannot be separated from the experience of division. This society is *historical* society *par excellence*. What seems to me to be condensed beneath the paradoxes of democracy is the status of power, for this power is not, as a certain contemporary discourse naively repeats, a mere organ of domination: it is the agency of legitimacy and identity. Now, as long as it appears detached from the prince, as long as it presents itself as the power of no one, as long as it seems to move towards a *latent* focus – namely, the people – it runs the risk of having its symbolic function cancelled out, of falling into collective representations at the level of the real, the contingent, when the conflicts are becoming sharper and leading society to the edge of collapse. Political power, as circumscribed and localized in society at the same time as being an instituting moment, is exposed to the threat of falling into particularity, of arousing what Machiavelli regarded as more dangerous than hatred, namely, contempt; and similarly those who exercise it or aspire to it are exposed to the threat of appearing as individuals or groups concerned solely to satisfy their desires. With totalitarianism an apparatus is set up which tends to stave off this threat, which tends to weld power and society back together again, to efface all signs of social division, to banish the indetermination that haunts the democratic experience. But this attempt, as I have suggested, itself draws on a democratic source, developing and fully affirming the idea of the People-as-One, the idea of society as such, bearing the knowledge of itself, transparent to itself and homogeneous, the idea of mass opinion, sovereign and normative, the idea of the tutelary state.

Since the advent of democracy, and in opposition to it, the body is thus revitalized. But it is important to point out that what is revitalized is quite different from what was once torn apart. The image of the body that informed monarchical society was underpinned by that of Christ. It was invested with the idea of the division between the visible and the invisible, the idea of the splitting of the mortal and the immortal, the idea of mediation, the idea of a production which both effaced and re-established the difference between the producer and that produced, the idea of the unity of the body and the distinction between the head and the limbs. The prince condensed in his person the principle of power, the principle of law and the principle of knowledge, but he was *supposed* to obey a superior power; he declared himself to be both above the law and subjected to the law, to be both the father and the son of justice; he possessed wisdom but he was subjected to reason. According to the medieval formula, he was *major et minor se ipso*, above and below himself. That does not seem to be the position of the Egocrat or of his substitutes, the bureaucratic leaders. The Egocrat coincides with himself, as society is supposed to coincide with itself. An impossible swallowing up of the body in the head begins to take place, as does an impossible swallowing up of the head in the body. The attraction of the whole is no longer dissociated from the attraction of the parts. Once the old organic constitution disappears, the death instinct is unleashed into the closed, uniform, imaginary space of totalitarianism.

Such, then, are a few thoughts which indicate the direction for a questioning of the political. Some readers will no doubt suspect that my reflections are nourished by psychoanalysis. That is indeed the case. But this connection is meaningful only if one asks oneself at which hearth Freud's thought was lit. For is it not true that in order to sustain the ordeal of the division of the subject, in order to dislodge the reference points of the *self* and the *other*, to depose the position of the possessor of power and knowledge, one must assume responsibility for an experience instituted by democracy, the indetermination that was born from the loss of the substance of the body politic?

# 10

# Pushing Back the Limits
# of the Possible

We do not know what the future will be of the mass movement which is currently shaking the communist regime in Poland. The uncertainty is such that even while writing this essay I ask myself whether Soviet troops will sweep into Warsaw before I have written the last line. This very day, 27 November 1980, most of the morning papers announced the beginning of a general strike in the Polish capital, although it was called off during the night as a result of a new and sudden concession by the government, which agreed to free two trade unionists who had been imprisoned a little earlier. Moreover, it agreed in principle to allow an inquiry to be conducted, within the police and the ministry of justice, into the responsibilities of those agents who have exercised repression against the workers. Were the arrests of the militants of Solidarity, which sparked off the last conflict, the result of a provocation by the hardliners within the party, or rather the action of the government? Whatever the case may be, the government gave way openly to the threat of the strike. However, at the very moment when the radio conveyed this information, we learned that the signs of a Soviet military intervention were increasing and that the Americans were taking them seriously enough to issue a new appeal to the Kremlin, urging them to allow the Poles to sort out their own affairs by themselves.

Thus the events unfold in rapid succession, but it is true that this haste has been there since the beginning of the strike at Gdansk. Test of strength follows test of strength, even though the confrontation between the power and the masses remains at the level of the symbolic. The last episode that we mentioned was preceded by many others, no less serious, and it may herald episodes which are more dramatic still and which will make it unnecessary for the

Russians to invade. Yet how can we discount the hypothesis of their intervention? It is not merely plausible: in view of the logic of the totalitarian system, it is probable. The Polish Communist Party cannot allow indefinitely its authority to be contested in fact and limited in principle by the action of independent unions; even less can it allow these unions, which it had hoped to bring under its control and to neutralize, to be caught up in a current of demands which they cannot canalize. Judging by all the information that reaches us, Poland is today a country where speech is bursting out in every sphere of society, where criticism and protest are set alight from one place to another and in all the major centres, from the factory to the university or the hospital. It is that country where, to an ever-increasing extent, the masses have become indifferent to the promises of the government and intractable to the advice of their own leaders, where it is no longer useful for those in command to issue threats or orders, where the foundations of legitimacy are crumbling.

Even in a democratic regime, such a situation could not continue without giving rise to a revolution. And yet a democratic regime is incomparably better equipped to accommodate and absorb the demands which are made. Its institutions organize and adjust the space of social conflict. The diversity of interests which are defined and expressed in the context of civil society provides the established power with the means to defend itself against the most energetic activities of contestation. The possibility of political change brought about through public opinion, of a displacement of the majority during the next elections, leaves many people with the hope of having some hold on the future. Thus we saw how French society could absorb the formidable effervescence which erupted within it in May 1968. The concessions of the government were effective at that time because they were credible; no one doubted that the Grenelle Agreements were carried out. The government's capacity to manoeuvre was facilitated by the attitude of a segment of the population, which was hostile to the revolutionary adventures and concerned to defend its interests and the established order. The loyalty of the army was assured, by virtue of its very position as the guarantor of both public order and the dominant interests. Finally – and no doubt this provides the best explanation of the survival of the regime – the development of the strike, whatever its magnitude and however varied its forms of contestation were, was embedded in a dynamic of conflict which, while normally contained within narrow limits and fragmented localities, is always recognized as inherent in democracy. May 1968 was an agonizing episode within a society which tacitly accepts to live at the pace of its conflicts, to make allowances for disturbance and opacity. May 1968 marked the eruption of an anti-authoritarian, anti-hierarchical, anti-bureaucratic speech, of a desire for freedom, equality and identity which are normally restrained, indeed repressed, but which are never excluded from social life.

In Poland the situation is altogether different. Faced with popular protest, the government makes substantial concessions. It promises to recognize the independence of the new unions; it promises to increase wages; it promises to limit censorship, to put an end to the control of news, to facilitate the spread of catholicism; even more, it promises to transform itself: authority passes into the hands of new men. However, these concessions are not credible, for the situation remains unchanged, the system of authority remains at the basis of social life, it is still organized around the party and this party itself is organized around its head, and the population does not have the capacity to choose its representatives.

Paradoxically, the government presents itself as in search of a consensus while it remains lodged in a power separated from society. From now on, its concessions will not work in its favour but rather will discredit it; they succeed in destroying that identification with the people, with the proletariat, which is supposed to provide its full legitimacy. Why should it wish to beg for support if in principle it embodied society? No doubt it has been a long time since the Poles – at least those who once had faith – have ceased to believe in the image of the communist incarnation. But it would be a mistake to play down the significance of the event which signals publicly the abandonment of this image. It would also be a mistake to imagine that the never-ending self-criticisms of communist leaders marked in the past the same desacralization of power. When Gierek took stock of the errors of the party or of its leadership, he did not in any way suggest that communist power had ceased to coincide with the people; he merely attributed its empirical errors to organizational failures, to the weaknesses of individuals who had not known how to occupy fully the place of power, to coincide with the people. He continued to insist on the occupation of this place and on the control of the decision-making apparatus, which in the future as in the past is in principle the preserve of the party. If disturbances took place in the factories or in the street, the leadership could certainly say that the party should take account of popular reactions, but that meant simply that the party should listen within itself to the voice of the people in such a way that the people would recognize its own voice in the party. The activity at Gdansk has a quite different significance; for there a split develops between the organ of power and the workers, in such a way that the former is unable to conceal its position as a particular actor confronting the claim to independence of the new unions: forced to make concessions, it falls from the symbolic position of the incarnating power.

Moreover, the vulnerability of the totalitarian system in a crisis situation stems from the fact that the internal social divisions are subordinated to a general division between the sphere of power and that of civil society. Poland is certainly not a homogeneous society; as elsewhere, particular interests clash within it. But it forms a common interest, an interest of civil society in opposition to the hold of the party and the bureaucracy. In these conditions, power, as soon as it is threatened, does not have a free reign to play on the oppositions between different social strata. And, by the same token, the support of the army is less certain. For if the army has doubts about the justification of its mission of protecting public security, if it does not see in a large segment of the population the signs of consent to the established order, if, lastly, it finds its function merged with that of the police, then the representation of its national role begins to vacillate. Finally, in contrast to democracy, the totalitarian system is constituted and maintained only by excluding every form of contestation. In this sense, as soon as these forms find sufficient strength to express themselves, they renew the test of its legitimacy at the same time as they mobilize themselves for specific objectives. A right is invented which opens up a field of action and thought freed from the tutelage of power. Thus the Polish workers expect not only those measures which would satisfy their demands: they are also giving themselves an unlimited capacity to take initiatives. Their demand is not only for a specific object, but also for the right to make demands. In short, the popular dynamic is not developing within the limits of the regime. Even though it does not seem to call into question the principles of the regime, even though, for example, the workers' leaders claim that they are not engaging in politics or even claim to recognize the leading role of the Communist Party, this dynamic has already moved beyond the closed space of totalitarianism.

Of course, one might well assume that the awareness of the dangers will put a brake on the opposition to the regime. But this awareness is more acute among the leaders involved in negotiations with the authorities than among those who sense a new liberty in the strike, who discover the strength of collective resistance and the vulnerability of power. The success achieved through action enlarges the field of the possible, while the image of an impassable limit becomes blurred.

What could the new leadership of the party do if the mass movement does not decline? The problem is not one of assessing the sincerity of the communists who are apparently won over to the formula of independent unions, nor one of gauging their patriotic sentiment. If the existence of the party is at stake, the Russians will appear as the only possible saviours. The moderates will give way to the hardliners or will form an alliance with them, or will themselves do the work of the hardliners. From now on, in any case, it may reasonably be supposed that Kania's strategy has never been dictated by anything other than a realist concern. His government has constantly combined attempts to corrupt trade unionists, manoeuvres of intimidation and concessions. The man himself was minister of state security. Are we fully aware of what that means in a communist regime? I read with some amazement the articles which, following the Gdansk agreement, celebrated the victory achieved by the two parties, the workers' representatives and the political leaders, as if a liberal communism had been established. It seems to me more plausible to assume that Kania had succeeded in playing for time and that this would work in favour of an attempt to restore the authority of the party. He is holding one end of the string that his opponents have grasped by the other end; he lets it be pulled, then holds it, then lets it be pulled again, in the expectation that the others will wear themselves out. After all, no one can say that he is mistaken. But it seems to me more likely that he will be led too far from his camp and that only the intervention of a third party, the Soviet giant, will prevent the party from collapsing. And this third party, it should be stressed, is not indifferent. The logic of totalitarianism is not to be found in the context of Poland, but initially in the context of what must be called the Soviet empire. The bureaucracy in the Kremlin sees its own power challenged, the order that it has established in Eastern Europe threatened, by the Polish workers. It expects results from Kania's strategy. It will not wait for its failure in order to act.

I am not among those who fear that an analysis of this kind implies a condemnation of the Polish movement. It is true that there is a way of

indicating the barrier of the impossible which would lead one to conclude that all action is futile. It is the way of passing judgement as a
spectator, without understanding that the representation of the
impossible helps to attenuate the sense of the possible. The Poles who
are struggling against the regime are not in the position of spectators
of their own life. They recognize themselves as actors in a system
which needs them in order to survive. If they take extraordinary
risks, it is because without them they would continue obediently to
maintain their own servitude. And the fact is that in facing these
risks, they have already pushed back the limits of the possible. The
existence of independent unions and the legalization of strikes, for
example, seemed incompatible with the logic of totalitarianism.
They have disrupted this logic, at least for a while. Whatever the
future may be, it is clear to all that a communist power has folded in
face of the active resistance of the masses and that the image of
Soviet power does not suffice to discourage collective initiative.

If one considers the last thirty years, one will recall that the revolt
of East Berlin was crushed in 1953, that of Hungary in 1956, that of
Czechoslovakia in 1968 – so many failures, one will say. But the
movement which is currently taking form in Poland is the heir of
these revolutions, developing new means of contestation which the
communist power has been unable, for the last four months, to contain. Moreover, it benefits from an historical experience acquired, in
part, in the same country, which was the site of conflict in 1956,
1970 and 1976. The maturity of the movement is apparent in many
ways: for instance, its capacity, particularly in the early phase, to
avoid street demonstrations which would expose it to repression, or
to avoid openly defying the communist power. I would add that even
in the USSR the criticism of the regime mobilizes an opposition,
admittedly scattered and still very small, but which spreads to the
outside world the themes of a resistance to totalitarianism.

The Polish intellectuals who actively supported the workers at the
risk of repression, and then supported the movement of Gdansk,
share the same sensibility as the Soviet dissidents, just as they know
themselves to be close to the Czech intellectuals or the persecuted
Hungarians. The idea that the power of totalitarianism does not
make action impossible has found expression in individual or collective initiatives – initiatives of groups or of the masses. In a sense, the
Polish movement goes further than these earlier movements, even
though in appearance it is less radical than the Hungarian uprising

was; for it moves beyond the dilemma of reforms *versus* the destruction of communist power – two perspectives which were opened up in Prague and Budapest – in order to assert, at a distance from that power, the autonomy of civil society, which is incompatible with the nature of the regime but which contradicts it from within, by ignoring, as it were, its principles.

In emphasizing the logic of totalitarianism, I do not at all wish to suggest that it is insurmountable, that it remains, despite the blows that it receives from time to time, invulnerable. What I rule out is the hypothesis of a stable compromise, in the context of a country in the Soviet bloc, between the requirements of the communist power and the democratic demands formulated by the workers, the intellectuals and, more generally, all the strata dominated by that power. The latter demands, such as they are expressed at the moment, point towards a new centre of power. But a situation of double power does not seem conceivable. One would fail to recognize the profound character of the conflict if one thought that the claims put forward could be satisfied without striking at the supremacy of the party. The problem is not one of respecting the latter, for it is not supremacy which characterizes the position of the party: power is total, or else the regime falls apart. In other words, what I rule out is the establishment of a democratic communism in which social conflict and opposition would be institutionalized. What we are observing, by contrast, is a *crack* in the totalitarian system. And I do not believe that this crack is accidental, the effect of circumstances whose conjunction would explain by itself the explosive effects. It is no doubt justified to call attention to the role played by catholicism in the crystallization of the Polish resistance. It has proved to be ineradicable, it has rendered possible the reconstitution of networks of socialization to which power had to accommodate itself and enabled alliances to be formed and information to be circulated, networks which are absent in other countries of Eastern Europe. Above all, it maintained a focus of legitimacy which was external to power and which enabled the Poles to defend themselves against the disintegrating effects of totalitarianism within society. Moreover, there can be no doubt that the economic crisis, by its very magnitude, fuelled the demands and led the population to the threshold of the intolerable. But having taken account of the role played by circumstances, it is important to recognize that the crack of which I am speaking develops along the lines of cleavage of the system.

## Two Sides of Totalitarianism

The most widespread accounts of the totalitarian system try to persuade us of its monstrous coherence and its perennial character. For their part, Western governments and the major political leaders tacitly accepted, up until the Helsinki negotiations and more or less explicitly during the latter, that the Soviet bloc not only had intangible boundaries but also – what amounts to the same thing – that it formed a legitimate ensemble of political entities. For Western governments to sign the Helsinki Agreement was, by accepting the fact of totalitarianism, to authenticate the idea of a part of humanity which lives beyond the iron curtain according to its own laws, of populations which form a single body with the power which subjugates them: such were the societies of Eastern Europe, locked in the definite horizons of their regimes, as if their populations did not aspire to freedom, as if these societies were not affected by the ferment of democracy, as if communist power was not exposed to the effects of the contradictions produced by its mode of domination. Despite the recommendations of certain sections, the general thrust of the Helsinki Agreement was unequivocal: the division between the democratic sphere and the totalitarian sphere was officially instituted. It had a geo-political and a historical significance: totalitarianism was in principle installed in the flow of time; and it was presented as insurmountable within its own boundaries. The future of the world was sketched out in terms of this division.

However, perhaps one should regard as more significant, although of less importance, the fact that the critique of totalitarianism, conducted by a minority which had recently shed its illusions about the blessings of Soviet socialism, most frequently projected the image of a flawless system of oppression, capable of effectively crushing all opposition, against which only heroic personalities – the dissidents – could protest. This critique was expressed in the name of a moral resistance against the violence of a state which concentrated in itself all the forces of coercion characteristic of modern states; and it left no other possibility than to try to apply pressure by protest on the harshest decisions taken by communist power against the persecuted opponents. The situation brought about by the invasion of Afghanistan and the international tension which followed it have somewhat modified the sensitivity to the nature of the Soviet regime. But in the best cases – I would dare to say, thinking of the complacency of French policy towards the Soviet Union – it merely increases the belief in the omnipotence of this regime and in a division of the world into two blocs, one of which, the totalitarian bloc, allegedly enjoys not only supremacy in weapons but also the cohesion of all its parts in the service of its expansionist aims.

Now even if it is true that, in military terms, there are indeed two camps (although their capacities for action could be assessed only by taking account of the interplay of forces which develop in the world independently of their will), and if it is also true that there is an essential difference between systems of a totalitarian type and systems of a democratic type, that should not make us forget that in reality the societies of the East and the West cannot be defined by the sole criterion of the power of their weapons and that they are the theatre of multiple conflicts, latent or manifest, which contradict the logic of the system. These contradictions are all the more remarkable in the East in that they are normally concealed, all the more formidable in that they are artificially contained. To forge the image of regimes which have apparently acquired the mastery of oppression is, in a certain way, to contribute to this concealment.

I hope that the reader will excuse me for referring to my own analyses, but the fact is that twenty-five years ago I already denounced this image as symmetrical to that of a radiant communism. What is common to both is the belief in the omnipotence of a system, in its capacity to translate itself, without remainder, into reality. Let me note in passing that one of the last avatars of this way of inverting the communist thesis while remaining dependent on it may be found in Zinoviev, when he replaces the idea of a People-as-One with the idea of a fragmented people in order to conclude, according to the same schema, that the regime responds to its desire; or when he replaces the idea of a luminous future with that of an interminable night, as if the lugubrious mechanisms of repetition have come once again to attest to the flawless logic which previously had worked towards the building of the good society.

In attempting to conceptualize totalitarianism, I always tried to distinguish between what it is ideally, in conformity with the project that it animates, and what it is in fact, that is, its actual development. In the past I did not have at my disposal the extraordinary testimonies which have emerged from the events of 1956 in Poland and Hungary and of 1968 in Czechoslovakia, or the great analyses of

Soviet society made by Solzhenitsyn. Today, the history of the last few decades seems to me to confirm and to clarify this distinction. On the one hand, totalitarianism is that system in which social division in all its forms is radically masked. There is no distance between the state and civil society; the state is presented as consubstantial with society: it is the social state, the proletarian state, society itself reduced to its active principle. In this sense, the state tends to be omnipresent in all sectors of social life. Its presence is assured by the party, whose ramifications develop everywhere and whose members become the agents of the Universal who act as doubles for each particular social agent, in the sphere of production as well as that of culture. Similarly, there is no distance between classes or, more precisely, no divisions which seem to be produced within the system; the class struggle, intensely declared, is attributed to the existence of social strata deriving from the past, to a bourgeoisie or a peasantry inherited from the old regime, or to the existence of groups manipulated by foreign imperialism. The dominant bureaucracy makes itself invisible and seems to dissolve in the homogeneous social body of socialism. Finally, for the same reason, there is no distance between the *place* of power identified with that of the people, the *place* of law and the *place* of the speech in which the ultimate knowledge of reality is announced. The party-state, or rather its governing organ, holds the principle of justice and the principle of truth together with the right of command. In this sense, a profound transformation of ideology takes place. Whereas ideology was organized around many centres in bourgeois democracy and was expressed in many languages, as it were, and in fragmented spaces (political, economic, legal, cultural), it now tends to become unified and to reduce all social representation to the same norms. As soon as power becomes omnipresent, the discourse of power seeks to efface its origin; it ceases to be that discourse on the social which, in bourgeois democracy, exhibited the position of those who spoke it in order to immerse itself in the social. Thus a power of discourse as such is constituted, a power which subjugates its agents, passes through them rather than developing within them, inscribes them in an impersonal knowledge which cuts them off from the experience of others and of things.

But we would be victims of the phantasy which inhabits this system if we imagined that it actually realized itself, that it could ever succeed in realizing itself, even in the heyday of Stalinism. We would be forgetting that social division is only masked, that power is in fact held by individuals who decide the fate of everyone, that classes continue to exist, that the bureaucracy forms a new dominant strata, that inequality exists in new forms, that the party, everywhere present, everywhere active, can only interfere in the factory, the office, the laboratory, in all the sectors of production and culture which continue to define themselves in terms of their own goals. We would be forgetting, finally, that the symbolic reference points of law, of knowledge and of reality may well have been denied, but not abolished; and that the prodigious expansion of ideology is paid for by the inability to maintain the criteria of legitimacy and illegitimacy, as well as those of the imaginary and the real. By shedding ourselves of the illusion which the totalitarian project seeks to substantiate, we can catch sight of the numerous contradictions which stem from the regime.

The fantastic attempt to efface social division, to absorb all processes of socialization into the process of state control, to push the symbolic into the real, is exposed to the threat of a violent return of all the signs of division and otherness. The power which dissimulates itself runs the risk of reappearing as the organ of oppression, towering over the whole of society and becoming the common target of all contestation. The party, which penetrates every milieu and exercises control over all activities, runs the risk of being seen everywhere as a parasite. The distance between those above and those below, and, more generally, inequality, runs the risk of being exposed. Finally, the all-pervading ideology runs the risk of provoking a generalized refusal to believe, a radical mode of disaffection which relegates it to the status of a pure political lie; the power of discourse collapses, leaving the image of the oppressive power without a protective screen.

Since the death of Stalin – the Egocrat, in Solzhenitsyn's terms, which sustained the image of the body of socialist society – numerous facts have emerged which attest to the erosion of the system. Both in the USSR and in the countries of Eastern Europe, where the weight of foreign oppression is added to that of internal oppression, the divide between the power and the people has deepened. The ideology has collapsed. With the decline of the legitimacy of the established regimes, bureaucratic cynicism and corruption became more prevalent, while the representation of disorder and illegality extinguished the faith in the values of socialism. Finally, modes of contestation have emerged which are not necessarily convergent, but which are united by the attempt to open a space outside the limits of power and outside the imaginary enclosure of the social – a space of right, a space of religion, a space of national identity.

While some people do not pause to consider these changes, being struck instead by the persistence of oppression, others draw the conclusion that we can no longer regard as 'totalitarian' those regimes which are incapable of securing the support of the population. Such regimes, it is said, can only rely on the police and the army; either they benefit from nationalist traditions where they are able to mobilize them, or they exploit the aspirations aroused by economic and technical development, or indeed they take advantage of the fragmentation of the subjected society. It seems to me to be more illuminating to grasp the totalitarian system in its history, to observe that the contradictions which it contained since its original formation have developed and to see that it has another side which has been apparent for a long time and which is coming increasingly to the fore.

The events of Poland are intelligible, it seems to me, only if they are situated in this history of totalitarianism; and, whatever the future may hold in store, these events have a significance which goes beyond the specific context of the present conflict. There can be no doubt that the Russian leaders know it. I said that they will probably be led to intervene militarily if the situation of double power continues. But their hesitation, their inability over several months to control the activity of the Polish workers by intimidation (in spite of the examples of Hungary and Czechoslovakia), indeed what must be called their tolerance – albeit forced – with regard to a challenge which arrives at their doorstep through the party of Gierek and then Kania, are as significant as an eventual intervention. We are told that the precedent of Afghanistan has placed them in difficulties with world opinion. But in view of the weakness of the response aroused by their invasion, the argument seems hardly convincing. We are told that the firmness of the warnings of the Americans could only incline them to prudence and that they are more wary of Reagan than of Carter. Perhaps. But the whole question is whether the necessity to re-establish order within the boundaries of their camp prevails over the possibility of a tension to which the West, and especially the Europeans, could probably not, in the long term, respond in a way which would be contrary to their economic policy and to what they regard as their security. It seems to me more plausible to believe that Poland has put the Soviet bureaucracy in an unprecedented situation; it faces a challenge which, as I said, is less radical than the Hungarian challenge but more disconcerting because it saps the foundations of communist authority and makes the population aware of its strength without apparently taking a political form. At Gdansk, the workers basically said to the leaders of the party and, through them, to the Russian leaders: 'We don't want your power, but we're taking charge, here and now, of the defence of our rights and interests.' This is what has created a situation hitherto unknown to all the communist powers; and it is by no means clear that the latter would be more successful in eliminating it by a single blow than by playing for time.

# Notes

## Editor's Introduction

1 For details of Lefort's publications and some of the commentaries of his work, see the Select Bibliography on pp. 331–3.

2 I offer a critique of Lefort's account of ideology in 'Ideology and the Social Imaginary', in my *Studies in the Theory of Ideology* (Cambridge: Polity Press, 1984), pp. 16–41.

3 See Rudolph Bahro, *The Alternative in Eastern Europe*, trans. David Fernbach (London: New Left Books, 1978).

4 An account of the circumstances surrounding the formation of Socialisme ou Barbarie may be found in 'An Interview with C. Castoriadis', trans. Burt Grahl and David Pugh, *Telos*, 23 (Spring 1975), pp. 131–55. See also Mark Poster, *Existential Marxism in Postwar France: From Sartre to Althusser* (Princeton: Princeton University Press, 1975), pp. 201–5.

5 See Cornelius Castoriadis, 'Les rapports de production en Russie', originally published in *Socialisme ou Barbarie*, 2 (mai–juin 1949), reprinted in Castoriadis's *La Société bureaucratique* (Paris: Union Générale d'Éditions, 1973), vol. 1, pp. 205–81.

6 This extended and somewhat polemical exchange with Sartre was conducted primarily in the pages of *Les Temps Modernes*; see especially Claude Lefort, 'Le marxisme et Sartre', 8 (1953), pp. 1541–70; Jean-Paul Sartre, 'Réponse à Lefort', 8 (1953), pp. 1571–629; and Claude Lefort, 'De la réponse à la question', 10 (1954), pp. 157–84. See also Claude Lefort, 'La méthode des intellectuels progressistes', *Socialisme ou Barbarie*, 23 (janvier–février, 1958). The essays by Lefort are reprinted in his *Éléments d'une critique de la bureaucratie* (Geneva: Droz, 1971).

7 The original text of 'Le totalitarisme sans Staline' contains lengthy quotations from the published texts of the Twentieth Congress and detailed analyses of the speeches and reports of the leaders and key

party members, including Khrushchev, Bulganin, Suslov and Malenkov.

8  For a brief overview of these debates, see David Lane, *The End of Social Inequality? Class, Status and Power under State Socialism* (London: George Allen & Unwin, 1982), chapter 5.

9  See Milovan Djilas, *The New Class: An Analysis of the Communist System* (London: George Allen & Unwin, 1966). The extent to which it is illuminating to regard the dominant individuals and groups in the USSR as constituting a 'class' is a debatable matter. For a good discussion of the relevant issues, see Alec Nove, 'Is There a Ruling Class in the USSR?', in *Classes, Power and Conflict: Classical and Contemporary Debates*, ed. Anthony Giddens and David Held (London: Macmillan, 1982), pp. 588–604.

10  The term 'civil society' refers, in its classical sense, to all those spheres of social life which are organized independently of the political action of the state.

11  Claude Lefort, 'Totalitarianism without Stalin', in this volume, p. 79.

12  Lefort's criticisms of certain tendencies in Socialisme ou Barbarie are expressed in 'Le proletariat et sa direction' (originally published in 1952) and 'Organisation et parti' (originally published in 1958), both reprinted in *Éléments d'une critique de la bureaucratie*. Lefort describes the circumstances which led to his break with Socialisme ou Barbarie in 'An Interview with Claude Lefort', trans. Dorothy Gehrke and Brian Singer, *Telos*, 30 (Winter 1976–7), pp. 173–92. For a somewhat different account, see 'An Interview with C. Castoriadis'.

13  Claude Lefort, 'Novelty and the Appeal of Repetition', in this volume, p. 124.

14  Lefort offered an assessment of the events of May 1968 in a collective work written by himself, Cornelius Castoriadis and Edgar Morin; see *Mai 1968: la brèche* (Paris: Fayard, 1968).

15  Claude Lefort, 'The Image of the Body and Totalitarianism', in this volume, p. 294.

16  Karl Marx and Frederick Engels, *Manifesto of the Communist Party*, in K. Marx and F. Engels, *Collected Works* (London: Lawrence and Wishart, 1976), vol. 6, p. 487.

17  Claude Lefort, 'The Image of the Body and Totalitarianism', p. 295.

18  Karl Marx, *Capital: A Critique of Political Economy*, ed. Frederick Engels (London: Lawrence and Wishart, 1974), vol. III, p. 830 (translation modified).

19  Karl Marx, *The Eighteenth Brumaire of Louis Bonaparte*, in K. Marx and F. Engels, *Collected Works* (London: Lawrence and Wishart, 1976), vol. 11, p. 185.

20  Ibid., pp. 103–4.

21  Lefort's account of the origins of a properly political discourse on politics and society was influenced by his extensive study of Machiavelli and the humanism of late fourteenth and early fifteenth century Florence. See especially his *Le Travail de l'oeuvre: Machiavel* (Paris: Gallimard, 1972); and 'La naissance de l'idéologie et l'humanisme', in his *Les Formes de l'histoire* (Paris: Gallimard, 1978), pp. 234–77.

22  Claude Lefort, 'Outline of the Genesis of Ideology in Modern Societies', in this volume, p. 201.

23  For a sustained discussion of the concept of the social imaginary, see Cornelius Castoriadis, *The Imaginary Institution of Society*, trans. Kathleen McLaughlin (Cambridge: Polity Press, forthcoming). An analysis of the relation between the concept of the social imaginary and the notion of ideology may be found in the essay cited above in note 2.

24  Claude Lefort, 'Outline of the Genesis of Ideology in Modern Societies', p. 224.

25  In analysing consumption in terms of a 'system of objects', Lefort draws on the work of Baudrillard; see especially Jean Baudrillard, *Le Système des objets* (Paris: Gallimard, 1968); and *La Société de la consommation: ses mythes, ses structures* (Paris: E. P. Denoël, 1970).

26  Lefort has made several recent contributions to this task; see especially 'Tocqueville: de l'égalité à la liberté', *Libre*, 3 (1978); 'Permanence du théologico-politique?', in *Le Temps de la réflexion*, no. 2 (Paris: Gallimard, 1981), pp. 13–60; 'Penser la révolution dans la révolution française', *Annales* (1980), pp. 334–52; 'Réversibilité', *Passé Présent*, 1 (1982), pp. 18–35; these essays are reprinted in Lefort's *Essais sur le politique* (Paris: Seuil, 1986). For a contemporary reappraisal of Guizot, see Pierre Rosanvallon, *Le Moment Guizot* (Paris: Gallimard, 1985).

27  Claude Lefort, 'The Logic of Totalitarianism', in this volume, p. 279.

28  Karl Marx, *On the Jewish Question*, in K. Marx and F. Engels, *Collected Works* (London: Lawrence and Wishart, 1975), vol. 3, p. 162.

29  Claude Lefort, 'Politics and Human Rights', in this volume, p. 270.

30  Lefort believes that, whatever one may think of the personal opinions of Solzhenitsyn, his writings are an important resource for a political reflection on the nature of Soviet society. Lefort offers such a reflection in a book-length study of *The Gulag Archipelago*: see Claude Lefort, *Un Homme en trop: réflexions sur 'L'Archipel du Goulag'* (Paris: Seuil, 1976).

31  Claude Lefort, 'The Image of the Body and Totalitarianism', in this volume, p. 298.

32  See Ernst H. Kantorowicz, *The King's Two Bodies: A Study in Mediaeval Political Theology* (Princeton: Princeton University Press, 1957).

33  See especially the following essays: 'L'insurrection hongroise', originally published in *Socialisme ou Barbarie*, 20 (1956–7); 'Retour de Pologne', originally published in *Socialisme ou Barbarie*, 21 (1957); and

'Une autre révolution', originally published in *Libre*, 1 (1977). These essays are reproduced in Lefort's book, *L'Invention démocratique: les limites de la domination totalitaire* (Paris: Fayard, 1981).

34 Claude Lefort, 'Pushing Back the Limits of the Possible', in this volume, p. 313.

## 1 The Contradiction of Trotsky

1 Leon Trotsky, *Stalin*, trans. Charles Malamuth (London: Hollis and Carter, 1947), p. 64.
2 Ibid., p. 18.
3 Ibid., p. 187.
4 Boris Souvarine, *Stalin*, trans. C. L. R. James (London: Secker and Warburg, 1939).
5 Trotsky, *Stalin*, p. xv.
6 Leon Trotsky, *My Life* (London: Thornton Butterworth, 1930), p. 432.
7 The work, it is true, was left unfinished, but Trotsky indicates in the Introduction that he intentionally gave a secondary place to the post-revolutionary period.
8 Trotsky, *My Life*, p. 453.
9 Trotsky, *Stalin*, pp. 403–4. (Here, and in what follows, the emphasis is Lefort's.)
10 *Writings of Leon Trotsky (1934–35)* (New York: Pathfinder Press, 1971), p. 173.
11 *New International* (Nov. 1934).
12 Trotsky's 'What happened and how', quoted in *Political Correspondence of the Workers' League for a Revolutionary Party* (March 1947), p. 27.
13 Trotsky, *My Life*, p. 414.
14 Ibid., p. 410.
15 Boris Souvarine, *Stalin*, pp. 362–3.
16 Trotsky, *Stalin*, p. 403.
17 Leon Trotsky, *The Revolution Betrayed*, trans. Max Eastman (London: Faber and Faber, 1937), pp. 97–8.
18 Souvarine, *Stalin*, p. 361.
19 Stalin, *October and the Permanent Revolution* (October 1924).
20 After the Thirteenth Congress, certain new problems concerning the domain of industry, the Soviets or international politics arose or became more clearly defined. The idea of opposing any platform to the work of the Central Committee of the Party with a view to their solution was absolutely alien to me. For all the comrades who assisted at the meetings of the Politbureau, the Central Committee, the Soviet of Labour and Defence, the Revolutionary Military Soviet, this assertion does not need proof. (Quoted in *Political Correspondence*)

21 Text of Trotsky's letter quoted in *The Bulletin of the Workers' League for a Revolutionary Party* (Sept.–Oct. 1947), p. 30.
22 Two extracts quoted in *Political Correspondence* are significant in this respect. In a speech to students from the Far East, Trotsky declares: 'We approve of the communist support given to the Kuomintang in China where we are trying to bring about a revolution.' (Reported by *International Press Correspondence*, May 1924.) Furthermore, to the Congress of Textile Workers, Trotsky says: 'The Trade Union Anglo-Russian Committee of Unity is the highest expression of this change in the European and especially British situation, which is operating under our eyes and is leading to the European revolution.' (Reported by *Pravda*, January 1926.)
23 Quoted in *The Bulletin* (Sept.–Oct. 1947).
24 Quoted by Souvarine, *Stalin*, p. 455.
25 Trotsky, *Stalin*, p. 403.
26 Ibid., p. 61.
27 Ibid., p. 64.
28 In this study, written in 1948, I merely allude to the crushing of the Kronstadt Commune and the repression practised by Bolshevik power against the workers' opposition movements. As far as Kronstadt is concerned, my sources were Voline's *La révolution inconnue* (republished in 1969 by Pierre Belfond) and an article by Victor Serge, 'Kronstadt', in *Politics* (April 1945). Since then, a great deal more information has been published. The following should be mentioned: Ida Mett, *La Commune de Cronstadt* (Paris: Spartacus, 1949); R. V. Daniels, 'The Kronstadt Revolt of 1921', *American Slavic and East European Review* (Dec. 1951); L. Schapiro, *The Origin of the Communist Autocracy* (London: London School of Economics, 1955), ch. XVI; George Katkov, 'The Kronstadt Rising', *St Anthony's Papers*, no. 6 (1959); *La Commune de Cronstadt, recueil de documents* (Paris: Bélibaste, 1969), which includes a translation of Kronstadt's *Izvestia* and extracts from the diary of an eye-witness, the anarchist Berkman; and P. Avrich, *Kronstadt 1921* (Princeton: Princeton University Press, 1970).

   As far as the repression of the opposition movements is concerned, see especially the testimony of Ciliga, analysed in my *Éléments d'une critique de la bureaucratie* (Paris: Gallimard, 1979), pp. 145 ff., and E. H. Carr, *The Interregnum, 1923–24* (Harmondsworth: Penguin, 1954), pp. 88–93, 276–8, 300–2. On the 'Workers' Group' see L. Schapiro, *The Communist Party of the Soviet Union* (London: Constable, 1960), pp. 276–7; R. V. Daniels, *The Conscience of the Revolution* (Cambridge, Mass: Harvard University Press, 1960), pp. 158–9. On 'Workers' Truth' see Daniels, *Conscience of the Revolution*, pp. 204 and 210, and *A Documentary History of Communism*, (New York: Vintage, 1960), vol. I, pp. 210–23; Schapiro, *Communist Party of the Soviet Union*, pp. 198–204.

29 Souvarine, *Stalin*, p. 319.
30 *Writings of Leon Trotsky (1934–35)*, p. 182.
31 Ibid., p. 179.
32 One may also compare this statement with the final lines of Trotsky's *Stalin* which completely contradict it:

> 'L'État, c'est moi' [I am the State] is almost a liberal formula by comparison with the actualities of Stalin's totalitarian regime. Louis XIV identified himself only with the State. The Popes of Rome identified themselves with both the State and the Church – but only during the epoch of temporal power. The totalitarian state goes far beyond Caesaro-Papism, for *it has encompassed the entire economy of the country as well. Stalin can justly say, unlike the Sun King, 'La Société, c'est moi'* [I am Society]. (*Stalin*, p. 421: Lefort's emphasis)

33 For example in the passage of his *Stalin* where, referring to the period that saw the liquidation of the kulaks, Trotsky writes: 'Thus opened the irreconcilable struggle over the surplus product of national labour. Who will dispose of it in the nearest future – the new bourgeoisie or the Soviet bureaucracy? – that became the next issue. He who disposes of the surplus product has the power of the State at his disposal.' (*Stalin*, p. 397)
34 Ibid., p. 406.

## 2   Totalitarianism without Stalin

1 Let us remember this formula from *My Life*:

> And the fact that today [Stalin] is playing first is not so much a summing-up of the man as it is of this transitional period of political backsliding in the country. Helvetius said it long ago: 'Every period has its great men, and if these are lacking, it invents them.' Stalinism is above all else the automatic work of the impersonal apparatus of the decline of the revolution. (Leon Trotsky, *My Life* (London: Thornton Butterworth, 1930), p. 432)

2 It is impossible for me to develop an economic analysis of the USSR within the limits of this study and I might, therefore, be criticized for presupposing that the problem of the class nature of the USSR has been solved instead of discussing it. The social inequality that I have described and the *de facto* separation between the state and the proletariat are not enough, for example, in the eyes of 'communists' who recognize them or in the eyes of Trotskyists, to characterize the USSR as a class society. The socialist foundations of the regime would appear to have been assured by the abolition of private property.

In an important study, Cornelius Castoriadis has amply criticized this last thesis. He has shown in a quite decisive way that the legal relations of property provided in themselves only a distorted image of the relations of production, that at the latter level the opposition between capital and labour is as radical in Russian society as in American or French society. Lastly, he has shown that it would be absurd to separate the sphere of production from that of distribution and that consequently the inequality of incomes circumscribes a particular social stratum whose shared 'privileges' express a collective appropriation of workers' and peasants' surplus value. In referring the reader to this article ('Les rapports de production en Russie', *Socialisme ou Barbarie*, 2 (mai–juin 1949)), I would simply add that socialism cannot be defined 'in itself', by the nationalization of the means of production and the collectivization of agriculture and planning – in other words, independently of proletarian power. In bourgeois capitalism there is an economic infrastructure that confers its real power on the dominant class, whatever the circumstantial character of the state may be. On the other hand, socialism cannot refer to an infrastructure, since it signifies the seizure by the proletariat of the means of production and the collective management of production. The dictatorship of the proletariat is essentially this new form of management. If the proletariat plays no part in this form of management, if it is reduced to the same role that it plays in capitalism, namely that of carrying out the decisions of others, then there is no longer any trace of socialism. The state bureaucracy then plans in accordance with the prospects and interests of all those who take part in its managerial functions. Nationalization and collectivization are formally at the service of society as a whole, but in reality at the service of a particular class.

3 Stalin's own role must not make us forget that there is a sort of internal logic in terror that leads it to develop to its extreme consequences, independently of the real conditions to which it was originally a response. It would be too simple to assume that a state could introduce terror as an instrument and then reject it once the objective had been attained. Terror is a social phenomenon; it transforms the behaviour and attitudes of individuals, and of Stalin himself no doubt. It is only after the event that its excesses can be denounced, as Khrushchev has done. As a phenomenon that exists in the present it is not an 'excess', for it constitutes social life.

4 I am referring to various studies, in particular to 'Mid-Century Russia', collected together in Isaac Deutscher, *Heretics and Renegades* (London: Hamish Hamilton, 1955).

5 I am using the classical term 'civil society' to refer to the totality of classes and social groups in so far as they are fashioned by the division of labour and determined independently of the political action of the state.

6  See Monnerot, *Sociologie du communisme* (Paris: Gallimard, 1949).

7  Recall this celebrated text of Marx:

The tradition of all the dead generations weighs like a nightmare on the brain of the living. And just when they seem engaged in revolutionising themselves and things, in creating something that has never yet existed, precisely in such periods of revolutionary crisis they anxiously conjure up the spirits of the past to their service and borrow from them names, battle cries and costumes in order to present the new scene of world history in this time-honoured disguise and this borrowed language. (Karl Marx, *The Eighteenth Brumaire of Louis Bonaparte*, in K. Marx and F. Engels, *Collected Works* (London: Lawrence and Wishart, 1979), vol. 11, pp. 103–4.

8  All references to Khrushchev's speeches are to the text published in *Cahiers du communisme* (mars 1956).

9  Ibid., p. 336.

## 3  What is Bureaucracy?

1  Karl Marx, *Contribution to the Critique of Hegel's Philosophy of Law*, in K. Marx and F. Engels, *Collected Works*, (London: Lawrence and Wishart, 1975), vol. 3, pp. 46–7 (translation modified).

2  Ibid., p. 46.

3  Ibid., p. 47.

4  Ibid. (translation modified).

5  Karl Marx, *The Eighteenth Brumaire of Louis Bonaparte*, in K. Marx and F. Engels, *Collected Works*, (London: Lawrence and Wishart, 1979), vol. 11, p. 185 (emphasis added by Lefort).

6  V. I. Lenin, *The State and Revolution*, in *Selected Works* (London: Lawrence and Wishart, 1969), p. 284.

7  See Max Weber, 'Bureaucracy', in *From Max Weber: Essays in Sociology*, ed. H. H. Gerth and C. Wright Mills (London: Routledge and Kegan Paul, 1948), pp. 196–264.

8  Alain Touraine, 'Situation du mouvement ouvrier', *Arguments*, 3, nos. 12/13 (1959).

9  Michel Crozier, 'L'ère du prolétariat s'achève', *Arguments*, 3, nos. 12/13 (1959).

## 5  Marx: From One Vision of History to Another

1  Karl Marx and Frederick Engels, *Manifesto of the Communist Party*, in K. Marx and F. Engels, *Collected Works* (London: Lawrence and Wishart, 1976), vol. 6, p. 482.

2  Ibid., p. 487.
3  As Maximilien Rubel pointed out, Marx said at the end of his life that reading the *Manifesto* (along with *The Poverty of Philosophy*) could serve as an introduction to the study of *Capital*.
4  Karl Marx, *Grundrisse: Foundations of the Critique of Political Economy*, trans. Martin Nicolaus (Harmondsworth: Penguin, 1973), p. 471.
5  Ibid., p. 472.
6  Ibid. (translation modified; emphasis added by Lefort).
7  Ibid.
8  Ibid.
9  Ibid., p. 473.
10  Ibid.
11  Ibid. (translation modified).
12  Ibid., p. 474.
13  Ibid., p. 475.
14  Ibid.
15  Ibid., p. 474.
16  Ibid., p. 475.
17  Ibid., p. 476.
18  Ibid., p. 486 (translation modified).
19  Ibid., p. 485
20  Ibid., p. 489.
21  Ibid., p. 491 (translation modified).
22  Ibid.
23  Ibid., p. 489.
24  Ibid.
25  Ibid., p. 494.
26  Karl Marx, *Capital: A Critique of Political Economy*, trans. Ben Fowkes (Harmondsworth: Penguin, 1976), vol. I, p. 479.
27  We must remember that Marx exploits anthropological material which had been systematically accumulated and deals with a social type which the English economists had thoroughly investigated before him.
28  Marx, *Capital*, vol. I, p. 439.
29  Ibid., p. 452.
30  Ibid., p. 457.
31  Ibid. (translation modified).
32  Ibid., p. 481 (translation modified).
33  Ibid., pp. 481–2.
34  Ibid., pp. 457–8.
35  Ibid., p. 459.
36  Ibid., p. 485.
37  Ibid., pp. 501–2 (translation modified).
38  Ibid., p. 503.

39  Ibid., pp. 544–5.
40  Ibid., p. 616.
41  Ibid., p. 617.
42  Marx, *Grundrisse*, pp. 105–6.
43  See especially Karl Marx and Frederick Engels, *The German Ideology*, in K. Marx and F. Engels, *Collected Works* (London: Lawrence and Wishart, 1976), vol. 5.
44  See 'Engels to Conrad Schmidt' (27 October 1890), in K. Marx and F. Engels, *Correspondence 1846–1895* (London: Martin Lawrence, 1934), pp. 477–84.
45  Karl Marx, *The Eighteenth Brumaire of Louis Bonaparte*, in K. Marx and F. Engels, *Collected Works* (London: Lawrence and Wishart, 1979), vol. 11, pp. 103–4.
46  Harold Rosenberg, 'Marx', in *Les Philosophes célèbres*, ed. Maurice Merleau-Ponty (Paris: L. Mazenod, 1956).
47  Marx, *Capital*, vol. I, pp. 165–6.
48  Karl Marx, *Capital: A Critique of Political Economy*, ed. Federick Engels (London: Lawrence and Wishart, 1974), vol. III, p. 827.
49  Ibid., p. 814.
50  Ibid., p. 822.
51  Ibid., p. 829 (emphasis added by Lefort).
52  Ibid., pp. 829–30.
53  Ibid., p. 830 (translation modified).
54  Marx, *The Eighteenth Brumaire of Louis Bonaparte*, p. 187.
55  Ibid., p. 112.
56  See ibid., pp. 186–8.
57  Ibid., p. 124.
58  Ibid., p. 125.
59  Ibid.
60  Ibid., p. 185.
61  Ibid., p. 127.
62  Ibid., p. 103.
63  Ibid., p. 106.
64  Ibid., p. 108 (translation modified).
65  Ibid., p. 105.
66  Ibid., p. 110.
67  Ibid., p. 111.
68  Ibid., p. 108.
69  Ibid., p. 110 (emphasis removed).
70  Ibid., p. 127 (translation modified).
71  Ibid., p. 128.
72  Ibid., pp. 128–9.
73  Ibid., p. 129.

74  Ibid.
75  Ibid., p. 168.
76  Ibid., p. 187.
77  Ibid., pp. 187–8.
78  Ibid., p. 190.
79  Ibid.
80  Ibid., p. 188.
81  Ibid., p. 193.
82  Ibid., p. 192.
83  Ibid.
84  Ibid., p. 186.

## 7　Politics and Human Rights

1  Karl Marx, *On the Jewish Question*, in K. Marx and F. Engels, *Collected Works* (London: Lawrence and Wishart, 1975), vol. 3, p. 162.
2  Ibid., pp. 162–4.
3  Ibid., p. 166.
4  Ibid., pp. 162–3.
5  Ibid., p. 163.

## 8　The Logic of Totalitarianism

1  Leon Trotsky, *Stalin*, trans. Charles Malamuth (London: Hollis and Carter, 1947), p. 421.
2  Marc Ferro, *La Révolution de 1917* (Paris: Aubier-Montaigne, 1976); *Des Soviets à la bureaucratie* (Paris: Gallimard-Julliard, 1980).

# Select Bibliography

## Writings by Claude Lefort

Books

*Mai 1968: la brèche*, with Jean-Marc Coudray (a pseudonym for Cornelius Castoriadis) and Edgar Morin (Paris: Fayard, 1968). This collaborative work is a reflection on the events of May 1968.

*Éléments d'une critique de la bureacratie* (Geneva: Droz, 1971). This volume is a collection of Lefort's early writings on politics, bureaucracy and totalitarianism. An abridged version of the volume was published in 1979 by Gallimard.

*Le Travail de l'oeuvre: Machiavel* (Paris: Gallimard, 1972). This is a lengthy study of the work of Machiavelli and of some of the most influential interpretations of his work. The study includes important discussions of the nature of interpretation and of the relation between Machiavelli's work and the development of modern societies.

*Un homme en trop: réflexions sur 'L'Archipel du Goulag'* (Paris: Seuil, 1976). This remarkable reflection on the work of Solzhenitsyn seeks to demonstrate its relevance to the analysis of totalitarianism.

*Sur une colonne absente: écrits autour de Merleau-Ponty* (Paris: Gallimard, 1978). Most of the essays in this volume are focused on the work of Merleau-Ponty.

*Les Formes de l'histoire: essais d'anthropologie politique* (Paris: Gallimard, 1978). This is a selection of essays which were originally published between 1951 and 1974. They deal with various themes in cultural anthropology and in social and political theory.

*L'Invention démocratique: les limites de la domination totalitaire* (Paris: Fayard, 1981). The essays which comprise this volume are concerned with various aspects of democracy and totalitarianism. They address theoretical issues as well as political developments in Eastern and Western Europe, from 1956 to the present day.

*Essais sur le politique* (Paris: Seuil, 1986). Most of the essays in this volume were originally published between 1980 and 1984. They explore a variety of themes in political theory.

## Articles

Most of Lefort's articles have been reprinted in the volumes cited above. The following list is a selection of recent articles by Lefort which have not yet been assembled in a collection.

'La politique et l'institution du social' (with Marcel Gauchet), *Texture* (1972).

'Entretien avec C. Lefort', *L'Anti-mythes*, 14 (1975). This is an interview with Lefort which was conducted on 19 April 1975. It has been translated into English and published as 'An Interview with Claude Lefort', trans. Dorothy Gehrke and Brian Singer, *Telos*, 30 (winter 1976–7).

'La Boétie et la question du politique' (with Pierre Clastres), in Etienne de la Boétie, *Le Discours de la servitude volontaire* (Paris: Payot, 1976).

'Maintenant', *Libre*, 1 (1977).

'Formation et autorité', in *Former l'Homme* (Neuchâtel: Rencontres Internationales de Genève, 1979).

'Introduction', in Maurice Merleau-Ponty, *Humanisme et Terreur* (Paris: Gallimard, 1980).

'La pensée politique devant les Droits de l'Homme', *Europa*, 3 (1980).

'Philosophie et non philosophie', *Esprit* (1982).

'Sur la nature des régimes de l'Est', *CFDT Aujourd'hui* (1982).

'De la démocratie', *Traces*, 7 (1983).

'How did you become a philosopher?', in Alan Montefiore (ed.), *Philosophy in France Today* (Cambridge: Cambridge University Press, 1983).

'Le corps interposé', *Passé Present*, 3 (1984).

'Entretien avec Claude Lefort', in *Entretiens avec Le Monde* (Paris: Éditions la Découverte et le Monde, 1985), vol. 6. This is another interview with Lefort, conducted by Christian Descampes on 7 November 1982.

'Arendt et la question du politique', *Forum*, 5 (1985).

'Hannah Arendt et le totalitarisme', in *L'Allemagne et le génocide juif* (Paris: Gallimard et Seuil, 1985).

## Writings on Claude Lefort

Howard, Dick, *The Marxian Legacy* (London: Macmillan, 1977). Chapter 9 of this book provides an overview of Lefort's work. The chapter reproduces Howard's earlier essay, 'Introduction to Lefort', *Telos*, 22 (winter 1974–5).

Poster, Mark, *Existential Marxism in Postwar France: From Sartre to Althusser* (Princeton: Princeton University Press, 1975). This excellent general survey of post-war French thought includes brief discussions of the formation of the group Socialisme ou Barbarie and of the debate between Lefort and Sartre.

Thompson, John B. 'Ideology and the Social Imaginary: An Appraisal of Castoriadis and Lefort', in *Studies in the Theory of Ideology* (Cambridge: Polity Press, 1984). This essay offers a critical analysis of Lefort's writings on ideology.

# Index

Index by Isobel McLean